An Overview Series Publication

Software Engineering

	Capability	Usability	Performance	Reliability	Instability	Maintainability	Documentation	Availability
Capability								
Usability								
Performance	●	●						
Reliability	●	○	●					
Instability		○	○	○				
Maintainability	●	○	●	○				
Documentation	●	○					○	
Availability	●	○	○	○	○	○		

●: Conflict One Another

○: Support One Another

Input cases valid and invalid

SYSTEM

QUALITY MEASUREMENTS

OBJECTIVES

ALARP - As low as reasonably practicable

Unacceptable Risk

Acceptable Risk

Global Metrics

Requirements

Design

Integration

Coding

Vali(

Product Quality
- Functionality
- Usability
- Efficiency
- Reliability

Process Quality
- Effectiveness of methods
- Use of standards
- Management

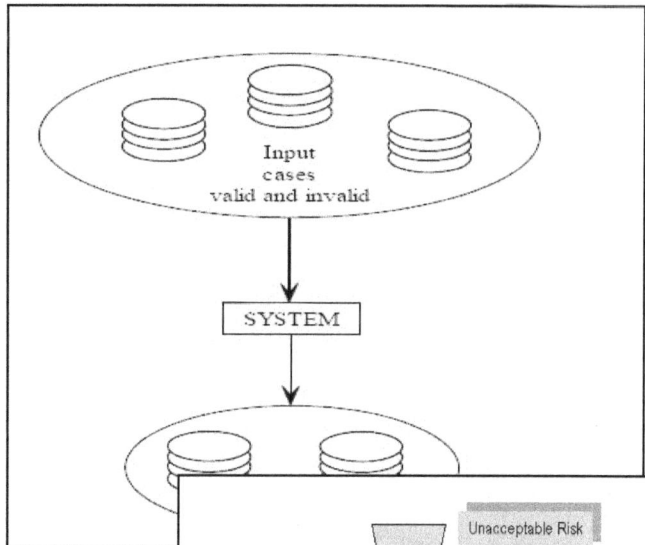

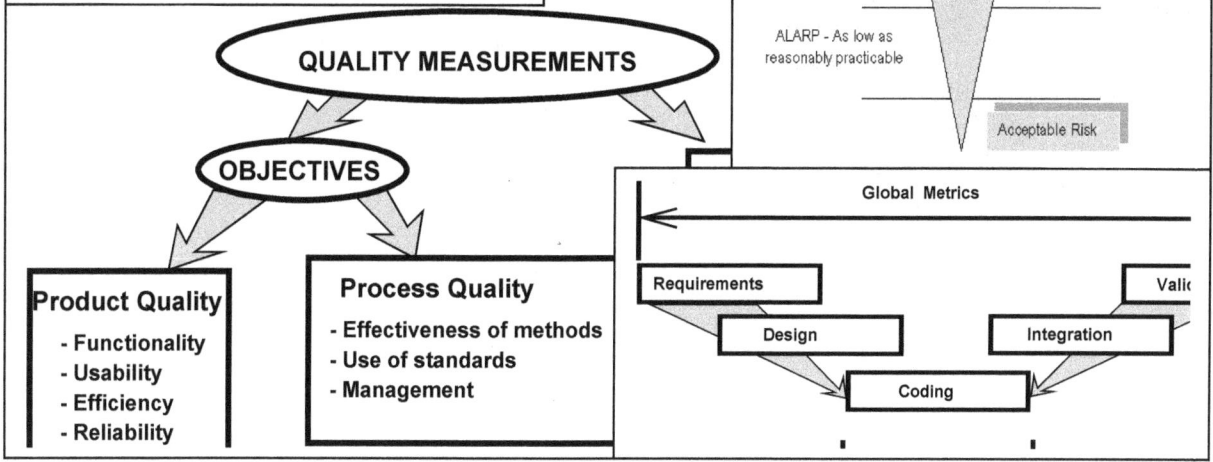

Dr. Goran I Bezanov PhD

This page is intentionally left blank

SOFTWARE ENGINEERING

AN OVERVIEW SERIES PUBLICATION

By Goran Bezanov PhD

MIG Consulting Ltd

31 Vicarage Road, London SW14 8RZ

British Library Cataloguing in Publication Data

A catalogue record for this book is available from the British Library

International Standard Book Number: 978-0-9558153-5-5

To my Sons
Ognen and Milos

This page is intentionally left blank

PREFACE

This text is a very brief overview of software engineering. My aim was to write a textbook that can be read and understood by readers who are not experienced software developers. It was my intention that, from this book they could gain sufficient understanding in order to know where to look for further direction. Additionally this book is geared towards software engineering rather than software development. This means that I will focus on aspects that a software engineer should know and so I will not cover any software programming aspects.

In chapter 1 I introduce aspects of software engineering that I consider relevant. Basic stages of software development are identified and some aspects of each stage briefly discussed. The main approaches to software engineering such as the waterfall approach; exploratory programming, prototyping and others are discussed. Most of these are covered in more details in later chapters of this textbook but in chapter 1 they are presented by way of an introduction. The very important concept of programming paradigms is also introduced and briefly discussed. The two most prominent paradigms namely procedural and object-oriented are briefly covered although more details are included in later chapters. The concept of a methodology is also considered and for the procedural paradigm, the Jackson Structured Method is presented as an example. For the object-oriented paradigm, the Booch methodology has been suggested, but since it forms a significant component of the Unified Modelling Language (UML) it has not been presented in detail in this chapter. Instead the reader is referred to Chapter 3 of this text where essential aspects of UML are covered.

Chapter 2 looks at modelling as a tool in software engineering. This is a very difficult topic to write about because modelling is used practically everywhere, in business, engineering, finance even in medicine and law. Models are intuitive to those that use them and they tend to evolve over time. For example the Booch methodology for Object Oriented Design (OOD) has been around for some 20 years. In that time Booch and others have refined it and it has been used in part to define Unified Modelling Language (UML), which is now de-facto standard in OOD. It is quite difficult to condense the complexity of the Booch method concisely into a single chapter of a textbook. That is, to present the material in such a way as to give the reader sufficient information to be able to use the method successfully in large projects. Therefore once again I have to say that this chapter provides an overview in modelling and the reader is encouraged to seek other text for a more detailed treatment of the subject matter.

In chapter 3 I briefly introduce UML, which is a way of describing systems that helps to visualise how they will behave once, built. It uses many diagrams with very clear syntax and rules, which makes it possible to be consistent when modelling systems. I describe here the essential aspects of UML so that the reader can become familiar with basic techniques of modelling using UML. I have provided simple examples of diagrams that can be extended to describe more complex systems.

Chapter 4 considers the requirement phase of software engineering. A brief mention of project management is also introduced because requirements are a significant part of project management. It goes without saying that without a solid description of the requirements any project will be doomed to failure. There are a large number of sources describing the components within a requirements specification and although most of these are valid, there are many variations and inconsistencies in terms of the terminology. For this reason I have simplified my text to group the requirements into user and system requirements and to consider these from the point of requirements definition and requirements specification. I consider this to be a straightforward approach that will satisfy most software engineering projects.

However, I do emphasise that other variants could be a better option in some projects. I also consider in this chapter the use of natural language and the inherent possibility of ambiguities, omissions and conflicts that accompany this form of requirements specifications. Program design language (PDL) is presented in this chapter as a possible means of translating natural language into a more precise specification.

In chapter 5 I cover the basic approach to software design. I consider the design process and how this relates to the programming paradigm as well as to the overall system architecture. With this in mind I recommend the 4+1 view of architecture as a means of developing the design. The approach towards implementing the design relies on many factors that relate to project management. I cover these factors briefly and their impact on design. I also consider quality and how this needs to fit into the design process. In this chapter I present an overview of real-time systems (RTS) design. In order to apply design principles I briefly cover some essential features of real-time systems such as scheduling policies. Actual steps in design of RTS are introduced and a simple example presented to describe this approach to design. The final section of this chapter introduces design of the user-interface.

Chapter 6 presents the advantages and disadvantages of prototyping. In some cases prototypes may not be necessary and using them could present additional problems in project management. In other cases they provide an invaluable tool without which, chances of success on the project would be diminished. A few popular approaches to prototyping are introduced but the main emphasis is on evolutionary, throwaway and incremental development approaches. I also cover briefly the extreme programming approach. It is not certain that all concerned would consider this to be an approach to prototyping but that is how it is presented here. The process of selecting a prototype for a given development is presented using example projects. This is largely dependent on the type of project and some general points to consider have been given. Ultimately the development team have to use common sense and also to consider the characteristics of each prototyping approach in order to select the most appropriate for their project.

Dependability is a qualitative feature and so it is difficult to measure. When describing dependability many authors consider that it spans across a number of dimensions. In chapter 7 I cover the dimensions of dependability and provide a few examples of projects that have failed as a result of some of these dimensions. The effects of implementing dependability are considered briefly and aspects such as failure and safety are considered. Reliability is a significant component of dependable systems and I briefly mention reliability metrics. Risk is a major factor and this is particularly important in safety-critical systems. I briefly consider hazard and safety analysis using the fault-tree approach. This is not exhaustive, and should serve merely as a guide towards explaining the principles of application of this approach.

In chapter 8 I consider the implications of software development for safety-critical systems. Hazard and risk analysis constitute a major aspect of these types of systems and I provide a brief outline of hazard classification and failure mode analysis. Failure mode analysis tools such as Failure Mode and Effects Analysis (FMEA) and Failure Modes, Effects and Criticality Analysis (FMECA) are presented briefly. These tools were originally designed for the process industry and have been suitably modified for use in software engineering. I provide some guidelines on the modifications that are required in this case. These methods are also used to assess the risk associated with failure modes and I offer a brief description of risk priority numbers and criticality analysis as a way of assessing risk. Hazard and Operability (HAZOP) is another method of hazard analysis that was first used in the chemical process industry, which can be adapted for use in software engineering. I describe the essential features here only and leave it to the reader to find further application of these methods to software engineering projects. At the end of the chapter I provide a simple example of a hazard analysis problem in safety-critical systems.

Chapter 9 looks at validation and verification of software products. To a large extent these rely on testing. The chapter briefly covers static and dynamic testing strategies and tools. I cover some basic strategies for testing such as thread testing and stress testing but these should only serve as examples because the approach to testing is generally developed in-house and therefore most organisations will have their own testing procedures. Finally the chapter considers interface testing. This is a particular type of testing which ensures that human beings are able to communicate effectively with the system through the user interface.

Chapter 10 covers testing from a software development point of view. The various stages of development are considered and suitable tests discussed. This subject area is very broad indeed and what has been presented can be considered as an overview rather than a prescribed approach to testing. It is accepted that most organisations will prescribe their own testing procedures however these will embody some of the aspects described in this text. I briefly cover white box and black box testing with emphasis on the procedures during testing. Equivalence partitioning is used as an example of white box testing to demonstrate how test data can be used to examine behaviour around the equivalence classes and the boundaries of their definition. Finally testing effectiveness assessment is presented since it is not uncommon for testing paranoia to settle in so that the organisation is not aware that they may be over-testing or indeed not using the appropriate testing methods. Assessing the effectiveness of tests is a means of dealing with this problem.

In chapter 11, I briefly cover quality in software engineering projects. This is a very important and also broad field in engineering and therefore it is difficult to cover all the important aspects. I consider some general points regarding quality and relate these to metrics that can be used to provide a measure of quality. I cover some generic software measures that were first introduced by IBM and HP and which are still valid. I provide example metrics and also try to explain where these fit within the overall software development cycle. I briefly cover quality assurance to include planning and control and consider any potential pit-falls.

Cost estimation in software engineering projects is covered in chapter 12. A large number of factors can impact on the cost of a project and Boehm's COCOMO models provide a good starting point for estimating cost. I describe the basic model type and then proceed to give some application details. COCOMO II is an enhanced version of the basic model and I briefly cover the essential features of this evolved model. As with the rest of this textbook, I emphasise that the main aim is to provide the reader with insight into a subject area, rather than going into details. For further reading the references given corresponding to each chapter are a good starting point.

This is my first draft and I shall revise and correct the errors in the next. Suggestions welcome to: mig@consultant.com.

Thank you

Goran Bezanov (September 2010, London)

This page is intentionally left blank

CONTENTS

CHAPTER 1 GENERAL CONCEPTS IN SOFTWARE ENGINEERING 1

1.1. INTRODUCTION 1
Waterfall approach 2
Exploratory programming 3
Prototyping 3
Formal transformation 4
Software development based on reusable components 4
1.2. PARADIGMS IN SOFTWARE ENGINEERING 6
Software development methodology 7
1.3. PROCEDURAL PROGRAMMING 7
Algorithmic design notation for sequence, iteration and selection 8
Sequence 9
Iterations 9
Selections 10
1.4. OBJECT-ORIENTED PROGRAMMING 16
History of OOD 17
Abstraction 19
Inheritance 21
Polymorphism 22
Encapsulation 22
Methodologies 23
1.5. CHAPTER SUMMARY 24
Exercises 25

CHAPTER 2 MODELLING 26

2.1. INTRODUCTION 26
Types of models 26
2.2. BASIC ASPECTS OF SOFTWARE MODELLING 27
Context models 27
Abstract modelling 30
Behaviour models 32
Architecture models 37
2.3. DOCUMENTING THE ARCHITECTURE 43
2.4. CHAPTER SUMMARY 44
Exercises 44

CHAPTER 3 UNIFIED MODELLING LANGUAGE **46**

3.1. INTRODUCTION 46
3.2. UML DESCRIPTION 46
   UML model types 47
3.3. UML DIAGRAMS.. 47
3.4. STRUCTURE DIAGRAMS 48
   Class diagram 48
   Component diagram.. 50
   Composite structure diagram 50
   Deployment diagram 51
   Object diagram... 52
   Package diagram 52
3.5. BEHAVIOURAL (DYNAMIC) DIAGRAMS 53
   Activity diagram 53
   State machine diagram... 54
   Use-case diagram 54
   Interaction diagrams.. 55
   Sequence diagram 55
   Collaboration diagram 56
   Interaction overview diagram.. 57
   Communication diagram.. 58
   Timing diagrams... 58
3.6. CHAPTER SUMMARY 59
   Exercises... 59

CHAPTER 4 REQUIREMENTS ENGINEERING **61**

4.1. PROJECT MANAGEMENT 61
   Project definition.. 61
4.2. PLANNING 62
4.3. FEASIBILITY ANALYSIS CASE STUDY 63
   Structure of a feasibility report... 64
   Proposing a solution and modelling.. 66
   Validation and verification.. 66
   Implementation... 67
   Commissioning... 67
4.4. REQUIREMENTS ENGINEERING 67
   Benefits of a requirements specification... 67
   Requirements definition... 70
   Requirement specification 71
4.5. WRITING A REQUIREMENTS SPECIFICATION 71
   Natural language specifications... 71
   Research in natural language methodology 75
4.6. PROGRAM DESIGN LANGUAGE (PDL)... 75
   PDL Uses 79
4.7. SOFTWARE REQUIREMENTS SPECIFICATION TEMPLATE 80
4.8. CHAPTER SUMMARY 81
   Exercises... 81

CHAPTER 5 SYSTEMS DESIGN **83**

5.1.   SYSTEMS ENGINEERING 83
5.2.   SOFTWARE DESIGN 83
Process considerations 84
Strategies 85
Human Factors 85
Project planning 87
Quality 88
5.3.   REAL TIME SYSTEMS (RTS) 89
5.4.   REAL TIME OPERATING SYSTEMS (RTOS) 92
5.5.   SCHEDULING 94
Scheduling levels 94
Three state diagram 94
Five state diagram 95
5.6.   SCHEDULING POLICIES 96
Pre-emptive 96
Non-pre-emptive 98
FCFS-First Come First Serve scheduling policy 98
SJF–Shortest Job First scheduling policy 99
SRT-Shortest Remaining Time scheduling policy 99
Highest Response Next (HRN) scheduling policy 99
Round Robin scheduling policy 100
Multi-level Feedback Queues (MFQ) scheduling policy 101
5.7.   DESIGN STAGES IN RTS 102
5.8.   USER INTERFACE DESIGN 105
GUI design considerations 106
Interface types 107
5.9.   CHAPTER SUMMARY 108
Exercises 109

CHAPTER 6 SOFTWARE PROTOTYPING **111**

6.1   INTRODUCTION 111
Advantages of prototyping 111
Disadvantages of prototyping 111
The prototyping process 112
6.2   TYPES OF PROTOTYPE 113
Quick and dirty prototypes 113
Detail design-driven prototypes 114
Non-functioning prototypes 114
Explorative prototypes 114
Experimental prototypes 114
Evolutionary prototypes 114
Throw away prototypes 115
Incremental development prototypes 117

6.3 EXTREME PROGRAMMING 118
  Simplicity and communication 119
  Feedback.. 119
  Courage.. 119
  Respect 120
6.4 AGILE METHODS 120
  Background to agile methods 120
6.5 CHOOSING A PROTOTYPING APPROACH.................................. 121
6.6 CHAPTER SUMMARY 123
  Exercises.. 124

CHAPTER 7 SOFTWARE DEPENDABILITY AND RELIABILITY 125

7.1. INTRODUCTION 125
7.2. DIMENSIONS OF DEPENDABILITY 126
7.3. EFFECTS OF DEPENDABILITY 128
  Costs 128
  Performance.. 129
7.4. FAILURE PROTECTION 129
7.5. SAFETY AND RELIABILITY 130
  Safety Terminology 130
  Example of reliability specifications 130
7.6. RELIABILITY METRICS 131
  Failure classification 131
7.7. HAZARD AND RISK ANALYSIS 133
  Fault-tree analysis 133
  Safety lifecycle 140
  Risk assessment 141
7.8. DESIGN RECOMMENDATIONS FOR DEPENDABILITY 142
7.9. CHAPTER SUMMARY 146
  Exercises.. 147

CHAPTER 8 SAFETY-CRITICAL SYSTEMS 149

8.1. INTRODUCTION 149
8.2. HAZARD AND RISK ANALYSIS IN safety-critical systems 149
8.3. FAILURE MODE AND EFFECTS ANALYSIS 150
8.4. FMEA / FMECA OVERVIEW.. 151
  Basic analysis procedure for FMEA or FMECA................ 152
8.5. RISK EVALUATION METHODS 152
  Risk priority numbers... 152
  Criticality analysis of risk 152
8.6. APPLICATIONS AND BENEFITS... 153
8.7. FMEA CONCEPT IN SOFTWARE LIFECYCLE MANAGEMENT...... 153
8.8. HAZARD AND OPERABILITY STUDIES (HAZOP)...................... 154
8.9. CHAPTER SUMMARY 157
  Exercises.. 158

CHAPTER 9   VALIDATION AND VERIFICATION 159

9.1.   INTRODUCTION 159
9.2.   TESTING TO VALIDATE THE SYSTEM 159
   Static analysis techniques 159
   Dynamic analysis techniques 161
9.3.   TESTING TOOLS 162
9.4.   TESTING STRATEGIES 163
   Strategies: 163
9.5.   INTERFACE TESTING 164
9.6.   LEVELS OF TESTING 165
9.7.   CHAPTER SUMMARY 165
   Exercises 166

CHAPTER 10   DEFECT TESTING 167

10.1.   INTRODUCTION 167
   Main approaches to testing 167
10.2.   WHITE BOX OR STRUCTURAL TESTING 169
   Code-inspections and walk-troughs 169
   Path testing 170
   Loop testing 171
   Domain testing 172
10.3.   BLACK BOX OR FUNCTIONAL TESTING 172
   Black box testing without user involvement 172
   Black box testing with user involvement 173
   Equivalence partitioning and boundary value analysis 174
10.4.   ASSESSING THE EFFECTIVENESS OF TESTING 176
   Points to consider for testing 177
10.5.   CHAPTER SUMMARY 180
   Exercises 181

CHAPTER 11 SOFTWARE QUALITY 183

11.1.   INTRODUCTION 183
   Total Quality Management 183
11.2.   GENERIC SOFTWARE QUALITY MEASURES 184
   Software metrics 184
11.3.   CURRENT METRICS AND MODELS TECHNOLOGY 186
   Metrics application 187
11.4.   METRICS CHARACTERISTICS 189
11.5.   IMPACT OF METRICS ON MODERN SOFTWARE ENGINEERING ... 189
11.6.   CORPORATE ATTITUDE TO SOFTWARE QUALITY 192
   Quality assurance 192
   Quality planning 193
   Quality control 193
11.7.   CHAPTER SUMMARY 194
   Exercises 195

CHAPTER 12 SOFTWARE COSTING **196**

12.1. INTRODUCTION 196
12.2. COCOMO COST ESTIMATION MODEL.. 199
  Estimation model development procedure 200
  Size estimation 200
  Software cost-modelling accuracy 201
12.3. ESTIMATION MODELS.. 201
  Small projects 201
  Large projects 201
12.4. COCOMO MODEL TYPES.. 202
  The basic COCOMO model... 202
12.5. DEVELOPMENT MODES FOR SOFTWARE COSTING 203
  Organic mode.. 204
  Semidetached mode 204
  Embedded mode 205
  Phase distribution of effort and schedule for organic mode projects 206
  Intermediate COCOMO Model 209
  The detailed COCOMO model 210
12.6. COCOMO II SOFTWARE COST ESTIMATION MODEL 211
  Cost Drivers.. 211
  COCOMO II effort equation... 212
  COCOMO II schedule equation.. 212
12.7. CHAPTER SUMMARY 213
  Exercises... 213
  References 215

APPENDIX I   SRS TEMPLATE... A0
APPENDIX II   PROGRAM DESIGN LANGUAGE (PDL)............................. A4
  PDL STANDARD.. A4
APPENDIX III   USER INTERFACE GUIDELINES A9
  Guidelines for user interface design A9

CHAPTER 1 GENERAL CONCEPTS IN SOFTWARE ENGINEERING

1.1. Introduction

Software engineering can be described as a discipline, which provides methods and tools for producing quality software while taking into account project constraints on the budget, timescales and resources. The institution of electrical and electronic engineers (IEEE) is a body that defines standards in many areas of engineering including software. According to the IEEE, software engineering can be defined as follows:

"The application of a systematic, disciplined, and quantifiable approach to the development, operation, and maintenance of software; that is, the application of engineering to software. " [1]

In order to help define the discipline the two words "software" and "engineering" can be taken separately. Thus "software" can be described as the code written by programmers to perform tasks that are required by the users.

And, "engineering" can be described as the process of applying scientific principles towards the practical design and construction of a solution to a presented task. Thus software engineering can be seen as just another branch of a broad engineering field. The different application areas of software systems share many of the common principles of engineering design and product development.

Software engineering involves all aspects of producing software for a given application. This includes the establishing the requirements specification of the system; system modelling, producing architectural and detailed design etc. In addition to this the system needs to be verified and validated. It is worth mentioning that typically these "non-programming" activities consume more than 50% of all development resources on a software engineering project. Testing techniques and tools, at different levels (unit, integration, and system) are needed throughout the project lifecycle. Due to the fact that software development is a human intensive process, management and quality control techniques should be used in order to run successful projects and produce quality systems.

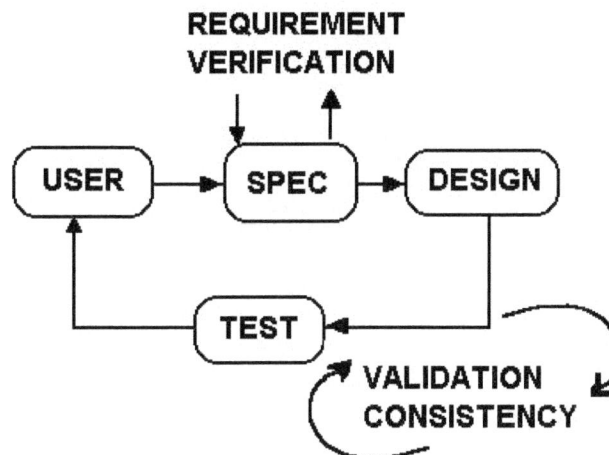

Figure 1.1 Requirements verification process

Thus it can be seen that there are many different components, which make up the discipline of software engineering. Some identifiable stages of the software development process are shown in figure 1.1 and can be briefly described as follows:

• **Software specification:** The functionality of the software and constraints on its operation must be defined. This stage is based on established user and systems requirements.

• **Software design and development:** Producing the software to meet the specification. This involves the design and implementation of the software.

• **Software validation and verification:** The software must be validated to ensure that it does what the customer wants. Using specific testing procedures performs validation and verification.

• **Software evolution:** The software must evolve to meet changing customer needs.

In theory at least, these stages of development ensure that well engineered software is reliable, efficient, user friendly and maintainable. In order to produce well engineered software a number of general approaches to software development can be defined. Some of these are briefly covered next.

Waterfall approach

This is perhaps the most intuitive approach to software development because the specific stages are completed in sequence, starting from a specification and progressing through the various stages in sequence. A simplified diagram is shown in figure 1.2, where it is seen that some stages are iterative, which means that they can be repeated until the outcome is satisfactory.

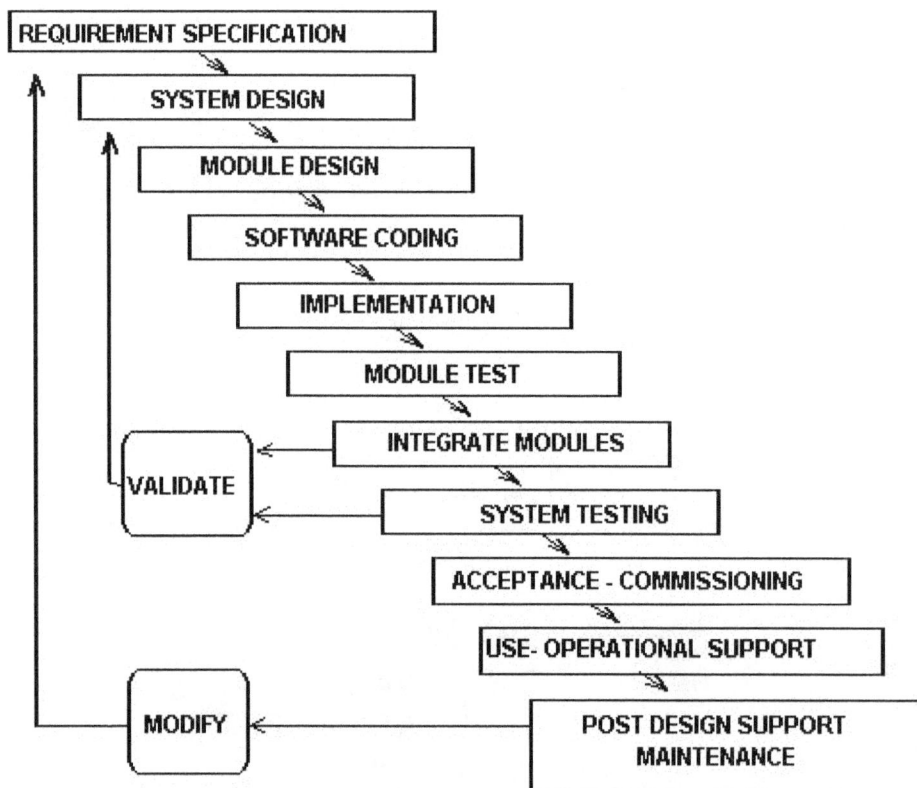

Figure 1.2. Waterfall approach to software development

This approach is suited to software projects that are relatively simple and where there are few unknowns. For example the development of a student record system that stores the information for students attending university courses. Although relatively bulky this type of system can be developed in stages according to the waterfall model. On the other hand, if for example you had to develop a computer game, where the creative input is largely undefined at the beginning, then it is difficult to apply the waterfall model to this type of software development.

Exploratory programming

This approach relies on developing a working system of the software as soon as possible and then modifying it until it performs adequately. This approach is best suited to projects that involve complex systems in which there are many unknowns and where the working environment is not well understood. For this reason exploratory software development methods should have a short development cycle. For example, this approach would suit a project to develop a computer aided software engineering (CASE) tool such as AUTOCAD.

Many advanced programming environments include CASE tools that support exploratory programming by making it easy and quick to try out different ideas. For example Google Apps and the Google App Engine assist software development by providing IT infrastructure through a set of applications that serve as a development platform for building new applications. [2]

Flash development under the Adobe Flash Platform provides tools to develop applications, content, and video that can run across different operating systems and devices. The Flash Platform consists of an integrated set of technologies that provide everything needed to deliver applications, content, and high-definition video to the widest possible audience. [3]

Smalltalk is perhaps the best-known example of an exploratory programming environment. The simplicity, effectiveness and elegance of Smalltalk are derived from its simple yet highly expressive syntax and the design of the various libraries of 'objects'. Smalltalk was the first, and remains one of the few, pure object-oriented programming languages. The ANSI Smalltalk Standard was approved on May 19, 1998." A large number of versions of small talk are available for different platforms and applications. [4] Smalltalk is very useful in exploratory programming because it allows programmers to create objects and try them out to see what happens, without having to compile a program. This makes programming easier, more fun, and less intimidating. Some programming languages that provide support for exploratory programming include Lisp, Smalltalk, Self, Factor, Oz, Obliq, Cecil, Dylan, REBOL, Tcl, and Python. [5]

Prototyping

Building a prototype is a well-established approach used in the development of engineering systems. For example, a small-scale prototype of an aircraft can give insight into flight behaviour before the complete system is built. This will save cost and time during development. In software engineering, prototyping is used in a similar fashion, which is to say that a prototype is initially built in order to identify system behaviour. Typically a prototype simulates only a few selected features of the target program, which may in fact be quite different from the eventual implementation. In this case the main purpose of a prototype is to allow users of the software to evaluate the design aspects featured in the prototype by actually trying them out rather than having to rely solely on documentation of the proposed design. Thus, software developers use feedback from the users of the prototype to determine if the software specifications match the user requirements. There is little point in making reliable, efficient software, which does not do what the users want. Prototyping can also provide insight into the accuracy of project management aspects such as the task schedules the proposed deadlines and milestones etc.

A variety of prototyping techniques exist and some of these are throwaway prototyping, evolutionary prototyping, extreme prototyping and incremental development. These will be covered later in chapter 6 of this text.

Formal transformation

Formal methods have been used in engineering for many years in order to prove mathematically that certain relationships hold true in given circumstances. It is generally considered that the design, which is underpinned by formal methods, can contribute to the reliability of the system. In software engineering, formal methods are a particular kind of mathematically based proofs that can be used to prove the correct functioning of a procedure. However, it is generally difficult to apply formal methods to event-driven systems because the occurrence of events is unpredictable. Some of the formal methods that are used in software engineering include logic calculi, formal languages, automata theory, and program semantics. These are used in many phases of the software development process including formal specification, verification and modelling.

During the requirements engineering phase, Formal methods allow a software engineer to create a specification that is more complete, consistent, and unambiguous than those produced using conventional or even object-oriented methods. In this event, set theory and logic notation are used to create a clear statement of facts (requirements). This mathematical specification can then be analysed in a formal manner in order to prove correctness and consistency. The resulting specification is less ambiguous than informal modes of representation because it has been created using a mathematical notation. [6]

In his publication, M.P. Ward provides a good example of how formal methods can be applied in software engineering. [7] In this paper Ward uses a complex sorting program as a case study for the analysis of a program by formal transformations. Besides a complex control flow, the program uses arrays to represent various linked lists and sets, which are manipulated in various 'ingenious' ways in order to get the best performance from the algorithm. Here the aim is to manipulate the program, using semantics-preserving operations, in order to produce an abstract specification. The transformations are carried out in the wide spectrum language (WSL) that includes both low-level program operations and high level specifications, and which has been specifically designed to be easy to transform. Thus it can be seen that research in formal transforms tends to be directed towards producing languages for direct transformation of a formal specification. It is widely accepted that graph transformation is a good candidate to form the backbone of such transformation languages. This topic includes the adaptation and integration of several ideas concerning graph rewriting, such as Story Diagrams, Triple Graph Grammars, controlled graph rewriting. [8]

Detailed study of formal methods is beyond the scope of this text and more information can be obtained elsewhere. A good starting point is the FM Europe website [9]

Software development based on reusable components

Software reuse is the process of creating software systems from existing code rather than building new software from scratch. The idea stems form the fact that much of the programming effort can be used in a variety of different software systems. For example, a routine to perform a binary search can be used in an Oracle database as well as in a search engine on the Internet. The main difference is the platform for which the code is written, but the algorithm remains unchanged. For a more specific example consider a software development enterprise that specialises in accounting software. It is very likely that they will have a stockpile of software procedures that can be reused in any future development projects. However, in reality re-use is not as simple as taking procedures off the shelf and compiling them into a program.

While organisations can reduce the time to market for a new product with this approach, they often face code duplication problems caused by cut and paste programming. In the event of errors being generated this duplication can also complicate the de-bugging process. In order to make re-use more appealing, new programming trends for reuse include formalising code development. This means that an interface must be defined for any newly written code that is intended for re-use. This can be analogous to a header file in protocol implementation, which is to say that the header defines how the contents are processed. In organisations that practice re-use, these are formally standardised into their software product line engineering procedures.

Perhaps it is useful to consider that early examples of software reuse are the libraries used in the 'C' programming language. Here a library of functions is stored in a header file, and the program can call any function, which is included in the header file without having to code that function explicitly. Thus for example, `printf` function is listed in the `stdi0.h` header file and any program that needs to use the `printf` function only needs to declare the `stdio.h` in the include statement. This is shown in the C program segment below.

```
#include "stdio.h"
void main()
{
    printf("This is a line of text to output.\n");
}
```

The above code segment would not compile correctly if the `stdio.h` file were not included in the source, because this would mean that there is no information about the `printf` function anywhere within the program. When the program compiles, the header file `stdio.h` is included in the compile process, and so the function `printf` is recognised by the compiler, since it is included in the `stdio.h` header file.

Following the development and evolution of Object-Oriented Programming (OOP) along with trends in standardising the development methodology with the Unified Modelling Language (UML) the idea of software reuse is an increasingly favoured approach to development.

Current research in reusable components appears to focus on making reuse faster, easier, more systematic, and to make it an integral part of the programming process. These were also some of the main goals behind the introduction of OOP and so it is not surprising that this is becoming one of the most common forms of software reuse.

A somewhat later approach to reuse is the so-called generic programming. This approach uses software "generators", which can create new programs of a certain type, based on a set of parameters that users select. Fields of study about such systems fall in the categories of generative programming and meta-programming, but these are beyond the scope of this text. [10]

1.2. Paradigms in software engineering

A programming paradigm refers to the fundamental style of computer programming. This is not the same as methodology, which refers to the approach taken towards solving problems in software engineering; Programming paradigms are distinguished in the concepts that are used to represent the elements of a program (such as objects, functions, variables, constraints, etc.) and the steps that compose a computation (assignment, evaluation, data flows, etc.). [11] Some of the programming paradigms that are in use today are listed in Table 1.1.

Table 1.1. A selection of programming paradigms currently in use

Agent-oriented	Component-based
Flow-based	Pipeline
Concurrent computing	Functional
Cell-oriented (spreadsheets)	Graph-oriented
Constraint	Logic
Event-driven	Structured
Procedural	Modular
Recursive	Object-oriented
Meta-programming	Domain-specific
Parallel computing	Process-oriented

If we researched into the evolution of programming languages we would find that to a large extent programming languages are designed around a particular paradigm. For example, Ada programming language was originally (cc 1980) designed for real-time systems applications and is still commonly used for those purposes. On the other hand, procedural languages were designed around a specific application area. For example, COBOL (Common Business Oriented Language). FORTRAN (FORmula TRANslation) and ALGOL (ALGOrithmic Language). All three of these languages use the procedural paradigm, which means that they rely on well defined sequence of actions which when implemented as a procedure will solve the required problem. Thus procedural languages were designed to support particular application area such as business, scientific, knowledge engineering etc.

With the rapid evolution of software following the introduction in the 1980s of the personal computer (PC) to the community as a whole, it became necessary to support a wider area of software applications within the computer community. Features of general-purpose operating systems such as Windows were extended to support multi-tasking and later multi-threading and also the general process and memory management features of the new operating systems were significantly improved. This broadening of software applications gave rise to the new paradigm, which is not based on procedures that are executed in a prescribed manner. Instead this new paradigm considers software components in a way that more closely resembles the real-world objects and tries to describe their behaviour under different conditions. This object-oriented paradigm gave rise to object-oriented languages (like Smalltalk, Eiffel and Java) that encapsulate data, and methods of manipulating the data, into a single unit called an object. The only way to access data is through the methods that are supported by the object. As a result of this, the internal workings of an object may be changed without affecting any code that uses that object.

In this text I will cover briefly these two paradigms, namely procedural paradigm and object-oriented paradigm, because they are the most common in current software engineering practice. Before describing these however it is worth mentioning a word or two about the role of methodology in software development.

Software development methodology

In software engineering a methodology helps in the design of software programs by ensuring that correct steps are taken at every design stage. This is true whether procedural or object-oriented programming paradigms are used. The methodology will be different for these paradigms but in either case it has rules that ensure that development is systematic and therefore less prone to errors in missing out components or including components that do not exist.

In a general sense, any methodology becomes invaluable when the system being designed is very complex and when it is difficult to trace all the control and data flows for all components. In these cases a clear and precise methodology for describing design will enable each component to be traced at every stage of development. Most often a software CASE tool (Computer Aided Software Engineering) is developed that will make the methodology easier to implement. In describing the procedural and OO programming paradigms some reference will be made to methodologies that are used to implement these.

In this text I shall briefly introduce Jackson Structured Programming (JSP) as a methodology used in procedural programming paradigm. For the object-oriented paradigm I shall refer to the Booch method, although a more appropriate representation is the unified modelling language (UML), which will be covered in chapter 3 of this textbook.

1.3.   Procedural programming

Procedural programming can sometimes be used as a synonym for imperative programming (specifying which steps the program must take in order to reach the desired state). Procedures, also known as routines, subroutines, or functions, describe a series of computational steps to be carried out. For this reason a procedural programming language provides a programmer with tools to define precisely each step in the performance of a task. Some good examples of procedural programs are the Linux Kernel and Apache Server. [12]

Procedural programming refers to the concept of describing a large and complex software program as being made up of a number of procedures, all of which combine to give the program its functionality. For example, imagine that you have to develop a program to calculate the VAT component of the cost of a given retail item. The software to do this would involve a very simple task of reading the item price as an input and returning the VAT percentage as the output (currently at 17.5%). For a more challenging development, assume that you are developing the software for an aircraft flight-simulator. Here the overall software effort is much more elaborate and you would be required to simulate complex relationships between systems. For example, the effect of changing altitude on performance of jet engines will need to be taken into account in order to provide a true simulation of aircraft behaviour in flight. Software systems of this type need to be developed as a combination of subsystems and modules, which enable a piecemeal type of development to take place. The concept of integrating modules and subsystems is then introduced to enable all software components to be brought together into a single executable program. This requirement to subdivide the program into executable components gave rise to procedures and consequently to procedural programming concepts.

Most programming languages can be used to program procedures that perform certain tasks, however the distinction is largely made between function oriented programming (FOP) which embodies the procedural concept and object-oriented programming (OOP) which is a different concept altogether. Thus, a distinction is made as to whether a programming language is Object-oriented and if not, then it is essentially procedural in nature. However, the procedural concept extends beyond the definition of the language that is used to develop the program. It is an approach to program design that is particularly useful to scientists and engineers, since it allows them to construct elegant data structures, which are needed in complex computational tasks. Arguably the most versatile programming language that supports procedural concepts is the 'C' programming language. Although it was primarily intended to run under UNIX, C is equally capable of running under Microsoft operating systems and other platforms, provided of course that a suitable compiler is in place to compile the C code for the required platform. It is perhaps worth mentioning at this point that C++ is a programming language that is derived directly from C and that supports both the procedural and the object-oriented paradigms. Nevertheless, returning to procedural programming we consider next a methodology of describing procedural programme design.

Algorithmic design notation for sequence, iteration and selection

At this stage we need to consider some modelling tools for procedural program design. In my opinion all programming efforts have as their aims to provide the user with a computational service. Very often this will involve the programmer and the user establishing a set of specifications that will guide the programmer in the design of the program and also help the user to identify the features that they want from the program. Therefore, before the actual programming is done it is necessary to describe program functionality in such a manner that even those who are not experienced in programming, can understand what the program will do at each stage. The Jackson Structured Programming (JSP) concept is commonly used in function oriented design. [13]

Broadly speaking, this concept describes all programming structures as a combination of the elementary components of sequence, iteration and selection (decision). The result is a functionally decomposed program offering the designer the possibility of creating the structure of the program to match that of the data. This concept is termed functional decomposition and the elementary components are defined as follows.

- **Sequence**, which has two or more parts occurring once each, in the order from left to right on the diagram.
- **Iteration**, which has one part, occurring zero or more times
- **Selection**, which has two or more parts of which one, and only one occurs once. (i.e. True/False)

To aid design we use a diagram to symbolise the interactions between these elementary components. The symbols used are as given in figure 1.3.

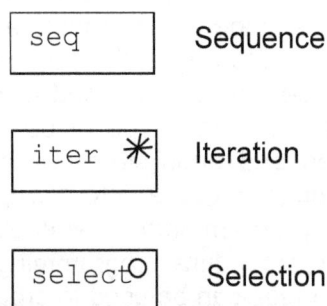

| seq | Sequence |

| iter ✳ | Iteration |

| select○ | Selection |

Figure 1.3. Basic procedural constructs

These elementary components can be combined to produce a program structure that is an arrangement of sequences decisions and iterations. Furthermore, this type of decomposition is equally applicable to data structures as it is to program structures. On a general point it may be said that if we are able to design a program whose structure corresponds to the data structure, then we achieve optimal program execution in speed and efficiency as well as accuracy. Let us consider each of these elementary components in turn.

Sequence

Very simply stated, sequences are program statements, which are executed in a prescribed order until there are no more statements to be executed or until a stop is encountered. Diagrammatically a sequence of actions to perform is depicted as rectangles linked by lines to indicate the level that they are at. The sequence starts at the top of the diagram with the top-level action. The next action is at the next lower level and in the sequence from left to right. For example, with reference to figure 1.4, if the sequence called `read` is made up of parts `read x`, `read y` and `read z`, in this order, the diagram would be as shown here.

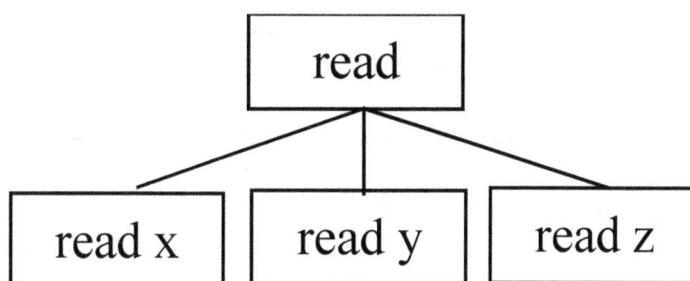

Figure 1.4 Graphic of sequence components

It was mentioned earlier that these structure diagrams could be used to represent both data and program structures. However, when relating them to program structures it is useful for us to convert them to a verbal notation that we call the schematic logic. [14]

Schematic logic is a translation of the basic elements of a sequence, iteration and selection into a logical constructs made up of simple statements. The statements `seq`, `iter` and `select` are used to signal the start of a component and each of them has to have an `end` to indicate that it has completed. When the schematic logic uses a statement to perform a task we use the `do` operator and terminate the statement with a semicolon (`;`). Thus, the schematic logic for the diagram shown in figure 1.4, would only use the `seq` component and would take the following form:

```
read        seq
            do read x;
            do read y;
            do read z;
read        end
```

Iterations

By definition, to iterate is to repeat the process in its entirety, as many times as there are number of iterations. Thus, for example if we were to calculate the values of

$y=x*2$ for the values of x starting at 0 and incremented until $x=4$ then there would be 5 iterations giving values corresponding to the table in figure 1.5.

x	0	1	2	3	4
y	0	2	4	6	8

Table of values for x and y

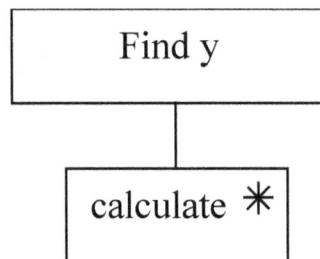

Figure 1.5 Graphic to show iteration

The diagram for this structure, called `find y` whose iterated part is `calculate` would be as shown here in the diagram. The asterisk (*) in the box for the iterated part indicates multiple occurrences of `calculate`, within `find y`. It must be stressed that `find y` is the iteration and that the multiplicity of `calculate` occurrences is an attribute of `find y` and not of `calculate`. Thus, in our example `find y` has 5 occurrences of the calculation $y=2*x$.

In programming terminology, iterations can be performed by the use of loops. A number of these are available in C and include the `do, while, do-while and for` loops. The schematic logic for the above diagram would only use the `iter` component and would take the following form:

```
find y     iter

           do calculate;

find y     end
```

Selections

Selections are based on decisions for which the answer is either yes or no, and in either case this leads to a particular event or process being invoked. In programming languages, decisions are invariably represented by `If` statements and these can also include `else` and `else-If` constructs. Additionally, there can be a number of levels of `If`-statements, which in programming terminology are referred to as `nested If` statements.

Diagrammatic representation of two-level nested `If`-statements is shown in figure 1.6. Here, the selection `Rail Ticket` has two further selections `Child` or `Adult`, each of which has parts `Single` or `Return`. The circles in the top-right corner of the boxes indicate that these are selections. (Or)

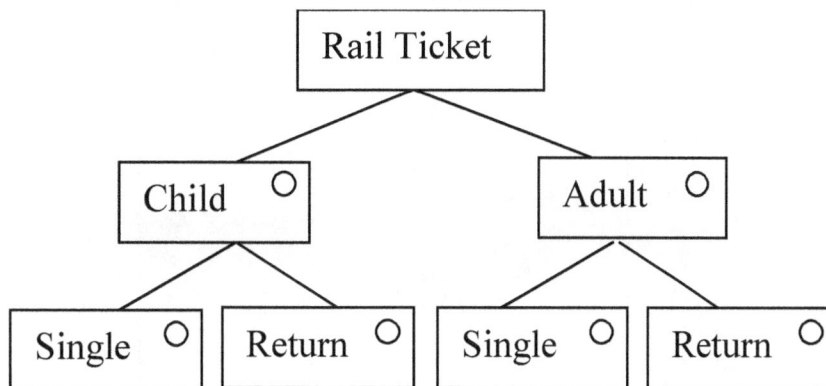

Figure 1.6 Graphic to show selection using two-level If statements

The schematic logic for this diagram would use only the `select` component and is of the following form:

```
Rail Ticket      select
                 do Child;
        Child         select
                      do Single;
        Child         or
                 do Return;
        Child         End

Rail Ticket      or
                 do Adult;
        Adult         select
                      do Single;
        Adult         or
                 do Return
        Adult         End
Rail Ticket      end
```

The elementary components discussed here are only useful when they combine to form complex structures. In order to maintain consistency in our representation of structures using the above elementary components we further assume that all structures will have a tree-type context. That is to say, there will only be one path to an element starting from the root at the top and working down the structure. In this manner we eliminate the possibility of errors due to inconsistencies that may arise when for example; two paths lead to the same point, and give differing results. Armed with the above graphical tools we are able to translate our design concept into a schematic logic that can then be further translated into a computer program.

Let us consider an example where we convert a schematic logic into a structure diagram. The schematic logic is given below and you are required to convert it into a structure diagram. The structure diagram solution is shown in figure 1.7 and we will consider the steps towards this solution next.

```
A seq
      B       seq
              do C;
              do D;
              E       iter
                      do F;
              E       end
      B       end
      G       select
              do H;
      G       or
              I       select
                      J select
                              do K;
                      J       or
                      do L;
                      J       end
              I       or
                      do M;
              I       end
      G       end
A     end
```

Solution:
Step 1: Annotate the schematic logic with lines to ensure where each component begins and ends. This is done so that we confirm that there are no errors and also to make it easier for us to follow the program logic. Thus I repeat the above listing and include the lines as annotations.

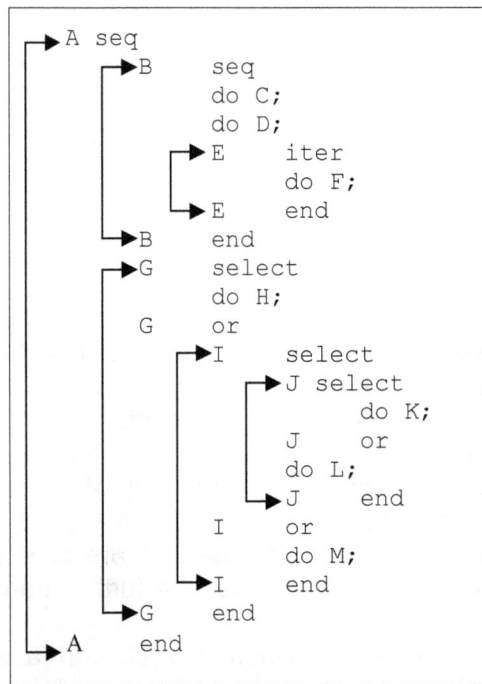

Figure 1.7 Schematic logic start-end links

The process of converting the schematic logic into a structure diagram is simply a matter of reading the schematic logic and as soon as an elementary component is found, placing a symbol for that component in the structure chart. Thus, we begin by noting that A is a sequence, which at the first level, evidently contains components B and G. Therefore, we produce the first component in our structure chart, which is a sequence component. This is shown in the figure Step 1 below.

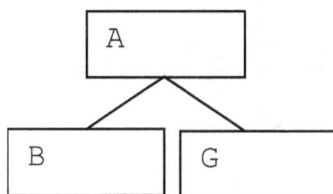

Figure Step 1

We proceed with performing the sequences in the prescribed order. Thus, B is the next component that we need to pursue. We note that B is another sequence, which has C, D and E as its component parts. C and D are statements to be executed and E is an elementary component, which is an iteration that has F as the executable part. We therefore append these to our Step 1 diagram and build a branch along the B path, as shown in figure Step 2.

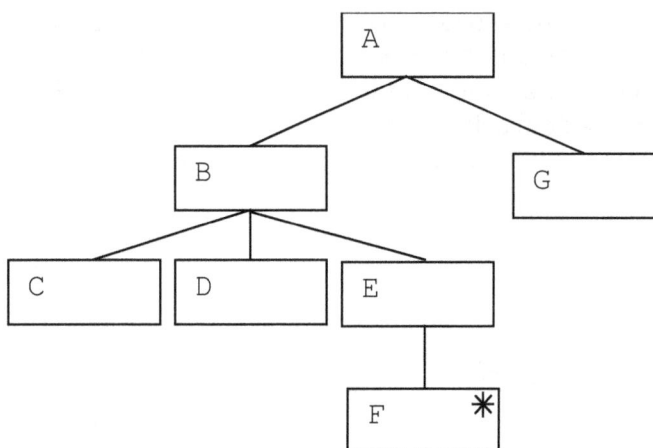

Figure Step 2

At this point the schematic logic reaches the end of B, which indicates to us that the B sequence has terminated. The logic then introduces the G element, which is a selection that chooses to execute H, which is a statement, or to perform I which is in fact another select. Therefore it is seen on the diagram that H and I are selection objects. Continuing on, it is seen that I is another select offering either M which is a statement, or the component J which is yet another select. The elementary component J is a select offering the choice of K or L, both of which are in fact statements that will terminate after execution. Armed with this information, we are ready to complete our structure diagram. The point on the structure diagram from which G needs to proceed is clearly seen in both the Step 1 and Step 2 figures. The complete structure diagram is shown in figure Step 3.

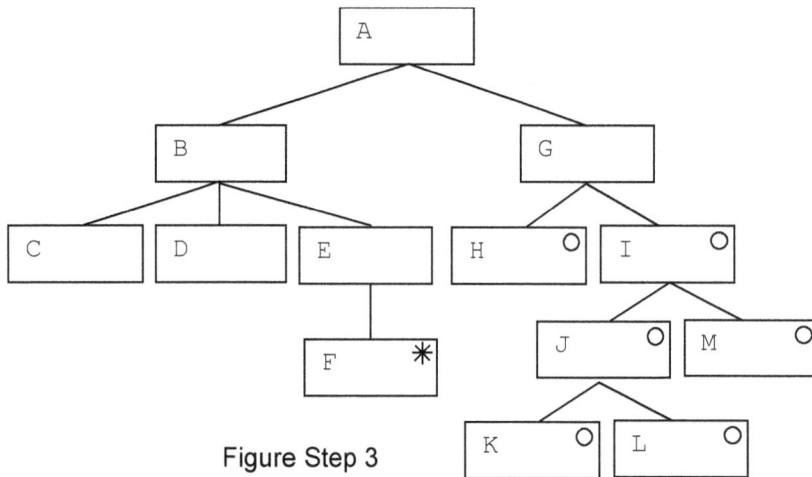

Figure Step 3

Example: Your task is to consider the structure diagram shown in figure 1.8 and produce the corresponding schematic logic. (Basically the reverse of the previous example)

The procedure for converting a structure chart to a schematic logic is equally straightforward. We simply follow the diagram in the correct order and when we come to an elementary component we declare it within our schematic logic and follow it through until it ends. If a statement is encountered we describe it with a do directive and terminate with a semicolon. We perform this action along every path starting from the root and moving down. Thus, we begin to translate the structure diagram shown in figure 1.8 below as follows.

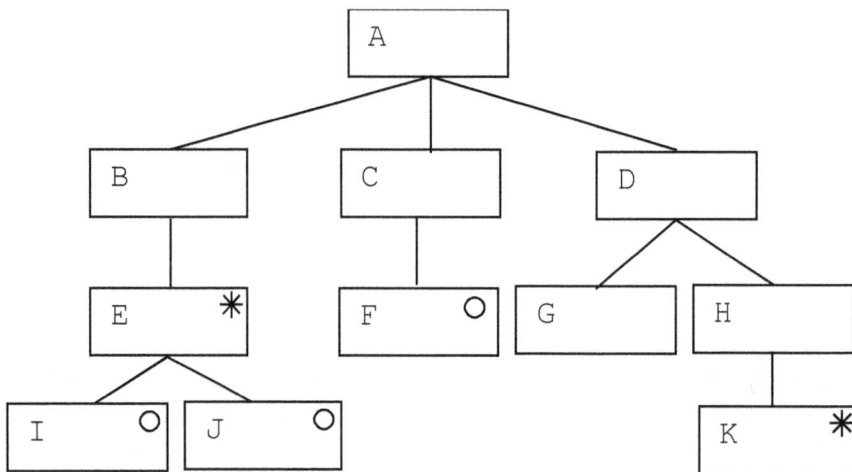

Figure 1.8 Structure diagram example

Solution:

From the diagram it is seen that A is a sequence of B, C and D. So starting with B we follow its full path. A quick glance at the diagram will indicate to us that the full path includes iteration and selection elementary components.

```
A       seq
        B       iter
                E       select
                        do I;
                E       or
                        do J;
                E       end
        B       end
```
Figure. Slide 1

We therefore proceed by considering each component in the B path, namely, E (an iteration) and I, J (selections). The resulting schematic logic segment is shown here in figure Slide 1. Having exhausted the B path the next path in the original A sequence is C. Here we have a select element that selects F only. We proceed to add the schematic logic for this noting that we must end it at the appropriate point. The schematic logic for the single select statement is shown in figure Slide 2.

```
............
        C       select
                    do F;
        C       end
......... .
```
Figure. Slide 2

Note that, in this particular example the select is irrelevant since there is no choice other than F. It is used deliberately to show that the structure can be represented even if it does not make programming sense. In fact a sequence instead of select would have given us the same result here. Also, note that both elementary components B and C have the same level of indentation on the schematic logic. This serves to indicate that they are sequences on the same level of the structure chart. Having completed the C element the next path to pursue is the D elementary component. This elementary component is a sequence G, H where G is a statement and H is another primary element, namely iteration. The schematic logic for this path is shown in figure slide 3.

```
.... . .
        D       seq
                do G;
                H       iter
                        do K;
                H       end
        D       end
........
```
Figure. Slide 3

The complete schematic logic is the collection of the above slides 1, 2 and 3 not forgetting of course to include the `end` directive corresponding to A.

1.4.   Object-oriented programming

As mentioned earlier around the mid to late 1980s the object-orientated paradigm gained momentum because of a need to develop and simulate an increasing variety of software applications and systems. At that time, the existing software methodologies made it very difficult to construct very large software systems especially if they were being developed by thousands of people spread across the globe. As mentioned earlier with object-oriented languages, data and methods of manipulating the data are kept as a single unit called an object and the only way to access the data is via the object's 'methods' (subroutines). Thus a software development process needs to consider what objects will be used, and what the properties of these will be. At this time we also consider classes in which to group similar objects. We also need to consider what methods an object will support.

There are a number of acronyms that are used in relation to the object-oriented paradigm and these are Object-Oriented Design (OOD), programming (OOP) and Analysis (OOA). Figure 1.9 shows the relationship between design, analysis and programming and this will be explained next.

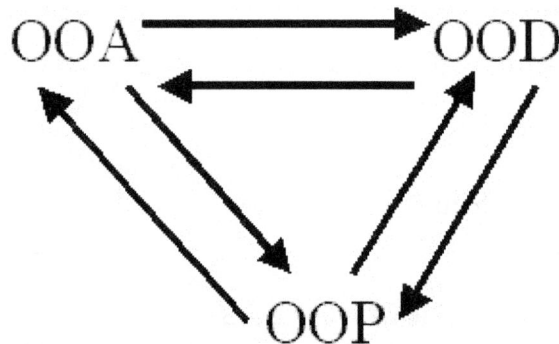

Figure 1.9. Relationship between design, analysis and programming

Good program designers usually approach design in an organised manner rather than just jumping in at the deep-end and beginning with the programming. In order to understand what they are trying to do and how they are going to go about it they need to carry out a great deal of research which will help to clarify the details of the design in their mind. This is where Object Orientated Analysis (OOA) can play an important role that is in enhancing the understanding of the problem that the client wants solved. This is usually followed by the Design stage (OOD) which focuses on how to implement a particular design solution which will then be used with the programming stage (OOP) to complete the full development cycle. A little more details of these stages will be described next.

Analysis stage
The analysis stage can be described briefly by the following bullet points,
- The development of the system model that describes the desired behaviour. Here the focus is on behaviour and not on the form of the system. (i.e. what it will look like)
- It is a statement of what the system does not how it does it.
- It is never an exhaustive answer to the problem. Rather it starts as an outline of the approach which is enhanced by analysis.

- It is not possible to carry out the complete analysis before the design is completed because design raises questions about behaviour and this impacts on the analysis stage.
- Analysis is never a stand-alone stage

Design stage

The design Stage is concerned with the following points:
- Creation of the architecture that will facilitate implementation.
- This stage does not stop until the final system is delivered to the client.
- The focus is on structure both static and dynamic and additional analysis may be required as a result of this.
- Build the system skeleton upon which all the rest of the implementation relies.

Programming stage

The programming stage uses both the analysis and design stages as a kind of blueprint of how to implement the overall design in the desired programming language.

However it has to be said that these stages do not always follow directly from one to another. Instead the overall development relies on the fact that each of the stages are adaptable. This means that that improvement and refinements can be made to one stage and these are then followed through to the other stages in order to maintain the integrity of the system. In this manner the overall development evolves rather than following a prescribed sequence of stages.

Figure 1.9 demonstrates the fact that each stage is not intended as a standalone component. The arrows linking each stage to the other two stages indicate that stages are flexible. Thus a refinement to one stage can be evaluated on the first pass and will be passed onto the other two stages. When these are updated their own impact on the first stage will be considered in a number of iterative passes.

History of OOD

The first ever object orientated language was Simula and it was developed in the 1960's by Kristen Nygaard and Ole Dahl as an extension of Algol 60. These early OO languages incorporated some of the key aspects of object-orientation, which are,
- Objects.
- Encapsulated classes.
- Inheritance.

Figure 1.10 depicts a simplified evolution of OOP languages. Here it can be seen that the most used object orientated languages today, i.e. C++ and Java derive from a combination of pure object-orientated languages and existing languages which were popular in industry. Consequently these are known as hybrid object-orientated languages. This is because they retained much of the syntax of popular existing languages while introducing new elements, which are necessary to implement OOD within a programming language. Having said that, most software developers consider these to be OOD languages and do not worry about the hybrid nature of their origins.

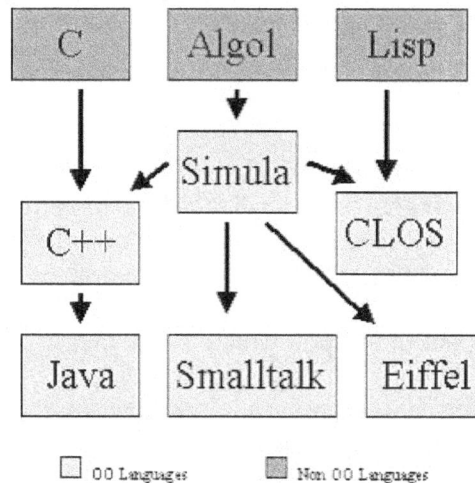

Figure 1.10. Evolution of OOP Languages

Pure object-orientated languages such as Smalltalk enforce the rules of the OO approach. They are focused on rapid development using powerful tools but they carry the restrictions that they are less concerned with performance and more with remaining true to the concept of OO. Hybrid languages derive from traditional mainstream languages, which have been extended to incorporate OO, but OO is not enforced and so it is up to the programmer to make sure that the correct rules have been followed. The advantages of hybrid languages are that they offer good performance, are portable and allow reusability of existing code. This enables developers to have a smooth migration from the traditional approach to the OO approach.

Object-oriented design considerations

Having briefly given the background to OO it is appropriate to consider some design aspects. Problems in the design of software systems mostly occur when the system is required to deal with complex situations, which are hard to conceptualise. For example, it is relatively easy to design software to control a cash point machine, but it is quite another matter designing software to submit Inland Revenue tax returns on-line.

The general idea behind the OOD approach is to represent a given problem by breaking it down into small chunks known as objects. Each of these objects is able to interact with other objects and all these objects together can be used to simulate the behaviour of the complete system. Thus we can simplify the design process by breaking everything that is too complex into smaller components that are easier to understand. We can then focus on designing the required behaviour for each of these objects and when we are satisfied we can assemble these to produce the design for the complete system.

Applying OOD

As would be expected the object is the foundation of OOD but how do we define an object? An object is not like a function or procedure in C or Pascal but more like a real world object, that has behaviour and state. In fact an object can have a finite number of states, and these will change according to the object's behaviour. e.g. a car can have the state 'ignition-off' but if you apply the behaviour to 'turn-on' the ignition then the state of the car will change.

The idea of breaking everything down into objects does not automatically make life simple and in fact doing so often complicates matters. That is to say, when a problem is divided into a large number of components, it becomes difficult to find out a solution because we have to search through a large number of individual components. Thus the concern is not only to solve the problem but also to identify which parts of a system we really need to deal with at any one time in the design. This introduces the concept of abstraction as a way of managing the complexity of a system.

Abstraction

Abstraction is the elimination of the irrelevant and amplification of the essential. This means that we remove anything that has no relevance to the problem that we are currently dealing with and only look at the essential parts, which we will need to know in order to solve a problem.

An example of abstraction is teaching someone to drive. When teaching somebody to drive we emphasise the important features of the car i.e. ignition, steering wheel, brakes etc. but we do not tell them about what type of engine the car has or how the fuel pump works or describe the detailed mechanics of the car. This is because when driving a car we use a high-level of abstraction so that everybody can have the ability to drive a car (admittedly some perform this task better than others).

On the other hand, mechanics must have a low-level of abstraction because they need to know how each part of the car works. There are further levels of abstraction at the mechanic level, as they may need to know what a battery does but not how it manages to perform this task etc. Thus it can be said that abstraction limits the details only to the level that is necessary for the system to function.

Identifying a Class

In order to construct objects we need to set up some kind of framework that objects obey so that anyone who understands the rules within this framework can look at a design and understand it. This is where the concept of a Class comes into play. A Class is a set of objects that share a common structure and a common behaviour. The Class is the blueprint, which we use in order to build objects, and it becomes an object when we fill in the details (initialise) the Class. In order to describe the concept of a Class consider figure 1.11.

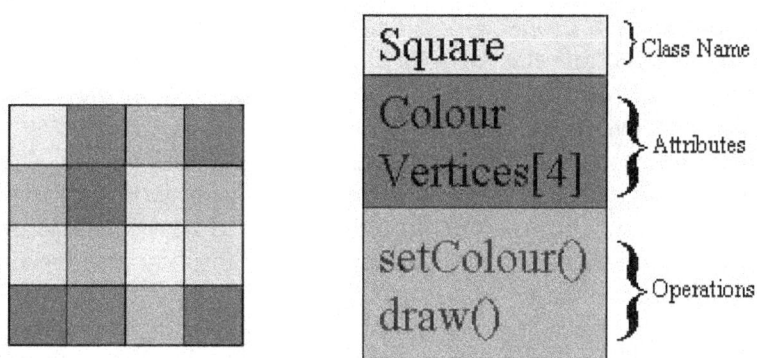

Figure 1.11. Class structure

Imagine a picture made up of squares as shown in figure 1.11. For this configuration we can make the following observations,

- Each square in the picture is an object, it has state (shade and position) and we can also describe behaviour that is attached to each square.
- We can change colour of squares or draw a new square.
- Each square is different but shares common features with other squares.

- We can abstract these commonalities.
- Each square has shared behaviour and the same sort of attributes
- We ignore the particular values of attributes and abstract (filter out unwanted information) in order to produce a Class of squares.

Thus a Class can be considered as a template for building new objects. It will only contain information about the attributes and operations, which are essential to the Class in order to implement a particular design. This means that the attributes and operations, which are important for one design project, may not cover all the states and behaviour scenarios that are important for another design scenario.

For example, consider the scenario of a washing machine. The amount of information required in order to implement the design of a controller for the washing machine compared with the information required in the design of a database to keep track of all the washing machines coming off a production line is vastly different. Yet both systems need to describe a washing machine class. Figure 1.12 shows a Class diagram of how classes are represented when designing an object-orientated system.

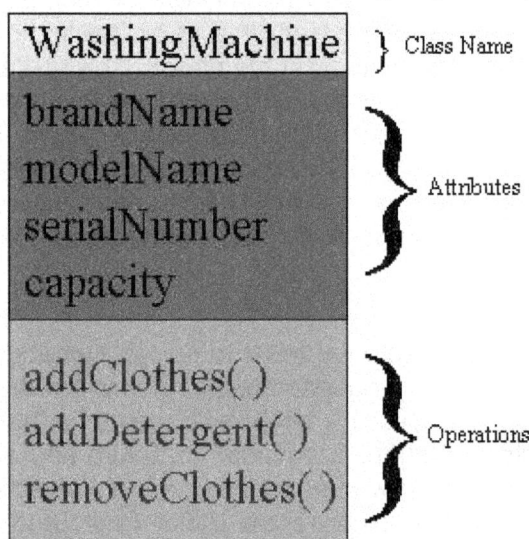

WashingMachine	} Class Name
brandName modelName serialNumber capacity	} Attributes
addClothes( ) addDetergent( ) removeClothes( )	} Operations

Figure 1.12. Washing machine Class

An attribute is a property of a Class. It describes the range of values that the property may hold in objects of that Class. In the washing machine example the attributes might be brand name, model name, serial number etc. An object will have a specific value for every attribute of a Class i.e. all of the above attributes will be initialised with values to produce an object. An operation is something that a Class can do or that you can do to a Class. An example operation for the washing machine might be add clothes, remove clothes, add washing powder, turn on etc. This is an example of higher-level abstraction, which applies to someone who wants to operate the machine on a daily basis.

Properties of classes

Perhaps the most important aspects of OO are the properties that are associated with classes and objects. The first concept we shall consider is that of inheritance. This is when one or more classes inherit state and behaviour from another Class. This can be achieved in the design process by removing common parts into a new Class, which is known as a super Class. Figure 1.13 shows an example of a system in terms of object classes. There are four classes shown, design, node, link and label. Each Class has its own attributes and methods. The arrows show the relationship between objects. If we wanted to create a superclass called Project we could collect properties such as name, description etc which are common to all members of the new superclass.

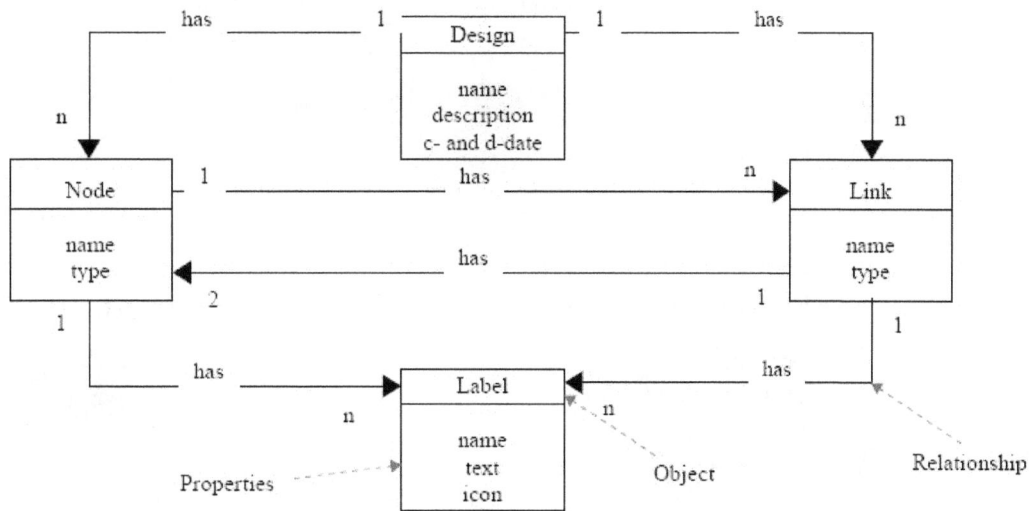

Figure 1.13. Interactions between classes

Inheritance

As an example of inheritance consider the picture of squares from the previous example. What if we wanted to introduce a new object such as a triangle along with the squares? The square has attributes such as colour and position with four vertices and a triangle will have attributes such as colour and position with three vertices. Similarities that can be removed in order to create a super Class are set the colour and draw shape (even if they are drawn differently). A Class can inherit three things namely,
- State e.g. colour
- Operations e.g. set colour (the shape Class knows enough to be able to set colour of any shape)
- The interface of an operation (i.e. what operation is achieved). It could be said that we do not care how shapes are drawn or what shape they are producing. For this situation the two subclasses and single super Class are shown in the diagram in figure 1.14.

The diagram shown in figure 1.14 describes a superclass called shape that has been created from the classes of triangle and square that share the common properties of colour and operations setColour() and Draw (). The sub-calsses of square and triagle inherit these properties and have other properties that are specific to their own class, and in fact these properties distinguish triangles from squares while both are in fact shapes.

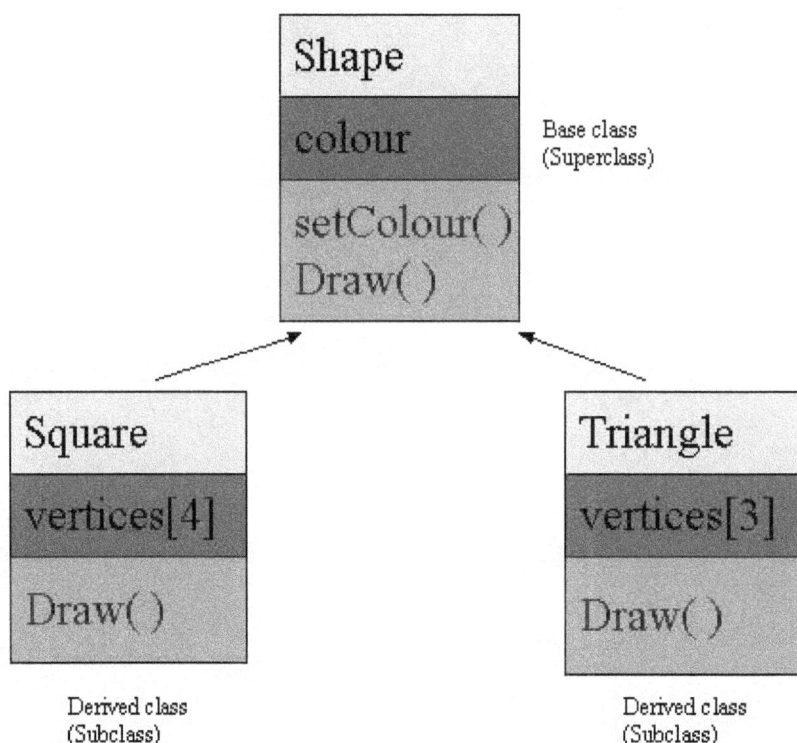

Figure 1.14. Classes inherit attributes from parent classes

Polymorphism

When we abstract just the interface of an operation and leave the implementation to subclasses it is called a polymorphic operation. Sometimes an operation has the same name in different classes but means different things. An example of this is that you can close a door, book, window, bank account etc. Clearly they all mean different things but have the same meaning (i.e. to close). This demonstrates that each Class knows how the operation should be interpreted in relation to that Class. This is known as polymorphism i.e. it allows the designer to maintain the terminology without having to make up artificial words to maintain a uniqueness of terms.

Encapsulation

When an object carries out its operations it hides those operations from the rest of the system so that we cannot see what is happening behind the scenes. For example we do not care nor need to know how the electronics within a CD player works, all that we want to know is the interface between the CD player and us i.e. how to eject, play, stop, move to next track etc. Therefore if we decide to change an object that has a relationship with another there would be no need to modify all related objects as long as the method of message sending remained the same. Consider again the CD example, if we wanted to upgrade our amplifier to a more powerful model we do not want to have to replace the CD player, tuner, tape cassette etc. It is this modularity, i.e. hiding the information that is not of concern to us, which makes OO design so useful.

Message passing

Objects use messages to communicate with each other. They are not usually concerned with the passing of data from one object to another but instead centre on the sending of a message telling an object to perform some kind of operation. We are not concerned with how an object does this but instead we need to be sure that the object will perform the action. In order for objects to communicate it is important to have a compatible interface, which both the server and the client can understand and use.

Associations

Objects have associations with each other, which help us to define the behaviour of objects. An example of an association is that I read a book, which is a one to one association, but I can also read papers and so there is an association with more than one Class. You can have bi-directional associations for example I live with my wife who also lives with me. This helps us build systems which model real life by understanding the relationships that objects have with each other.

Aggregation

This is when an object can be made up of several other objects. For example a computer is made up of a monitor, keyboard, processor, mouse, speakers etc. This is important because it allows us to represent common occurrences, which mimic the real world that we live in.

Methodologies

There are a number of methodologies, which can be followed to help us to implement an OOD. Typically these methodologies prescribe a sequence of steps to produce a number of graphical representations of what we are trying to design. These graphical tools help us to communicate our design concepts to the client in a way that they or the staff working for them can understand. By doing this we can ensure that we are producing exactly what they require from us without them needing to understand how you will go about creating the final product. [15]

There are many different methodologies that are used in industry and more recently a unified approach to describing OO design has evolved. Unified Modelling Language (UML) is not a methodology as such; rather it is a language that can be used to model a design. This means that the design could have been conceived using a specific methodology, and before it is implemented we can represent it using UML. UML is a de-facto standard in OOD and we will consider some aspects in Chapter 3. Implementing a design methodology is flexible in that the ordering of steps in design stages is not pre-defined. There is a general flow or sequence that has to be followed but this can be changed during the design stage. The following steps are given as a guideline.

Steps:

- **Write use-cases:** These are mini scenarios of the system. Here a section of the system that can be seen working on its own is isolated and tested for single usage. This test helps to identify the requirements.
- **Develop message flow diagrams for use-cases:** These show the messages flowing between classes and also give a clear picture of the Class interaction in a use-case.
- **Develop collaboration diagrams:** These diagrams show how classes and sub-systems are related and also how these interact with other classes and systems. There is a great deal of elaborate analysis in this section in order to achieve a definitive set of diagrams for the design.
- **Identify classes:** One way of identifying classes is to list the nouns that are extracted from requirement documentation and discussions with users. The key nouns are the provisional classes of the design. Further stages in the design process should make it possible to filter out the classes more precisely.

- **Identify Class attributes:** The attribute of a Class is that information which the Class is known to possess and which the Class must remember at all times in order to maintain its state. A property of a Class is therefore not necessarily an attribute.
- **Identify responsibilities (methods):** Collecting a list of verbs that are affiliated to the nouns does this. These are then used to identify actions that are performed on the nouns. This leads to the identification of methods.
- **Identify subsystems:** These are major portions of the system that can be seen as isolated for the purpose of design. The aim here is to reduce complexity of the complete system by breaking into more manageable sub-systems. The isolation of these subsystems must be made along sensible lines so that their functionality can be ascertained and tested. A good way to isolate subsystems is to look for classes that have a strong coupling and to group these together into a sub-system.
- **Identify contracts:** A contract is the most fundamental responsibility of a Class. The Class must fulfil these as part of its existence. All classes and sub-systems have contracts and these must be identified.
- **Develop Class-inheritance hierarchy:** Prudent use of inheritance can greatly reduce the amount of data stores and therefore a suitable choice of inheritance must be made at an early stage of design.
- **Develop message flow diagrams for methods:** Similar to the message flow diagram for classes this serves to define relationships between methods.
- **Implement methods:** - Methods can be contracts that are 'public' and these should be implemented first as they are known. Methods that are Private are the 'support' methods and these can be implemented at a later stage when more information is available.
- **Test methods:** - All classes must be unit tested. This means that each Class must be looked at individually and tested against the information available. i.e. message flows, collaboration diagrams etc. This is particularly true for public methods.
- **Develop function tests:** - Since software development is in stages, the use-cases can be used to perform function tests for any software that is written.

The above steps are consistent with UML and therefore these will be covered in Chapter 3.

1.5. Chapter summary

In this chapter I introduce aspects of software engineering that I consider relevant. Basic stages of software development are identified and some aspects of each stage briefly discussed. The main approaches to software engineering such as the waterfall approach; exploratory programming, prototyping and others were discussed. Most of these are covered in more details in later chapters of this textbook but here they were presented as an introduction to software engineering. The very important aspect of programming paradigm was introduced and briefly discussed. The two most prominent paradigms namely procedural and object-oriented were introduced. The concept of a methodology was also considered and for the procedural paradigm, the Jackson Structured Method was presented as an example. For the object-oriented paradigm, the Booch methodology has been suggested, but since it is a significant component of the UML it has not been presented in this chapter. Instead the reader is referred to Chapter 3 of this text where UML is briefly covered.

Exercises

1.1. Describe giving examples as appropriate the essential features of the following approaches to software development,
   1. Waterfall approach
   2. Exploratory programming
   3. Prototyping
   4. Formal Transformation
   5. Software development by based on reusable components

1.2. Draw a structure diagram for an automated cash point machine (ATM). I suggest that your system should offer the only following options:
   1. Balance enquiry
   2. Cash withdrawal
   3. Transaction printout
   In all cases the ATM should authenticate your personal identification number (PIN). However, you are free to make any assumptions as guided by your own experience.

1.3. Produce the schematic logic for the ATM structure diagram that you obtained in question 1.2 above.

1.4. Explain the main differences between procedural programming and object-oriented programming. Use your library, the Internet and other resources to provide you with the required information.

1.5. What is structured programming and why is it important for the data structure to coincide with the program structure? Use your library, the Internet and other resources to provide you with the required information. Hint: Jackson Structured Programming (JSP).

1.6. Describe the Object-properties and Class and how they fit into OOD.

1.7. Explain with examples what is Abstraction?

1.8. Explain with examples what is Inheritance?

1.9. Explain with examples what is Polymorphism?

1.10. Explain with examples what is Encapsulation?

1.11. Explain with examples what is a Software Methodology.

CHAPTER 2 MODELLING

2.1.   Introduction

Modelling is a very broad term and there are many ways to interpret it. Whatever model we use, the main purpose is to simulate something that we wish to make. For example, mathematical models are used in engineering to describe the behaviour of physical systems. In software engineering models are used to represent software systems and the data within. Therefore it is evident that software modelling is somewhat different from mathematical modelling. In software engineering all models tend to describe some aspect of system behaviour. Therefore models are useful in many stages of the product lifecycle from requirements, through design and testing as well as commissioning and maintenance.

In engineering terminology the term system is generally used to describe a collection of components that interact and work together to accomplish a certain task or function. System models are used to describe how these components interact to accomplish the functionality of the system. They focus on describing the interaction of a system with its environment and in the majority they use a graphical notation, which in many cases is easier to understand than written natural language.

Models describe the system boundaries and help to make the system functionality more transparent. However, as models are abstract and often based on assumption they are not valid in all situations. Thus every model has a designation where it fulfils a particular aim. This means that the same model may not necessarily be valid or consistent for other designations. Which model is being applied depends on the target group and on the information the model will communicate.

For example let us assume that we wish to model the behaviour of a waiter in a restaurant. There are many aspects that influence the behaviour of the waiter, and some of these are the restaurant manager, the chef in the kitchen, customers and others. However our model only needs to focus on the waiter and his behaviour, which will include taking orders and delivering these to the table. Other details of preparing the food etc are not of concern in the model of a waiter.

Modelling saves time and cost by providing a simulated environment in which to analyse the system. Errors that are identified during the modelling stage can be rectified before final production of the system. A number of iterations can be done in a simulated model so that potential problems can be identified and rectified before the final build.

Types of models

As software engineering as a discipline evolved, many models were developed to help in all stages of design and development. Early programming efforts in 1980's tended to adopt the functional programming model where emphasis was placed on describing software as procedures and functions that perform specific tasks. Models that are used for this are function-oriented representations such as the JSP (discussed earlier), Yourdon structured method (YSM) and others. Around the early 1980s the focus in software design shifted towards object-oriented design. Consequently modelling effort also moved towards the object-oriented domain. This effort produced independent modelling methodologies some of which include work by Grady Booch at Rational Software, Object Modelling Technique by Rumbaugh and the work of Ivar Jacobson on use-cases. More recently it became apparent that a standard for modelling in software engineering was required. This led to the development of the unified modelling language (UML) which is an accepted standard of the Object Management Group (OMG).

I recommend to anyone involved in software engineering to learn UML because it is used in the vast majority of software houses as a basis for modelling OO software development. The individual methodologies that have been developed are not necessarily redundant because UML is a modelling language, rather than a methodology. This means that UML can be used to represent software models that have been developed using an unrelated software methodology. Describing UML would require a textbook in its own right and therefore a detailed description will not be provided in this text. Instead a very brief overview will be given in chapter 3 of this text in order to introduce the reader to the essential aspects of UML. At this point I will leave UML and return to briefly explain some basic aspects of modelling.

2.2. Basic aspects of software modelling

Context models

Context models show the system and its relationship with other systems and sub-systems. The first model of a system that is usually produced is a context diagram. Context diagrams are used to define the boundary between the system that is being developed and its environment. Therefore the focus is on the interfaces that the system needs to have to external entities. These entities are represented by named boxes and connected using directional arrows. My context diagrams always have a central block that represents my system, which connects to other blocks that have interfaces represented by arrows. For example, assume that I have been given 8 weeks to perform a feasibility study on a subject of my choosing and that I have to produce a report and deliver a short presentation. Given this initial requirement my context diagram would be as shown in Figure 2.1.

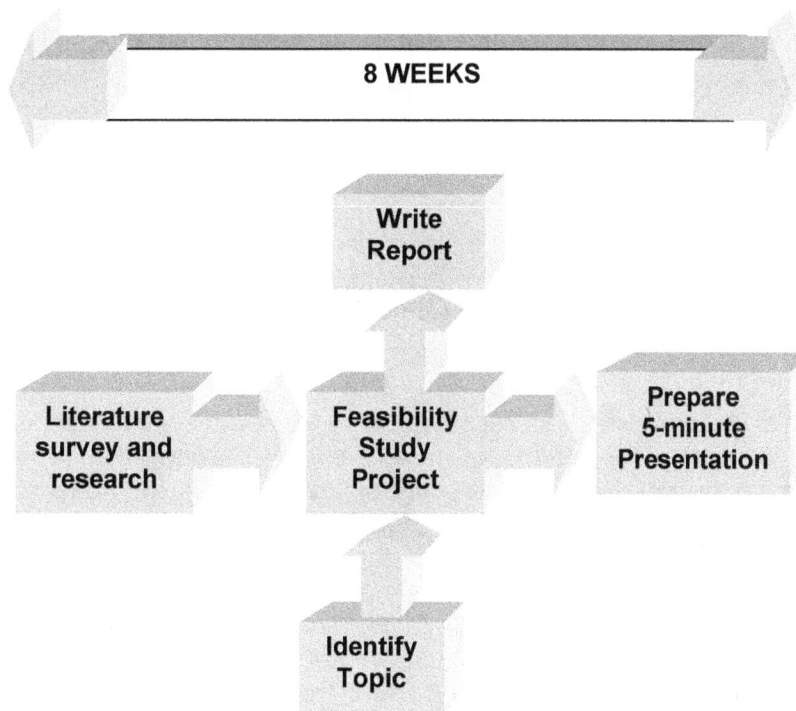

Figure 2.1. Context diagram

The important thing to note is that the context diagram is produced early on and as I spend more time on the project, things will become clearer, so that I may refine my design. In figure 2.1, I have my inputs, which is my literature survey and research, as well as my effort to write the report and prepare the presentation. My outputs are also identified on the diagram, as well as the overall time-scale. A context diagram is a starting point and it is normally extended to subsystems and subcomponents in order to provide an overall context (as the name implies). It is used to identify the salient aspects of the project, such as the inputs and the outputs, and the main functional components without going into any significant detail. These can be broken down into smaller sections at a later stage, but the context diagram should be simple and only needs to identify the main components and the relationship between these.

It is worth noting that the context diagram of figure 2.1 is fairly simple in that there are only four interfaces that the system needs to support. In a more elaborate project, with more interfaces, the context diagram would become more complex. In these projects the context diagram would use full lined arrows to describe information flow and dashed line arrows to describe any controls. A hypothetical example is shown in figure 2.2. Here a part of a student record system is shown.

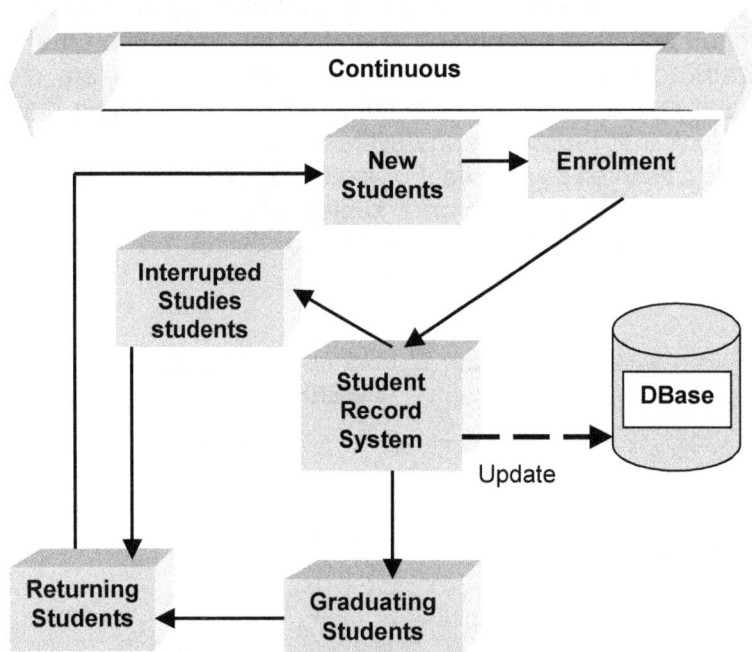

Figure 2.2. Hypothetical context diagram with information and control flows

This system needs to record information about students that are currently attending courses. The information flow is shown between the various subsystems and the main system. For example, control flow is shown as a dashed lined arrow to the database because there is an action that needs to be performed. Namely the database needs to be updated with the appropriate information whenever any changes are made. This is an over-simplified example, used mainly to show the concept of information flow and control flow. The context diagram should be as simple and as clear as possible because it usually serves to define an approach to manage the project. If the initial context is correct then the subsequent stages of project management will become more manageable.

Whenever you start thinking about any project I suggest that you draw a context diagram. Simply start with a central bubble, which is the main aim of your project and then show the interfaces that you need in order to achieve this aim. It will certainly not be the last model of the system that you will use, but it is a good starting point.

It is seen from these examples that context diagrams use boxes and lines to describe the relationship between the main system and its subsystems. This type of model identifies the different subsystems and their interaction with the main system in a simple and clear manner so that the reader can get a good idea of the system structure. It also enables us to split the project into different subsystems that can be developed separately and integrated later on. Context diagrams can also be used to specify interfaces because they show which systems interact with each other.

Generally the context diagram has no information on the data and control flow and the diagram does not indicate the properties of the different subsystems. Thus, the context diagram only gives a rough overview of a system and its components. Different context models are produced for different applications. The first example above used a context model to describe a project to produce a feasibility report. This has nothing to do with software modelling. The second model showed the context of a student record system that is software based and uses a database as a data repository. These types of models are sometimes referred to as repository models. There is an abundance of literature describing various models but in this text, I shall only consider some of the basic model types.

Repository Model

This model is used for systems using a common (central) data source (referred to as data repository). Using this model, all data is stored centrally which offers the following advantages:

- Central backup and security, which adds to system and data security and eases management.
- There are no interfaces between the subsystems. That is, data always flows through the repository which is the focal point for all subsystems.
- It is possible to share very large amounts of data efficiently provided that the repository can support it. (i.e. Oracle is a very powerful database management system (DBMS))
- New subsystems can easily be integrated without having to change other components. However, the new subsystem must be compatible with the data repository interfaces.

The repository model identifies the data boundaries and defines them precisely and all operations on data is made through the central repository. Although this model is very useful the fact that data is centralised can also cause serious challenges for developers. Some of these are,

- User rights and data management can be complex.
- The repository is a single point of failure.
- The system accessing the data should have a standard method of recovery, or at least the different methods should be compatible otherwise problems can arouse when a system produces a failure.

Example

Figure 2.3 shows an example of a repository model where it can be seen that communication between different software subsystems of a company is not established directly. (i.e. between HR, CS and Management). Instead each subsystem only has access to a data repository (common to all subsystems) where all data are stored centrally.

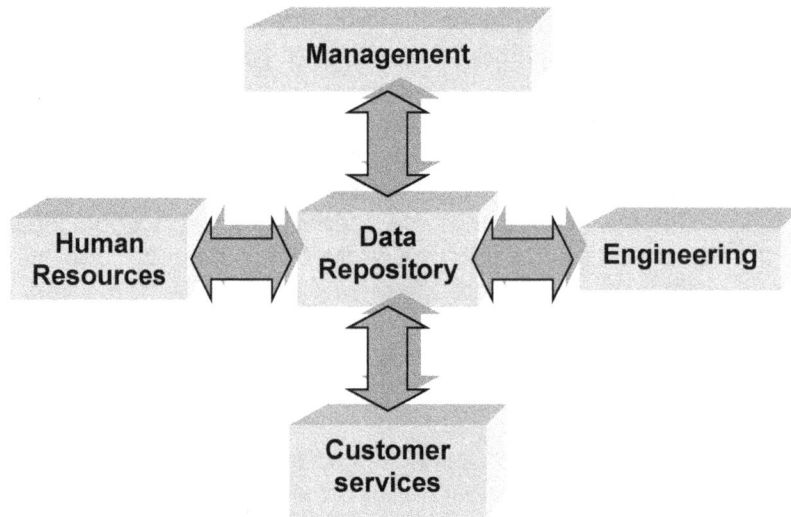

Figure 2.3. Repository model

Abstract modelling

This type of modelling is most commonly used to describe the system architecture. The reason that these are called abstract is because they represent conceptual relationships. For example the seven-layer Open System Interconnect (OSI) model defines 7 layers that can be used to describe all communications. [16]. This model is totally abstract, which means that it cannot be used on its own. It can only be used to describe communications between systems. It also happens to be a layered model where each layer represents a sub-system, which communicates only with its preceding and following layers. The following are main features of the layered model,

- Small changes to one layer do not affect other layers as the interfaces of each layer stay the same.
- The system can be developed incrementally.
- A developed layer can be put into service while other layers are still under development.
- If the interfaces of a layer are changed only the preceding and following layers may be affected, not other layers.
- As data is processed in different layers troubleshooting may be difficult because the source of error is difficult to trace.
- As each layer requires a certain amount of management, many layers can cause a significant management overhead.
- Some services within a layer are accessed directly by some systems. This can cause complicated data flows and also any change to the layer can affect outer systems that are accessing it. (This can sometimes be a contradiction to one of the benefits).

Example

As an example, figure 2.4 shows the abstract model of the Windows 2000 O/S architecture. This is a layered model in that each layer communicates only with the one above and below. Note that we are using this to illustrate the layered abstract model, rather than to explain the Windows 2000 architecture. The model of figure 2.4 shows the architecture is divided into two parts, the User mode and the Kernel mode. User mode refers to all the applications, services, system processes and the environment subsystem, all of which use the dynamic-link library (DLL) in order to access the kernel mode. The kernel is part of the O/S that provides the very basic services for all other parts of the operating system. For example, all processor services are performed in kernel mode and before accessing the hardware these services need to pass through a hardware abstraction layer (HAL). The Windows HAL provides a link to the hardware interfaces such as buses, I/O devices, interrupts, interval timers, DMA, memory cache control etc.

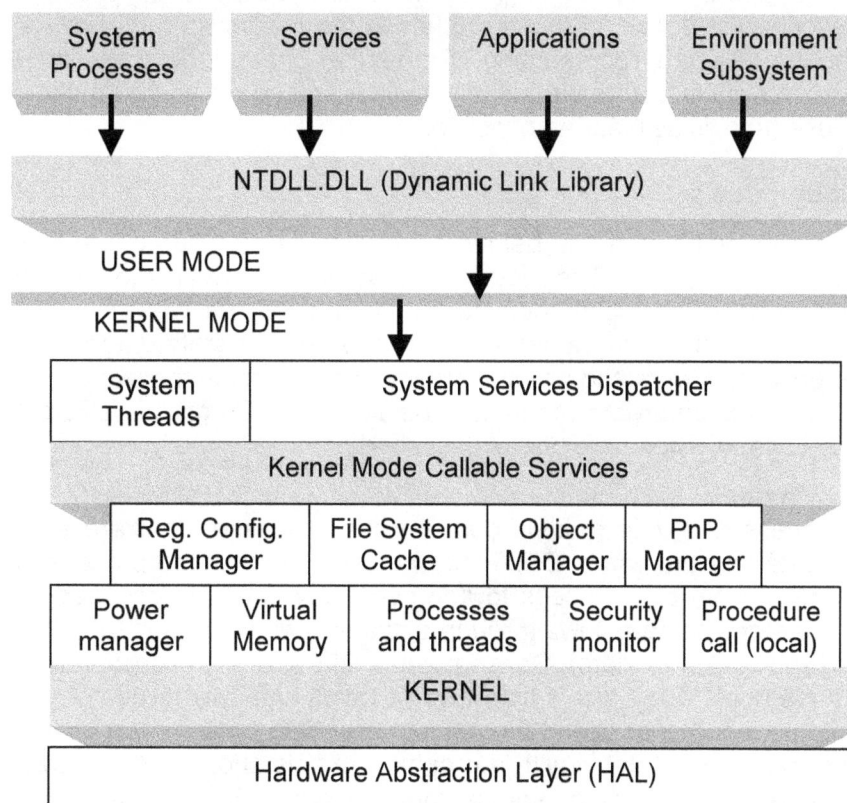

Figure 2.4. Simplified Windows NT 2000 Kernel Architecture [17]

Abstract models do not have to be layered and can take various forms in order to represent different abstractions of systems. Just to give you an analogy consider that as a person, I could be modelled in different abstractions. For example, you could model my behaviour as a lecturer in the context of which you would know what I am doing and how. On the other hand my children could model me as a parent and describe my behaviour from that standpoint. Thus, although I am the same person in both cases, the two models are different because they are taken from different perspectives. These two perspectives represent two different levels of abstraction of the system (in this case me). In terms of software models abstractions can refer to data processing, systems interfaces, entity relationships, object interaction, stimulus-response in real-time systems and many others. Some examples and a brief description of types of abstract models, which might be produced during analysis, are:

- **Data-processing model**: Data-flow diagrams show how data is processed at different stages in the system. This model is concerned with describing the sources and sinks of data. Where does data begin and how it travels through the system? What operations are made and how the data are modified?
- **Composition model:** Entity-relationship diagrams show how the entities in the system are composed of other entries and describe their relationships.
- **Architectural model:** Architectural models describe the main subsystems, which make up the system.

- **Classification model:** Objects, Class/inheritances diagrams show how entities have common characteristics.
- **Stimulus-response model:** State-transition diagrams show how the system reacts to internal and external events. This is commonly used in real-time systems.

The important thing to keep in mind when you are using modelling is that you must describe the details of these models to the reader so that they can understand what the models are representing. Remember that models are there to help us visualise the system before we actually build it and so we should make every effort to make these models as clear as possible.

Behaviour models

As the name implies, behaviour models are used to describe the overall behaviour of the system. They focus on how entities within the system interact and include entity relationship models (as in databases) as well as stimulus/response models (such as state diagrams). As mentioned earlier state diagrams show how the system reacts to events and are particularly useful in real-time systems. The two most common types of behaviour model are the Data Flow Diagrams (DFDs) and the State Machine diagram. These are briefly described next.

Data-flow model

Process and data models describe the processes that are supported by the system. Data flow diagrams (DFD) may be used to show the processes and the flow of information from one process to another. They can also be used to describe the processing steps as data flows through a system, which means that they describe the sources and sinks of data. Consequently DFDs are a constituent part of many analysis methods. They are simple and relatively intuitive to use so that developers and customers can understand them. Data flow diagrams can be used to represent a system at any level of detail with a graphic symbols showing data flows, data stores, data processes, and data sources/destinations. (See figure 2.5) Their basic characteristics are as follows,
- DFDs show how the input is transformed into the output by a sequence of functional transformations.
- These diagrams do not contain control information and are only concerned with data transformations.
- DFDs are an integral part of a number of design methods and most CASE tools support DFD creation.

An advantage of DFDs is that they show transformations without making assumptions about how they are implemented. For example a system described using DFDs in this way could be a single program using separately code units for each transformation. In this way the transformations are implemented using separate routines that operate on common (shared) variables. Alternatively, it may be implemented as a number of communicating tasks such that the result is governed by the variables as they are communicated between tasks (i.e. at run-time). It is also possible to implement the system by a combination of these methods. Thus, the DFD representation is independent of the implementation details.

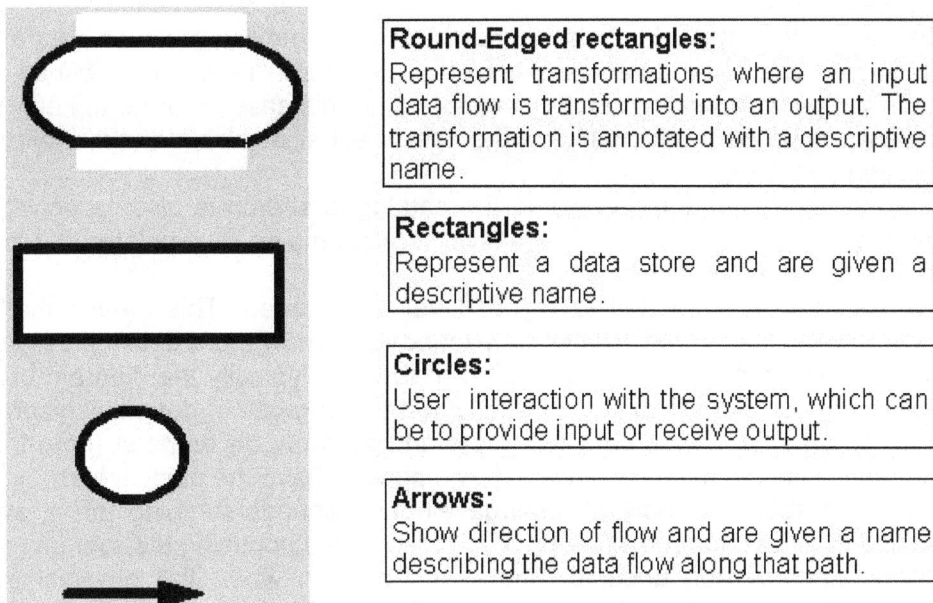

	Round-Edged rectangles: Represent transformations where an input data flow is transformed into an output. The transformation is annotated with a descriptive name.
	Rectangles: Represent a data store and are given a descriptive name.
	Circles: User interaction with the system, which can be to provide input or receive output.
	Arrows: Show direction of flow and are given a name describing the data flow along that path.

Figure 2.5. DFD Notation symbols

DFD diagrams are designed to be fairly intuitive so that readers can easily understand them. To help with this key words 'and' + 'or': are also used. These have their usual meanings as in Boolean expression and are used to link data flows when more than one data may be input or output from a transformation. An example of a DFD showing the process of retrieving a catalogue item from a data store is shown in figure 2.6.

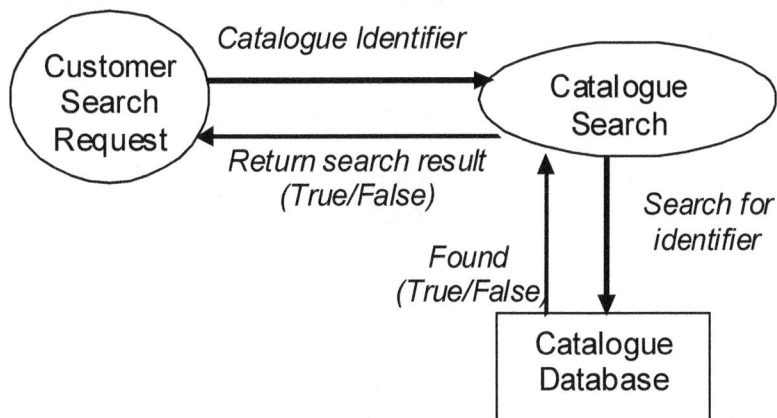

Figure 2.6. Example DFD

Here,

• The customer represents user input/output. In this example the same user inputs data and also receives the output from the system. Therefore a single symbol representing the user is shown.

• The label of the data flow (above the arrow) shows that an identifier is supplied with the request. In this case it is a catalogue identifier.

• The Data Flow symbol represents movement of data into the process that searches the database.

• The process transforms the data from an identifier to a search item in the database. For this reason it is represented as a round edged rectangle (ellipse in my case).

• The Data Store symbol represents data that is not moving (delayed data at rest). In this case the data stored is a list of all catalogue items. The results of the search will vary depending on the system, but in this case, in order to keep things simple we describe a response that the item is either available or not available for collection by the user.

• The Process symbol representing the catalogue search is also responsible for returning the search results. This activity transforms or manipulates the original data into the results of the query.

DFDs can be expanded to higher levels if required. This means that each process or transformation symbol can be expanded to show more detail. If this is done then the new diagram is said to be at a level above. (Typically the diagram of figure 2.6 is said to be level 0). Thus it can be said that the purpose of data flow diagrams is to provide a semantic bridge between users and systems developers. (note that the word semantic implies "meaning"). Data flow diagrams have the objective of,

• Reducing the likelihood of user/developer misunderstanding of a system, resulting in a need to redo systems or in some cases not using the system at all.

• Not having to redo documentation from scratch when the physical system changes. Since the logical system, WHAT gets done often remains the same when technology changes documentation can be modified rather than re-written.

• Reducing systems inefficiencies when a system gets implemented relatively early in the design stage. DFDs provide very clear models of the system even in early stages of design.

• Being able to evaluate system project boundaries or degree of automation, when the scope of the project is not entirely clear at the outset. In other words they can be used to specify project scope.

DFDs are well suited to function-orientated design which is in contrast to object-orientated design.

State machine models

State machine models (or finite state machines) are used to model the behaviour of a system in response to internal or external events. Therefore, these models describe all of the system states and also the events, which cause transitions from one state to another. In contrast to DFDs, state diagrams do not show the flow of data within the system.

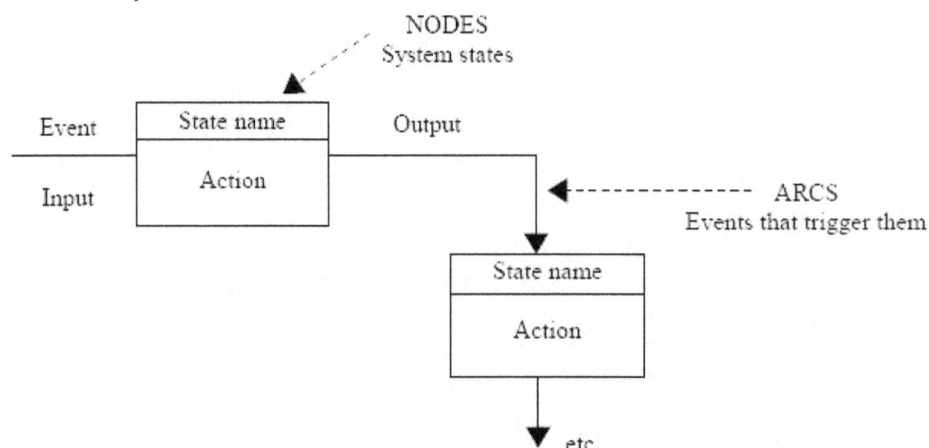

Figure 2.7 State diagram shows the states and transitions

This type of model is particularly useful for modelling real-time systems because these are often driven by stimuli from system's environment. A state machine model of a system assumes that, at any instant in time the system is in only one of its possible states. When a stimulus is received, this usually triggers a transition to another state, from a number of possible states as shown in figure 2.7.

As mentioned earlier state diagram models are predominantly used in real-time systems. For instance the state diagram model of a microwave oven could be described as shown in figure 2.8.

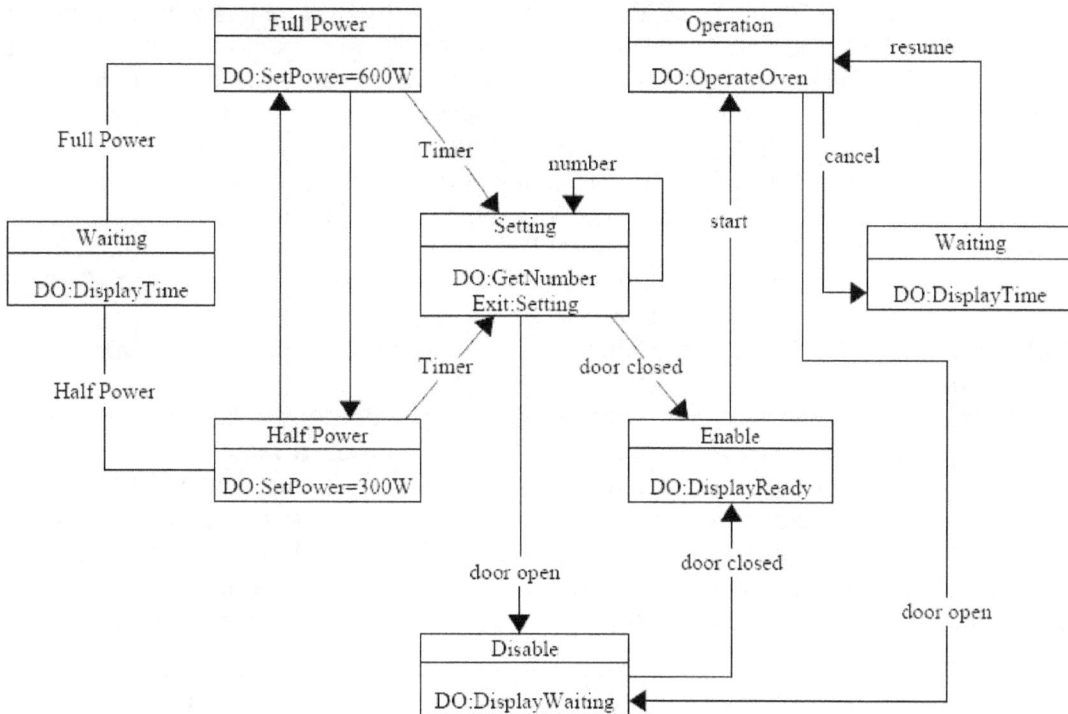

Figure 2.8. State diagram model of a microwave oven

The microwave oven model is commonly used to describe state machines because it is very intuitive and easy to understand. Normally the states will be derived from the system specification and transition between states would be used to develop the state diagram. However, in order to explain the state diagram as a modelling concept, we can do the reverse here, that is to say, start from a state diagram and show how it has been derived. Thus, from figure 2.8 we can identify that there are seven states, which the microwave can have. Reading from left to right these are,

0 Waiting State 0 - Idle	1 Waiting State 1 - Half Power	2 Waiting State 2 - Full Power	3 Waiting State 3 - Setting	4 Waiting State 4 - Enabled	5 Waiting State 5 - Disabled	6 Operation

Events cause transition between states. The events that the microwave system identifies are also shown in the diagram. These events operate on states and each state has at least one event that operates on it. Sometimes two events are associated with a state, such as for example the timer event and the number event both operate on the setting state. The events for the microwave are,

Full Power	Half Power	Timer	Number	Door Open	Door Closed	Start	Cancel	Resume

Behaviour is described by a state-transition table, which identifies each possible state transition within the system. An example transition table for the microwave state diagram of figure 2.8 is shown in figure 2.9. To create this table we need to include events, which trigger transitions in each state. Thus for example, with reference to figure 2.9, the State 0 (waiting state0 – idle) identifies with two events (Full-power and Half-power), either of these events will cause state transition into the next state corresponding to the given power rating. Note that I have named the states so that they are representative of their power rating. From either of these two states transition into state 3. (Setting) is achieved by the timer event. Also note that before state 3 is entered there is still the option to select either of the power levels. However, once in state 3, this option is no longer available. From state 3, two transitions are possible. These are either to state 4 (enabled), which is triggered by the door-closed event, or to state 5 (disabled), which is triggered by the door open event. State 6 (operation) can only be reached from the enabled state and this is triggered by the start event. Once in the operation state the door open and the cancel events both cause a transition to the disabled state.

Note that to read the state transition table, you look at the current state in the columns and scroll down the rows to see which event has a state transition in that column. If there is a transition against an event then the new state is listed in the intersection of the column for the state and row for the event that triggers the transition. This can be seen from figure 2.9 where for example in the waiting state0-idle; there is a state transition to state 2 when the event Full Power occurs. Also in the same initial state the event Half Power will trigger a state transition to state 1.

States	Waiting State 0 - Idle (0)	Waiting State 1 - Half Power (1)	Waiting State 2 - Full Power (2)	Waiting State 3 - Setting (3)	Waiting State 4 - Enabled (4)	Waiting State 5 - Disabled (5)	Operation (6)
Events							
Full Power	2	2	-	-	-	-	-
Half Power	1	-	1	-	-	-	-
Timer	-	3	3	-	-	-	-
Number	-	3	3	-	-	-	-
Door Open	-	-	-	5	-	-	5
Door Closed	-	-	-	4	-	4	-
Start	-	-	-	-	6	-	-
Cancel	-	-	-	-	-	-	5
Resume	-	-	-	-	-	-	-

Figure 2.9. State transition table for the microwave example

The state diagram model provided here represents simple operations of a microwave oven. It is not complete because for example it shows that once started, the microwave does not stop unless the door is opened. Also when the cancel button is activated the only option is to resume from where it stopped, not to restart.

Nevertheless I am only concerned here with providing you with an overview of how state-machine models are constructed, so that you can appreciate what is going on.

Architecture models

These are abstract models that are used to describe the overall architecture of the system. At this level there are a variety of different models some of which depend on the various 'stakeholders' of the system: end-user, developers, systems engineers, project managers, etc. Each of these requires a different view of the system and the model should also be able to handle separately the functional and non-functional requirements.

Philippe Kruchten of Rational Software Corporation presents a clear description of a model for describing the architecture of software-intensive systems. This model uses multiple, concurrent views which address the individual needs of different stakeholders. [18] To describe software architecture, Kruchten defines a model, which is composed of multiple views,

- **Logical view**, which is the object model of the design (when an object-oriented design method is used),
- **Process view**, which captures the concurrency and synchronisation aspects of the design,
- **Physical view**, which describes the mapping(s) of the software onto the hardware and reflects its distributed aspect,
- **Development view**, which describes the static organisation of the software in its development environment.

System architecture can be organised around these four views, and then a fifth view describing a few selected use-cases, or scenarios is used to illustrate the interactions between the four views of the model. This is depicted in figure 2.10 where the four views are all linked together by the scenarios, which is the fifth view. Consequently Kruchten has named this the "4+1 view" of software architecture.

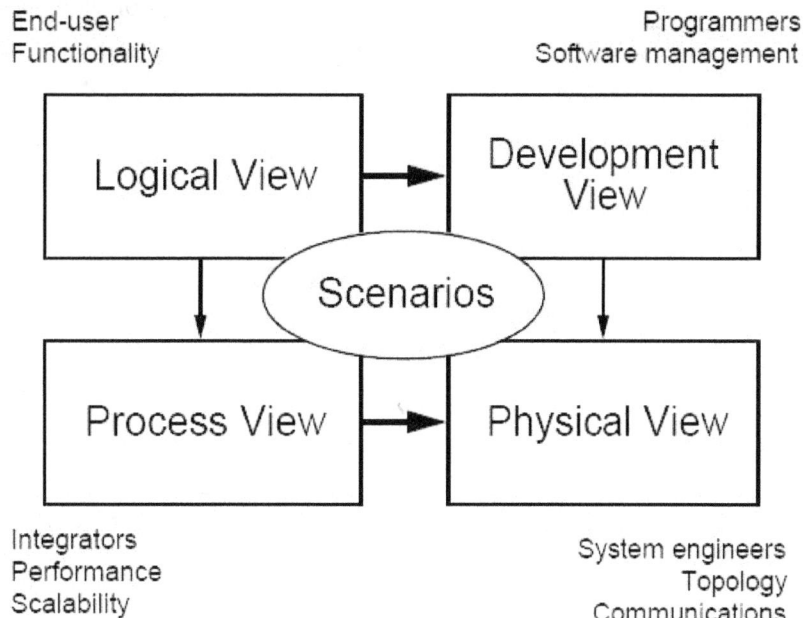

Figure 2.10. The 4+1 view of software architecture [18]

In order to illustrate the difference between the views Kruchten provides a number of examples. These are briefly introduced next, with a note that full explanations are given in the original paper by Kruchten. [18]

The Logical Architecture

The logical view is concerned with primarily the functional components of the system and how these are related. Logical architecture design is the next step after the conceptual design. Note that we can define conceptual design to be an abstract design which includes only the most important components and entities. (Similar to a context diagram mentioned earlier) These components may include major technology systems such as external systems that are needed for overall functionality. Therefore logical design can be described as a more detailed design, which includes all major components and entities plus their relationships. Consequently the data flows and connections are detailed in this stage. The target audience are typically developers or other systems architects. However, it is possible to create logical designs for business purposes to ensure that all components and functionality are well understood.

Logical designs do not include physical server names or addresses. However they do include any business services, application names and details, and other relevant information for development purposes. Note that object-oriented design and function-oriented design have different logical architectures. To illustrate the 4+1 approach, Kruchten describes the object-oriented decomposition of the logical view.

The Object-Oriented Decomposition

The system is decomposed into a set of key objects or object classes, taken from the problem domain. Logical architecture can be represented by means of Class diagrams and Class templates. For example consider the model of a PABX telephone exchange shown in figure 2.11.

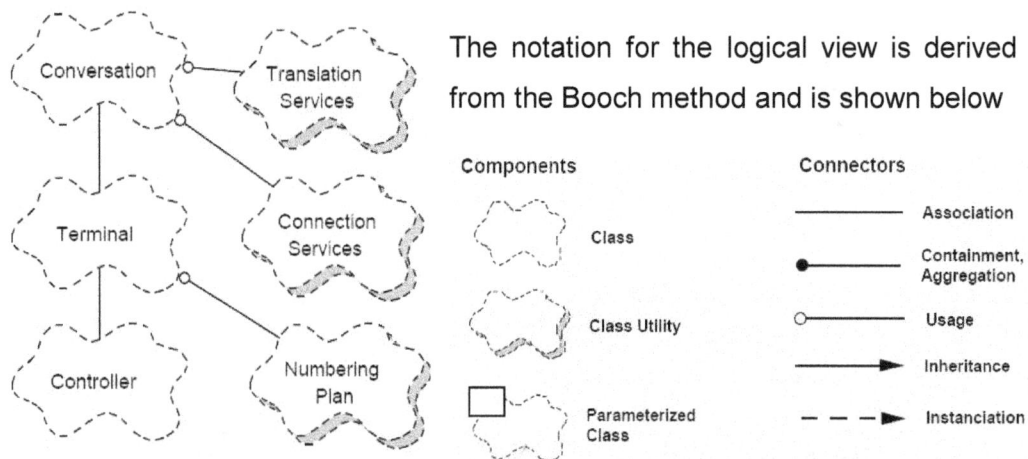

Figure 2.11. Logical architecture diagram for a PABX system

Figure 2.11 shows conversation, terminal and controller classes and the Class utilities that relate to them. It should be clear from this diagram that the controller Class is in association with the terminal Class only. The conversation Class is also in association only with the terminal Class, which identifies the terminal Class as the intermediate Class between the controller and conversation classes.

The terminal Class requires the numbering plan Class utility while the conversation Class requires the Class utilities of translation and connection services. Whilst the logical view provides the link between classes, the actual description of the diagram requires more details. Thus in relation to figure 2.11 it needs to be explained that a PABX system establishes communications between terminals so that people can talk to each other. A terminal in the diagram is shown as a Class and it may be a telephone set, an ISDN line, etc. and different interface cards support different lines (or modes of communication). The line controller object decodes all the signals on the line interface card. Thus it is seen from the logical view diagram that the controller Class has a direct association with the terminal Class. However the details of this association are not included in the logical architecture diagram.

The responsibility of the terminal object is to maintain the state of a terminal, and negotiate services on behalf of that line. For example, it uses the services of the numbering plan to interpret the dialling in the selection phase. For this reason the diagram depicts a usage relationship between the terminal Class and the numbering plan. The Conversation Class utility represents a set of terminals engaged in a conversation and this is represented on the diagram by an association between the terminal Class and the conversation Class. Once again, the details of this association are not provided in the diagram.

Conversation Class uses translation services (directory, address mapping, routes), and connection services to establish a voice path between the terminals. These are shown in the diagram as usage relationships between the conversation Class and the Class utilities of connection and translation.

From the above it can be seen that this is a very simple model which is used to illustrate the idea of a logical architecture diagram rather than to identify the complexity that can be achieved using this model.

The Process Architecture

According to the prescribed 4+1 model the process view takes into account some non-functional requirements such as for example performance and availability. It addresses issues of concurrency and distribution, fault-tolerance, and how the main abstractions from the logical view fit within the process architecture.

A process is a grouping of tasks that constitute an executable unit. Processes represent the level at which the process architecture can be controlled (i.e., started, recovered, reconfigured, and shut down). In addition, processes can be replicated in order to distribute the processing load, or to improve availability. For this view the software is partitioned into a set of independent tasks. Here, a task is defined as a separate thread of control, which can be scheduled individually on one processing node. It is possible to distinguish between: major tasks, which are the architectural elements that can be uniquely addressed and minor tasks, that are additional tasks introduced locally for implementation reasons (cyclical activities, buffering, time-outs, etc.). Major tasks communicate via a set of well-defined inter-task communication mechanisms: synchronous and asynchronous message-based communication services, remote procedure calls, event broadcast, etc. Minor tasks may communicate by shared memory.

Figure 2.12 depicts a simplified process model for a PABX system. Here it is seen at the top of the diagram that a single terminal process handles all the terminals. All controller objects are executed within one of the three tasks that comprise the controller process. The diagram does not contain the details and therefore an explanation would normally be required. For example the following details may be used to explain the controller process. A task with a relatively low cycle-rate scans all inactive terminals (scan rate of approximately 200 ms). Any terminal becoming active is placed in the scan list of the high cycle rate task (10ms), which detects any significant change of state, and passes them to the main controller task.

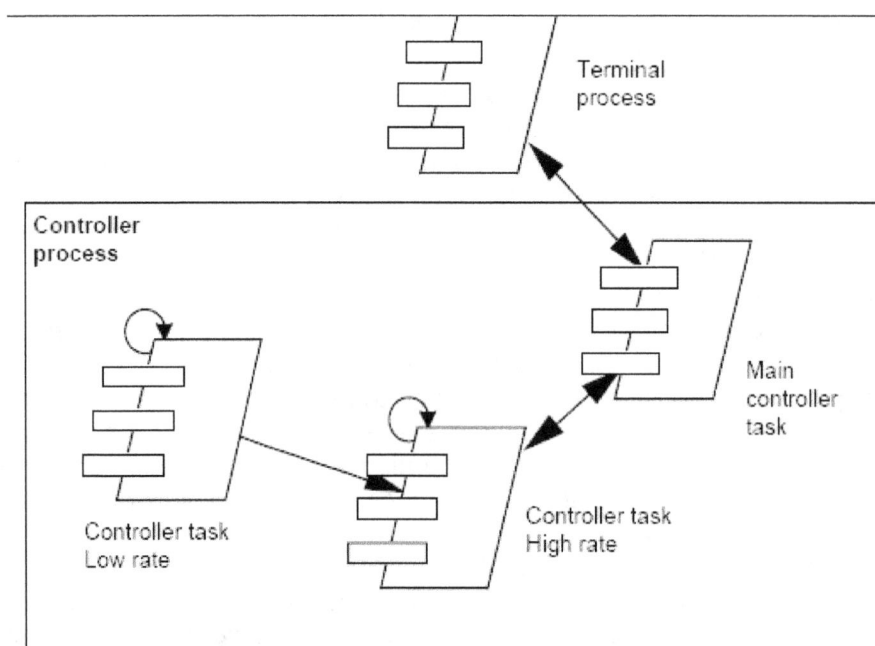

Figure 2.12. Process model for PABX system

The main controller task interprets the changes and communicates them by message passing to the corresponding terminal. Here message passing within the controller process is done via shared memory.

Communication between the controller process and the terminal process is done by message passing as indicated by the double-headed arrow linking the two processes. Once again it must be said that information presented here is only designed to explain the purpose of the process view, and it is not intended here to provide a detailed account of the PABX process model.

The Development Architecture

The development view focuses on the actual software module organisation in relation to the software development environment. This view is intended for developers and therefore the software is packaged in small chunks (program libraries, or subsystems etc.) that can be developed by a small team of developers. In this view it is quite common to use the layered model. This means that subsystems are organised in a hierarchy of layers, each layer providing a narrow and well-defined interface to the layers above it.

For the most part, the development architecture takes into account internal requirements related to the ease of development, software management, reuse or commonality, and to the constraints imposed by the toolset, or the programming language. The development view serves as the basis for requirement allocation, i.e. for allocation of work to teams (or even for team organisation), for cost evaluation and planning, for monitoring the progress of the project, for reasoning about software reuse, portability and security.

In order to minimise the development effort of very complex networks with dependencies between modules careful consideration needs to be given to the number of layers used. In order to support the development of simple release strategies layer-by-layer it is recommended to define 4 to 6 layers of subsystems, with each layer having a well-defined responsibility. The design rule in this case is that a subsystem can only depend on subsystems that are in the same layer or in layers below.

The Physical Architecture

The physical architecture takes into account primarily the non-functional requirements of the system such as availability, reliability (fault-tolerance), performance (throughput), and scalability. Figure 2.13 shows the basic structure of a physical architecture diagram for the PBX example considered earlier. The software executes on a network of computers, or processing nodes. The various elements identified such as networks, processes, tasks, and objects all need to be mapped onto the various nodes. It may be necessary to describe several different physical configurations: some for development and testing, others for the deployment of the system at various sites or for different customers. The mapping of the software to the nodes therefore needs to be highly flexible and have a minimal impact on the source code itself.

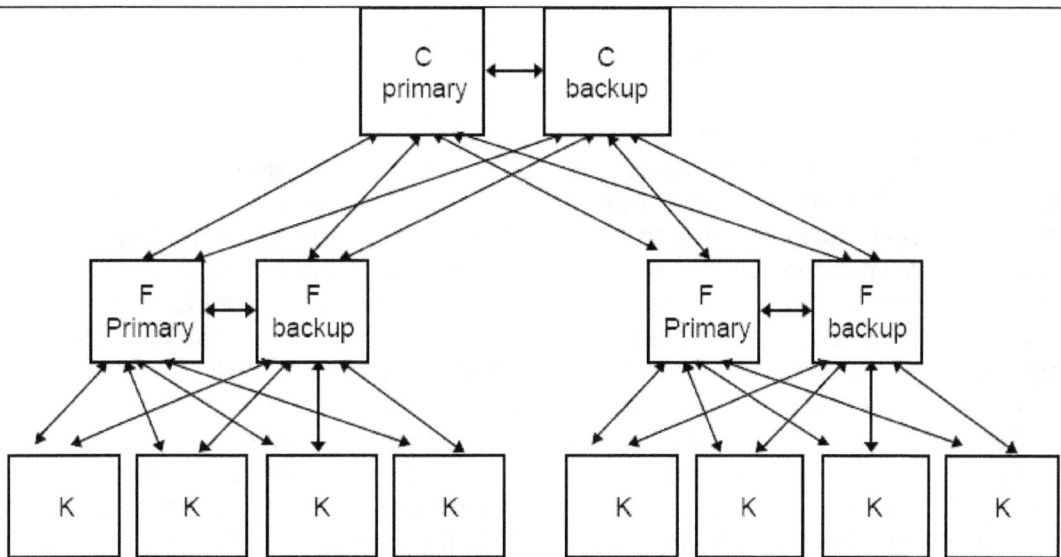

Figure 2.13. Physical architecture diagram PBX

Scenarios

Scenarios are needed in order to integrate the four views within a common task. The four view can be shown to work together seamlessly by the use of a small set of important scenarios. These are general use-cases that are in some sense an abstraction of the most important requirements. Their design is expressed using object scenario diagrams and object interaction diagrams. These scenarios serve two main purposes:

- To discover the architectural elements during the architecture design
- As a validation role after this architecture design is complete, both on paper and as the starting point for the tests of an architectural prototype.

Example of a Scenario

Fig. 2.14 shows a fragment of a scenario for the small PABX. The corresponding script according to the numbered sequence is as follows,

(1) The controller of Joe's phone detects and validates the transition from on-hook to off-hook and sends a (2) message to wake up the corresponding terminal object. The terminal allocates some resources, and tells the controller to emit some dial tone. (3) The controller receives digits and transmits them to the terminal. (4) The terminal uses the numbering plan to analyse the digit flow. (5) When a valid sequence of digits has been entered, the terminal opens a conversation.

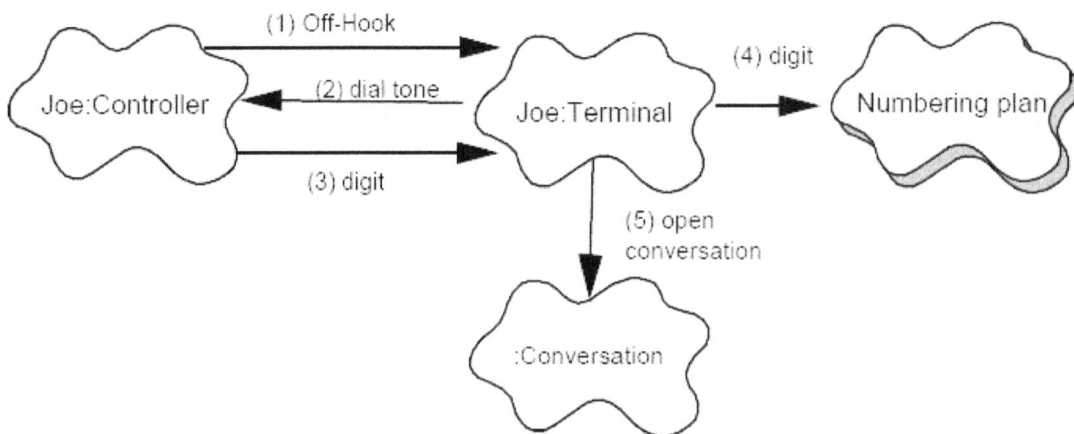

Figure 2.14. Example scenario for a small PABX

Correspondence between the Views

Consistency between views is a requirement for accurate modelling of the architecture. Elements of one view are connected to elements in other views, following certain design rules and heuristics. In other words, from the logical to the process view important characteristics of the classes of the logical architecture are translated into the process architecture. For example Class attributes such as autonomy, persistence, subordination and distribution in the logical view will have implications in the process view. A brief explanation is provided next.

• **Autonomy**: are the objects active, passive, protected? An active object takes the initiative of invoking (starting or triggering) other objects' operations or its own operations and has full control over the starting of its own operations by other objects. Conversely, a passive object never invokes spontaneously any operations and has no control over the starting of its own operations by other objects. A protected object never invokes spontaneously any operations but performs some arbitration on the invocation of its operations.

• **Persistence**: are the objects transient, permanent? Do they cause the failure of a process or processor?

• **Subordination**: does the existence or persistence of a particular object depend on another object?

• **Distribution**: are the state or the operations of an object accessible from many nodes in the physical architecture, from several processes in the process architecture?

In the logical view of the architecture each object is considered to be active, and potentially "concurrent," i.e., functioning "in parallel" with other objects. No further consideration is given in the logical view to degree of concurrency that is required for the object. Consequently, when this object is used in the process architecture, in order to support concurrency each object has to be implemented with its own thread of control. In reality this is not always possible because of the huge programming overhead that this imposes. At the same time in the process view, the benefits of exploiting concurrency are invaluable for several reasons namely,

• To react rapidly to certain classes of external stimuli, including time-related events.

• To take advantage of multiple CPUs in a node, or multiple nodes in a distributed system.

• To increase the CPU utilisation, by allocating the CPU to other activities while some thread of control is suspended waiting for some other activity to complete (e.g. access to some external device, or access to some other active object).

- To prioritise activities (and potentially improve responsiveness).
- To support system scalability (with additional processes sharing the load).
- To separate concerns between different areas of the software.
- To achieve a higher system availability (with backup processes).

It is possible to determine the appropriate degree of concurrency and define the set of processes that are needed. However this is beyond the scope of this text and Kruchten directs the reader to the original paper for further reading. [18]

2.3.   Documenting the architecture

The documentation produced during the architectural design is captured in two documents:

- A Software Architecture Document, whose organisation closely follows the "4+1" views (see figure 2.15)
- Software Design Guidelines, which captures (among other things) the most important design decisions that must be respected in order to maintain the architectural integrity of the system.

If you were preparing an architecture level report I would recommend that you use the template provided here in figure 2.15. This is not because the template is the best around, but rather it is because there are so many variations and alternative documentation templates that you just need to select one and go with it. When you are employed, it is likely that the organisation that employed you will have a worked out approach to documentation.

Title Page
Change History
Table of Contents
List of Figures

1. Scope
2. References
3. Software Architecture
4. Architectural Goals & Constraints
5. Logical Architecture
6. Process Architecture
7. Development Architecture
8. Physical Architecture
9. Scenarios
10. Size and Performance
11. Quality

Appendices
A. Acronyms and Abbreviations
B. Definitions
C. Design Principles

Figure 2.15. Outline of a Software Architecture Document

2.4. Chapter summary

This chapter covers modelling as a tool in software engineering. This is a very difficult topic to write about because modelling is used practically everywhere, in business, engineering, finance even in medicine and law. Models are intuitive to those that use them and they tend to evolve over time. The principles of modelling are generally quite straightforward however the systems that they are used to model can be quite complex. Consequently, a complex system leads to a complex model and students of software engineering are required in a relatively short space of time to assimilate some very complex modelling concepts. For example the Booch methodology for OOD has been around for some 20 years. In that time Booch and others have refined it and as we mentioned it has been partly used to define UML. It is quite difficult to condense the complexity of the Booch method into a chapter of a textbook in such a way that it can be understood. That is, to present the material in such a way as to give the reader sufficient information to be able to use the method successfully in large projects. Therefore once again I have to say that this chapter provides an overview in modelling and the reader is encouraged to seek other textbooks for a more thorough treatment of the subject matter.

Exercises

2.1. Explain giving examples the significance of context models in software engineering.

2.2. Distinguish between different types of abstract models.

2.3. Behavioural models can be represented using DFDs or state transition diagrams. Compare and contrast these two types of behaviour models using examples as appropriate.

2.4. Using DFD develop basic models for a cash-point machine. These are usually called ATM (Automatic teller machine). Make assumptions as required but focus on data flow modelling.

2.5. Repeat question 2.4 above, but now use state charts. Make the required assumptions but focus here on states during transactions, and the events that cause state transitions.

2.6. Distinguish between the four basic views in architectural modelling. Give examples why each view would be useful and at which stage of the software product lifecycle.

2.7. For the earlier example of an ATM system, make the necessary assumptions, and develop the architectural model based on the above 4+1 principle. Remember to include scenarios that would enable you to integrate the four architectural views.

2.8. Write a short report along the recommended structure for you design in question 2.7 above.

2.9. Consider the design and documentation of the ATM in questions 2.7 and 2.8 and contrast it with the answers to the ATM problems in questions 2.4 and 2.5. What I would like for you to do is discuss if and how the object-oriented approach of the 4+1 method compares with structured approach of the DFD and state diagrams.

2.10. Explain the advantages and disadvantages of using the following types of models in software engineering applications,
   i) Abstract machine model.
   ii) Repository model.
   iii) Client-Server model.

2.11. Produce a conceptual architecture design for a security system in a modern building with the following specification. (Make any assumptions that you feel are necessary).

> The system is intended to protect against intrusion and to detect fire. It should incorporate smoke sensors, movement sensors and door sensors, video cameras located at various places in the building, all of which are under computer control. An operator console where the system status is reported, and external communication facilities to call the appropriate services such as police, fire, etc. is also specified.

CHAPTER 3 UNIFIED MODELLING LANGUAGE

3.1. Introduction

UML was designed to work with object-oriented (OO) methodologies for software development. As mentioned in chapter 2 of this text, OO means that the system is considered as being made up of a collection of objects that interact with each other. Typically these objects belong to a Class of objects with similar properties, and the system is therefore defined in terms of classes, objects and their properties. Object-Oriented Analysis and Design (OOAD) is an object-oriented approach for developing a software system. The OOAD process enables you to implement the key aspect of object orientation, such as abstraction, inheritance and encapsulation as mentioned in chapter 2 of this text. In addition, the OOAD process enables you to identify entities in a problem domain in relation to real-life objects. Simple designs can be implemented quite easily but more complex systems require a systematic approach to design and documentation so that the project can be managed successfully throughout its lifecycle. UML provides as standard for the design and documentation of OOAD.

3.2. UML description

UML is not a development methodology by itself however; it was designed to be compatible with the leading object-oriented software development methods of its time (for example OMT, Booch method, Objectory). [19] Since UML has evolved, some of these methods have been reworked in order to take advantage of the new notations (for example OMT), and new methods have been created based on UML. Perhaps the best known of these methodologies is IBM Rational Unified Process (RUP). There are many other UML-based methods like Abstraction Method, Dynamic Systems Development Method, and others, designed to provide more specific solutions, or achieve different objectives.

Unified Modelling language is a standard language for modelling a software system. It is used to model a software system and uses diagrams for representing the various tools of a software system. Therefore using UML enables a developer from any background to identify the tools in the analysis and design of a software system. It is also used as a language for communication across teams.

UML is a combination of diagrams and notations. The diagrams and notations are precise and are understood by developers and designers of software who are familiar with UML. This enables all the team members in a software company to coordinate and communicate with each other during project development. The language used for communication is simple, easy to use and it must be understood by all team members. Diagrammatic representation is used extensively in UML because it is relatively easy to comprehend and interpret. Thus UML can also be used as a language for communication among teams of software developers.

Finally, UML can be used to design a Meta model. Note that a meta-model refers to the most basic aspects of the component that we want to model. In the most limited cases, meta-models support only the data definitions of an application; these mechanisms have similar expressive capabilities to those of a UML Class diagram. You can design a Meta model by using UML to identify the semantics for an existing UML model. This is to say that the meta-model describes only the core (meaning=semantics) of an existing UML model. For example, designers who use ready-made tools to design models for a system can use a Meta model. Meta-models are pure in their simplicity and so there is less chance of making mistakes. Another feature provided by UML is that it enables you to specify, construct, and document a software system. UML is used to specify all the decisions taken during software development. The model designed using UML can be mapped directly to an object-oriented language such as java, C++ or Smalltalk.

Although UML is a necessary tool in software engineering there are cases where it has some disadvantages. For example UML is not beneficial if an application needs to be developed in a short period of time. In addition UML is not really applicable if a small amount of functionalities need to be added to an existing module.

UML model types

UML model types are classified depending on the information they represent. Models can be classified on the basis whether they represent static or dynamic information about a system. Another way of classifying models is based on what is accomplished in the model. According to the second classification, models are classified as either analysis or design models. These types are briefly described next.

Static Model: Static models identify the structural properties of the problem domain. In addition, the various components of the system, their internal properties and relation between the components are described. Entities that are present in a problem domain form structural properties of the system. For example, in an inventory system, the details of customers, products and suppliers are the structural properties of the system.

Dynamic Model: In the dynamic model, entities identified in the static model are mapped to classes. The behaviour of classes is identified and represented. For example, in an inventory system, adding customer details and modifying customer details constitute the behaviour of the customer Class.

Analysis Model: In the analysis model a problem domain is analysed to identify relationship between the entities in the problem domain. For example to develop an inventory system you identify a relationship between the accounting clerk, manager and the supplier. The entities identified in the static model are represented in the analysis model.

Design Model: In the design model, the classes that form a software system are identified and represented. For example, consider an inventory system designed for a problem domain. In this problem domain "Customer" is one of the classes of the inventory system. The analysis and design model may contain static and dynamic aspect of modelling a system.

3.3.   UML diagrams

There are twelve diagrams supported under UML. Four are structural, five are behavioural and three are used for model management, which include packages, subsystems and models. It is very important to distinguish between the UML model and the set of diagrams of a system. A diagram is a partial graphical representation of a model. The model also contains documentation such as written use-cases that drive the model elements and diagrams. This is sometimes referred to as a semantic backplane. Although UML is evolving there is a general tendency for UML diagrams to represent two distinct views of a system model these are,

- **Static (or structural) view:** This view depicts the static structure of the system using objects, attributes, operations and relationships. The structural view includes Class diagrams and composite structure diagrams.
- **Dynamic (or behavioural) view:** This view describes the dynamic behaviour of the system by showing collaborations among objects and changes to the internal

states of objects. This view also includes sequence diagrams, activity diagrams and state machine diagrams. Figure 3.1 shows the two views arranged in a hierarchy of diagrams. These basic components of these two views are briefly described next.

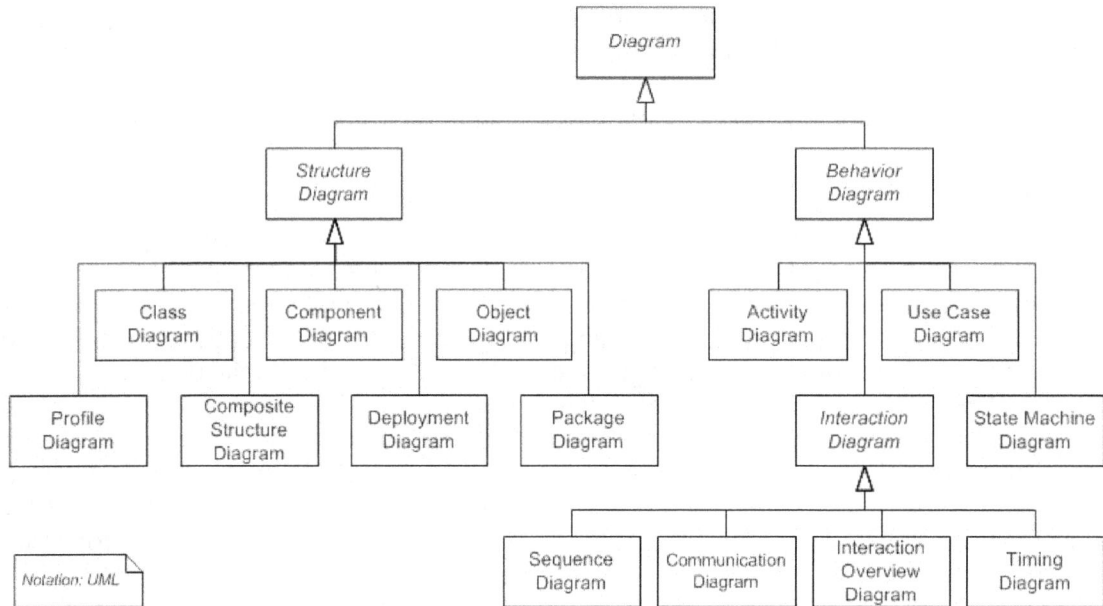

Figure 3.1. UML diagrams hierarchy

3.4.   Structure diagrams

Structure diagrams focus on the contents of the system being modelled. [20] The models in this category are,

Class diagram

The Class diagram is perhaps the most important in the OO paradigm. It describes the structure of a system by showing the classes within, their attributes, and the relationships between them. Class diagrams are used for a wide variety of purposes, including both conceptual/domain modelling and detailed design modelling. The notation for representing a Class diagram is shown in figure 3.2, which is fairly self-explanatory.

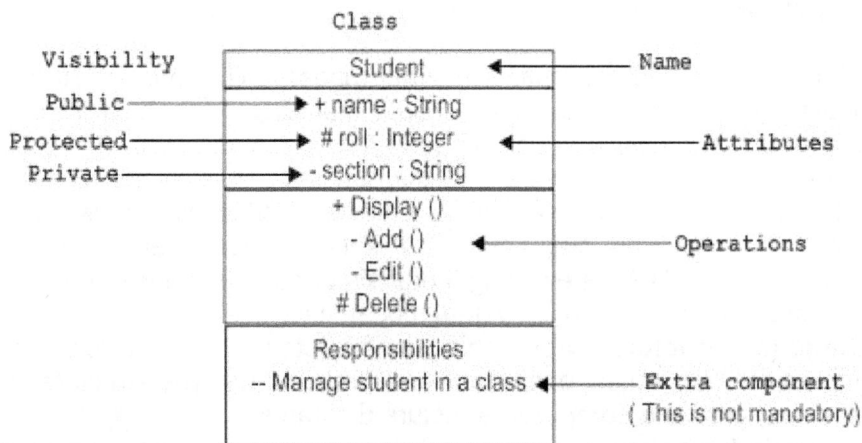

Figure 3.2. Notation for representing a Class

A Class diagram also represents behaviour of classes. For example, in an order management system the Order Class includes the operations: confirm, close, as depicted in the figure 3.3

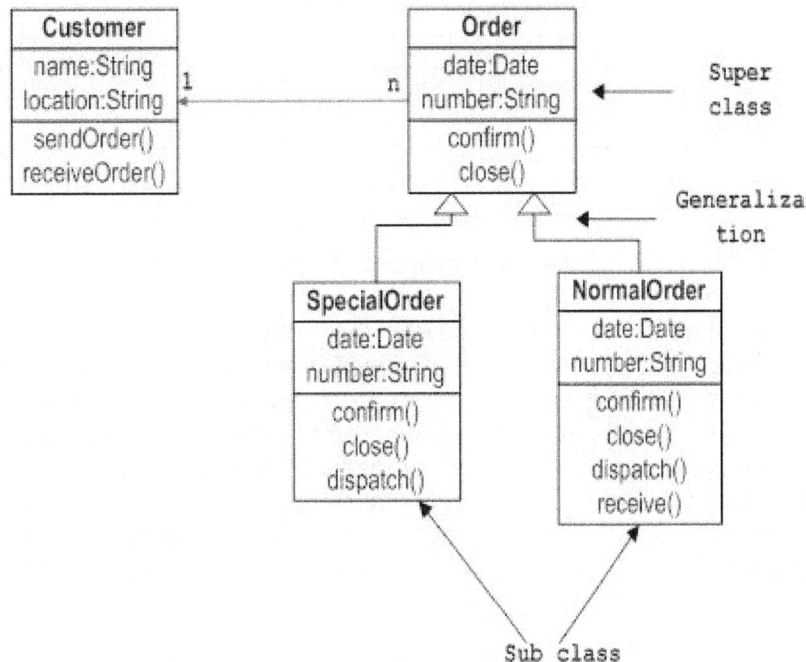

Figure 3.3. The UML Class diagram order management system

The reason why Class diagrams are so important is that they define the core components of the complete system model. Consider any system and try to describe classes that it contains. For example, what are the classes in an ATM system (i.e. cash-point machine)? We have all used one and we know what it does, it takes our cashpoint card and pin and based on a menu of services allows us to chose a particular one. It also does some basic security checks and acts to retain the card in some cases. Therefore based on this what are the classes?

The simple rule to identify classes is to consider the objects that make up the system. We know that classes are made up of objects that have similar properties. Thus we identify objects by considering the nouns in the system. In the ATM these are, user, balance, statement, account, and others. Properties of objects are typically described by adjectives i.e., overdrawn, in credit, wrong number etc. Methods are the actions that are performed on objects and these are defined within the classes. To find out what possible actions the system could support we think of verbs. Thus for an ATM the possible methods are, withdraw, deposit, balance enquiry etc.

Once we have a collection of objects, properties and methods (i.e. nouns, adjectives and verbs) we can organise them into classes. A good Class structure will make the complete system model easy to read and represent. It is for this reason that I said earlier that the Class diagram is perhaps the most important diagram in OOD. Next we consider some other diagrams that are used in UML, but before venturing into that it has to be said that none of these diagram is useful on its own. It simply does not make sense because each diagram models a particular feature, and the complete picture can only be seen after all the features have been modelled.

Component diagram

As the name implies a component diagram depicts how a software system is split up into components and it also shows the dependencies between these components. The notation is shown and annotated in figure 3.4.

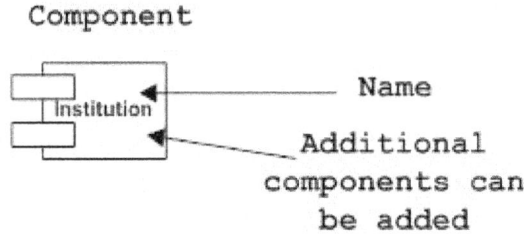

Figure 3.4. Component diagram notation

The component diagram shows the dependencies among software components, including the classifiers that specify them (for example implementation classes) and the tools that implement them; such as source code files, binary code files, executable files, scripts and tables. An example component diagram is shown in figure 3.5 where a system is shown composed of a user interface component, a controller component, database component and the main model component. Dotted arrows between components indicate that there is an association between them but no details are provided in the component diagram. For this we use other types of diagrams.

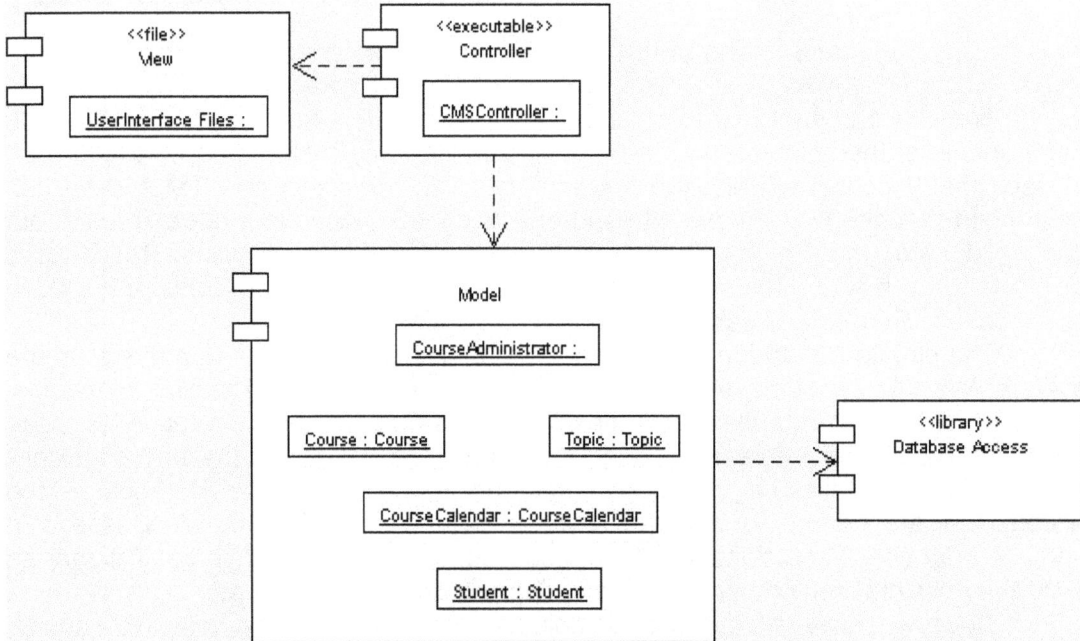

Figure 3.5. Component diagram

Composite structure diagram

Diagrams of figure 3.6 and 3.7 describe the internal structure of a Class and the collaborations that this structure makes possible. The composite structure diagram allows the modeller to describe the relationships between elements that work together within a class.

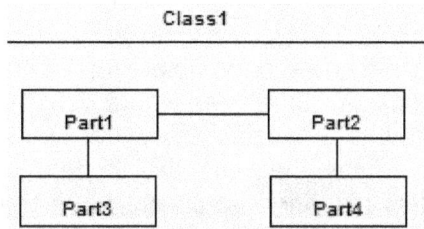

Figure 3.6. Notation for a composite structure diagram

Note that the structure diagram is similar to a Class diagram, but it also shows parts and connectors. The parts are not necessarily classes within the model and they do not represent particular instances, but they may be roles that classifiers could play. The parts are shown in a similar manner to objects. The composite structure diagram is used to show the runtime architectures of classes. Which is to say, how the class behaves while it is executing (running)?

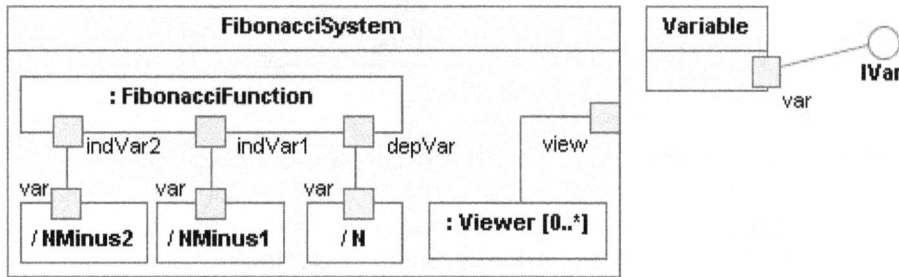

Figure 3.7. Composite structure diagram [20]

Deployment diagram

A deployment diagram serves to show how the system looks when it is implemented. This will typically include a model of the hardware used in the system and the execution environments and tools deployed on the hardware. An example deployment diagram of an on-line order management system is shown in figure 3.8.

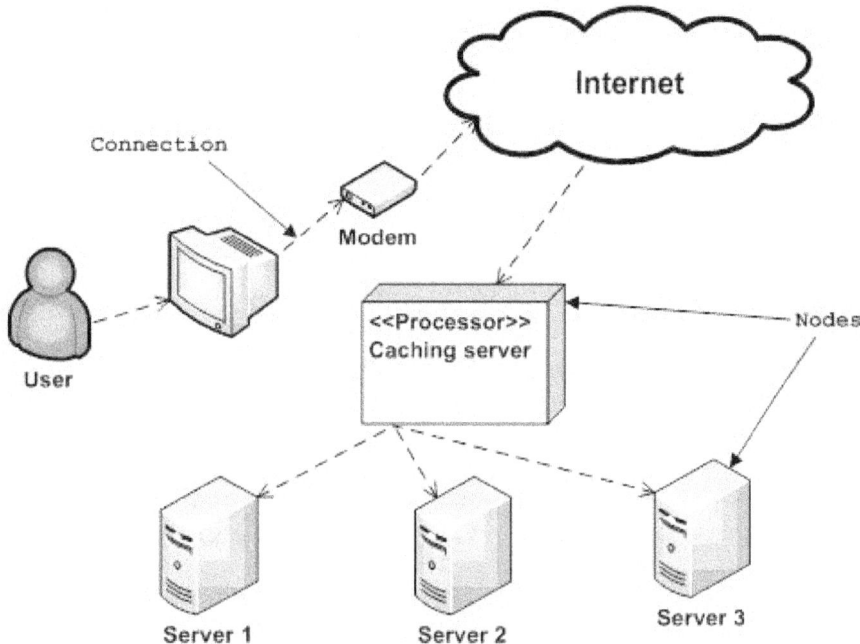

Figure 3.8. Deployment diagram example order management system

Object diagram

An object diagram shows a complete or partial view of the structure of a modelled system at a specific time (see figure 3.9). An object is an instance of a Class, which means that it is a specific entity that has specific value of the attributes and specific behaviour. In the diagram, the student object belongs to the student class. Note that the class identifier would not have the specific values in the fields shown but the object diagram would.

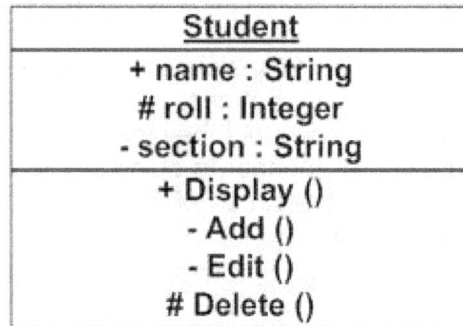

Student
+ name : String # roll : Integer - section : String
+ Display () - Add () - Edit () # Delete ()

Figure 3.9. Object notation diagram

For example, in the Class of all vehicles an example could be a make of Mercedes Benz, a type of saloon cars, a model name E280 and possibly a serial number. Figure 3.10 shows an example of how to represent objects in a UML diagram for an order management system. Within a Class of Customer we identify a sub-class of Order. Each instance of an Order class is a unique object with a unique number. Furthermore, a subclass of orders is identified which have a special attribute and a separate identifier.

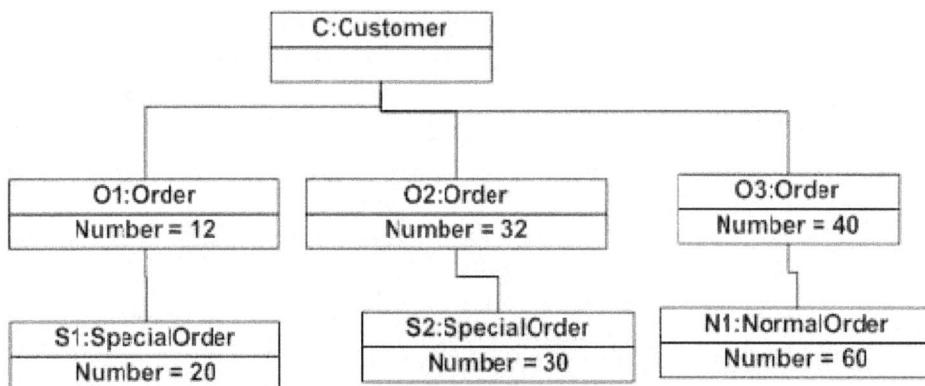

Figure 3.10. Object diagram

Package diagram

These diagrams depict how a system is divided into logical groupings and they also show the dependencies among these groupings. The notation used in package diagrams is shown in figure 3.11. Here it is seen that a package is used to group components and to provide a namespace for this group. Components that can be used to define a group are classes, objects, use cases, components, nodes, node instances etc. and thus all of these can be organised as packages.

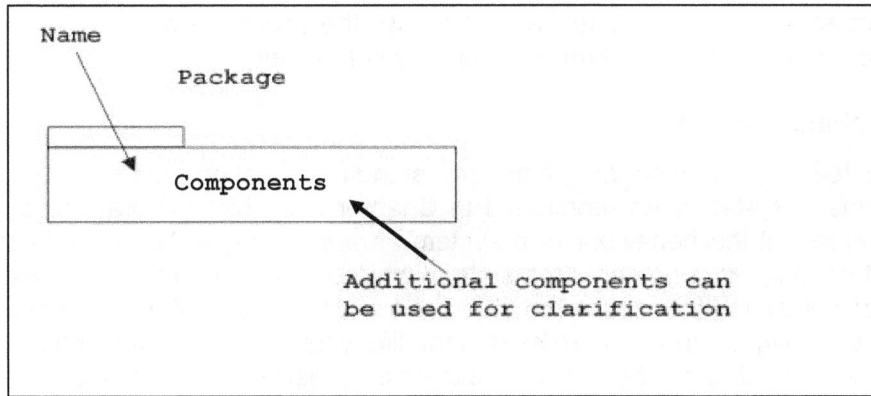

Figure 3.11. Package diagram

3.5. Behavioural (dynamic) diagrams

Dynamic diagrams emphasise what must happen in the system being modelled. They include,

Activity diagram

As the name implies, activity diagrams represent the operational step-by-step workflows of components in a system as shown in figure 3.12.

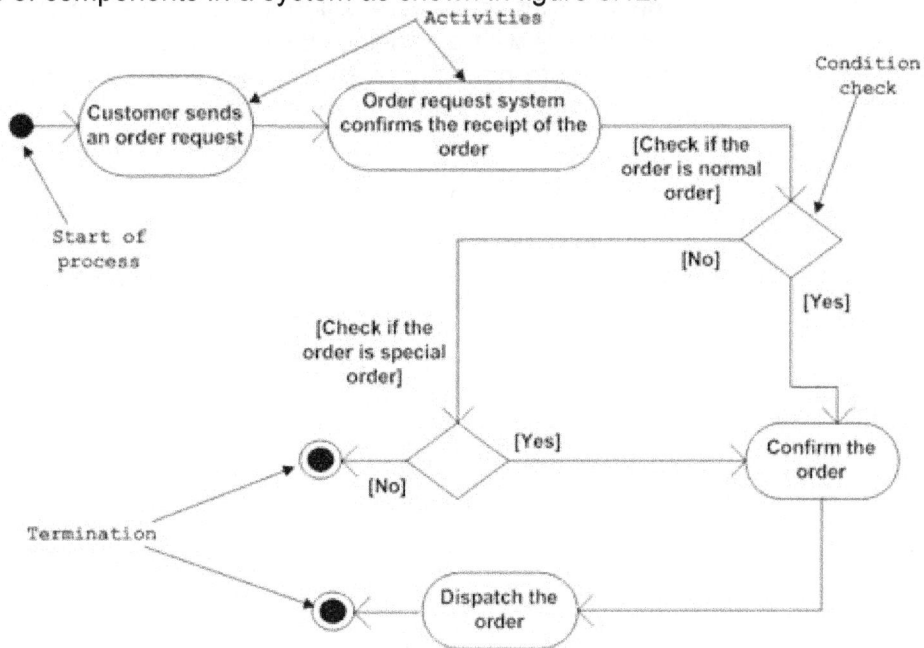

Figure 3.12. Activity diagrams order management system [21]

In this diagram an activity diagram shows the overall flow of control of an order management system. In many ways UML activity diagrams are the object-oriented equivalent of flow charts and data flow diagrams (DFDs) used in function-oriented (structured) development and they are used to model the dynamic aspects of a system. Therefore, an activity diagram represents the sequence of activities performed by a Class. It describes the behaviour of a Class when it receives messages communicated between objects that are interacting in the system. For example, consider the order management system in figure 3.12. The activity diagram can be used to represent the flow of activities in the ordering procedure. Reading from left to right and following the directions of arrows the sequence of activities that make up the order management system are relatively self-evident.

State machine diagram

Finite-state machine diagrams are standard notation that can be used to describe many systems. As mentioned in Chapter 2 of this text state diagrams are used to represent the behaviour of a system as a selection if its identified states. In OOD a state diagram represents the state in which a particular object can exist and it also describes events that cause the object to transit from one state to another. In this way the state diagram in OOD represents the lifecycle of a single object from the time it is created until it is destroyed. For, example, consider the status of a candidate before joining an organisation, initially the candidate applies for a job. The candidate attends an interview and if selected, the candidate is employed. The state diagram can be used in this situation to represent the various states of a candidate. Eventually the candidate may retire or indeed change jobs and all these are events that trigger the state transition of the candidate as an object.

Note that in OOD a system typically consists of many objects. The changing status of multiple objects cannot be represented in a single state diagram. Figure 3.13 depicts a state transition diagram to process an order. Initially the system is idle, until an event triggers the first transition. The order request is an event that triggers a transition to an intermediate state. This requires a decision on which option is used for the delivery. This decision in turn triggers a transition to the next state etc. You could identify with this if you compare it with an on-line payment and order system that we are all familiar with. Here you are normally taken through a set of menus and after filling details, you click an icon to take you to the next state of the application. Thus, clicking on a particular icon is an event that triggers a transition to another state.

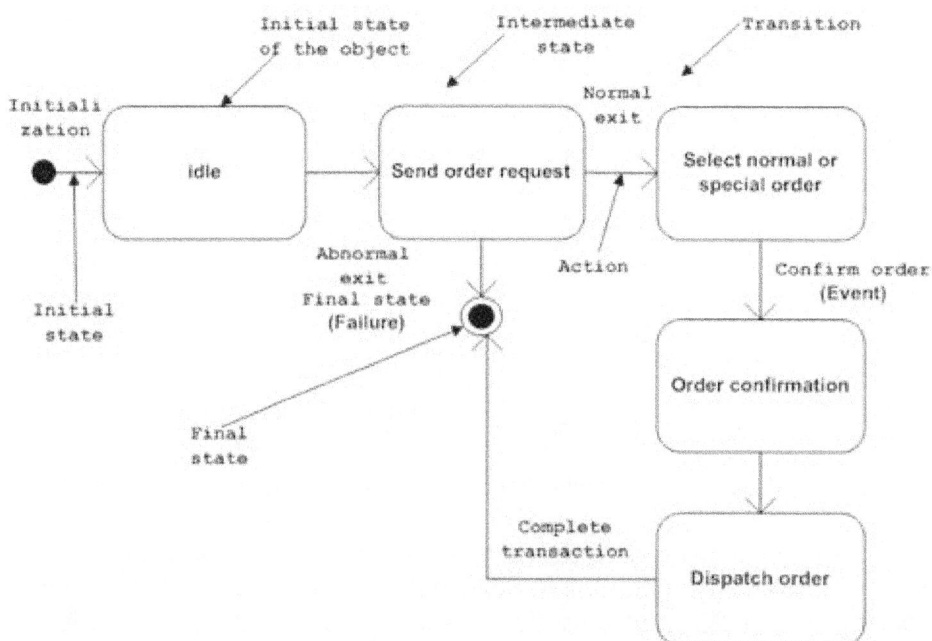

Figure 3.13. State diagram example order management system [21]

Use-case diagram

Use-cases are mini-scenarios of the system. They are used to simplify modelling so that we can get an idea of behaviour without using the complete system model. The diagram representing use-cases shows the functionality provided by a system in terms of users (actors), their goals represented as use-cases, and any dependencies among these use-cases. Actors interact with the system directly. A use-case is a specific transaction between actors and the system. There can be many use-cases for any system, but a use-case isolates each particular transaction and models that independent of all others. Figure 3.14 is an example of a use-case diagram in UML notation. Here the annotations are provided for guidance in Courier font but you would not normally annotate your diagrams in this way. The actor in figure 3.14 communicates with the use-case, which in this example is called 'register student'. Other use-cases could be pay fees, check qualifications etc.

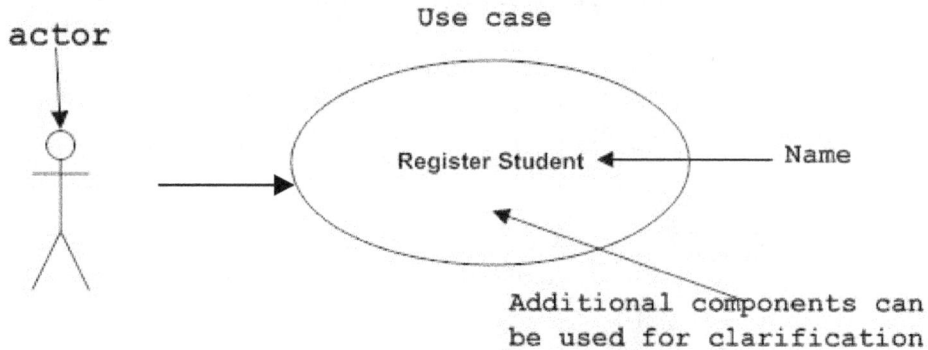

Figure 3.14. The UML use-case diagram

As another example, consider a situation in which an accounting clerk generates pay-slips for employees in a payroll system. The accounting clerk is an actor because the accounting clerk interacts with the payroll system directly. The accounting clerk generating pay-slips is the use-case in this example.

Interaction diagrams

Interaction diagrams depict the flow of control and data between components in the system being modelled. From the name 'interaction' it should be clear that the diagram is a part of dynamic behaviour of the system. This interactive behaviour is represented in UML by two diagrams known as a Sequence diagram and a Collaboration diagram. The main purpose of both these diagrams are similar but they differ in that sequence diagrams focus on the time aspect of a sequence of messages while collaboration diagrams focus on the structural organisation of objects that send and receive messages.

Sequence diagram

Sequence diagrams illustrate how objects communicate with each other in terms of a sequence of messages. Optionally a sequence diagram can be used to indicate the lifespan of objects relative to those messages. The focus of sequence diagrams is to describe messages between objects in temporal (i.e. related to time) or chronological (i.e. related to sequence) order. Thus, you would create a sequence diagram when you want to explicitly represent the sequence of message flows in a system. To describe such a sequence of messages consider an example of what happens when you use a mobile phone to dial a number. A possible sequence is shown in figure 3.15. Here the messages are clearly shown in sequence from pressing buttons through digitising and emitting tone etc. It has to be said that all these diagrams are designed so that they are easy to interpret, and therefore it is not necessary to go into a great deal of explanation about what they represent.

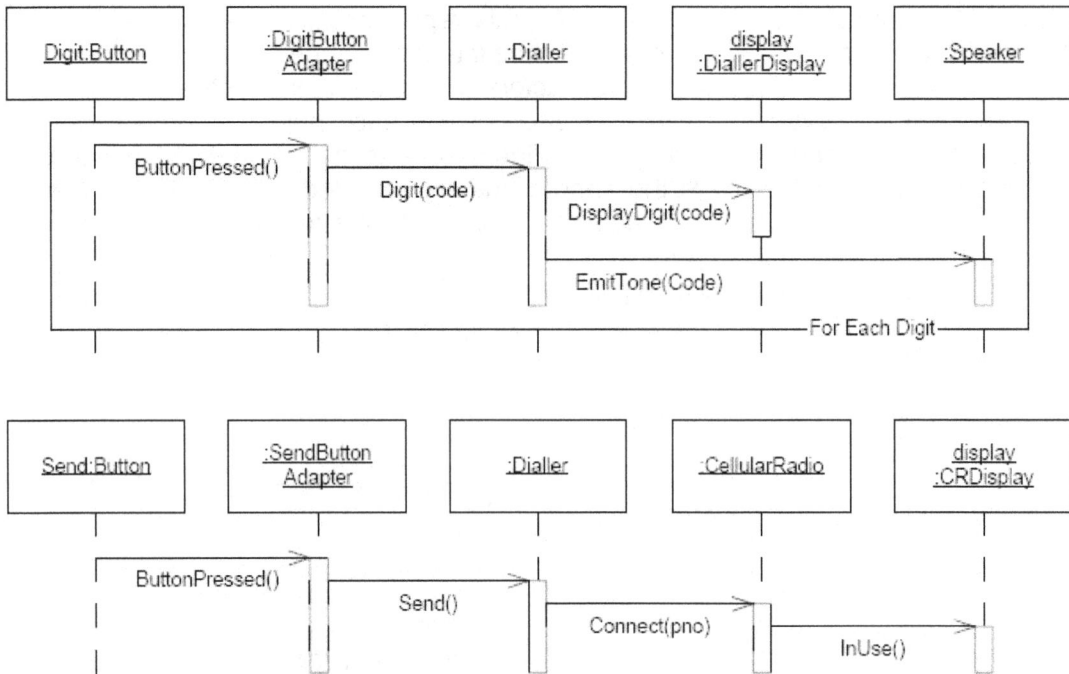

Figure 3.15. Sequence diagram example of a cellular phone

Collaboration diagram

As mentioned earlier collaboration diagram focus on the organisational structure behind the objects that are communicating in terms of sequenced messages. (See figure 3.16) They represent a combination of information taken from Class, Sequence, and Use-case Diagrams describing both the static structure and dynamic behaviour of a system.

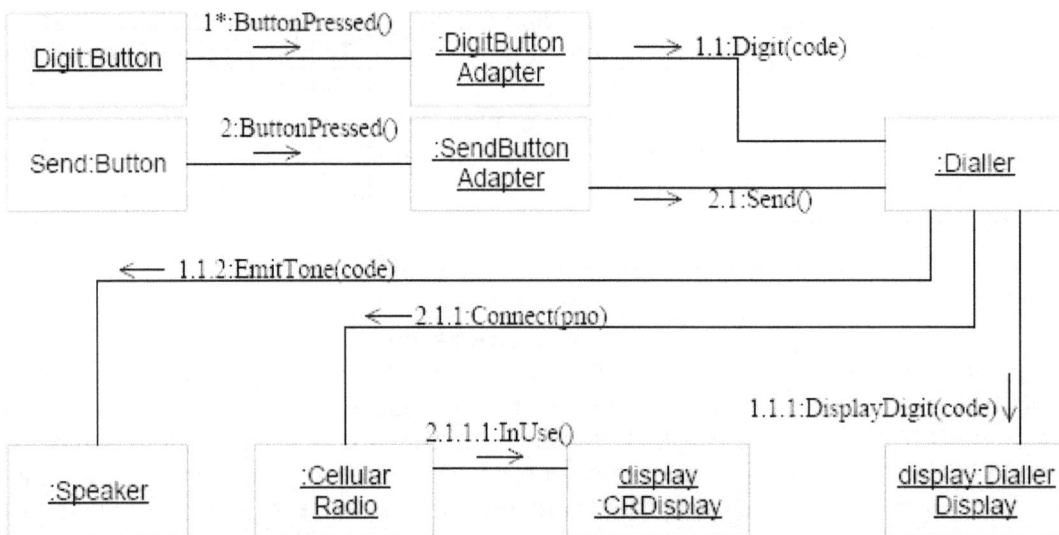

Figure 3.16. Collaboration diagram example cellular phone

As the name implies, the emphasis here is on the links between objects, which describe how objects collaborate (or work together). In contrast to sequence diagrams, collaboration diagram do not emphasise the order in which object interact. Collaboration diagrams are used to represent relationships between objects in a software system and they also represents how various objects interact with each other. You create a collaboration diagram if you need to explicitly represent a relationship between the various objects in a system. Figure 3.16 is an example of a UML collaboration diagram for a cellular phone, which should be relatively self-explanatory. If you are familiar with database design, then you will understand collaboration diagrams, because they naturally fit into database models.

Interaction overview diagram

These are types of activity diagram in which nodes are used to represent interaction diagrams. An example diagram is shown in figure 3.17 where it is seen that each node/activity within the diagram represents another interaction diagram. (i.e. event selected, performance selected) Note that Interaction Overview diagram is a new addition in UML 2.0. It describes a high-level view of a group of interactions combined into a logic sequence, including flow-control logic to navigate between the interactions.

Figure 3.17 shows the interaction activity diagram for a theatre booking system. There are three classes, display performance for selected event, date and also confirmation. The user interacts by selecting an event or cancelling selection. Performance date and event are supplied to the user via the selection box (diamond shape) and from here the appropriate event and date are booked, which is to say [event selected] and [performance selected]. In this simple diagram all interactions are represented between the user and the system classes.

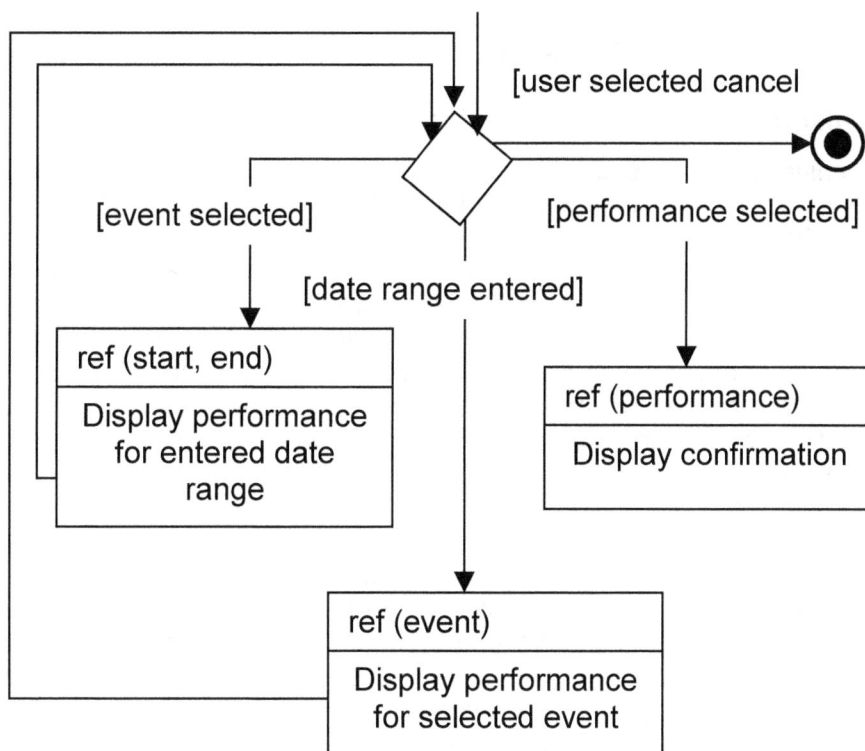

Figure 3.17. Interaction overview diagram

Communication diagram

Communication diagram is slightly different than the collaboration diagram although it too considers interaction between objects. We can say that it is a scaled down version of the earlier UML collaboration diagrams. The distinguishing factor of the communication diagram is the link between objects. This is a visual link and it is missing in sequence diagrams. Note that in sequence diagrams only the messages passed between objects are shown and there is no indication of inks between objects. In contrast the communication diagram is used to specify just the links between objects. This also prevents the modeller from making the mistake of using an object diagram format as the basis for messaging. In other words it forces the modeller to use separate diagrams for messages and for links between objects. A Communication diagram may model synchronous, asynchronous, return, lost, found, and object-creation messages.

Figure 3.18 shows a communication diagram with four objects and three links. Each object on a Communication diagram is called an object lifeline.

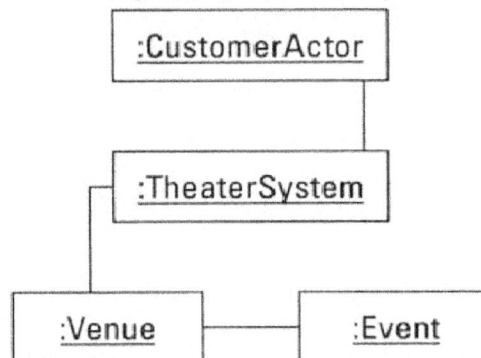

Figure 3.18. Communication diagram [21]

Timing diagrams

Timing diagram is another addition in UML 2.0. It is an optional diagram designed to specify the time constraints on messages sent and received during an interaction between objects. It can be used to signal the change in state or condition of an object over time. Typically it is used to show the change in state of an object over time in response to external events where the focus is on timing constraints. (See figure 3.19) It basically deals with the time of events over the entire lifecycle of an object. Therefore, a timing diagram can be defined as a special purpose interaction diagram which focuses on the events of an object in its lifetime. It is basically a mixture of state machine and interaction diagram. The timing diagram uses the following time lines:
1. State time line
2. General value time line

A lifeline in a timing diagram forms a rectangular space within the content area of a frame. It is typically aligned horizontally to read from left to right. Multiple lifelines may be stacked within the same frame to model the interaction between them. Thus from figure 3.19 the Sd single lifeline is a rectangular space defining a lifeline. To its right, aligned horizontally is another example of a lifeline (i.e. Sd double lifeline). Each of these is stacked within the same frame to show the interaction i.e. event, performance.

Sd Single lifeline example	Sd Double lifeline example
Event	Event
	Performance

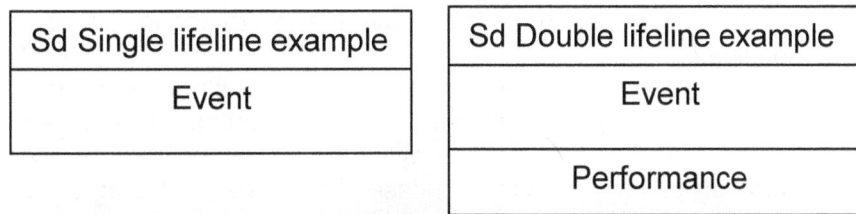

Figure 3.19. Timing diagram example

It can be seen from the above that learning to use UML properly is a skill that is acquired over time. UML encapsulates many of the tools that have been used in the existing modelling methodologies and unifies these under a common language and syntax for representing each of these tools.

There are many examples of UML diagrams available on the Internet and also there are numerous publications that describe the UML approach. A useful starting point is the UML 2.0 introduction website. [22]

3.6. Chapter summary

In this chapter I briefly introduce UML. It should be quite clear that UML is a way of describing systems that helps to visualise how a system will work once it is built. The language uses many diagrams with very clear syntax, which makes it possible to be consistent in modelling systems. Like any language it takes time to master UML. I have shown here the essential features of UML so that the reader can become familiar with some aspects of modelling using UML. The simple examples of diagrams that I have provided can be extended to describe more complex systems, and getting the system right is a matter of trial and error. What I mean to say is that you draw UML diagrams to model the system and as the model evolves you can notice mistakes or something that you have omitted. You then refine the model so that it looks like you want it to. UML representation is also a very good way of documenting design. This helps others to understand your design and it also makes software maintenance and re-use significantly easier to implement. I also emphasise that particular UML diagrams on their own do not make much sense, and that only as a collection of diagrams do they begin to model the system in a way that developers can understand.

Exercises

3.1. Is it a good idea to have a standard for representing models in software engineering? Discuss the merits and consequences of using a standard such as UML to model systems in software engineering.

3.2. How does UML use diagrams to represent systems? Using examples as appropriate, discuss why both static and dynamic types of diagrams are needed to represent a system?

3.3. Why is a Class diagram one of the most important diagrams in OOD?

3.4. In OOD how would you go about identifying classes, objects, properties and methods of objects and classes?

3.5. Consider a scenario in which an accounting clerk generates pay-slips for employees in a payroll system. Making any assumptions necessary identify the classes in this scenario, the objects that they contain and the properties and methods associated with these.

3.6. List and briefly discuss the relevance of static diagrams in system modelling.

3.7. List and briefly discuss the relevance of dynamic diagrams in system modelling.

3.8. Consider a scenario in which an accounting clerk generates pay-slips for employees in a payroll system. The accounting clerk object is an actor because it interacts with the payroll system directly. The accounting clerk generating pay-slips is the use-case. Draw use-case diagram to describe all the possible transactions that could be modelled in this scenario.

3.9. For any one use-case that you identified in Q3.8 develop a full UML model to include dynamic models. State any assumptions that you make.

CHAPTER 4 REQUIREMENTS ENGINEERING

4.1.   Project management

Project management is a very broad discipline and there are a large number of resources that can be accessed on–line as well as in published literature. [24,25] Project management generally concerns the management of resources in order to deliver results. The resources can be: people, materials, buildings and premises, IT and communications, storage, plant and equipment, finance, administration, marketing, human resources, legal, technical and scientific etc. The project deliverable could be: products, services, purchasing, selling, training, education, culture, customer service and relations, quality, health and safety, new product development, new business development; and in any combination. A very important element of project management is the delegation of responsibility for the project. Depending on the size of the project the levels of responsibility will vary but in a very general sense it has to be said that all projects should identify persons that are responsible at every stage in the project. For a start every project must have a project manager, who is responsible for performing the following tasks,

- **Planning the project:** Very simply stated, a good plan saves time and reduces the cost of the project. Or, alternatively defined, a bad plan costs time and money, reduces profit and can easily result in a loss and/or bankruptcy.
- **Estimating the cost and establishing the budget**: Budget is a very important factor since it establishes the limits to which costs can be taken. Ultimately cost is the driving factor behind the majority of resources that are needed in a project.
- **Identifying and acquiring necessary resources** (People, Equipment, etc.) productive teams can significantly improve project efficiency. Skills that are needed in a project need to be resourced during the planning stages so that costs can be determined.
- **Managing the project** (to the schedule and within budget): Not everything can be planned. There are always potential problems that cannot be foreseen. Contingency plans need to be in place in order to mitigate the effects of unforeseen problems.

Managing a project typically involves a number of stages. As projects vary so the project management approach will have to be modified to suit them, but in general project management can be divided into the stages given in Figure 4.1. These stages will be describe briefly next.

As seen in Figure 4.1 there are a number of stages in the lifecycle of a project.

Project definition

This involves establishing the requirements, which will serve to guide all the other stages of the project. For example, a requirements document will be used to plan the activity, model any proposed solutions and evaluate these models. Requirements will be needed during the implementation stage as well as commissioning. Thus, it is seen that a significant amount of effort is needed to accurately establish the project requirements. The next stage in Figure 4.1 is project planning.

4.2.　Planning

Accurate planning of projects is a very complex and challenging task. There are a large number of project management tools that are available to assist with planning. Many of these are software tools, which implement a variety of established algorithms. Some of the more advanced of these rely on theoretical concepts such as decision support systems (DSS), Queuing theory, Markov analysis, forecasting as well as tools such as linear programming, network modelling, goal programming, scheduling with PERT/CPMs etc. [26]

The Internet is a very rich resource for locating these tools, and some will also be offered on a free trial period. The difficulty here is that before you can apply any of these tools, you need to learn how to use them. This takes time and it has to be evaluated against the available resources. In the early stages of project management it is a good idea to spend time thinking about the project, sketching a few ideas using a pencil and paper and trying to find out any potential difficulties. For example, the context diagram described in chapter 1 is a good starting point when planning any project.

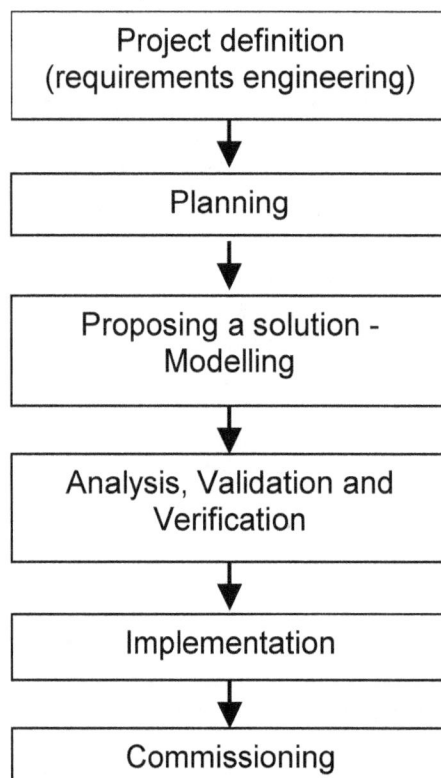

```
┌─────────────────────────────────┐
│      Project definition         │
│  (requirements engineering)     │
└─────────────────────────────────┘
                │
                ▼
┌─────────────────────────────────┐
│           Planning              │
└─────────────────────────────────┘
                │
                ▼
┌─────────────────────────────────┐
│     Proposing a solution -      │
│           Modelling             │
└─────────────────────────────────┘
                │
                ▼
┌─────────────────────────────────┐
│     Analysis, Validation and    │
│          Verification           │
└─────────────────────────────────┘
                │
                ▼
┌─────────────────────────────────┐
│        Implementation           │
└─────────────────────────────────┘
                │
                ▼
┌─────────────────────────────────┐
│         Commissioning           │
└─────────────────────────────────┘
```

Figure 4.1. Stages in project management

After only a short period of time spent on researching into management techniques, it becomes clear that a vast amount of literature is available on the subject. The problem with this is that we do not have time to read all of it and must therefore focus on defining only the relevant components. As a matter of interest, when I typed, "project management" into a search engine of my browser, it returned 118 Million results. Therefore, it is left to the reader, should they find this course of action necessary, to pursue further research into management science and techniques. .

As far as this text is concerned, only the very basic aspects will be covered, and these will help to manage simple projects in software engineering. If a more complex project needs to be managed then resource to more advanced management techniques will be required.

Planning and organising are essential to the success of any project. A project involves inputs and outputs as well as deadlines. Planning and organising activities and resources to achieve the desired outputs within time and budget are a major component of project management. In the present age of the Internet it is relatively easy to find software tools that can help with project management. There are numerous software tools for managing projects that also include planning and organisational software and many vendors offer free trial periods on their product. For example, Table 4.1 lists some project management templates that can be downloaded for free from a vendor of project management applications. [27]

Table 4.1

Project Initiation	Risk Management
Project Planning	Issue Management
Project Execution	Quality Management
Change Management	Project Closure

Whilst these templates, and project management resources are very useful, it has to be said that they are only as good as our ability to use them. Once again we are faced with the need to do some research. This is necessary to establish a timed relationship between the available resources and the project deliverables. Typically a project would be broken down into a number of tasks (or work packages) and each of these will be allocated the resources that are needed. This is so that each of the tasks can be done relatively autonomously which means that for example different teams could be allocated to different tasks. By doing this it is also possible to do tasks in parallel which means that large projects to be managed more efficiently. Using a tool such as a Gantt chart, a timescale is provided to indicate the sequence in which tasks occur and also when deliverables are to be expected. It is usual to include milestones in a Gantt chart as indicators of progress throughout the project. It is very likely that different teams will be involved in different tasks and in complex projects this can present problems. Where a number of different teams are working on different tasks, at some stage these separate efforts need to be integrated and tested as a complete unit. It has to be said that planning occurs throughout the project and the starting plan is quite often significantly different to the one produced later on in the project lifecycle. We consider next an example of a feasibility study, which is often a starting point that is used to determine if it is worth going ahead with the main project.

4.3.   Feasibility analysis Case Study

A feasibility study is used to provide an analysis of the objectives, requirements, and system concepts for a proposed project or activity. Typically a feasibility study is done in order to help decide if the activity should proceed or not. For example, I can do a feasibility study to determine if I should re-mortgage my home and use the money to buy a holiday home in Spain. On the other hand I could do a feasibility study to determine if the installation of a Wind Farm in Kent would be a good investment for a client. Additionally, the detail to which a study is taken will depend on the resources that are available. Quite often, a preliminary study can be used to determine if there is a need to perform a more detailed feasibility study, which would require more resources. Thus a feasibility study can vary in the detail to which it is performed.

The following is a very simple case study that can provide some guidance to undertaking a feasibility study and preparing a feasibility report. Please note that this case study is only used here as a guide. It is a hypothetical case in an engineering discipline; I have chosen the 'games' area as an example of something topical in software engineering. However, it is important to note that there are many different ways to approach a feasibility study. To a large extent this will depend on the subject of the feasibility study, the knowledge domain, the timing and budget constraints as well as the experience of the team that is charged with undertaking it. For example if you are considering the feasibility of upgrading an existing e-mail system based on a Unix mail server to a Microsoft Exchange Server, then your approach will include the evaluation of the existing system and the also the features of the proposed system etc. On the other hand this approach is not suitable if you are working out the feasibility of say, the installation of a 1MW wind turbine on a farm near Hastings in Kent. In this case, there is no existing system to compare to and improve upon. Instead the feasibility will consider planning and environmental conditions and impact on the community, as well as the practical business issues of cost and returns on investment. In all cases a feasibility study needs to rely on common sense and professional know-how so that as far as possible the potential for success of a project can be assessed.

Structure of a feasibility report

Every feasibility study will be unique, but in general the following report structure can be used as a guide. In order to give you an idea of what each section of this feasibility report should contain, I am assuming that we have a request from a client to produce a preliminary report on the feasibility of developing a new game to be hosted on a the Internet and freely used by clients within a common web browser application. The client has given me one week to produce a report that she can take to investors.

Client brief

> *Dear Goran,*
>
> *I am meeting a client in a week's time who is interested in funding a web hosted game development project to develop an on-line gaming infrastructure where clients can play the game and the revenue will be generated by banners that advertisers pay for. As you can imagine, the more clients that play the game, the higher the revenue that advertisers will be prepared to pay. When I meet with her, I should like to have a preliminary feasibility study of such an enterprise, which I hope will interest her enough to fund a full study. Could I ask you to prepare a feasibility report, and also a short PowerPoint presentation for me to take to the meeting?*
> *I am sorry that this is short notice, but if we can manage to interest her, I am assured that we will be engaged as consulting engineers on the project.*
> *Your sincerely*
>
> *Dana Urban*
> *Managing Director*

With this client brief I am able to sketch out a preliminary schedule of activity. My time resource is 7 days and my initial schedule is as given as a Gantt chart in table 4.2. I drafted my initial time schedule based on my experience in the subject and my understanding of what is required. My reasoning in allocating the time resources as per Gantt chart is as follows.

- I have no previous experience in games development projects, and I do not have anyone that I can ask to help me.
- I believe that the quality of my feasibility study is determined by how much time I can spend on researching and understanding the technology that is available.
- I also need to understand the commercial aspects of such a project and
- I am also aware that I need to consider the infrastructure issues.

For this reason I have allocated the bulk of my time to information gathering and research activities. I shall use the library and the Internet to obtain the information that I require. Based on my understanding of the subject, I consider that the most important aspect is to become informed on the technical considerations of assessing the development infrastructure. I need to use the Internet as a platform, so that means I will need a development platform that is supported by all browsers. Flash comes to mind but I have also heard of Google.doc as documentation system used for similar developments. This part of my activity I have called the environmental considerations in my plan. Thus, I have allocated 6 days to the task of research and information gathering.

Table 4.2. Gantt Chart

	Duration (Days)						
	1	2	3	4	5	6	7
Background research	▓	▓	▓	▓	▓	▓	
Technical Considerations		▓	▓	▓	▓		
Commercial Considerations		▓	▓	▓	▓		
Environmental Considerations			▓	▓	▓	▓	
Report writing				▓	▓	▓	
PowerPoint Development						▓	▓
Milestones				1		2	3
M1 - Complete research							
M2 - Produce Report							
M3 - Produce PowerPoint Presentation							

This allocation also takes into account my experience in the software engineering industry, as a result of which I do not need to read up on aspects of software engineering project management since I am quite experienced in these matters. Even though I have allocated 6 out of 7 days to research, it can be seen from Table 4.2 that some of this time will be shared with report writing and preparing the presentation.

From my previous experience I estimate that about 20 hours are required to prepare the report and power point presentations for this study. Therefore my simple reasoning is that I take this away from the week, and whatever is left I allocate to research. Table 4.2 shows that I intend to start my report writing on day 4. I believe that after 3 days of research I should be in the position to contribute some useful information to the report. A day or so later, I intend to begin work on the PowerPoint presentation. The information contained in the report will be used in the presentation, so I am intending to start the presentation work on day 6.

To help me with timing, I have included milestones 1, 2 and 3. Milestone 1 is the time that I finish my researching. In my view this is an extremely important aspect of planning, i.e. knowing when to stop an activity. I have learned from my past experience that I can get carried away with research and I am aware that this could run into my report preparation time and compromise the quality of my report and presentation. Milestones 2 and 3 are my deadlines for producing the report and presentation respectively.

This is a very simple example of the steps that are generally taken in project planning, and it should help you start on any software engineering project. As with modelling discussed earlier, planning is also largely intuitive. We plan to the best of our ability, but sometimes events happen that make us change our plans. It is always good to consider any events that are likely to impact on our planning and to build into our plan contingency measures to account for these.

There are other aspects that must be included in any plan and one of the overriding factors is the cost of development. Costing will be covered in Chapter 12 of this text, but it is worth mentioning that it should be included in the feasibility report example shown here.

Proposing a solution and modelling

Chapter 2 of this text described modelling as a resource that can potentially identify problems that are not easy to spot during the planning phase. Additionally, by identifying these problems before the implementation stage, modelling can save time and reduce costs. Modelling as a general term is very broad. On the one hand, making the necessary assumptions and describing relationships using some combination of mathematical equations can model anything that we can perceive in the physical world. On the other hand, if we are considering a system or a process, we can use graphical and analytical techniques to model the behaviour of the components within. In software engineering for example, the Universal Modelling Language (UML) is used to describe everything involved in a software development project. Chapters 2 and 3 of this text covered modelling and the general tools used to develop system models in both procedural and object-oriented paradigms.

Whatever the project, a project manager must be able to identify at which stage of the project it is necessary to apply modelling and also which types of models are appropriate for the project. As with any other resource, modelling takes time and has a cost associated with it. The project manager must be able to judge if the modelling effort is cost effective. When all the models have been completed the proposed solution can be identified. If the application area of the project is well known, and the team is experienced in delivering similar projects, then a labour intensive modelling effort may not be cost-effective. On the other hand, if little or no experience is available, and there are a large number of unknowns a dedicated, labour intensive modelling effort may well be a very cost-effective option. Once again, it is up to the project management team to make these decisions.

Validation and verification

With reference to Figure 4.1, after the modelling stage there follows a stage during which we need to analyse the proposed solution in order to determine if the solution satisfies the requirements. Validation considers if the proposed solution meets the user requirements as specified in the requirements document. Thus, validation is concerned with answering the question "are we building the correct system"? Verification on the other hand considers whether the system is being built in a correct way. That is to say, verification is concerned with the analysis from the planning and execution point of view rather than the functional perspective. In the event that errors are identified as a result of these analyses, the project manager will need to address this and apply the required corrective measures.

Implementation

The next stage is the implementation stage. If all other stages have been completed in a satisfactory manner, then the implementation stage should be quite straightforward. If not, problems will occur that will require a return to some of the previous stages, and if necessary even as far back as the requirements stage. It is of fundamental importance that all the possible errors have been rectified before this stage is reached. If a design error is built into the implemented system, it could be prove to be very difficult to identify and very expensive to correct.

Commissioning

The final stage is commissioning. Here the project is delivered to the client, and it is measured against the original set of agreed requirements. At each stage a document is produced to describe the activities of that particular stage.

Some more details on requirement engineering in software projects are presented next.

4.4.   Requirements engineering

Every project needs to be specified accurately so that the parties involved in the project know what their obligations are and the boundaries of their responsibility. In many cases the parties involved will have different backgrounds and therefore a different perspective on the project. For example, the financier of the project may not appreciate the technical complexity of the task in hand, whist the technical director, may not realise the costs involved in the marketing and distribution of the finished product. As there are varieties of projects, so every project will have a somewhat different approach to requirements specification.

There are a very large number of sources that refer to the different requirements specifications. For example in the area of software development, SRS refers to the software requirement specification document. The IEEE [28] is an excellent source for definitions of system and software specifications. For example, designers of real-time, embedded system software, will use IEEE STD 830-1998 as the basis for software specifications. A similar standard used for the specification of systems is the IEEE STD 1233-1998. However, for most purposes in smaller systems, the same templates can be used for both types of specifications.

A database applications company that outlines the requirements, which they want clients to satisfy before they are engaged on a project, gives a more practical example. [28] Here the database developers are informing the client about the information that they need in order to undertake a database development project. The requirements are very precise and clearly stated. It is not at all clear how these requirements fit in with the IEEE standards, but nevertheless they serve the purpose of defining the requirements from the client end.

Benefits of a requirements specification

A well-researched and precise requirements document will serve to help the smooth running of the project throughout its lifecycle. Some areas that this will influence are as follows, [29]

Legal basis: It can serve to establish the basis for agreement between the clients and the suppliers on what the project will provide.

Reduced development effort. A formal requirements document encourages the various parties concerned to consider rigorously all of the requirements before design begins. This helps to reduce effort in subsequent redesign, modifications and retesting. Careful review of the requirements can reveal omissions, misunderstandings, and inconsistencies early in the development cycle when these problems are easier to correct.

Provide a basis for estimating costs and schedules. The description of the product to be developed can be used as a realistic basis for estimating project costs. This in turn helps both the clients and the suppliers because they can both make business decision based on this.

Provide a baseline for validation and verification. Project can be validated much more easily if a good requirement document is in place.

Although mainly dealing with software engineering, Somerville gives a very good treatment of requirement analysis. [30] Here, the desirable characteristics of requirements specifications given in are as follows. Requirements specifications should be: [31]

- **Complete**: specification must precisely define all the situations that can be anticipated and the manner of the response to these.
- **Consistent**: there is no conflict between individual requirement statements.
- **Unambiguous**: A statement of a requirement is unambiguous if it can only be interpreted one way.
- **Modifiable**: Statements that are related must be grouped together and those that are not, must be separated. Arranging the requirements document into a logical structure can help with this.
- **Ranked**: Statements are ranked according to their importance in the organisational structure.
- **Testable**: It should be possible for all statements in the requirements specification to be tested according to a pass or fail criteria. If this is not possible, then alternative, quantifiable assessment criteria should be identified.

Even though the above relate primarily to software requirements specifications, they are very general and can therefore be applied to almost any project. That said the above do not really provide us with a way of producing a requirement specification. Within the confines of this text and pertaining to projects that primarily involve science and engineering, the requirements document should be structured according to Table 4.3.

Table 4.3 User and System requirements

User requirements	System requirements
Requirements definition: This is the definition of the aims from the **user** perspective. What is the system or project aiming to achieve? These should be defined to a point where the project can proceed with an acceptable level of risk.	**Requirements definition:** This is the definition of the aims from the **system** perspective. What is the system or project aiming to achieve? In contrast with user requirements, these should also consider resource implications on system development. (i.e. have we done something like this before?)
Requirements specification: Effectively these are the objectives that need to be met in order that the aims can be satisfied. This will normally consist of functional and non-functional requirements as described below.	**Requirements specification:** These are objectives as outlined in the user requirements, but from the systems perspective. It should be clear that some objectives would be different when looking at the system as opposed to the user requirements.

As seen in Table 4.3 the requirements document is divided into two sections. The section on user requirements deals with the functional and non-functional requirements from the user perspective. A somewhat different perspective is the system requirements where the aims consider the system rather than the user. Here the resource implications are taken into account. It is evident that both the user and the system requirements need to be satisfied in order that the project can have a chance of being successfully completed. The functional and non-functional requirements are briefly defined as follows,

Functional requirements: As the name implies, these refer to functions that the system provides for the user. Therefore these requirements are statements that describe how the user and the system are expected to react to particular inputs. In other words functional requirements specify particular behaviour of a user and or a system, or the interaction between these.

Non-functional requirements: In a general sense these relate to quality and attempt to quantify the value-added components of a system and a user. Generally these will be related to the functional requirements since they operate in the same environment. For, example, if the system is a manufacturing process, and the user is a process operator, then non-functional issues could be the timing constraints on the services or functions offered by the system. On the other hand, if a project were to design a new architecture for a game console, which is based on RISC technology, then the non-functional requirements would include constraints on the development process, standards, etc. Typical non-functional requirements include, reliability, scalability, cost etc. It is worth mentioning that because of their qualitative nature these are usually identified using metrics. [32]

The above describes a general template for producing a requirements document for typical projects in science and engineering that are carried out by students at university as part of their course requirements. Please note that this is only a template and the reader is encouraged to consider other sources for further directions. However, the above template is very simple to use and it should provide a solid starting point for specifying project requirements for simple projects.

It has to be said that in a very general sense, the requirements document is also important because it can be used as the basis of a contract between a client and the supplier of a service. In this respect the requirements document can help to identify difficulties in the early stages of the project. There is one small concern however when preparing a requirements document. Namely the question arises, how much details should be included in the requirements document? On the one hand, specifications that include a lot of details are safer from a legal standpoint since it is precisely stipulated what the system will do and how it will be implemented. But, with this level of detail, who is to say that the client may not engage a cheaper supplier to work to that specification. On the other hand, a loosely written specification will protect the designer, but it may introduce misunderstanding between the client and the supplier of the service. Clearly a compromise is needed between these two extremes and the project manager must decide where to draw the line between disclosure of sensitive design details and legal protection on system specifications. It is generally recommended that the requirements document should go as far as it is legally safe towards specifying the system to include implementation details. In fact, it should go as far as the point where any more detail would compromise the securing of the contract for the supplier.

Figure 4.2 shows the documents that need to be included as part of the requirements engineering process. This is by no means exhaustive, and different projects may need a different set of documents. Nevertheless, the documentation indicated in Figure 4.2 is a useful template to start with, that can be refined as the need arises.

Requirements definition

Perhaps the best place to start with requirements definition is the title of the project. The title for the project can usually be derived from the initial requirements. This initial requirement can originate from a number of sources, such as for example a supervisor, a client, an invitation to tender, an offer of a research grant or from own initiative. In academic research, it is common to arrive at a title after discussions with a professor who will typically be in the position to define the project quite precisely. In the world of politics, you could be asked by your boss to organise and run a campaign for a candidate in a presidential election. On the other hand in the commercial sector, a manager or a director may ask you to re-organise the department to improve efficiency. In engineering, perhaps your company has just won a contract to build a nuclear power station, and you are going to be the project manager. If you are working as a design engineer for Formula 1, then perhaps your boss has asked you to improve the design of the car so that it performs better in the next season

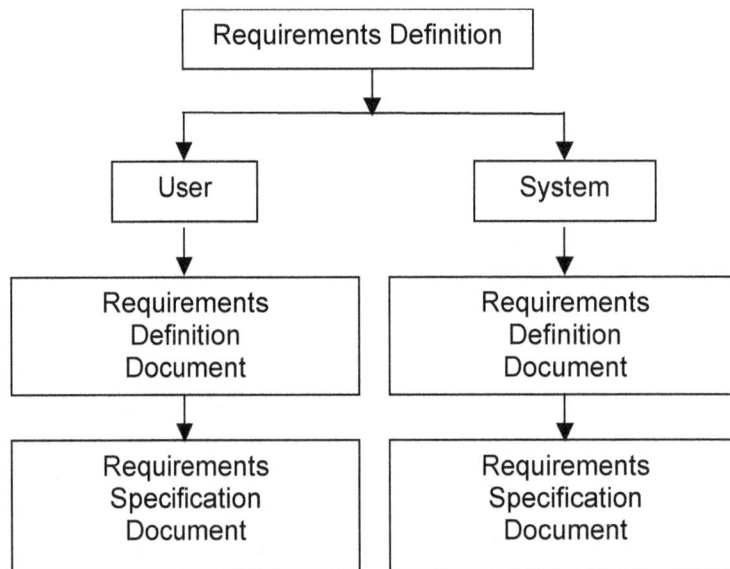

Figure 4.2. Requirements documentation

It should be clear therefore that there are innumerable ways that we can arrive at the title for a project. As mentioned earlier, research is needed to establish the project aims. Therefore, having arrived at the title how do we begin researching?

The place to begin with research is at the point of ignorance. This is to say that I shall begin at that point where my knowledge about the subject stops. In most cases we will be required to undertake research in the area of our expertise. This saves time and resources, because the person that has been asked to do the research already knows a lot about the subject. But, having said that, recent graduates do not generally have the experience of senior engineers and managers, and when they are asked to do any research, they have to begin at a lower level. There are also implications regarding resources, which are to say, do we have access to the required literature and other resources, such as perhaps literature about a similar project?

Whilst it may be possible in some cases to define project aims without doing any research, it is suggested that the first deliverable in a project is the requirements definition. Research activity that is involved in obtaining a requirement definition typically involves three stages, requirement elicitation, analysis, and documentation. From a pragmatic perspective, requirements definition strives for requirements that are good enough to allow the team to proceed with design, construction and testing at an acceptable level of risk.

Requirement specification

Having obtained the requirements definition the next stage is to produce a requirement specification. This entails going into more details in explaining how the requirements definition will be interpreted and implemented. For this reason the requirements specifications documents must be free of any ambiguities, omissions and conflicts in the requirements definitions. Within the context of this text, the requirement specification document is a refinement of requirements definition to identify the objectives and the steps towards achieving these.

As a guideline, in projects in science and engineering, where often there are elements of hardware as well as software, the following should be addressed in a requirements specification,
- Define the functions of the system.
- Define the Hardware / Software functional partitioning.
- Define the performance specification.
- Define the hardware / software performance partitioning.
- Define safety requirements.
- Provide installation drawings/instructions.
- Provide Interface Control Drawings (ICD's, External I/O).

Thus it is seen that a requirements specification should define the full functionality of the system, which includes both the functional and non-functional components. After the requirements have been established the next phase of the project is to establish a plan of activity.

4.5. Writing a requirements specification

In a typical software engineering projects the requirements definition includes statements in natural language describing the requirements of the system. This would usually be the starting point and would normally change as discussion between client and software engineers progress.

The stage after this would be to produce a requirement specification, which describes the services of a system (as detailed as possible). If appropriate formal methods may be used at this stage as discussed in Chapter 1. In the requirements specification stage the design, features of the software should be covered in sufficient detail in order to provide legal protection and at the same time not to give too much information away so that the client can engage someone else on the project. Therefore this section describes the software design in detail using models and any other tools such as for example the use of prototypes to determine the correct specification.

One of the first stumbling blocks of producing a specification is the natural language description of the system. Typically this is the first description of a system. However natural language may be too abstract for describing the specification and therefore it is likely to lead to incorrect interpretation of the initial requirements. We will consider some issues relating to natural language specification next.

Natural language specifications

The starting point in requirements definition is the natural language description of what is required. This will normally take the form of a written document that acts a starting point for establishing an agreed requirements definition. Natural language is universal, flexible, and widespread, but unfortunately also inherently ambiguous.

Ambiguity is a major problem in requirements specification because the different readers of the requirements specification may understand what is written differently. If the engineer's understanding of the document differs from that of the customer then the customer is likely to be dissatisfied with the resulting product. This is because the software developers design and implement a system that does not behave as intended by the customers.

Nevertheless natural language is very common in all human activity and therefore it cannot be eliminated from the requirements process. To help with project specifications it is therefore necessary to identify any ambiguities, omissions and conflicts from a natural language specification.

- **Ambiguities**: To find any ambiguities in a specification it is necessary to identify the adjectives and verbs. Most common ambiguities occur when an adjective or verb is not described fully, or when it is introduced without any further information on the exact definition of the feature, for example: The system will process the credit card. Here the ambiguity is seen in the verb 'process' in other words, what will the system do has been left ambiguous?

- **Conflicts**: In a natural language specification, conflicts refer to inconsistencies between two or more actions within the requirement document. For example: The credit card will be returned after three unsuccessful attempts. The conflict is in that elsewhere there is a statement that a credit card will be retained after three unsuccessful attempts. Here the conflict is in the action performed after three unsuccessful attempts. (There is also an omission here because I don't specify attempts at what?)

- **Omissions**: These relate to the omission of a feature or functionality that was included but which is not described further. In other words, the feature is described, but not in a great enough detail. Developing the requested feature without additional information is not possible without the risk of misunderstandings between the different parties (e.g. customer and developer). In the above example of conflict I omitted to say what the attempts were, ie. Attempts at logging into the system by providing the correct PIN number etc.

During the requirements engineering phase it is therefore important to carefully analyse any specification that is written in natural language and to consider in detail any ambiguities, omissions and conflicts. It is also important to resolve these before proceeding to subsequent stages of software development. In order to explain the implications of these let us consider an example.

Example:

Discover ambiguities or omissions in the following statement of requirements which form part of a ticket issuing system.

> *An automated ticket issuing system sells rail tickets. Users select their destination, and input a credit card and personal identification number. The rail ticket is issued and their credit card account charged with its cost. When the user presses the start button, a menu display of potential destination is activated along with a message to the user to select destination. Once a destination has been selected, users are requested to input their credit card. Its validity is checked and the user is then requested to input a personal identifier. When the credit transaction has been validated, the ticket is issued.*

Solution:

Software system requirements are classified according to, functional, non-functional and domain requirements. In order for the requirements to be as complete as possible these three areas should be covered in sufficient detail to prevent any ambiguities from arising or important details being left out. Note that the presented solution is also provided in natural language. This is to say that we are presenting arguments as to why something is not clear and how we can rectify this.

Ambiguities:

The first area where there could be an ambiguous interpretation of the requirements is that the domain in which this automated ticketing system will operate has not been defined. What is the intended location for this system and as such the range of possible destinations that can be selected from? For example, is it realistic that somebody could buy a ticket from a machine located in London for a destination in Bermuda for example? This could be interpreted as a valid action according to the requirements given above.

In the above requirements what type of credit card can be used? Under this statement we could specify that only one type of credit card may be used, i.e. Visa and the ambiguity would be removed. However, this is not a realistic solution to the problem, because it would exclude a large portion of the customer base, as everybody does not have the same type of credit card. On this point we may also suggest that there is an omission in the specification. Namely, perhaps the system should support the use of debit cards such as Switch and Maestro, which are widely used by the customer base.

When the validation of a card is carried out what type of checks are done? Does the machine check that the number string matches the number string stored as PIN for that credit card and whether it has a valid expiry date? Clearly the banking system would not accept this as a valid security check and would probably require the machine to check with their computer system to make sure that the card does exist, has not been reported stolen etc. which would imply that the system has access to a database of all valid credit cards. In this example we have identified an ambiguity that has led to further possible omissions in the specification

These points briefly show how ambiguities in a statement of requirements can cause problems. At the same time we have to be realistic about what the system needs to do and therefore the natural language should describe this as precisely as possible, For example, I could design a system that would be placed in a London train station selling rail tickets to New York. The system only allows users who have a gold Amex card to use the machine. The card only has to have a credit card number that matches the layout for the gold Amex and the correct validity date in order to be accepted by the machine. The machine would then prompt the user to enter any sixty digits number as their personal identifier. The ticket that would be printed out would be on a plain piece of paper and have the destination and price paid displayed on it.

The system outlined above could be free from ambiguities, omissions and conflicts, but the resulting system would not be useful to anybody. This highlights the need for clarity in the statement of requirements and also the logical approach to providing a solution to the original problem.

Omissions:

There are many possible omissions in the statement of the requirements given above. This is because the statement itself serves only as an example and as such it is not detailed enough. You should be able to learn from this example how to identify omissions even in cases where the statement of requirements is more refined. As stated earlier one obvious omission that the statement of requirements does not include the domain of the system or the possible scope of the system. For example is the system location and also the scope of the service that it should provide. Also the statement of requirements does not include any timescale for the delivery of the system. Do they want the system to be ready in a weeks time or three years time? There is also no mention of the response time for the machine. Clearly a system that takes about ten minutes to process the purchase of a ticket would lead to massive queues building up and make the machine unworkable in a real life situation.

There is no indication of the lifespan of the system i.e. how long will the system be in operation? This plays a major factor in the complexity of the system in terms of the need to upgrade the system to include new stations, types of credit card systems etc that would incur extra development costs. Who is the target user? Does the system have to account for users who have little experience of using new technology? Is the system designed for people with little experience of technology? Then it would have to include the ability to assist the user with how to operate the machine. Will the machine have to provide additional information to other users such as engineers, sales departments etc. In which case the machine would have to incorporate the ability to store information about transactions carried out, service logs etc. Does the system have to be expandable so that at latter dates additional functionality can be added such as the ability to use notes and coins?

The requirements makes no mention of displaying the cost of tickets to the user and no provision for different types of tickets such as singles, returns etc. Is it realistic to expect the user to purchase a ticket without knowing how much they are paying for it? Does the machine reset to a pre-configured condition once a ticket has been purchased? There is no mention of the credit card being returned to the user after a transaction and no receipt for transactions carried out has to be printed. What type of ticket is to be issued? Does it have to incorporate information on a magnetic strip on the back of the card so that it can work with other systems? Are there any legacy systems in operation that the new system must work in conjunction with or will this be a system constructed from scratch?

The omissions considered above show that natural language statement specification need to be very long and precise if they are to cover the full system specification. They are given here purely as an example, but they do serve to show how much detail the specifications need to go into.

Conflicts

The requirements do not clarify as to where the personal pin number used by each person comes from. Is it unique to each transaction? Or is it the same one used when they use an ATM? Does the machine give the number to the user or do they have to go somewhere else to obtain a pin?

Information about the level of security to be incorporated into the system is not consistent. There is mention of a personal identification number, which appears to be in conflict with the personal identifier.

From this example it should be fairly clear that natural language specifications must be carefully scrutinised so that all parties concerned have the same interpretation of the requirements. Before a requirement specification is complete there are important questions that need to be asked by the developer otherwise they run the risk of producing a system that does not meet requirements and consequently leading to a great deal of wasted time and money for all parties. This situation can cause much difficulty in software engineering project. For example, the company that commissions a project modifies the requirements because they have realised at later stages that the system being designed does not fully meet their criteria due to misinterpretation of the requirements by the designer. Such amendments at later dates of the project lifecycle can lead to work that took months to carry out being scrapped because it is not possible to carry out the modifications due to technical difficulties. This in turn leads to project costs spiralling out of control and deadlines being overshot.

Research in natural language methodology

It is worth mentioning that natural language processing is receiving attention in research such that dedicated methodologies of translating natural languages into formal specification are being developed. For example B. R. Bryant [33] proposes a methodology for the formal development of software systems from a user's requirements specification in natural language into a complete implementation, proceeding through the steps of formal specification, and detailed design and implementation in an automated manner. The proposed methodology is based upon the theories of two-level grammar (TLG) and object-oriented design and takes advantage of the existence of several software design tools. The authors claim to have developed an iterative transformation process from the natural language specification into the final implementation. This process also includes a specification development environment to assist the user in formulating the specification, as well as the designer component to help in accomplishing this transformation. It is suggested by the authors that the underlying formal specification methodology may also be used in the final development of the implementation.

This is just an example of research in the area of natural language specification and the reader is encouraged to seek further clarification by researching into references provided in literature. The IEEE publication by Bryant mentioned here is a good start as it provides a list of useful references to follow.

4.6. Program Design Language (PDL)

It is possible to reduce the problems in natural language specification, mentioned earlier by describing the system in a language that is similar to natural language but has the flavour of a programming language. PDL is a common coding technique where you write out the code in a language as close to plain English as possible. It is quite common for programmers to use the term pseudocode to represent a format similar to the PDL. The structure of the PDL is less descriptive than natural language so that it can be very precise. The format is therefore sufficiently simple to be understood by everyone and complex enough to describe the functionality of the system.

In software programming there is often reference to the level as being low-level (i.e. Assembly, Byte Code) or high-level (C++, Java etc.). Simply stated, reference in this case to low or high-level languages, is made with respect to how close the programming language is to plain spoken English. In general, the closer it is to spoken English, the higher the level of the language. For example an assembly listing of a simple programme adding two numbers together could look like this:

```
MOV BL,01H; Load register BL with value 01 hexadecimal
MOV AL,0FH; Load register AL with value 0F hexadecimal
ADD AL,BL; Add the contents of registers AL and BL, store result in AL
MOV [300],AL; Write the result in AL to memory location 300H
INT 20; Return to DOS
```

An example in C doing more or less the same thing would look like this:

SUM=1+15;

C is a higher level language than assembly and the statements in C that add two numbers are a lot easier to write than in assembly. However, it is worth noting that the computer hardware executes all code as binary values, and the code written in a low level language is often much more efficient than the binary code that is produced from a high-level language after the program has been compiled.

When we talk about programming languages in terms of levels, the point of reference is the spoken English language. The above shows that C coding is closer than assembly to the way we would describe the addition of two numbers in plain English. Thus, the closer the code comes to looking like English, the "higher" its language level becomes. If we were to compare ways to print a word on the screen in C++ and QBasic, it should be relatively obvious that QBasic is a higher level language than C++:

Code in C++ - *cout << "hello world" << endl;*

Code in QBasic - *PRINT "hello world"*

From this it can be seen that PRINT is much closer to the English word than `cout` is. Thus it can be said that PDL is the highest-level language description of code. When you code in PDL, you are coding in plain English and not in computer code. In fact, you can write code in PDL and then use it to construct a routine in any computer language since you never used a piece of language specific code. This is most useful in software engineering because it allows the designer to describe the way that code will perform without using any specific programming language.

Consider the following example specification presented in two distinctly different levels of PDL. Both descriptions refer to the same functionality of code and apply to programming with graphics objects as used in the games industry. The basic functionality that must be provided is to prevent access to the graphics object while we are drawing it. [34]

PDL specification Example A

```
Lock the drawing surface to prevent access by other programs and check for errors.
Get mem_pitch of the surface using (int)ddsd.lPitch.
Get *video_buffer to draw to using ddsd.lpSurface.
if pixel_mode == random then
        Create three random values for x, y and color.
else if pixel_mode == linear then
        Increment x value by 1.
        Create a random value for color.
end if
video_buffer[x+y*mempitch] = color
Unlock the surface and check for errors.
        return 1
```

PDL specification Example B

```
Prevent the drawing surface from being accessed by other programs while we draw.
Retrieve the memory pitch of the surface memory so we do not draw out of bounds.
Retrieve the location of the surface so that we can draw to it successfully.
If the pixel mode is set to random
        Create three random values that we can assign to the x, y and colour attributes of the pixel.
Else if the pixel mode is set to linear
        Update the horizontal position of the pixel.
        Create a random value for the colour of the pixel.
End If
Plot the pixel on the screen.
        Release the surface for general use once again.
        Return TRUE that the pixel was plotted.
```

At first glance example B appears to be closer to plain English than example A. Furthermore looking at example A the first sentence uses the term "Lock a surface". This can cause some confusion because such a phrase can easily be attributed to DirectX and its Lock() function, which can be misleading. The same applies to the term Unlock. Example B is much clearer on this by using the terms "prevent" and "release". Additionally example A uses direct reference to variable names, which is generally not advisable in PDL. Finally in example A we have the ending "return 0". This is a language-limiting statement, which is specific to the C language. After going through above points, and comparing them to Example B, it should be possible for you to understand what PDL should look like. In general, the higher the level a PDL takes the easier it is to understand by everyone on the project. A word of caution may be appropriate at this juncture. Like any high level description PDL can become too complicated. Therefore writing PDL specifications is generally an iterative process. Write it once, and then start to break it down as far as you can without quite reaching code level while maintaining the basic rules of PDL.

Although there is no standard for the description of PDL, more often than not people tend to adopt a convention based on programming languages. In terms of functionality it is possible to use constructs in procedural programming to describe PDL. Note from chapter 1 that almost any algorithm can be described in terms of sequences, decisions and iterations. Therefore all PDLs use these components. For OOP the PDL tends to take on the style of a programming language such as Java or C++. Rather than going into detail here I have included in Appendix II a short description of some basic PDL features. At this stage I shall provide a few examples of PDL and if you need more details please refer to Appendix II.

Example PDL

Example for a game-board function. [35]

```
FOR X = 1 to 10
  FOR Y = 1 to 10
    IF gameBoard[X][Y] = 0
      Do nothing
    ELSE
      CALL theCall(X, Y) (recursive method)
      increment counter
    END IF
  END FOR
END FOR
```

The above is adequate in that the PDL describes the structure of the code. A slightly better choice of PDL would be to omit unnecessary steps such as the do nothing clause in the above PDL. The resulting PDL code is shown below.

```
Set moveCount to 1
FOR each row on the board
  FOR each column on the board
    IF gameBoard position (row, column) is occupied THEN
      CALL findAdjacentTiles with row, column
      INCREMENT moveCount
    END IF
  END FOR
END FOR
```

The next example shows how PDL is used to write comments in the source file. Note that the double slashes are indented.

```
public boolean moveRobot (Robot aRobot)
{
    //IF robot has no obstacle in front THEN
        // Call Move robot
        // Add the move command to the command history
        // RETURN true
    //ELSE
        // RETURN false without moving the robot
    //END IF
}
```

Example Java implementation

In the following example note that source code statements are interleaved with PDL. Comments that correspond exactly to source code are removed during coding.

```
public boolean moveRobot (Robot aRobot)
{
    //IF robot has no obstacle in front THEN
    if (aRobot.isFrontClear())
    {
        // Call Move robot
        aRobot.move();
        // Add the move command to the command
history
        cmdHistory.add(RobotAction.MOVE);
        return true;
    }
    else // don't move the robot
    {
        return false;
    }//END IF
}
```

Note also that PDL when used in OO paradigms tends to adopt Java type declarations for functions and methods. Therefore it is assumed that anyone reading the PDL is familiar with basic Java syntax. Thus an example PDL for OOP could be as follows. In this example the PDL is written in a syntax that is similar to C++ or Java. This means that functions and variables are defined before they are used. Thus all the functions are declared before the main {} statement. We all know that the main{} function is the first executing function in C, C++ and Java. Following these declarations the programme uses loops and If-Then structures to describe behaviour. Here the specification is for a simple theatre booking system. Clients use a credit card to pay for a theatre performance and during the selection process they can choose from available seats. The last part of the code also includes telephone reservations. The code is not a complete specification but it serves to show how a Java-looking PDL can be used to specify a system. Have a look through this code and make sure that you can follow what is going on.

```
number GetCard();
bool ValidateCard(cardnumber);
Message(message_text);
ShowSeats(List Seatdata);
List GetSeat();
ReturnCard();
PrintTicket(List Seats);
UpdateSeatData(List BookedSeats);
DebitCard(Cardnumber, value);
Bool GetConfirm();
main()
{        if (card detected)
            {  CardNo = GetCard();
                if (ValidateCard(CardNo) == False)
                  { Message(CardInvalidMsg); ReturnCard(); Exit; }
                else
                  { ShowSeats(List Seatdata);
                    do {  SeatChoice = List GetSeat();
                         if (!validseat) Message(ChoiceInvalidMsg);
                         Message(EndList);
                         }while(!endlist);
                    if (Getconfirm() == True)
                      { PrintTicket(SeatChoice, cost);
                    UpdateSeatData(SeatChoice);
                        DebitCard(Cardnumber, cost); }
            }
        if (telephone) { GetBookingData(SeatChoice, cost);
                UpdateSeatData(SeatChoice);
            DebitCard(Cardnumber, cost); }
}
```

PDL Uses

Part 1: Functions Review

In all software engineering projects it is necessary to ensure that functions and subroutines do exactly what they are intended to do. Software engineers and project managers do not want to waste time going over endless lines of code to learn whether or not the routine does what they want it to. PDL provides them with a concise description of what the code will do without being programme specific. This also means that clients that are not familiar with programming can also change the wording of a routine to better match specification. This is a cost-effective way of modifying the program architecture. In other words, rather than taking out lines of code and figuring out the impact of this on the rest of the programme, a modification could easily be described by a change in a single line of PDL.

Part 2: Code Documentation

It has been suggested that PDL is a useful tool in documenting software. [35] The high level nature of PDL allows it naturally to be used for commenting programme code. Therefore you could use the PDL as a comment before the coding. Example B introduced earlier can be used as an example of this. As an example, consider Example B again but with PDL used as comments before the C++ coding.

```
// Prevent the drawing surface from being accessed by other programs while we draw.
lpdds7->Lock(NULL, &ddsd, DDLFLAGS, NULL);

// Retrieve the memory pitch of the surface memory so we do not draw out of bounds.
int mempitch = (int)ddsd.lPitch;

// Retrieve the location of the surface so that we can draw to it successfully.
UCHAR *video_buffer   = (UCHAR *)ddsd.lpSurface;

// If the pixel mode is set to random
if (pixel_mode == RANDOM) {
        // Create three random values that we can assign to the x, y and color attributes
of the pixel.
        UCHAR color   = rand()%256;
        int x         = rand()%800;
        int y         = rand()%600;
}
//Else if the pixel mode is set to linear
else if (pixel_mode == LINEAR) {
        // Update the horizontal position of the pixel.
        pixel_x++;

        // Create a random value for the colour of the pixel.
        UCHAR color   = rand()%256;
} // End If

// Plot the pixel on the screen.
video_buffer[x+y*mempitch] = color;

// Release the surface for general use once again.
lpdds7->Unlock(NULL);

// Return TRUE that the pixel was plotted.
return 1;
```

It is very common for programmers to code first and later to add comments. Or at least do this at the same time. Here we are considering that documenting the code is done first with PDL, which is the reversal of the conventional process of documenting. Not only is this a convenient way of documenting the code, but it also serves to double check that the code does what the PDL describes.

4.7.   Software requirements specification template

Documenting requirements is a complex task and most software houses will adopt their own style. When you consider all the aspects that contribute to requirements engineering it should be quite obvious that documenting all these requires a significant amount of effort. As a guide, Appendix I offers an example template for your consideration. It is likely that when you engaged on a specific software engineering project, that you will be asked to produce documentation according to the in-house template, but until such time it is useful to consider an example templates shown in the appendix.

4.8. Chapter summary

This chapter considers the requirement-engineering phase of software development. A brief mention of project management is also introduced because requirements are a significant part of project management. It goes without saying that without a solid description of the requirements any project will be doomed to failure. There are a large number of sources indicating the components in requirements specification and although most of these are valid, there are many variations and inconsistencies in terms of what terminology is used etc. For this reason I have simplified my text to group the requirements into user and system requirements and to consider these from the point of requirements definition and requirements specification. I consider this to be a straightforward approach that will satisfy most software engineering projects. However, I do emphasise that other variants could be a better option in some projects. I also consider in this chapter natural language specifications and the inherent possibility of ambiguities, omissions and conflicts. Program design language (PDL) is seen as a possible means of translating natural language into a more precise specification. PDL is also seen as a useful tool for documenting projects in software engineering.

Exercises

4.1. Discuss why planning is important in software engineering projects.
4.2. What do you see as the main purpose of a feasibility study?
4.3. What is the purpose of a Gantt chart?
4.4. Describe using examples as appropriate the main stages of project lifecycle in software engineering.
4.5. What are the benefits of requirements engineering?
4.6. Distinguish between requirements definition and requirement specification in the context of requirements engineering.
4.7. Giving examples explain the difference between functional and non-functional requirements in software engineering projects.
4.8. What are the main problems of natural language specifications?
4.9. The requirement phase of software development is a major part of the software engineering process. Discuss the general approach to defining user requirements, and the documentation that is needed to support it. In your answer include a description of the characteristics of a good requirements specification and the type of information that this would include.

4.10. For the outline specification of a theatre ticket issuing and booking system given below, identify the ambiguities, conflicts and omissions in the statement of the requirements.

> St*atement of the requirements:*
>
> The system will provide tickets for a performance and debit the accepted credit card that is inserted into the machine. If this is unsatisfactory a ticket will not be issued and a suitable message displayed. The customer must select a seat. Telephone bookings can be made in advance, the tickets being issued against the appropriate card. Cancellation is the reverse process.

4.11. For the ambiguities, conflicts and omissions that you have identified in Q 4.10 above explicitly state how they can be resolved.

4.12. You are a consultant on a project for a small software company producing computer games and teaching material. The client is asking you to design a computer application to run on a personal computer that will help to teach children aged 9-11 basic mathematics. You have arranged the first meeting with the client where you are determined to obtain all the information that is necessary for you to prepare a formal specification for the software development.

> In your answer to this question prepare the information that you will take to this meeting. You may choose to include the following components:
> i. List of questions to establish functional and non-functional requirements.
> ii. A suggested initial model of the system architecture to help you discuss requirements with the client.
> iii. A suggested work plan to include prototyping techniques that you wish to propose.
> iv. A preliminary budget to provide the client with an idea of the cost of your consulting services.
>
> For all of the above state any assumptions made, and explain the reasoning behind your choice

4.13. Describe what PDL is and what are the possible uses for PDL in the requirements stage of software engineering.

4.14. Write example PDL specifications for the following systems, i) ATM ii) enrolling students onto a course.

CHAPTER 5 SYSTEMS DESIGN

5.1. Systems engineering

In engineering terminology a system is generally used to describe a collection of components that interact and work together to accomplish a certain task or function. In many engineering systems these components include software as well as hardware and consequently system design will also include information about the processes, which constitute the system.

In many modern engineering systems, software is the overriding component in terms of cost and complexity. Good software engineering practices and tools can therefore make a substantial difference, even to the extent that they may be the main factor behind the success of the project. The distinction between software and systems engineering is consequently somewhat vague. For comparison Table 5.1 provides a brief distinction between these categories. [36]

Software Engineering	Computer Science	System Engineering
It is concerned with the practicalities of development and delivering useful software. It is part of system engineering.	The systematic study of algorithmic processes that describe and transform information: their theory, analysis, design, efficiency, implementation, fundamentals and application.	System Engineering is concerned with all aspects of computer-based systems development, including hardware, software and process engineering.

5.2. Software design

In some ways it can be said that requirements specify what a program should do while design specifies how the program should do it. Design is also seen as a means of ensuring reliability. Software design usually involves breaking a large program down into many smaller programs, such that those smaller pieces together do the work of the whole program. In this way it is possible to separate the issues of architecture, or overall program concept and structure, from the problems of actual coding, which can also solve problems of actual data processing.

Design stage also defines a programming template, including the specification of interfaces, which can be shared by different teams of developers working on various parts. Finally, design specifies the program independently of the implementation language platform, thereby removing language-specific limitations, which could inadvertently creep into the design. [37]

We have mentioned in earlier chapters the fact that projects are made up of a sequence of stages beginning with requirements stage and ending with a commissioning stage. Design, development and testing happen between these two stages of development. The modelling tools that were mentioned in chapters 2 and 3 are used throughout the design and development stages in order to ensure that development agrees with the specifications. Validation and verification stages take a formal approach to assessing whether the system that was designed meets all the requirements and also whether we have built the system in the correct way. More on these in later chapters, but for now we will concentrate on design.

Software design is the process of implementing the specifications that are contained in the requirement documentation. By definition design implies creativity, and for this reason design engineers must understand the system that they are designing. They must also know the limitation of the technology that is being used, as well as appreciate the constraints that are imposed by the available time and financial resources. It is not always expected of the design engineer to build the best possible system. This is because the best possible is also likely to be most expensive, and the design has to take into account whether in fact the system needs to be the best possible in order to satisfy its specifications. Thus the design engineers have to consider quality and cost aspects as well as functional requirements. All of these will be part of the requirements engineering process and so design begins with a formal consideration of the systems specifications. It is the design stage that is used to convert these specifications into a format ready for implementation of the system. Typically design can be considered as being made up of three stages,

- **Process**: what are the stages of design?
- **Strategies**: how to go about it?
- **Quality**: how to measure it?

All of these stages merit considerable effort and all of them will have a direct relationship with the specifications. In all cases modelling is required to ensure that design is proceeding correctly. Therefore it is clear from the start that design follows the software-programming paradigm.

Process considerations

At the start of our design effort we need to decide which paradigm we are working with. In chapter 1 I focused on two of the most common paradigms, namely procedural and object-oriented. Thus we need to decide if our system is better suited to procedural or object-oriented representation. Although we did not discuss other paradigm flavours there are distinct features of embedded and real-time systems as well as safety-critical systems that are essentially different paradigms. Whatever the case, we need to establish at the outset the paradigm that the design will follow. (Refer to chapters 1 for a short list of programming paradigms that are currently in use). Choice of paradigm will have a bearing on the stages identified above, with perhaps more emphasis on the process and the strategies stages.

The requirements engineering stage will not always decide for us which paradigm to adopt. Quite often we need to make this decision at the design stage. For example consider a relatively simple software system to control the working of a microwave oven. If you look back to chapter 2 you will find a model of a microwave system. The model is shown as a state diagram in figure 2.8.

Given this task how do we go about producing a design?

First of all which paradigm is we going to use? Well in my view this is a real-time systems. It is not necessarily safety-critical and I would favour the OO paradigm. This is because I can easily identify the objects; their states and how they react to events form the state diagram. Would I have been wrong to adopt a procedural paradigm? Well the answer is not necessarily so. It is quite possible for me to use data flow diagrams to represent events and their impact on processes that are taking place in a microwave oven system. The state diagram indicates the sequence of transitions between states and this fits in well with the procedural components of sequence, decision and iteration. Therefore it can be said that either choice of paradigms is suitable. In contrast consider the requirement to design an on-line computer game to be played by users accessing the application on the Internet and using their browser to run the game. Which paradigm are we going to recommend? Perhaps you would need to do some research before making a decision but this requires an OO paradigm. The environment that games run on are designed for OO operation and any new application will rely on the application programming interface (API) which itself is designed around the OO paradigm.

These two brief examples serve to show that the decision is usually relatively easy to make for experienced software engineers. In general it can be said that standalone systems which do not require many interfaces can be designed using the procedural paradigm. By contrast systems that require complex interfaces are better suited to OO paradigms.

Having decided on how to select the paradigm the next stage is to develop the architecture of the system. The 4+1 model describe in chapter 2 is a good approach that is suitable for both of the paradigms considered earlier. This should help to produce a clear design in the four views, namely Logical view, Process view, Physical view, Development view. It will also provide a selection of scenarios to observe the integrated architecture across the four views. The way to apply the 4+1 approach is to break down the system into subsystems and to apply this approach at subsystems level. When all the subsystems have been completed these should be integrated in order to describe the overall system architecture.

During the process stage it is very important to give due attention to interface design. In particular, systems that require complex user interaction must adopt appropriate level of design of the user interface. Thus when a system is broken up into subsystems, particular attention should be paid to the user interface subsystem, for which special considerations should be made. Some essential aspects of user-interface design will be covered later in this chapter. Please refer to appendix III for more detailed example considerations in user interface design.

Strategies

Having established the overall system architecture we need to decide on the mechanism to implement our design. To a large extent this stage depends on the size of the task. Very large software systems will require different strategies from stand-alone developments of bespoke software. For example, consider a project to develop software that enables individuals in the UK to complete and submit their self-assessment tax returns on-line. Typically the deadline for on-line submissions is the 31st of January in the tax year to April. For one reason or another most submissions are filed on the deadline date. So, assuming that we have the process stage sorted out and we have all the subsystems represented in the 4 architectural views, how do we go about implementing this? The answer lies in management of software engineering projects. One of the first things to consider in software project management are the human factors. These are briefly covered next.

Human Factors

Typically, teams of software programmers using engineering principles that include both the technical and non-technical aspects undertake software engineering projects. To be effective, software managers must understand their staff as individuals and understand how these individuals interact. An understanding of human factors can help identify possible ways of increasing productivity. Some issues relating to human factors are introduced next, but I have to say that this is a much broader field of enquire than I am proposing to cover in this text.

Group Working

In the vast majority of cases software engineering is part of a group activity. In typical software engineering projects approximately half of the programmer's time is spent interacting with other team members, 30% working alone and 20% in activities such as travel and training. This must be taken into consideration when organising a software engineering project because it will be necessary to consider personalities within groups as well as the means of communications and lines of responsibility.

Personalities in Groups

Perhaps more than in other engineering disciplines, within software engineering there is much diversity in the abilities of individuals. Programming can be very abstract and those that are good at abstraction may not always be able to appreciate the more concrete aspects of project management. The ability to correctly identify the human resources that are needed is key to the success in a software engineering project. Some salient features of personalities within a group are given next.

Task-oriented: This type is motivated by the work itself. In software engineering, they are technicians who are motivated by the intellectual challenge of software development.

Self-oriented: This type is principally motivated by personal success. They are interested in software development as a means of achieving their own goals.

Interaction-oriented: This type of individual is motivated by the presence and actions of co-workers.

The most successful groups are made up of people from each Class with the group leader being mostly task-oriented. Group loyalties, leadership, ego-less programming and interaction are also very important factors. Some other factors that influence productivity in teamwork are given next.

Privacy: Programmers require an area where they can concentrate and work without interruption.

Outside awareness: People prefer to work in natural light and with a view of the outside environment.

Environment: different people have different opinions on decor. The ability to rearrange the workplace to suit working practices and to personalise that environment is important.

Information storage: Much of software development requires the coding of knowledge-based information. Therefore memory organisation within the system is key to the way that information is organised and consequently to the way that the system is programmed.

Communication within groups

It is well known that effective communication between members of a development group is essential if the group is to work efficiently. Factors which impact on the effectiveness of communications includes: The group size, structure, physical work environment and status and personalities within the group.

More formal group communications can be structured as either centralised or decentralised networks. As the name implies a centralised network has a pivotal person through whom all communication takes place. On the other hand in a decentralised network communication takes place between individual members and not though one pivotal person.

Both types of communications are acceptable but it is generally considered that centralised networks are better suited to projects that involve relatively simple and routine tasks where the challenge is logistical rather than technically complex. Decentralised networks are better suited to complex tasks.

Project planning

Software project management encompasses the knowledge, techniques, and tools necessary to manage the development of software products. This means that managers need to create a plan for software development, using effective estimation of size and effort, and to execute that plan with attention to productivity and quality. Within this context it is also necessary to consider topics such as risk management, alternative lifecycle models, development team organisation, and effective management of technical personnel. Large software projects typically include a variety of specific plans to implement the strategy, these would normally include, [38]

- Program master plan
- Management plan
- Development plan
- Configuration management plan
- Quality assurance plan
- Maintenance plan
- Test plan
- Integration plan
- Documentation plan
- Transition plan
- Firmware development plan

A large number of software CASE tools exist to aid management of software engineering projects. Details of these tools and indeed the underlying management theory are beyond the scope of this text. I shall confine myself to listing some desirable features of CASE tools for software project management. These are as follows,

1. Project reporting and tracking

Managers are always under pressure to get the project delivered on time and there is a temptation to overlook the need to document and track changes in software projects.

2. Estimating and scheduling

To avoid history repeating itself it is good to use software to retrieve historical data about previous projects. This can serve to improve cost estimates and time schedules.

3. Automating workflows

Keeping track of workflows, who does what and by which deadline is a very important aspect of software project management? The issue here is not to monitor individual performance, but rather to identify and deal with potential bottlenecks.

4. Assignment of resources

This links with item 3 above. Improved assignment of tasks to individuals and groups can avoid redundancy in project resources.

5. Project communications

Effective communication between teams is invaluable in project management. Communications should also be transparent and secure. There should be contingency measures in case important team members are absent form the project.

6. Project team collaboration

Team collaboration is an issue that touches on individual personalities. In general it is good to schedule meetings between different teams in order to test consistency within the overall project.

Quality

Quality is best achieved by careful consideration of standards, effective development techniques, and periodic technical reviews. In software engineering quality is usually seen through metrics. Software metrics will be covered in more details in chapter 10 of this text, however a brief mention relating to quality issues during the design stage are covered next. A scheme that could be used for evaluating software quality factors is given below. [37]

Software quality factors

Understandability

Are variable names descriptive of the physical or functional property represented? Do uniquely recognisable functions contain adequate comments so that their purpose is clear? Are deviations from forward logical flow adequately commented? Are all elements of an array functionally related?

Completeness

Are all necessary components available? Does any process fail for lack of resources or programming? Are all potential pathways through the code accounted for, including proper error handling?

Conciseness

Is all code reachable? Is any code redundant? How many statements within loops could be placed outside the loop, thus reducing computation time? Are branch decisions too complex?

Portability

Does the program depend upon system or library routines unique to a particular installation? Have machine-dependent statements been flagged and commented? Has dependency on internal bit representation of alphanumeric or special characters been avoided? How much effort would be required to transfer the program from one hardware/software system or environment to another?

Consistency

Is one variable name used to represent different logical or physical entities in the program? Does the program contain only one representation for any given physical or mathematical constant? Are functionally similar arithmetic expressions similarly constructed? Is a consistent scheme used for indentation, nomenclature, the colour palette, fonts and other visual elements?

Maintainability

Has some memory capacity been reserved for future expansion? Is the design cohesive—i.e., does each module have distinct, recognisable functionality? Does the software allow for a change in data structures (object-oriented designs are more likely to allow for this)? If the code is procedure-based (rather than object-oriented), is a change likely to require restructuring the main program, or just a module?

Testability

Are complex structures employed in the code? Does the detailed design contain clear pseudo-code? Is the pseudo-code at a higher level of abstraction than the code? If tasking is used in concurrent designs, are schemes available for providing adequate test cases?

Usability

Is a GUI used? Is there adequate on-line help? Is a user manual provided? Are meaningful error messages provided?

Reliability

In a general sense this can be described as the probability that software performs its intended functions correctly in a specified period of time and under stated operating conditions. Some aspects of programming that impact on this are; Are loop indexes range-tested? Is input data checked for range errors? Is divide-by-zero avoided? Is exception handling provided? However reliability is also affected if there is a problem with the requirement document.

Efficiency

Have functions been optimised for speed? Have repeatedly used blocks of code been formed into subroutines? Has the program been checked for memory leaks or overflow errors?

Security

Does the software protect itself and its data against unauthorised access and use? Does it allow its operator to enforce security policies? Are security mechanisms appropriate, adequate and correctly implemented? Can the software withstand attacks that can be anticipated in its intended environment? Is the software free of errors that would make it possible to circumvent its security mechanisms? Does the architecture limit the potential impact of yet unknown errors?

User's perspective

In addition to the technical qualities of software, the end user's experience also determines the quality of software. This aspect of software quality is called usability. It is hard to quantify the usability of a given software product. Some important questions to be asked are:

- Is the user interface intuitive (self-explanatory/self-documenting)?
- Is it easy to perform simple operations?
- Is it feasible to perform complex operations?
- Does the software give sensible error messages?
- Do widgets (software components) behave as expected?
- Is the software well documented?
- Is the user interface responsive or too slow?

The above concerns relate to all paradigms in software engineering design. I have already discussed procedural and object-oriented paradigms. Next I shall briefly consider aspects of real-time systems.

5.3. Real Time Systems (RTS)

Real-time systems have timing constraints associated with their performance such that they are required to respond to their environment in a timely fashion. Consequently these systems monitor and interact with their environment. Interaction with the environment is usually through input and output devices. Inputs come from sensors. Outputs go to actuators. Examples of sensors and actuators are given below.

Input Sensors	Output/Actuators
Pressure	Servomotor
Temperature	Hydraulic devices
Light	Displays
Shaft encoders	Displacement devices

As mentioned earlier, time is critical in real time systems and all real time systems are required to respond within specified time limits, which are often called timing-constraints. This does not have to be in nanoseconds for all systems because the inertia of the system may not react to such fast responses. For example, the Anti-lock Braking System in a car is a real-time system. The principle aim of this system is to prevent the wheels from locking when the brakes are applied. A controlled actuator is used to apply and disengage the brakes at high frequency in order to prevent the wheels from locking. Typically, this on-off braking action is applied at approximately 1kHz. Thus the real-time constraint is determined here by taking into account the stopping action of the brakes, the inertia of the car and the dynamics of braking, rather than the capability of software and hardware to execute as fast as possible. Real time systems can be classified according to types of constraints. These are,

- **Soft real time systems**: Soft RTS is a system whose operation is degraded if the timing constraint is violated. This means that the system does not fail in its operation if the timing constraint is not satisfied but rather that the operation is degraded.
- **Hard real time systems** : Hard RTS is a system whose operation is incorrect if timing constraints are violated. This system will fail if the timing criteria are not satisfied.

Real time systems rely on stimulus (sensor information) to initiate action or response, using actuators as shown in Figure 5.1. Software is needed to process the input and determine the required outputs and this is done according to a prescribed control algorithm.

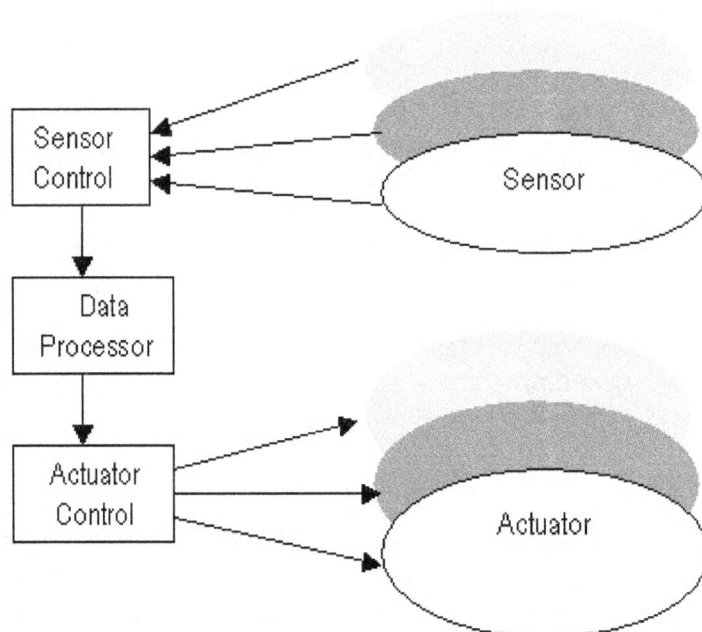

Figure 5.1 Sensors and Actuators in RTS

Stimuli can be periodic which means that they occur at regular intervals. Or Aperiodic which means that there is no interval associated with the stimulus i.e. over-speed alarm on a train. By design Aperiodic signals are often interrupt driven. This makes sense because we do not know when these will occur and so it makes sense to interrupt the system when these occur. On the other hand, periodic signals are often polled because we know the frequency with which these occur. In some cases periodic signals can be interrupt driven through a synchronisation with system clock.

Interrupt driven

Figure 5.2 shows a process that can be interrupted and these are also called pre-emptive processes. When an interrupt occurs the Interrupt Service Routine (ISR) takes over from the main process.

Event driven (pre-emptive)

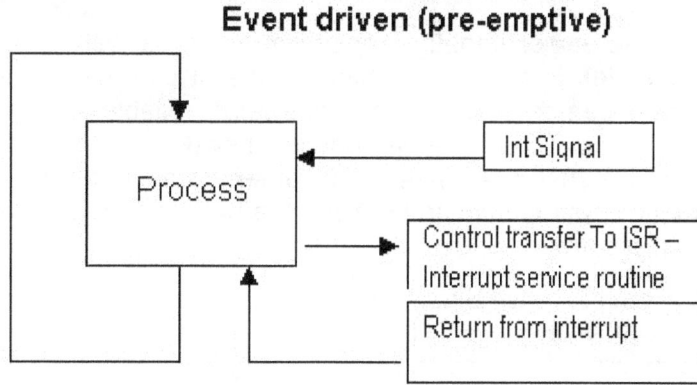

Figure 5.2 Interrupt driven control

In a multitasking environment where many interrupts occur at the same time the problem of deciding which interrupt to service is resolved by an interrupt priority mechanism. Figure 5.3 shows the alternative to interrupts, where the program uses polling in order to determine if an alternative process needs servicing. These occur periodically and are determined by the programmer.

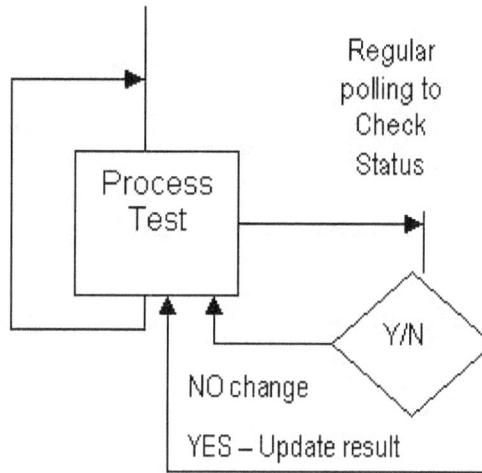

Figure 5.3. Polling based control

In simple real time systems with only a few tasks needing to run concurrently we use a foreground–background model where the interrupted task is in the background whilst the interrupting task is in the foreground. The status of tasks can interchange depending on the interrupt frequency.

In complex real time systems there are too many combinations of tasks that need to be executed and control of priority is much more difficult. In such systems we identify the so-called real time systems executives, which control the allocation of resources (CPU, memory, etc.) to tasks in accordance with a scheduling policy. When many processes are executing concurrently within a real-time system, there needs to be a mechanism for controlling execution and satisfying the real-time constraints. In this case it is necessary to use a dedicated real-time operating system. A real-time O/S (RTO/S) is similar to a general purpose O/S but the emphasis is that it has features which support concurrency of processes and threads. Some aspects of RTO/S are briefly considered next.

5.4. Real Time Operating Systems (RTOS)

As mentioned earlier, real-time does not mean as fast as possible, instead it means that it operates in a timely fashion so that it can interact with its operating environment which demands a known, consistent, reliable and repeatable, timing performance. A typical RTS arrangement is shown in figure 5.4. The distinctive feature of a RTOS is that it is typically implemented as a kernel. In this sense the kernel acts as a layer of abstraction between the hardware layer and the applications layer where the tasks are running.

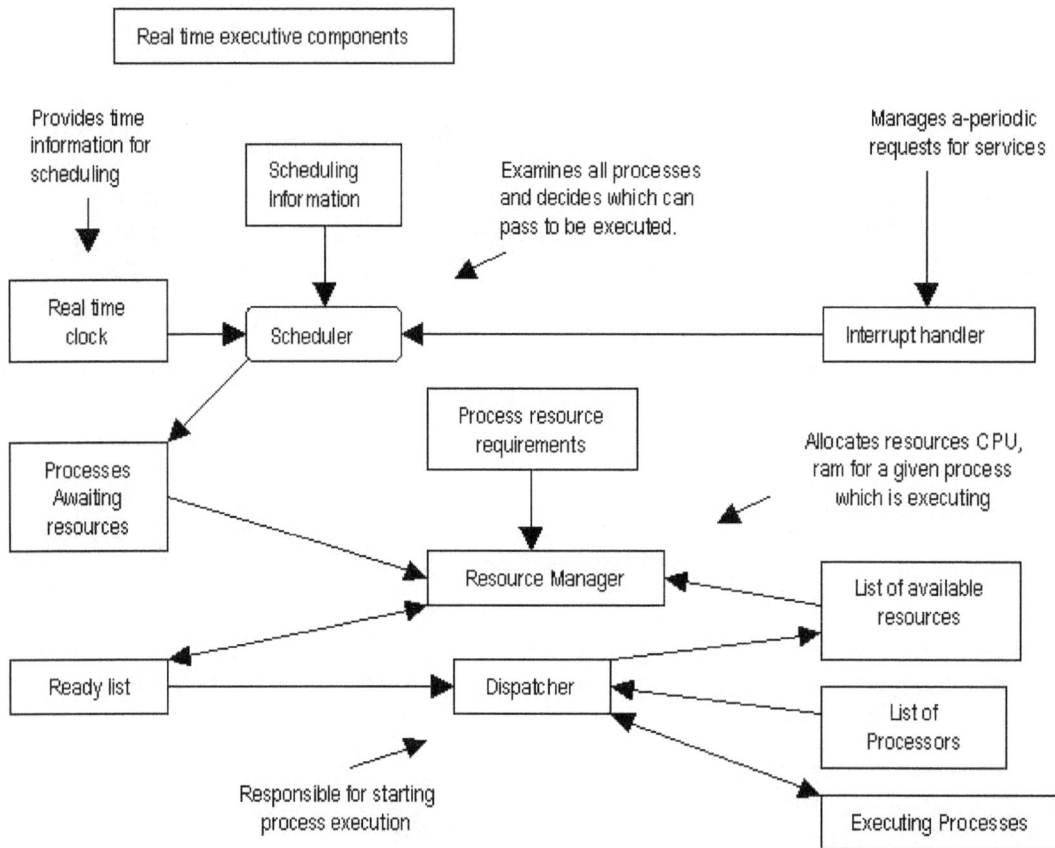

Figure 5.4 Typical RTS arrangement

The kernel in this context provides the services for the applications requiring access to hardware and also acts in such a way as to hide the activities between the two layers. While it is possible to implement an embedded program without using a real-time kernel, a well established, proven kernel can save on development time. There are a large number of RTOS kernels on the market, and in general they all act as an interface between the application software and the system hardware. At the same time a RTOS kernel provides several categories of services to application software. These include: task management, dynamic memory allocation, and basic timer services.

The main distinction between a real time O/S and a general purpose O/S is the approach to timing for internal operations. In RTOS, the kernel timing is rigidly controlled. In this way, the operating system services consume established amounts of time. For example, in RTOS the expression of a timing constraint is as simple as: T *(display _value) = constant.* Thus, whatever the effects of other functions within the multitasking RTOS, the time to display a value will be constant. For this to happen the kernel in a RTOS has to be designed to cope with these constraints. The basic functional components of a RTOS kernel are shown in Figure 5.5. Here the central function is task management. In simple terms a task is an instance of execution of a programme, and when many tasks are running at the same time, that is to say concurrently, they have to be managed in such a way that they do not adversely affect each other.

Figure 5.5 shows that the central job of the RTOS kernel is task management. In a multi-tasking environment, more than one task ere executing and these may require access to resources such as memory and I/O at the same time. The task management software must ensure that these resources are available. Common problems such as deadlock and mutual exclusion need to be prevented in the kernel. At the same time, a RTOS kernel must enforce timing constraints, for this reason timing control is essential and consequently a timer strictly controls each kernel service. Synchronisation between tasks is also required, and quite often adjustments to timing are required in order to account for communication delays between tasks.

Scheduling the execution of tasks is one of the major functions of any multi-tasking O/S, but in RTOS this is job is complicated by the real-time constraints. For this reason RTOS could never replace a general-purpose multitasking O/S and vice-versa. This is because the performance of a RTOS is geared towards satisfying the timing constraints, and this comes at the expense of flexibility that is offered by the general purpose O/S. In small, embedded applications, the RTOS may not need to manage many tasks, and therefore the scheduling of tasks is quite straightforward. However, modern embedded systems can be very complex, and the RTOS is required to perform complicated allocation of CPU, memory and other resources. It is therefore prudent to consider some general principles of scheduling.

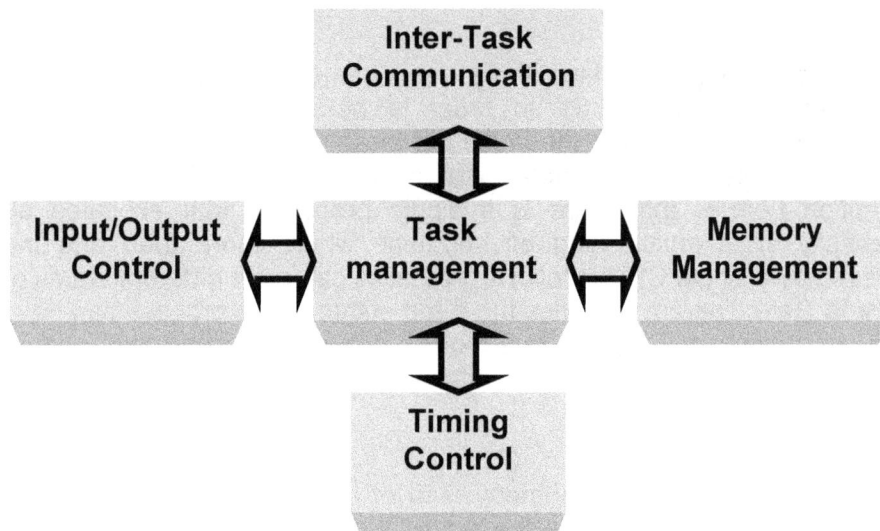

Figure 5.5 RTOS Kernel functions

The kernel is responsible for task management and the way that this is done is by using dedicated scheduling algorithms. Some general aspects of scheduling are discussed next and specific reference to real time systems will also be covered.

5.5. Scheduling

In a multi-tasking environment, whether real time or general purpose, the operating system has the job of determining the sequence and timing of the execution of processes. Schedulers are software programs that are designed to implement particular scheduling policies. These scheduling polices can be divided into three levels,

- **High-Level** (or long term or job scheduling)- Deals with decisions whether to admit a new job to the system processor (CPU). All jobs enter the system into the READY queue.
- **Medium-Level**- decides whether to temporarily remove a process from the CPU or to re-introduce the process (to balance processor loading).
- **Low-Level** (short-term or processor scheduling)- Decides which ready process to assign to the CPU.

In order to maintain consistency schedulers work according to a prescribed policy, such as for example (First Come First Serve (FCFS), Shortest Job First (SJF) etc). Time slicing is often applied with scheduling policies in order to allocate a prescribed period of time to a task. For example, in a time-slicing environment the kernel may interrupt each process after a few milliseconds to switch control to another process.

Schedulers that work at different levels have different tasks, but in a general sense, the objectives of scheduling are as follows,

- Provide maximum process throughput.
- Allocate jobs to the processor according to a policy. This way processes are treated consistently.
- During busy periods, in order to prevent CPU over-load, it should avoid further loading (e.g. inhibit any new job or new users) or alternatively reduce the level of service (i.e. increase response time).

Scheduling levels

Scheduling is divided into three levels namely High Level (HLS), Medium Level (MLS) and Low Level (LLS). In order to better describe the various levels of scheduling it is necessary to introduce the three state and five state process models. These models describe the states that a process can take during execution. The assumption here is that there is a single processor that executes all the tasks sequentially. In a multitasking environment, where more than one task is being processed by a single CPU, it follows that tasks can be in different states of execution. The three state diagram identifies the three states that a process can have, as ready, running and blocked. The five state models allow the blocked and ready states to be suspended, and therefore these two states are added to the basic three states.

Three state diagram

In a multitasking environment each of the many processes can be in one of three distinct states. These are the ready, blocked and running states as shown in Figure 5.6. A process traverses between these states under the control of schedulers.

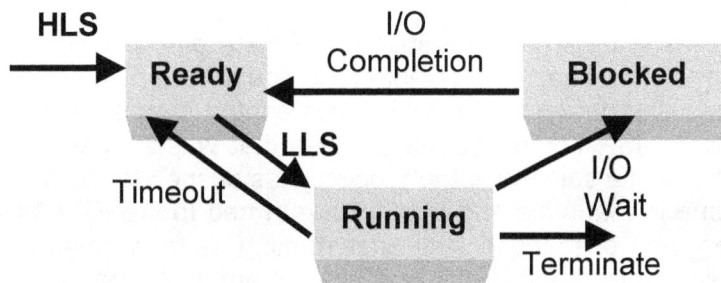

Figure 5.6 Three state diagram

With reference to Figure 5.6, it is seen that a process enters the system to the READY state via the High Level Scheduler (HLS). In multitasking there is a queue of processes in this state and therefore it is necessary to maintain a linked list of their respective process control blocks (PCBs) so that the order in which processes are scheduled can be controlled. When the CPU is free to accept a process, it is the job of the Low Level Scheduler (LLS) to determine which of the processes that are in the READY queue, should be allocated to the CPU. The process that is in the running state can exit that state in one of three ways. Namely, it can terminate or it can be timed out by the scheduler in which case it is returned to the READY queue. It can also leave the running state if it enters an I/O wait and in this case the LLS sends the process into the BLOCKED state. If the process goes into a BLOCKED state then the LLS will place the next process in the READY queue into the RUNNING state. When the I/O wait for the BLOCKED process is complete, it is placed by the LLS into the READY state and its PCB joins the linked list queue. Note that the only path into the RUNNING state is through the READY state.

Five state diagram

The five-state diagram arises from the operations of the Medium Level Scheduler (MLS) where a process that is in READY or BLOCKED or RUNNING state can be SUSPENDED. This gives rise to two more states namely, the READY SUSPENDED and BLOCKED SUSPENDED states as shown in Figure 5.7.

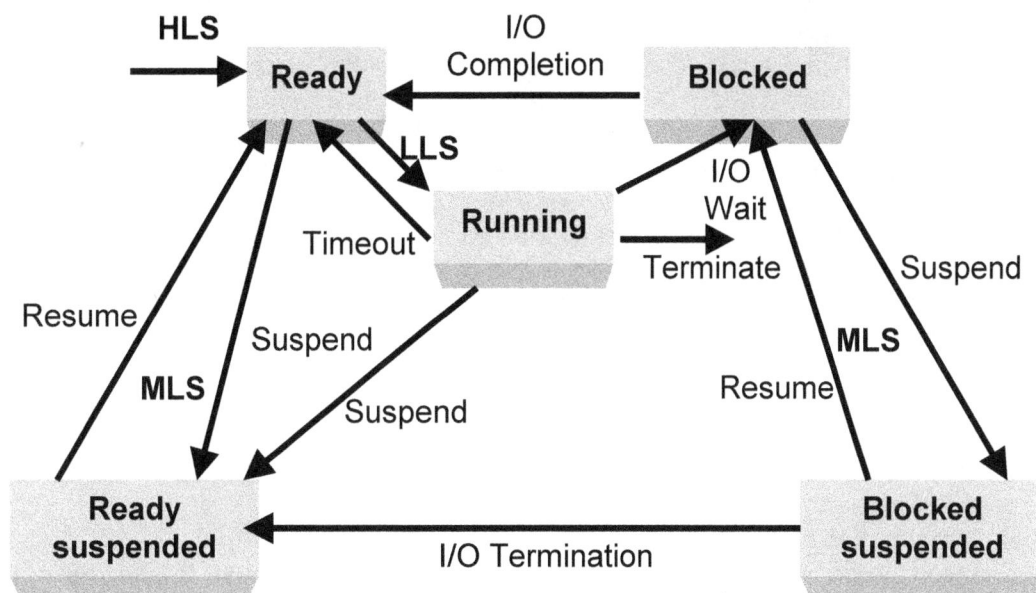

Figure 5.7 Five state diagram

The reason to temporarily suspend a state can arise from a number of O/S related actions. For example, an interrupt could cause the CPU to suspend the currently executing process in order to pass control onto an interrupt service routine (ISR). When the ISR completes the process that was suspended can be resumed. However it has to be said that if the process was suspended form the running state, it cannot resume in that state and has to be returned to the READY queue. Therefore the transition from suspended state into running state is always through the ready state. This is because there is only one point of entry into the running state and this is from the ready queue. A brief description of typical scheduling policies is given next.

5.6. Scheduling policies

Scheduling policies are the rules, which are used to decide whether a particular action is taken. In process terminology these actions refer to processes, and so can range from suspending, resuming, loading a process etc. These policies are therefore used to decide how to schedule the activities of different tasks in a multitasking environment. In multitasking systems tasks are divided in two major categories, namely pre-emptive and non-pre-emptive depending on whether they can be interrupted or not. The latter are more common in embedded and real time systems, so that the timing constraints can be satisfied. A brief description of both categories is given next.

Pre-emptive

In the pre-emptive scheme LLS may remove a process from the RUNNING state in order to allocate another process to the CPU. The cost of this in processing time is the added overhead of context switching. Note that a context switch is the term used to describe the switching of processes that are in the running state. Nevertheless, this timing overhead may be justified in cases where a long process is in danger of monopolising the processor. Additionally, pre-emptive multitasking allows the computer system to more reliably guarantee each process a regular time-slice of CPU time. For this reason most RTOS kernels schedule tasks using a scheme called "priority-based pre-emptive scheduling." Here, each task is assigned a priority by the programmer, and the task with a higher priority is allowed to pre-empt (i.e. interrupt) a task with a lower priority.

Additionally, external I/O can be used to trigger the execution of a task via an interrupt service routine (ISR). In this case the ISR is vectored to the interrupt and the hardware interrupt controller assigns the interrupt priority. Note here that the term 'vectored' simply means that an interrupt is assigned a location in memory where the ISR is located. For example, the Intel 8059 interrupt controller can support 8-levels of interrupts, and additionally can be cascaded to support 64 levels of hardware coded interrupts. The 80x86 processor reserves the lower 1Kbytes of memory to store 256 vectors that are used to identify interrupts as type 0-255. Intel reserves types 0-31, and the programmer can use all the other types. The Intel 80x86 CPU locates the ISR in memory by multiplying the interrupt type number by 4.

When an interrupt occurs, the kernel controls the execution on an ISR. In the event that a number of interrupts occur at the same time, the kernel must decide which to execute first and this is done by assigning priority to interrupts. The general response of the kernel following an interrupt is as follows,

1 Complete the current instruction.
2 Based on priority value of the interrupt, determine which task to allocate to the processor.

3 Save the conditions of the current state, this is normally done by a PUSH onto the STACK of the program counter and the segment registers if these are used. But generally, the location where execution has stopped is pushed onto the STACK so that the program can return to it.

4 Run the ISR. Note that the ISR is a software routine that ends with an instruction to POP the items that have been stored on the STACK. This enables the program to resume from the point at which it was interrupted.

These 4 steps together constitute a context switch, which was mentioned earlier. (For example on an Intel 8086 this takes a minimum of 50 microseconds)

Interrupt priority

The basic principle of priority-based interrupt is seen in Figure 5.8 where three tasks are being scheduled by the RTOS kernel. Here it is shown that the task with the lowest priority is Task1 and the highest priority task is Task 3. This may not be immediately clear and therefore a brief explanation is required.

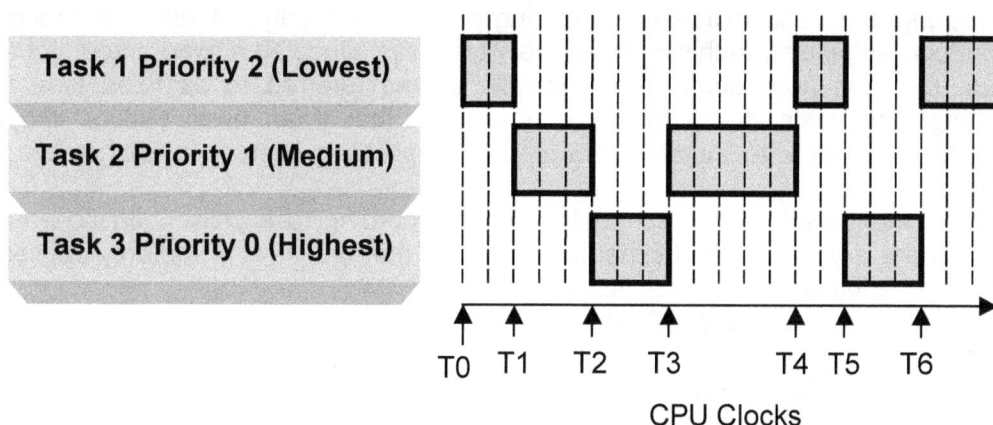

Task 1 Priority 2 (Lowest)

Task 2 Priority 1 (Medium)

Task 3 Priority 0 (Highest)

T0 T1 T2 T3 T4 T5 T6

CPU Clocks

Figure 5.8: Timeline for Priority-based Pre-emptive Scheduling Examples

Assume that time is shown on the x-axis and increases from left to right. Task 1 begins executing at T0 and there are no other tasks running at this time. At time T1, Task 2 with medium priority requires the CPU, and because it has a higher priority than Task 1, it pre-empts it and takes over the CPU. Which is to say that Task 2 is executing and Task 1 has been stopped. At time T2, Task 3 requires the CPU and because it has a higher priority, it pre-empts the currently running task, which is Task 2. At T3 Task 3 completes and releases the CPU. At this time the scheduler has a choice to allocate either Task 1 or Task 2 to the CPU. Looking at their priorities, Task 2 has a higher priority, and therefore gets the CPU. When Task 2 completes at T4, the CPU is allocated to Task 1. At T5 Task 3 decides to run again, and interrupts Task 1. At T6 Task 3 completes and CPU is given to Task 1.

From this brief explanation it is seen that the principle of priority based scheduling is quite straightforward. At any time that a task needs to run, the kernel checks to see if the task currently executing has a higher priority. If it does not then it can be pre-empted so that the higher priority task can run. The programmer of the system must ensure that each task is assigned the appropriate priority based on the functional requirements of the system.

Non-pre-emptive

In general purpose operating systems, where time constraints are not so critical, the allocation of tasks to the CPU can be scheduled according to a non pre-emptive principle. Non-pre-emptive means that, once a process has been allocated to the CPU it runs until it completes and the CPU cannot be taken away from that process. The only time the process will relinquish the CPU is when it terminates, or when it enters the BLOCKED state. Another, more drastic way to leave the READY state is when a non-mask able interrupt (NMI) occurs. (i.e. power loss). In non-pre-emptive systems, response times are more predictable because incoming jobs cannot displace waiting jobs, even if they have higher priority. In this case the priority of a task is irrelevant, because the scheduler works on a policy that does not take into account how important a job is. It has to be said that embedded real time systems, do not always need to use the pre-emptive scheduling principle. Soft real time systems do not need to comply with strict timing constraints that hard real-time systems do, and so they can be implemented using non-pre-emptive policies.

Another type of scheduling that is no longer very common is cooperative multitasking that was used in the Windows 3.1 O/S. In this scheme, in order to enable multitasking, each application when running would periodically relinquish control back to Windows scheduler. In this manner every task was allocated a fixed amount of time to run. In some applications this principle is also referred to as fixed time task switching. The main disadvantage of this is in that if an error occurs and the application is unable to transfer control to the operating system, it may freeze the system.

As mentioned earlier, schedulers work according to a prescribed scheduling policy. There are 6 Low level scheduling policies that are most commonly applied to process scheduling, these are as follows,

(SJF)   Shortest Job First.
(FCFS)   First Come First Serve.
(RR)   Round Robin.
(SRT)   Shortest Remaining Time.
(HRN)   Highest Response Ratio Next.
(MFQ)   Multilevel feedback queue.

FCFS-First Come First Serve scheduling policy

This is a non-pre-emptive policy that schedules tasks based on the order that they arrive. The size of tasks is not considered and consequently this policy favours long jobs over short jobs. This is because the waiting time to run time ratio is smaller for long jobs than for short jobs. Table 5.2 shows the typical ratios that can be expected with this policy. Here is seen that shortest job (P3) has the highest wait-to-run time ratio. (12)

Table 5.2

Process	Estimated run-time (T_{ER})	Waiting time (T_W)	Ratio (T_W) /(T_{ER})
P1	10	0	0/10=0
P2	2	10	10/2=5
P3	1	12	12/1=12
P4	100	13	13/100=0.13

SJF–Shortest Job First scheduling policy

This is another non-pre-emptive policy and it works on the basis that it schedules the shortest jobs first, leaving the longer jobs for later. The assumption here is that once the short jobs have been completed, and no more are left, the longer jobs can proceed. This avoids delaying the short jobs by waiting for long ones to finish. With SJF if there are a large number of shorter job there is a risk that the longer job suffers longer waits, and therefore may result in job starvation. For SJF an estimated run time must be available for each process and could be supplied by Job control Language (JCL). Table 5.3 shows the typical ratios that can be expected with this policy. Here is seen that in comparison to the FCFS, all jobs have a lower wait-to-run-time ratio. However the highest ratio is for the longest job (P4).

Table 5.3

Process	Order SJF	Estimated run-time (T_{ER})	Waiting time (T_W)	Ratio (T_W) /(T_{ER})
P1	P3	1	0	0/1=0
P2	P2	2	1	1/2=0.5
P3	P1	10	3	3/10=0.3
P4	P4	100	13	13/100=0.13

SRT-Shortest Remaining Time scheduling policy

This is a pre-emptive variation of SJF that uses a timeout to context switch between jobs. It uses a time stamp to monitor the length of jobs and schedules these according to the principle of Shortest Remaining Time (SRT) policy. With this policy the job with the shortest time to completion is processed first. Each job runs for the duration of the timeout and then a new calculation is done to determine which of the remaining jobs are the shortest. Table 5.4 shows an example of the performance of this policy. Although this policy has the overhead of keeping a time-stamp, it is seen to be fair to all jobs, and more importantly, it guarantees that no jobs will be starved of CPU time.

Table 5.4 SRT

Process	Time	Order	Units of time elapsed FROM START						
	Unit	SJF	1	2	3	4	<--- >	13	14
P1	10	3	10	10	10	9		0	-
P2	2	2	2	1	0	-			-
P3	1	1	0	-	-	-			-
P4	100	4	100	100	100	100			99

Highest Response Next (HRN) scheduling policy

HRN is also a pre-emptive policy derived from SJF, which has been modified to allow the longer jobs to have a chance to complete. This modification involves calculating a dynamic priority after each unit of execution time. It is based on a calculated priority value and the formula is as follows,

$$P = \frac{T_W + T_{RT}}{T_{RT}} \qquad (1.1)$$

where,
P- calculated priority
T_W- waiting time
T_{RT}- running time

Looking at the equation 1.1 it is clear that P is never less than 1. For example, assume two processes P1 and P2 with run times of 5 and 10 units respectively have been waiting for 1 unit time. Their priority values can be calculated from (1.1) as follows,

$$P_1 = \frac{T_W + T_{RT}}{T_{RT}} = \frac{1+5}{5} = 1.2 \text{ and } P_2 = \frac{T_W + T_{RT}}{T_{RT}} = \frac{1+10}{10} = 1.1$$

From the result it is seen that process P1 has a higher priority value and therefore takes precedence over P2.

Consider another example. Assume process P4 has a run time of 100 units and has been waiting for 12 units of time. At this time, another process P5, with a run time value of 10 units joins the queue. Another unit of time later, after P4 has waited for 13 units of time, P5 has been in the queue for 1 unit time and it has a running time of 10 units of time. The priority calculation for P4 and P5 would be,

$$P_4 = \frac{T_W + T_{RT}}{T_{RT}} = \frac{13+100}{100} = 1.13 \text{ and } P_2 = \frac{T_W + T_{RT}}{T_{RT}} = \frac{1+10}{10} = 1.1$$

In this situation even though P4 is a long job the priority has moved up higher than P5, which has shorter running time but joins the queue later. Table 5.5 show the calculated priorities for a range of process lengths.

Table 5.5 HRN with the Priority calculated priority value

Process	Estimated run-time (T_{RT})	Waiting time (T_W)	Priority value (T_W+T_{RT}) /(T_{RT})
P1	10	0	10/10 =1
P2	2	10	12/2 =6
P3	1	12	13/1 =13
P4	100	13	113/100 =1.13

Round Robin scheduling policy

Round robin is a common scheduling scheme where processes are allocated the CPU in a rotating fashion with a timeout signalling the change form one process to the next. (See figure 5.9) A process is selected from ready queue in a First In First Out (FIFO) sequence. Processes are assigned a quantum of time to run on the CPU, which must not be exceeded. As soon as the time quantum expires, an interrupt occurs and if the process that has been executing has not finished it is placed at the back of the FIFO queue. If the process has finished then it is removed and a new process joins the back of the FIFO queue. A hardware timer that generates an interrupt at pre-set intervals usually provides the time quantum. This policy is pre-emptive which only occurs at expiry of quantum time.

Perhaps the most significant feature of this policy is that it guarantees the completion of even the longest jobs. Since each process is allocated a quantum, and when this has expired, it moves to the back of the queue, every process remains in the queue until it has completed. Thus, for n processes in the queue and a fixed time quantum (Q), then each process gets a proportion of CPU time given by,

$$P_{CPU} = \frac{1}{n}$$

With the allocation of a fixed number of Q time units, it follows that no process waits longer than $T_W = (n-1) \times Q$ time units. The main disadvantage of this policy is the significant overheads because each quantum time generates a context switch.

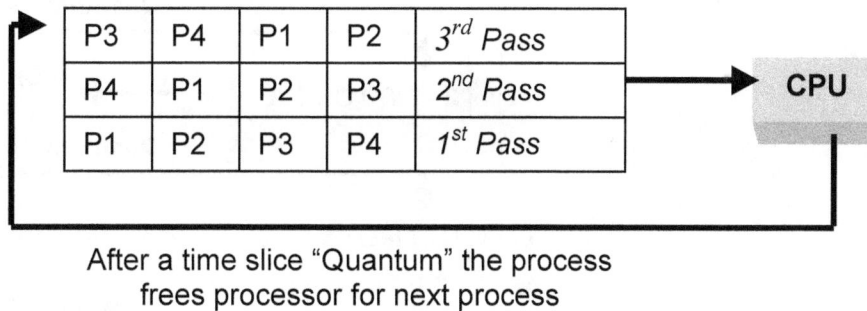

P3	P4	P1	P2	3rd Pass
P4	P1	P2	P3	2nd Pass
P1	P2	P3	P4	1st Pass

CPU

After a time slice "Quantum" the process
frees processor for next process

Figure 5.9 Round Robin Process Swapping

Choice of time quantum is very important with the round robin scheduling policy. It should not be too short because this will increase the frequency of context switch. Since every context switch takes CPU time this can lead to a condition called 'thrashing', where the CPU spends all its time context switching and not running any processes. On the other hand if the context switch is too long, that could introduce idle time, when the process has terminated and the quantum has not elapsed. (Typically quantum = *10-20 mS*). Figure 5.9 represents round robin scheduling.

Multi-level Feedback Queues (MFQ) scheduling policy

MFQs are a combination of FIFO queues arranged at different hierarchical levels in accordance with the level of CPU requirements. The highest level in the hierarchy consists of short processes and the lower levels contain processes that are longer. MFQs combine several levels of FIFO queues with a time quantum applied to limit processor time given to each process. Every process enters at the highest level of the MFQ. As the process runs, if it uses up its quantum, it will return to the back of the FIFO queue at the lower level. This will be repeated so that every time the quantum is exceeded the process will drop to the level below. The highest level is for processes with the shortest CPU time since these will complete before they are relegated to lower levels. Consequently, lower levels consist of processes that have progressively longer CPU time requirements. Transition from the higher level to the one below it is achieved by providing a timeout (quantum Q). This is seen in Figure 5.10, which shows that a new process enters at the highest level, and progresses down the levels for as long as it does not complete. The lowest level in this hierarchy offers a round robin scheduling policy. Here the longest jobs reside because they have dropped all the way down the hierarchy. At this level these processes will remain until they terminate and they will receive CPU time according to the RR policy. In this manner MFQs ensure that ALL jobs are given a chance to complete.

MFQs can be made adaptive by recording the level at which each process terminated when it was last in the queue. The next time that the same process runs instead of placing it at the highest level of the MFQ, it will be placed at the level that it exited. In this manner the process will not waste time in the higher levels where it will not complete. This is an attempt to provide an adaptive policy which treats processes on the basis of their past behaviour.

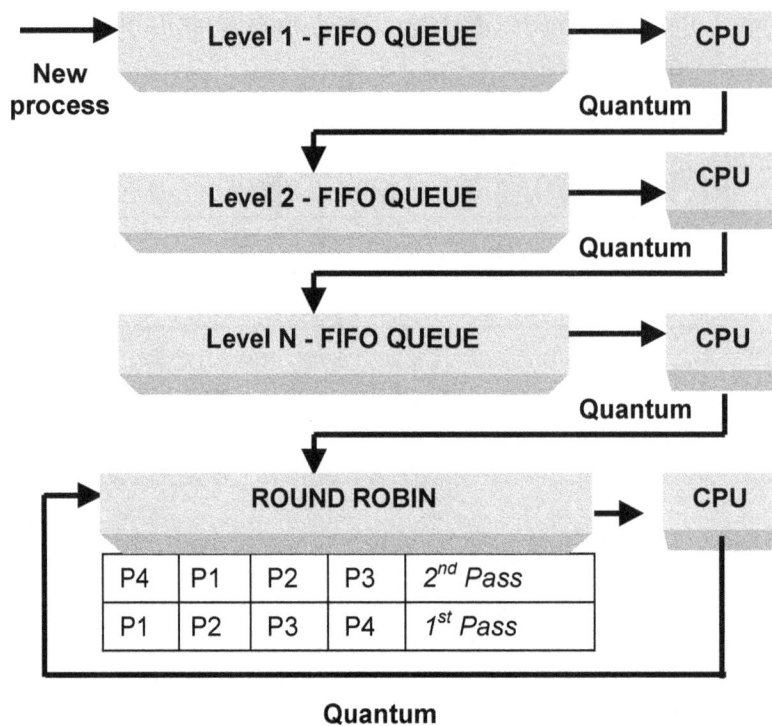

Figure 5.10 Multi-level feedback queues.

5.7. Design stages in RTS

It was mentioned earlier on that real time systems are characterised by timing constraints. Consequently the design of a real time system differs from other software systems because the response times must be considered in early stages of the design process. Events (Stimuli) are generated by sensors and these are processed by the system software so that the appropriate response can be obtained for the system. Figure 5.11 shows the relationship between sensors, actuators and the process.

Stages in the design process of RTS are:
1. Identify the stimuli that the system must process and the associated response. Typically these are tabulated. (See example below)
2. For each stimulus and associated response, identify the timing constraints, which apply to both stimulus and response processing.
3. Integrate the stimulus and response processing into a number of concurrent processes.

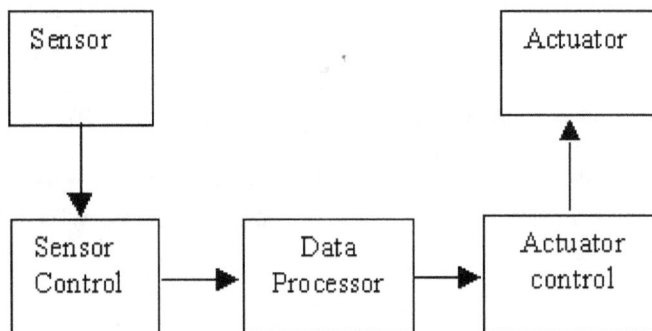

Figure 5.11 RTS processing

4. For each stimulus and response pair, design algorithms to carry out the required computations. Algorithm designs often have to be developed relatively early in the design process to give the indication of the amount of processing required and the time required to complete this. This will impact on the achievable timing constraints of the design. For example, if a software loop to produce a pulse on the output port of a microprocessor requires 5 microseconds of CPU time, then the maximum achievable frequency of pulses at the I/O port is 200kHz.

5. Design scheduling systems, which will ensure that processes are started in time to meet their deadlines.

6. Integrate the system under the control of a real time executive.

Example

You are required to design a real time system to control the operation of the terminus light train at Gatwick airport. The initial brief states that the system will monitor train speed and if this is exceeded the brakes will be applied automatically to reduce the speed to the required limit. The track is divided into a number of segments and these are used to service two trains going in opposite directions. Each track segment has a red light signal, which indicates that the track segment should not be entered.

Identify the stimuli that must be processed by the on-board train control system and the associated responses to these stimuli.

Produce the system architecture diagram.

Solution

The outline is very brief and therefore we need to specify more details in order to develop our design. Note that this example is only used to illustrate the steps in the design process only. Consequently it is not intended to produce a complete and detailed design. In order to make the system safe we need the following,

1. The system must be programmed to monitor train speed. The maximum allowed train speed is 50 kph. A transmitter on the track continually broadcasts the information on the status of the signal that controls the track segment. The train receives information from the trackside transmitter when it is within 10 metres of the trackside transmitter and the time required for the track segment information is 50 milliseconds. This is Periodic. Sensors on the train should be designed to provide information about the current train speed (updated every 500 milliseconds) and the train brake status (updated every 200 milliseconds). Note that the inertia of a moving train dictates the rate of speed monitoring. Therefore reading speed every half a second is sufficiently frequent to detect changes in time to react to them. Also note that the trackside transmitter has 50 milliseconds to transit signal to the train about the speed. Therefore train speed cycle has to be long enough to accommodate this.

2. If the speed of the train exceeds the maximum track speed by 5-10 kph then the trackside transmitter sends information to the control room to signal over-speed status. The time for sending the signal information and broadcast the track segment is 50 milliseconds. This signal triggers the audible alarm in the train control room to sound the over-speed warning. This process is not regular because it happens only occasionally, consequently it is Aperiodic.

3. In the event of the speed of the train exceeding the segment speed limit by more than 10kph the brakes are automatically applied to the train without control room involvement. The sensor detects a segment speed to be more than the maximum speed of 10 kph and the train brakes are automatically applied until the speed falls to the segment speed limit of 50 kph. This process will have to take into account the 50

millisecond speed signal timing and the speed monitoring process that has a timing requirement of 500 millisecond. Thus, applying the brakes process can be synchronised with the train speed process to run at 500 milliseconds. This process is Aperiodic because this process is not expected to occur at regular intervals. However, once this process is started it is periodic at 500 ms all the while the speed is in excess of 10 kph of the limit.

4. If the train enters a track segment that is signalled with a red light, the train protection system applies the train brakes and reduces the speed to zero. In this state, the train brakes are applied within 20 milliseconds of the time when the red light signal is received. This timing is selected because the timing of the signal to be sent is 50 ms. Therefore any response must be faster than that. Brakes are applied until the train stops. An audible alarm in the control room signals to the crew that danger is present. This process is aperiodic since it only occurs when red light signal is not obeyed.

For this proposed system the following table indicates the stimuli/response and timing constraints.

Stimuli	**Timing requirements**	**Response**
Trackside transmitter (Broadcasts segment identifier and speed limit).	50 milliseconds required.	On-board train control system compares information with on-board data.
Trackside transmitter (Broadcasts status of signal controlling track segment).	50 milliseconds required.	On-board train control system compares information with on-board data. When the train enters a track segment that shows a red light the train brakes are applied (within 20 milliseconds of the time when the red light signal is received) until the speed is zero.
Current Train speed.	Status Updated every 500 milliseconds.	When limit is exceeded by more than 5 kph, warning is sounded in driver's cab. When limit is exceeded by more than 10 kph brakes are automatically applied (within 500 milliseconds of the time when the excess speed has been detected) until the speed equals the segment speed limit.
Train Brakes.	Status Updated every 500 milliseconds.	Automatically released or applied depending on the speed of the train.
Red light process	Brakes applied within 20 milliseconds.	Automatically applied when on the red light status of the train. Persists until train stops.

The process architecture is shown in figure 5.12. All the stimuli are identified on the diagram with a frequency that they occur with. The overall response frequency of the system is calculated to be larger than the sum of the individual stimuli frequencies. (i.e. (2+20+50+2=74Hz, so choose 100Hz for overall response). Since frequency is the inverse of time, the higher frequency indicates shorter period.

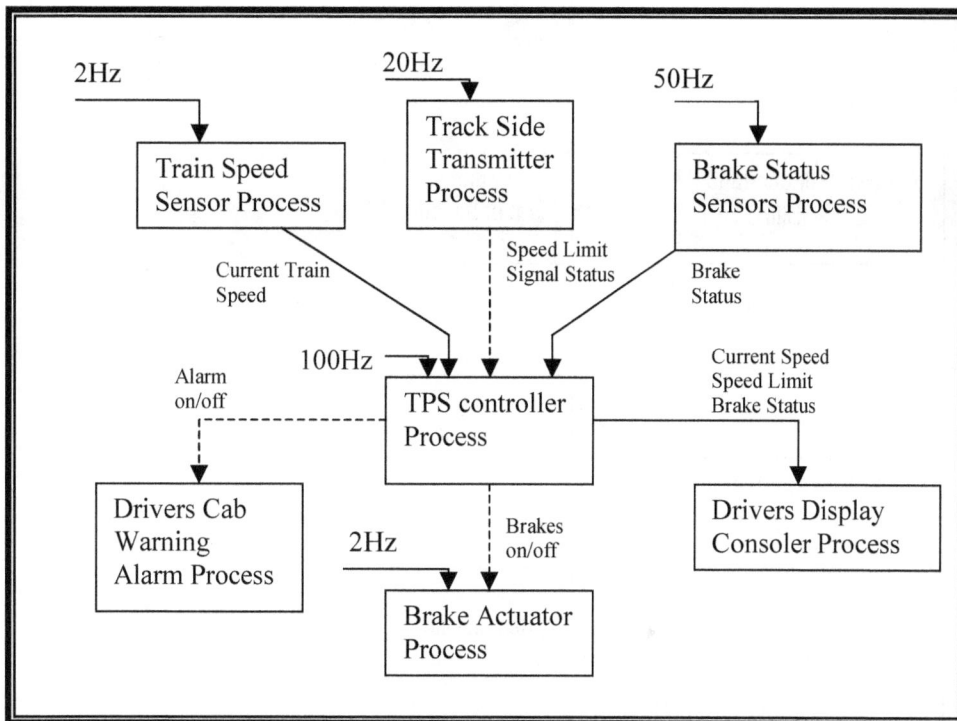

Figure 5.12. Train protection system architecture

The above is a simplified treatment of a real-time and also safety critical system. Proper treatment would require much more detailed analysis of every aspect but I am only providing an outline design example here to illustrate the principle. In the above example I have not described the algorithms for each stimulus-response pair. This should be fairly intuitive and straightforward so it is left to the reader to explore this aspect. Next I will briefly consider user interface design.

5.8. User interface design

User interface is very important in all software design as system users often judge a system by its interface (rightly or wrongly) rather than its functionality. Poor interface design means that many software systems are never used. User-interface design will necessarily be a part of the overall system design, however if a system is broken down into smaller parts then the user-interface can be considered at that level. Figure 5.13 shows a diagram of the user-interface design process.

Reading from top to bottom it is first necessary to analyse and understand user activities so that the interface can be designed with the desired features. At this stage only a paper-based solution is provided and this is presented to the user for evaluation. The next step is to produce a prototype. This can be done in a visual programming environment (i.e. VisualBasic) so that it can be produced quickly and modified easily. The user will evaluate the prototype and suggest any modifications. This will result in a dynamic prototype, which will be used as a basis for design of the executable version of the interface. During this step final consultation with the user will take place in order to make any final modifications. The executable interface could be developed in a language different to the one used for prototyping. During the prototyping stages the designer needs to take into consideration aspects of the interface, which are beyond user satisfaction. Some of these considerations are presented next.

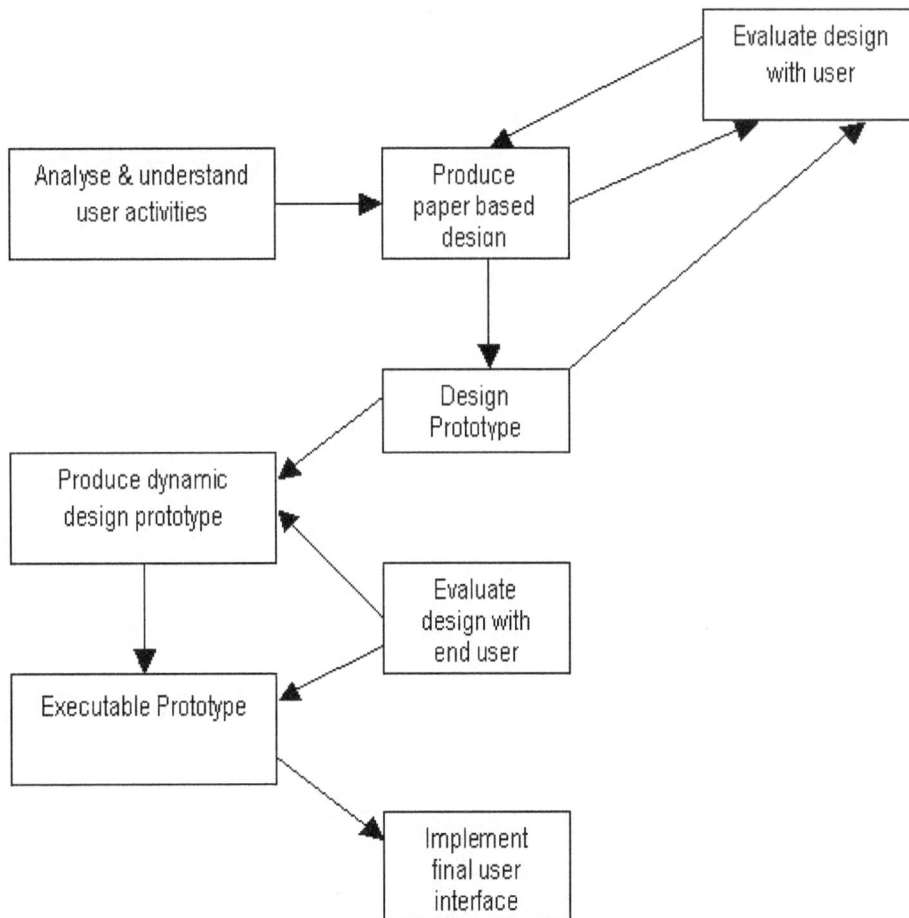

Figure 5.13. User interface design process

GUI design considerations

When designing a user interface it is necessary to bear in mind the amount of information that is presented to the user. It is quite easy to clog the interface with too much information making it difficult for users to interact with it in a suitable way. Some considerations for interface design are as follows,

- **Static vs. dynamic:** Is the interface animated and if this is a requirement
- **Precise vs. relative:** Some interfaces are better used when relating to something. For example a change in the value of shares on the stock market is perhaps more relevant than the actual value of stock.
- **Textual, numerical or graphical:** This is an obvious distinction and needs to be considered both in terms of the user and the type of information that needs to be presented.
- **How often updated:** Updating too frequently may cause the user to become overwhelmed with information.
- **Colour: number of colours,** changes, consistency, and pairings. Visual impact of colour is very important and can impact on the users' ability to process information.

Other issues that the designer needs to take into account are summarised in table 5.6.

Table 5.6 User Interface Design considerations

Principle	Description
User Familiarity	- Interface should use terms and concepts drawn from experience of users. The interface should use the language that the user is familiar with. It should use known icons and verbal terms (e.g. Microsoft standard print icon, design of an oven or a plane cockpit.)
Consistency	- Interface must be consistent where possible with comparable operations used in a similar manner, if possible, similar interfaces (e.g. Graphics Suite: save the picture as. OR. Export the picture as. Should look similar)
Minimal Surprise	- Users should never be surprised with interface behaviour. (default screen if required). Use of default screens and icons. (e.g. Blue screen for system freezing is an example of minimal surprise!)
Recoverability	- A mechanism to recover from errors. The system should have a possibility to recover from problems without or with only little user interaction. Standard screens should be used if necessary. (e.g. (not very helpful but anyway) Dr. Watson from MS NT)
User Guidance	- Interface must provide useful feedback to user including a help facility. Buttons and labels must be meaningful. Software should have a user-friendly. Help function. (e.g. ?-menu or F1 key in Windows OS)
User diversity	The interface should provide appropriate interaction facilities for different types of user. Each user group should only get the information it requires. Not too little and not too much. The interface should therefore be able to interact with different types of user. (Manager, HR, Sales, Development) (e.g. Web interface for Perry-library compared with the staff interface)
Usability Attributes	The user should be able to judge the quality of an interface by considering these attributes. Some of these are mentioned next.

Usability Attributes
- **Learnability**: How long does a user need to become productive with the system? Is staff training required?
- **Speed of operation:** Is the reaction time of the system adequate to the need of the user. Are there unacceptable waiting times for the user?
- **Robustness**: Is the system tolerant to user faults (or general fault tolerant)?
- **Recoverability**: .How good is the system in recovering from errors?
- **Adaptability**: Is the system (interface) tied to a specific model of system?

Interface types

The following is a brief consideration of different interface types. For each type considered I provide some advantages and disadvantages, which may be taken into consideration during design.

Direct manipulation: This interface attempts to model the 'information space' as seen by the user. For example a word processing package attempts to present the text so that it looks like the final report or textbook to the user. Users are able to manipulate the model in order to give it characteristics that they prefer. The resulting manipulation provides immediate changes and this works well for most classes of user.

Advantages: control, ease of learning, immediate feedback

Disadvantages: modelling, keeping track, memory usage (e.g. MS software), speed of response

Menu driven: User is presented with a pre-configured selection of choices (menus). A hierarchy of menus can be arranged to limit the number of choices at each level. This approach suits occasional users who are able to use the interface quite effectively even if they are not very familiar with it. Examples, Macintosh o/s, Windows, most program development environments.

Advantages: no need to memorise commands, little typing skill needed, avoids some errors, context obvious (to m/c) used with help

Disadvantages: menu structures can be repetitive; keeping track of what was done is difficult, speed of operation particularly for experienced users.

Command driven: Users type commands on the prompt using the keyboard. The number and syntax for these commands determines the operations that can be performed. This was the first computer interface in use and is still popular with regular users and software developers. examples MSDos, Unix.

Advantages: Relatively easy to implement, for most part commands use natural language, commands can easily be combined, concise

Disadvantages: Commands have to be learned as well as the syntax for any options, prone to typing errors, have to know commands even to use help.

The choice of which type of interface to use rests with the software design team. It is also important to consider the type of user that will be the main operator of the software. For this reason it is quite common to find that the design of the interface is often a mixture of types e.g.: menu + sort-cut commands, direct manipulation + menus or commands (i.e. WP, SSHEET). It is also common for some systems to have more than one interface, for example a system to monitor services in a building would have different interfaces for a technician and for a manager. The manager may be informed that a fault has occurred in a particular sector of the building while the technician would be given the full details of the fault.

The above treatment of user interface design is intended to give the reader a basic understanding of the process. More information can be obtained from dedicated text on the subject. For further reference I include in Appendix III examples of guidelines for interface design that are currently in use.

5.9. Chapter summary

In this chapter I cover the basic approach to software design. I consider the design process and this relates to the programming paradigm as well as to the overall system architecture. With this in mind I recommend the 4+1 view of architecture as a means of developing the design. The strategy or the means of implementing the design relies on many factors related to project management. I cover these briefly and their impact on the design. I also consider quality and how this needs to fit into the design process. I consider briefly real-time systems design. In order to apply design principles I briefly cover some essential features of real-time systems such as scheduling policies. Actual steps in design of RTS are introduced and a simple example presented to show the approach to design. The final section introduces design of the user-interface. Some general considerations are presented and discussed.

Exercises

5.1.   Explain what you understand by the term systems engineering and how you would define a system?

5.2.   Software design is a broad discipline, and it can be divided into three main areas, process, strategy and quality. Using examples as appropriate discuss how these three areas are dealt with during design.

5.3.   Assume that you are in charge of a project to design software that enables individuals in the UK to complete and submit their self-assessment tax returns on-line. Describe briefly the process, strategy and quality issues that would be part of your design. State any assumptions that you make.

5.4.   Why should you take into considerations management issues while designing a software system? After all you are a designer, not a manager.

5.5.   Describe the various plans that you should take into account during the strategies design stage.

5.6.   Your boss has approved a budget to purchase a CASE tool to help with project management. He has asked you to prepare an outline of the features that such a tool should have. Prepare a document identifying these features and explaining why you consider them to be important.

5.7.   Describe how quality influences design in software engineering.

5.8.   You are a senior software manager for a games developer and you have to prepare the release of a new game that your organisation has developed. The game is played for free by on-line users under a browser (Internet Explorer or Mozilla Firefox). Revenue is generated by hosting banners of advertisers on the game website and the fees for this are proportional to the number of users playing the game. From this brief explanation, stating any assumptions that you consider relevant, discuss the quality issues that you would recommend to your design team in order to increase the chances of success of the launch of your new game.

5.9.   What are the distinguishing features of real-time systems?

5.10.   Describe the 3-state and the 5-state process models.

5.11.   What are the three levels of scheduling that apply to the state diagrams of Q 5.10 above?

5.12.   Explain the principle of priority based pre-emptive scheduling as used in RTOS kernels.

5.13.   How are tasks allocated priorities in a RTS application?

5.14.   Non-pre-emptive polices use-scheduling algorithms to decide what tasks to schedule next. This makes sense because these tasks cannot be pre-empted. But, how do pre-emptive policies schedule tasks?

5.15.   With reference to the relevant stages in the design process of a real time system, explain why the overall system response times must be considered early in the design process.

5.16. You are a software engineering consultant invited to design a security system in a modern building. The building services manager tells you the following information,

> The system is intended to protect against intrusion and to detect fire. It should incorporate smoke sensors, movement sensors and door sensors, video cameras located at various places in the building, all of which are under computer control. An operator console where the system status is reported, and external communication facilities to call the appropriate services such as police, fire, etc. is also specified.

   i. Produce a table indicating the sensor equipment that you can recommend and timing information as well as responses that you expect from these.
   ii. Describe the algorithms that are needed to match responses to stimuli.
   iii. Draw an architecture diagram for your design.

5.17. Why is user-interface design important in software engineering projects?

5.18. What are the main considerations in user-interface design?

5.19. What are the main types of user-interface?

5.20. An insurance broker requires a software application that will enable its staff to calculate the insurance premium that clients have to pay. The calculations are based on well-established company formulas and the procedure for decision-making is also very clear. The managers' main concern is the human computer interface (HCI), which she believes, needs to be designed to optimise the efficiency of processing applications. Using this application as a design example, explain the various stages of a GUI interface design.

CHAPTER 6 SOFTWARE PROTOTYPING

6.1   Introduction

Prototyping is the process of developing a trial version of a system (a prototype) or its components or characteristics in order to clarify the requirements of the system or to reveal critical design considerations. [40] In other words prototyping provides a means for both the engineer and the user to 'test drive' software to ensure that it does what it is supposed to do. Furthermore, by having a prototype of a system engineers are able to improve their understanding of the technical issues governing its operation.

Software prototyping is the process of creating an incomplete version of a software program, which can be used to let the users have a first idea of the completed program or allow the clients to evaluate the program. The methodology for creating prototypes is based on building a working model of the system and using this to help with designing, implementing, testing, and installing the system. Thus it can be seen that a prototype serves as an additional stage of software development that can help with clarifying design issues. While this is useful it also means that the time and other resources spent on building a prototype must be taken into account. Thus there are some advantages of prototyping and some disadvantages. We briefly discuss these next. [41]

Advantages of prototyping

Reduced time and costs: Prototyping can improve the quality of requirements and specifications provided to developers. Because changes cost exponentially more to implement as they are detected later in development, the early determination of what the user really wants can result in faster and less expensive software.

Improved and increased user involvement: Prototyping requires user involvement and allows them to see and interact with a prototype allowing them to provide better and more complete feedback and specifications. The presence of the prototype being examined by the user prevents many misunderstandings and miscommunications that occur when each side believe the other understands what they said. Since users know the problem domain better than anyone on the development team, increased interaction can result in a final product that has higher tangible and intangible qualities. Thus the final product is more likely to satisfy the users' expectations for look, feel and performance.

Disadvantages of prototyping

Insufficient analysis: The focus on a limited prototype can distract developers from properly analysing the complete project. This can lead to overlooking better solutions, preparation of incomplete specifications or the conversion of limited prototypes into poorly engineered final projects that are hard to maintain. Furthermore, since a prototype is limited in functionality it may not scale well if the prototype is used as the basis of a final product, which may not be noticed if developers are too focused on building a prototype as a model.

User confusion of prototype and finished system: Users can begin to think that a prototype, intended to be thrown away, is actually a final system that merely needs to be finished or polished. This can lead them to expect the prototype to accurately model the performance of the final system when this is not the intention of the developers. Users can also become attached to features that were included in a prototype for consideration and then removed from the specification for a final system. If users are able to require all proposed features be included in the final system this can lead to feature creep. Developers can also become attached to prototypes they have spent a great deal of effort producing. This can lead to problems like attempting to convert a limited prototype into a final system when it does not have an appropriate underlying architecture.

Excessive development time of the prototype: A key feature of prototyping is that it is supposed to be done quickly. If the developers lose sight of this fact, they may try to develop a prototype that is too complex. When the prototype is thrown away the precisely developed requirements that it provides may not yield a sufficient increase in productivity to make up for the time spent developing the prototype. Users can become stuck in debates over details of the prototype, delaying implementation of the final product and holding up the development team.

Expense of implementing prototyping: the start up costs for building a development team focused on prototyping may be high. Many companies have development methodologies in place, and changing them can mean retraining, retooling, or both. Many companies tend to just jump into the prototyping without bothering to retrain their workers as much as they should.

A common problem with adopting prototyping technology is high expectations for productivity with insufficient effort behind the learning curve. In addition to training for the use of a prototyping technique, there is an often-overlooked need for developing corporate and project specific underlying structure to support the technology.

The prototyping process

The process of prototyping involves the following steps,

1. Identify basic requirements: Determine basic requirements including the input and output information desired. Details, such as security, can typically be ignored. The outputs at this stage are,
- Establishing Objectives → Prototyping Plan
- Define Functionality → Outline Definition

2. Develop Initial Prototype: The initial prototype is developed that includes only user interfaces. The output at this stage is,
- Develop Prototype → Executable Prototype

3. Review: The customers, including end-users, examine the prototype and provide feedback on additions or changes. The output at this stage is,
- Evaluate Prototype → Evaluation Report

4. Revise and Enhancing the Prototype: Using the feedback both the specifications and the prototype can be improved. Negotiation about what is within the scope of the contract/product may be necessary. If changes are introduced then a repeat of steps #3 ands #4 may be needed.

Prototypes can also be used to establish and validate the software requirement. They can help the customer to identify their requirements more precisely by enabling the customer to experience (a part of) the later system with a mock up. Prototyping can also be used to help the developers to identify the critical parts of the system.

Figure 6.1 shows an illustration of the prototype process.

```
                    ┌─────────────────────────┐
              ──────▶│  Prototype Specification │
                     └─────────────────────────┘
                                  │
                                  ▼
                     ┌─────────────────────────┐
              ──────▶│  Prototype Development   │
              │      └─────────────────────────┘
              │                   │
              │                   ▼
              │      ┌─────────────────────────┐
              │      │  experiment with Prototype│
              │      └─────────────────────────┘
              │                   │
              │                   ▼
              │                  ╱╲
              │                 ╱  ╲       yes
              │                ╱Proto╲ ─────────▶
              │                ╲type  ╱
              │                 ╲accepted╱
              │                  ╲╱
              │                   │ no
              │                   ▼
              │      ┌─────────────────────────┐
              └──────│  Prototype Specification │
                     └─────────────────────────┘
```

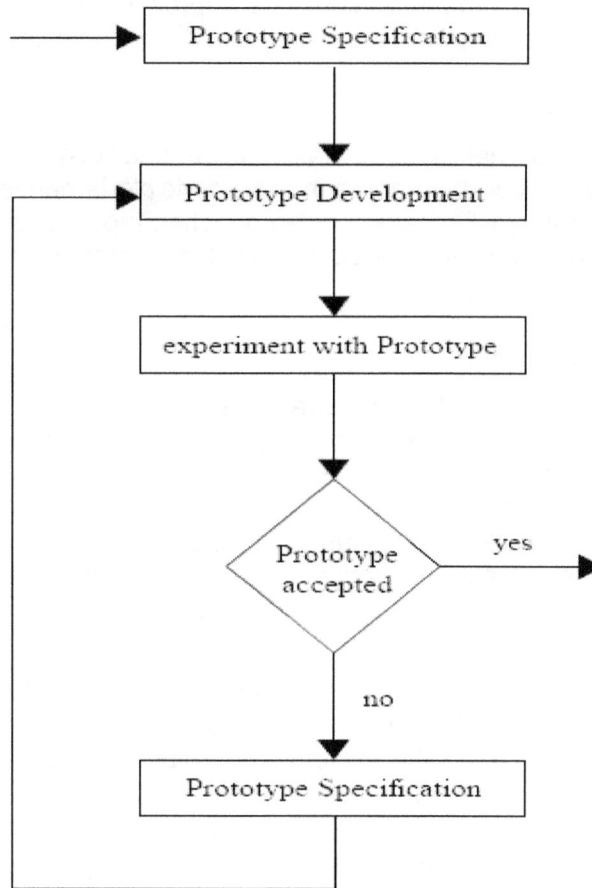

Figure 6.1. Prototype process

6.2   Types of prototype

There are many different types of prototypes and they are designed for different applications. In essence prototyping can be classified into the following categories,
  • Complete Prototypes: All essential functions are given. This is very rare. All experiences provide a basis for the final specification.
  • Non-complete Prototypes: Here only some sub-systems like user interface, architecture and components are built. These are very common.
  • Re-usable Prototypes: Essential parts of the prototype are used for the implementation. These are common where software development centres on similar products.
  • Throwaway Prototypes: This prototype is used to demonstrate the system concept. It will not be delivered to the customer. It should be noted that no developed parts are taken through to the final product.

Based on the above classification several different prototype methodologies have been developed and some of these are presented next.

Quick and dirty prototypes

As the name implies this approach focuses on quickly bringing up a version of a system, then modifying it until the customer can grant minimal approval. This is quite common but is limited to small-scale projects where it is relatively easy and cheap to produce a quick prototype. With this approach care must be taken so that something intended to be temporary does not actually become permanent.

Detail design-driven prototypes

Software houses that develop fairly large and complex systems (i.e. tax accounting software) favour this approach. The principle is derived from engineering disciplines where ``prototype" means a pre-production model of a system. The model is "test-driven" to uncover any defects, and the prototype refined until all the requirements have been satisfied.

Non-functioning prototypes

More often than not this approach is adopted in the early stages of requirements analysis. The idea is to provide the customer with visual examples of inputs to and outputs from system processes. With this approach no data are actually input, nor are results computed and output. There is very little opportunity for identifying functional requirements because of the lack of interactive experimentation. However it can be used as a preliminary stage in small-scale projects.

Explorative prototypes

The purpose of this kind of prototyping is to obtain a full description of the system specification. It provides insight for the developers into how many solutions are possible in order to create the system. Developer can discuss the feasibility of implementation of different options. As a result they could decide to develop a prototype for verifying the usability. This includes the functionality and the modification. In general explorative prototyping is used for analysis and system specification.

Experimental prototypes

The aim of experimental prototypes is a full description of the specification for each sub-system. This is then used as a basis for the final system implementation. The efficiency of the sub-systems can be verified. This type of prototyping is used at the development of each component and of the system. The interaction between all components can be verified by using this type of prototyping.

Evolutionary prototypes

As the name implies this type of prototyping evolves into a working software product. Development begins with an easily modifiable and extensible working model of a proposed system. This is not necessarily representative of a complete system, but it provides users with a physical representation of key parts of the system before implementation. Therefore we start with an easily built, readily modifiable, ultimately extensible, partially specified, working model of the primary aspects of a proposed system. The goal is to evolve the prototype into the final system, which implies that the requirements should be fairly precise before development can proceed. Because of the evolutionary nature of development the techniques of evolutionary prototyping can be applied concurrently with structured analysis at the beginning of the project and with structured design during the tuning phase. Basic characteristics of evolutionary prototyping are shown in figure 6.2.

In summary therefore, evolutionary prototyping is used for systems where the system complexity is in the data and NOT in the system functionality. This applies for example for databases or management software. Key feature of this system is the user interface and not the system structure behind that interface.

This method is mostly suitable for small projects with well-understood system functionality. As the user tests the interface of their later program, there is a good interaction between the user and the development team. The main disadvantage may be that there will be lots of minor changes during a project, which are difficult to track and to document.

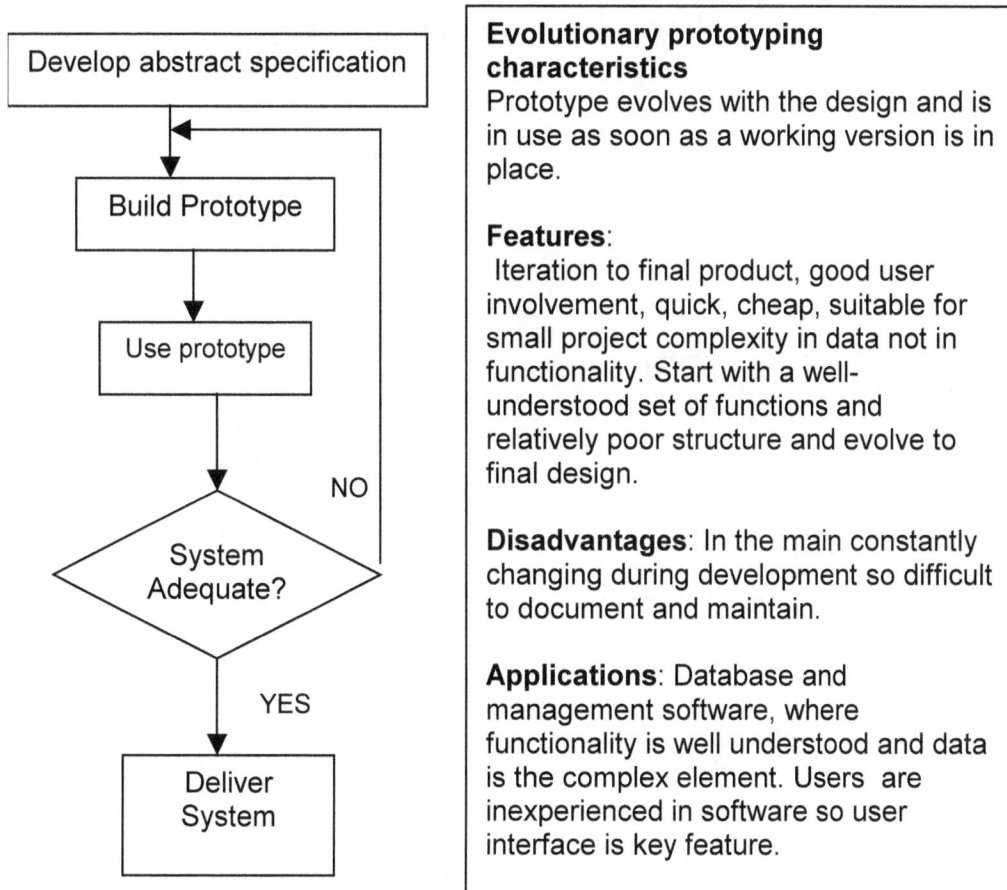

| Develop abstract specification | **Evolutionary prototyping characteristics** Prototype evolves with the design and is in use as soon as a working version is in place. |

Evolutionary prototyping characteristics

Prototype evolves with the design and is in use as soon as a working version is in place.

Features:
 Iteration to final product, good user involvement, quick, cheap, suitable for small project complexity in data not in functionality. Start with a well-understood set of functions and relatively poor structure and evolve to final design.

Disadvantages: In the main constantly changing during development so difficult to document and maintain.

Applications: Database and management software, where functionality is well understood and data is the complex element. Users are inexperienced in software so user interface is key feature.

Develop abstract specification → Build Prototype → Use prototype → System Adequate? — NO (loops back to Build Prototype) / YES → Deliver System

Figure 6.2. Evolutionary prototyping characteristics

Example

A system to monitor student access to the building shall be installed to track the students and their working behaviour. This system needs only a few operations, but must deal with a huge amount of data. The features are well defined at the beginning. A lecturer starts developing the software and tests its functionality. After having found a few bugs and missing features the prototype is improved. After all staff are satisfied with the functionality, the prototype can be put into production being release 1.0. The software evolves through a number of versions over time. Each version based on the previous.

Throw away prototypes

Throwaway or Rapid Prototyping refers to the creation of a model that will eventually be discarded rather than becoming part of the finally delivered software. The basic approach is shown in figure 6.3.

```
┌─────────────────────────────────┐     ┌──────────────────────────────┐
│  Develop abstract specification │     │ Throwaway prototyping        │
└─────────────────────────────────┘     │ characteristics              │
              │                          │ Prototype developed with     │
              ▼                          │ limited functionality in     │
      ┌─────────────────┐                │ order to enable users to use │
      │ Build Prototype │                │ it so that the requirements  │
      └─────────────────┘                │ can be established.          │
              │                          │                              │
              ▼                          │ Suitable for large projects  │
      ┌─────────────────┐                │ where functionality is not   │
      │    Evaluate     │                │ clear at the outset.         │
      │    prototype    │                │                              │
      └─────────────────┘                │ Formal development to final  │
              │                          │ product therefore good       │
              ▼                          │ structure and documentation. │
        ╱─────────────╲                  │                              │
       ╱  Satisfactory ╲                 │ Can be expensive with long   │
       ╲      ?        ╱                 │ development time.            │
        ╲─────────────╱                  │                              │
              │                          │ We start with unknown        │
              ▼                          │ components and the outcome   │
      ┌─────────────────┐                │ is a formal specification    │
      │     System      │                │                              │
      │  Specification  │                │ Main disadvantages: (Beside  │
      └─────────────────┘                │ cost)                        │
              │                          │ No consideration for non-    │
              ▼                          │ functional requirements. So  │
      ┌─────────────────┐                │ extra work needed to         │
      │ Develop software│                │ establish these.             │
      └─────────────────┘                │                              │
              │                          │ Applications: Complex        │
              ▼                          │ engineering, scientific, AI  │
      ┌─────────────────┐                │ tools, where problem domain  │
      │ Validate System │                │ is not well understood. Some │
      └─────────────────┘                │ safety critical systems,     │
              │                          │ where good performance is    │
              ▼                          │ needed for efficient and     │
        ╱─────────────╲                  │ well structured code.        │
       ╱    System     ╲                 │                              │
       ╲   Adequate?   ╱                 └──────────────────────────────┘
        ╲─────────────╱
              │
              ▼
      ┌─────────────────┐
      │ Deliver System  │
      └─────────────────┘
```

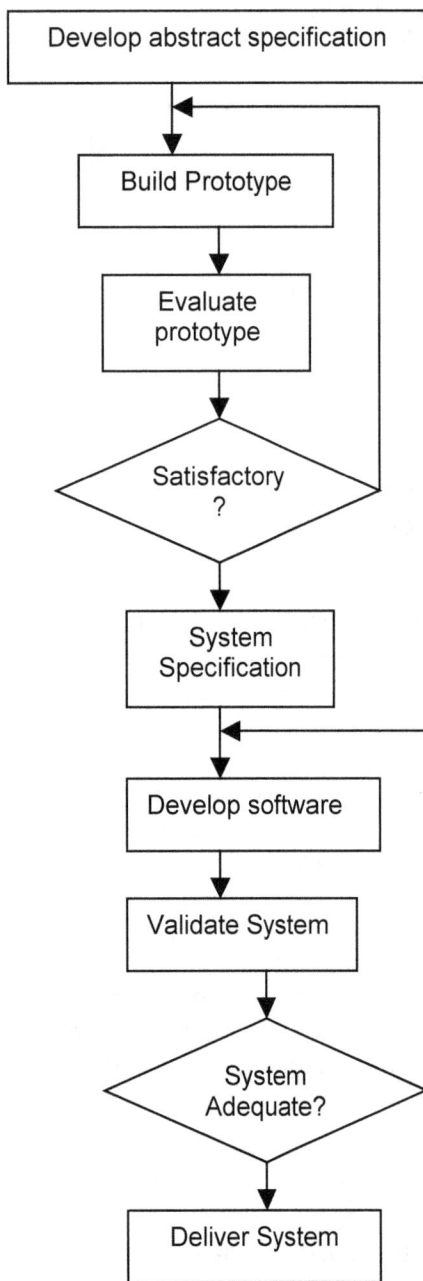

Figure 6.3. Throwaway prototyping characteristics

After preliminary requirements gathering is accomplished, a simple working model of the system is constructed to visually show the users what their requirements may look like when they are implemented into a finished system. Thus the main features of throwaway prototypes are,

- A product is designed to be used only to help the customer identify requirements for a new system
- The product cannot be implemented or even evolved into a deliverable system - only the derived requirements will be maintained, often results in tools that are unsuitable for use in production systems.

Throwaway prototyping is often used for systems with a complex functionality where the requirements are difficult to establish. Here the focus is to clarify system requirements and to provide additional information for process risk analyses. Basic features of throwaway prototyping are shown in figure 6.3.

When the prototyping is finished the throwaway prototype will be not used for any further software development. The final system is then designed from scratch by using the information gained with the throwaway prototype. This kind of prototyping can be used in large projects. The output of the prototyping phase is a formal system specification. This specification and the fact that the system is not based on the prototype leads to a good (software) structure and a clear documentation. The disadvantages may be increased development time, which can lead to higher project costs. Additionally this prototyping method does not consider non-functional requirements. These must be established separately.

Example

Student record system software shall be introduced in LSBU to help with administration. Because the current application does not offer the features required, and the staff cannot specify the requirements exactly. Students start programming a user interface with some 'dummy' data and calculations. The staff use this in order to test the functionality and eventually requests further features. This causes a new iteration of prototyping. In the end, when staff are satisfied with the features offered, a formal system specification is written and a professional software company is assigned to program a new application based on the specification made by the students. The prototype developed by the students is not used for further development. The software house delivers and installs the first version of its new software. This is validated by the staff and could if required be improved further.

Incremental development prototypes

This methodology does not need the design of any prototype. It is applicable for big databases where the structure is well known early on. The customers have to commit themselves to the main system requirements in the very beginning of the project. Once the project is started, a change to the system requirement causes a rework of all stages (requirements, design and implementation). It is also necessary that system designers commit to particular design strategies before the project is started. Basic characteristics of incremental development are shown in figure 6.4. In some ways the incremental development follows the rules of the Waterfall Model. First the customer defines the most important features of the system. These high-priority features are implemented first and delivered as the basic framework to the customer. All delivered components will not be changed again, except when errors occur. In the next increment lower priority features are developed and implemented in the framework, which is already in use or being tested by the customer. This ensures that the most important features of the system are tested most extensively and that errors in this part of the system are less likely than in lower prioritised components.

The advantage of this approach is that the customer is able to use the implemented feature and does not have to wait until the whole system is delivered. Furthermore an overall project failure is less likely because some components will have been successfully delivered to the customer during the early stages of the project.

Example

A software engineering department at a London university has decided that purchasing an off-the-shelf student record system (SRS) is too expensive and therefore they intend to build their own system. The head of department begins by consulting staff and together they produce a clear set of requirements for the SRS system. In order to make use of the system as soon as possible, the design team produces the overall system architecture and quickly implements the most urgently needed features. (i.e. Tuition fees management and adding/removing students). These features are implemented in version 1 of the software and staff begin using the system with these features. The department continues developing the system in increments and as each increment is completed it is integrated with the working prototype. Thus other features are implemented step by step until the student record system is complete.

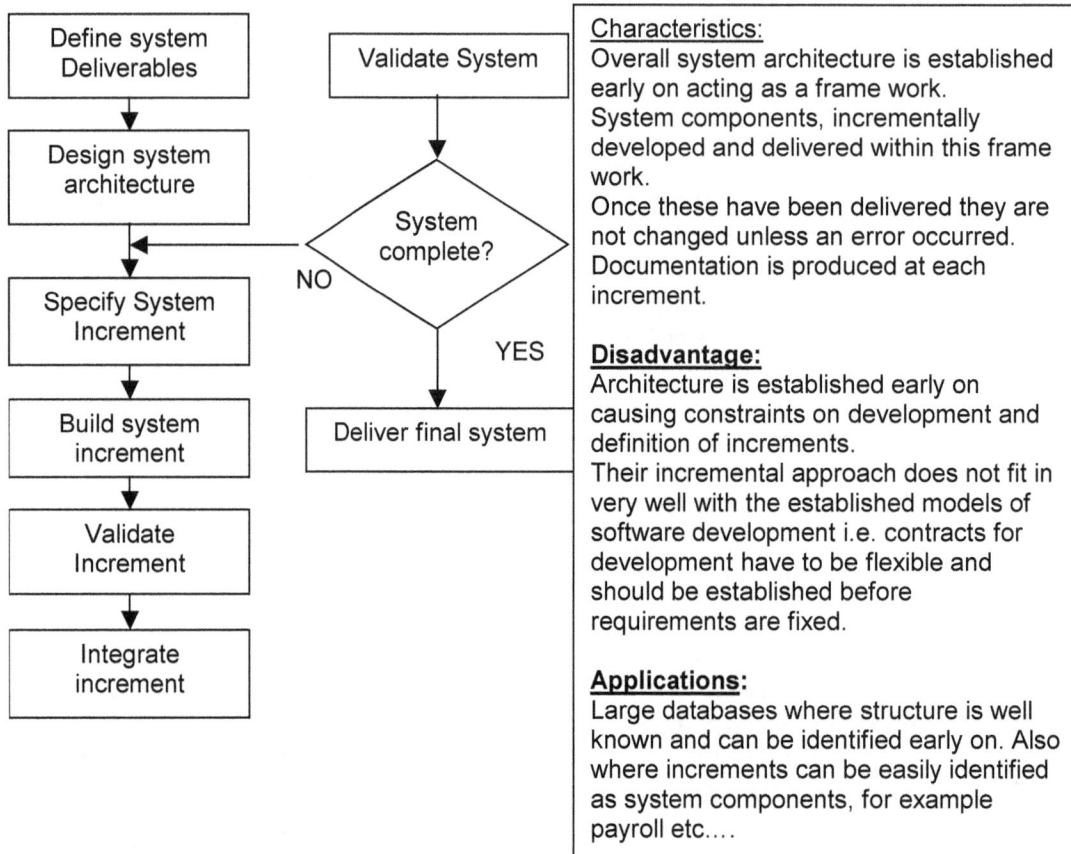

Flowchart	Characteristics:
Define system Deliverables → Design system architecture → Specify System Increment → Build system increment → Validate Increment → Integrate increment	**Characteristics:** Overall system architecture is established early on acting as a frame work. System components, incrementally developed and delivered within this frame work. Once these have been delivered they are not changed unless an error occurred. Documentation is produced at each increment.
Validate System → System complete? — NO → / YES → Deliver final system	**Disadvantage:** Architecture is established early on causing constraints on development and definition of increments. Their incremental approach does not fit in very well with the established models of software development i.e. contracts for development have to be flexible and should be established before requirements are fixed. **Applications:** Large databases where structure is well known and can be identified early on. Also where increments can be easily identified as system components, for example payroll etc....

Figure 6.4. Incremental development prototyping characteristics

6.3   Extreme programming

Extreme programming (XP) is a relatively new concept that appears to have similarity with prototyping. [42] For this reason I have chosen to include it in the chapter that deals with prototyping. It is possible that some authors may consider extreme programming to be a paradigm rather than a prototyping method, but that is not material at this stage. I am simply trying to describe an approach to software development that has appeared in the late nineties and is gaining momentum. This approach is based on upholding five values,

- Simplicity
- Communication
- Feedback
- Courage
- Respect

Simplicity and communication

By identifying these values the approach aims to give all developers a shared view of the system, which matches the view held by the users of the system. For this reason Extreme Programming relies on simple designs, common metaphors, collaboration of users and programmers, frequent verbal communication, and feedback. In this manner XP techniques can be viewed as methods for rapidly building and disseminating institutional knowledge among members of a development team. Furthermore simplicity in design and coding should in most cases improve the communication process. Which is to say that most programmers in the team will be able to understand a simple design.

In some ways XP is similar to evolutionary prototyping because it encourages starting with the simplest solution. Extra functionality can then be added later. However the difference between this approach and the evolutionary approach is that the focus on designing and coding is based on what should be done today rather than what is needed for some point in the future. It can be argued that this is a disadvantage because we are not taking into consideration future needs. However there is a school of thought, which considers that this is more than compensated for by the advantage of not investing in possible future requirements that might change before they become relevant. Which is to say that designing and coding for uncertain future requirements implies the risk of spending resources on something that might not be needed.

Feedback

Within Extreme Programming, feedback relates to different dimensions of system development:
- <u>Feedback from the system:</u> by writing unit tests, or running periodic integration tests, the programmers have direct feedback from the state of the system after implementing changes.
- <u>Feedback from the customer:</u> The functional tests (aka acceptance tests) are specified by customers and testers. From these they will get concrete feedback about the current state of their system. This review is planned once in every two or three weeks so the customer can help to steer the development.
- <u>Feedback from the team:</u> When customers come up with new requirements in the planning stage the team directly gives an estimation of the time that it will take to implement.

Feedback is also closely related to communication and simplicity. Flaws in the system are easily communicated by coding a unit test, which proves that a certain piece of code will break. Direct feedback from the system tells programmers to re-code this part. A customer is able to test the system periodically according to the functional requirements (aka user stories).

Courage

Several practices embody courage. One is the principle to always design and code for today and not for tomorrow. This is an effort to avoid getting bogged down in design and effort to implement something that is not needed at the present time. Courage enables developers to feel comfortable with re-factoring their code when necessary. This means reviewing the existing system and modifying it so that future changes can be implemented more easily. Another example of courage is knowing when to throw code away: courage to remove source code that is obsolete, no matter how much effort was used to create that source code. Also, courage means persistence: A programmer might be stuck on a complex problem for an entire day, then solve the problem quickly the next day, only if they are persistent.

Respect

The respect value is manifested in several ways. In Extreme Programming, team members respect each other because programmers should never commit changes that break compilation, make existing unit-tests fail, or that otherwise delay the work of their peers. Members respect their work by always striving for high quality and seeking for the best design for the solution at hand through re-factoring.

By adopting the four values mentioned earlier leads to respect from others in the team. Nobody on the team should feel unappreciated or ignored. This ensures high level of motivation and encourages loyalty towards the team, and the goal of the project. This value depends on the other values, and is very much oriented towards the people in a team.

Thus it is seen that XP begins with five values as given above. The principle is then extended into fourteen principles and further into twenty-four practices [43] The idea is that practices are concrete things that a team can do day-to-day, while values are the fundamental knowledge and understanding that underpins the approach. Both values and practices are needed, but there is a big gap between them - the principles help bridge that gap. Many of XP's practices are old, tried and tested techniques, yet often forgotten by many, including most planned processes.

One of the most striking practices in XP is its strong emphasis on testing. While all approaches mention testing, most do so with a pretty low emphasis. However XP puts testing at the foundation of development, with every programmer writing tests as they write their production code. The tests are integrated into a continuous integration and build process, which yields a highly stable platform for future development. XP's approach here, often described under the heading of Test Driven Development (TDD) has been influential even in places that have not adopted much else of XP.

6.4   Agile methods

This may not be a recognised prototyping technique, but it is a relatively new approach to software development where development proceeds in short time frames, and the team meets frequently face-to-face to review progress. Rather than having an unchanging specification, feedback during development can result in the goals changing. The team can quickly respond to these changes and hence the term agile-methods.

Background to agile methods

Software development methodologies have been the main driving force of software engineering for many years. All of these prescribe a disciplined process for development, which is based on sound engineering principles. The main aim of these methodologies is to make software development more predictable and more efficient. They do this by developing a detailed process with a strong emphasis on planning inspired by other engineering disciplines - which is why some refer to them as engineering methodologies (another widely used term for them is plan-driven methodologies). [43] Perhaps the most frequent criticism of these methodologies is that they are bureaucratic. Which is to say that there is so much detail in steps to follow the methodology that the pace of development slows down.

Agile methodologies were developed in reaction to these methodologies. For many people the appeal of agile methodologies is their reaction to the excessively prescriptive and detailed approach of the engineering methodologies. Agile methods attempt a useful compromise between no detail and too much detail, providing just enough detail to gain a reasonable pay-off. The result is that agile methods have some significant changes in emphasis from engineering methods. The most immediate difference is that they are less document-oriented, usually emphasising a smaller amount of documentation for a given task. In many ways they are rather code-oriented: following a notion that the key part of documentation is source code. Furthermore agile methods are distinguished by the following characteristics,

- **Adaptive rather than predictive.** Engineering methods have a tendency to plan out a large part of the software process in great detail for a long span of time, which works well until things change. Consequently their nature is to resist change. On the other hand agile methods welcome change. They try to be processes that adapt and thrive on change, even to the point of changing themselves.
- **People-oriented rather than process-oriented.** The goal of engineering methods is to define a process that will work well whoever happens to be using it. Agile methods assert that no process in itself is able to compensate for the skill of the development team. Therefore the role of a process is to support the development team in their work.

A very concise and informative article that puts XP above and agile methods into perspective would make an interesting read. [43]

6.5 Choosing a prototyping approach

From the description of the different approaches to prototyping it can be seen that different projects will suit different prototypes. When deciding which approach to adopt the software engineer needs to consider the answers to the following critical questions,

- How complex is the system to be built?
- Which critical objective of software development must be achieved by prototyping?
- How much user involvement is required during prototyping?
- Do we have a good understanding of the requirements?
- Is the prototype simply the first version of the final product?
- Is the prototype to be used only to experiment with various design alternatives?
- Are we prototyping to test the requirements specifications?
- Will the prototype use actual data and allow the user to test what-if scenarios during demonstrations?
- Will there be any possibility of evolving the prototype into the final product?

There are many other questions that could be asked but the above should be enough as a starting point. Let us consider an example next.

Example

You are a software engineer responsible to deliver a project to develop a decision support system that will enable users to translate natural language specifications into a formal software specification. Comment on the advantages and disadvantages of the following development strategies:

(a) Develop a throwaway prototype using a prototyping language such as Smalltalk. Evaluate this prototype and then review requirements. Develop the final system using C++.

(b) Develop the system from the existing requirements using Java and then modify it to adapt to any changed user requirements.

(c) Develop the system using evolutionary prototyping using a prototyping language such as Smalltalk. Modify the system according to the user's requests and deliver the modified prototype.

Solution

You may realise that the software development effort to develop a translator from natural language into formal specification is a tremendously difficult task. Reference to Chapter 4 of this text will serve to remind you of the problems in the accuracy of natural language specification. A brief description of the formal specification indicates that this is a complex system that requires much development effort. You can make your own judgement about the complexity and other issues so that you can provide the necessary arguments to support the choice of the prototype that you recommend. A possible solution is given next.

(a) Develop a throwaway prototype using a prototyping language such as Smalltalk. Evaluate this prototype and then review requirements. Develop the final system using C.

A large part of the effort to build a prototype is wasted because you cannot use the prototype at the end of the day. The prototype is only used for specifying the user requirements and get experience in the domain (for instance: testing new algorithms). After the prototyping is "finished" the programmer is experienced in solving the given problems (can solve the problems better in the real system) and the user requirements are well known.

This type of development is advisable if the effort for the prototype is less than for the whole project. This is true for large projects. The prototype will be written in a language such as Smalltalk which is object oriented (OO). These OO languages enable the programmer to create a whole system relatively quickly and with less effort, albeit that there is less quality and stability. Nevertheless the result is a prototype system that can be used to define the requirements. After the requirements are specified and all tests are done, the prototype will be thrown away and the final system will be built from scratch. Throwaway prototyping helps to reduce the risk that the whole project fails and as a result increases customer satisfaction (less changes in the delivered system are necessary).

(b) Develop the system from the existing requirements using Java and then modify it to adapt to any changed user requirements.

This resembles the quick and easy approach to prototyping. Java is a useful language for this because it is object-oriented and also virtually platform independent. A fairly good application can be developed relatively quickly and modified as the requirements change. However this approach is risky because it can lead to a lot of effort spent on implementing changes. Thus, for this approach to be appropriate, clear user requirements should be known at the beginning of development. This is because the effort, which is needed to correct a system that is based on wrong user requirements, increases very fast with the development progress. For example: If the requirements are for a motor vehicle, after a motorcycle is developed it is impossible to change it to a car without enormous effort. For this reason changes in requirements during development should be minimised as far as possible.

This development strategy is only suitable for small project such as real-time systems. In small projects the effort that is needed to build a throwaway prototype is too high/expensive in comparison with the whole project. In this particular strategy the system is a prototype written in Java, which is developed quickly and then enhanced to the required system. The effort to build a throwaway prototype can be saved by using this approach, but the quality may be less if the requirements are not well known in advance.

(c) Develop the system using evolutionary prototyping using a prototyping language such as Smalltalk. Modify the system according to the user's requests and deliver the modified prototype.

This is similar to point (b) shown above. In general it is not a good idea to deliver a product in a prototyping language. These languages are optimised to be able to build a system very fast. This possibility results lower quality (for example instability). This strategy is only suitable for demonstration purposes (or very special applications) because of the lower quality and the (special) prototyping language of the system. If the system should be delivered it must be written in the required language (not in a prototyping language).

6.6 Chapter summary

In this chapter I considered the advantages and disadvantages of prototyping. In some cases prototypes may not be necessary and could cause extra problems in project delivery. In other cases they may be an invaluable tool without which chances of success on the project would be significantly diminished. A few popular approaches to prototyping were introduced but the main emphasis was on evolutionary, throwaway and incremental development approaches. These were discussed in more detail and some examples given. Extreme programming (XP) is also presented in this chapter as an example of prototyping. It is not certain that all concerned would consider XP to be an approach to prototyping but that is how it is presented here. The last aspect covered was a brief overview of the process of selecting a prototype for a given development. This is largely dependent on the project type and some general points to consider have been given. Ultimately the development team have to use common sense and also to consider the characteristics of each prototyping approach in order to select the most appropriate for their project.

Exercises

6.1. Why is prototyping necessary in some software development projects and not in others?

6.2. What are the main advantages and disadvantages of prototyping?

6.3. Describe the prototyping process, and explain what are the alternatives to prototyping.

6.4. Describe the main types of prototype and their salient features.

6.5. What is extreme programming? Do you think that it can be considered as a prototyping approach? Explain your reasons.

6.6. You are a software engineering manager responsible for a number of software development projects in your company. You need to decide which prototyping approach to recommend for each project. It is in your interest to deliver the software on time and within budget, as well as to satisfy the client requirements for the systems that your team produces. For the following project descriptions, discuss what prototyping techniques you would suggest. State any assumptions made and explain the reasoning behind your choice.

Project 1: A knowledge-based application that will help sellers to decide to accept or reject an offer to buy products in bulk.

Your client offers discount prices for products if purchased in large quantities. Buyers can save on the product price, but they have to pay for carrying large inventories. You need to develop a computerised decision support system (DSS) that will aid the sales department in deciding whether to sell a given quantity of a given product at the offered price. This decision is based on a well-known economic order quantity (EOQ) formula, which states;

$$EOQ = \sqrt{\frac{2 \times annual\ usage \times annual\ cost}{unit\ price \times holding\ cost}}$$

Project 2: A database system is required to maintain control of records in a dental surgery.

Records for all patients are held in five carousels each having 1000 trays. A database will contain data on patient's number, last visit, next scheduled appointment and other information. This database will be used to aid searches and to prepare letters to patients.

When a patient record is required, the patient's number is entered into the database and the carousel corresponding to the record rotates to the appropriate position. When in position, the system presents the relevant tray and releases the patient's record file.

CHAPTER 7   SOFTWARE DEPENDABILITY AND RELIABILITY

7.1.   Introduction

Dependability of a system is a measure of the degree of trust that users have in the system. It reflects users confidence that the system will operate as expected and that it will not fail during normal use. In software engineering dependability focuses on user satisfaction regarding a software system. It is difficult to measure dependability of software because this is inherently a qualitative issue. For example we can say that the system is dependable because we estimate that the probability of failure on demand (POFOD) is 1 in 1000. Thus we use a metric POFOD to describe the dependability of the system. To get a measure of the metric we can perform tests and determine that out of 1000 uses of the system it failed one time. There is no absolute guarantee that the system will maintain this level of performance in the metric that we are using, but it is an indicator of dependability. In general therefore dependability is expressed in a relative metric ranging from low to ultra-dependent. Ultra-high dependable systems cannot be proved to be 100% dependable, as the costs (and effort) rise exponentially with the improvement of the dependability.

Users often reject unreliable systems, because their use does not satisfy expectations and needs of the user. Additionally low dependability can cause high costs, loosing valuable staff motivation and working time.

Example: Consider a corporate computer network servicing 1000 users across a number of offices within a building. The network is organised as a domain and the primary domain controller (PDC) looks after network access by users and computers. When the PDC of a domain is out of service and no backup BDC is installed, whole companies can be forced to a stand-still, because staff cannot log on to their computers. Consequently dependability of the whole network rests on how dependable the PDC is. If a BDC is configured in this network, the dependability of the network increases even if the dependability of the PDC does not change.

In order to put software dependability into perspective I will briefly consider a report produced by the British Computer Society (BCS). BCS, which is the Chartered Institute for IT in the UK, promotes wider social and economic progress through the advancement of information technology science and practice. In December 2006 at the Royal Society in London, BCS organised a 'Thought Leadership Debate' aimed at exploring issues surrounding the development of software and how it impacts on our everyday lives. The 45 participants were all senior people from IT suppliers, commerce, industry, the public sector and universities. The result was a short report describing the state of the industry and for those interested in software engineering this provides a very useful read. [44]

According to this report, there are still many software engineering projects that are specified using ambiguous natural language (NL) statements and vague diagrams, implemented in ill-defined programming languages with well-known and inherent weaknesses, in the hope (against all logic) that testing the resulting mess will somehow lead to a usable product. A large proportion of software engineering projects are cancelled and those that do survive are usually over budget and full of vulnerabilities. The US National Institute of Science and Technology has calculated that poor quality software costs the US economy nearly one per cent of GDP. The report considers that the software industry is reputably years behind where it should be, a fact, which often leads to unusable products.

The report further suggests that currently much of the available software only delivers a percentage of what it is supposed to. Users often put up with bugs in order to get the benefits of software, and finding themselves in a situation where they often do not know enough about the product in order to formulate a useful complaint.

While the report identifies the problems it also provides guidelines as to how this can be rectified. There are a number of recommendations and some of these will be discussed later in this text, after we consider some general aspects of dependability.

7.2.   Dimensions of dependability

In software engineering 'dependability' is not the same as having software meet the needs of users. For example, a software product could have disappointing set of features that fail to meet expectations of the users, but nevertheless it is dependable because it never does anything that could not be expected. On the other hand, in safety-critical systems, dependability is the main quality requirement over and above functionality and user satisfaction.

In the past there were a number of significant failures in software, however only those that are spectacular come to the attention of the public. Following are a few examples in the space exploration area supplied by the European Space Agency (ESA). [45]

Mariner 1 (July 1962): - Cause: omission of a hyphen in a computer instruction
Ariane 501 (June 1996): - Cause: un-handled software exception
Titan IV-B (April 1999): - incorrect parameter in the attitude control system
Mars Climate Orbiter (September 1999): - failed translation of imperial units into metric units
Mars Polar Lander- Deep Space 2 (December 1999): - Cause uncertain but the testing activity was found not adequate

Dependability covers the engineering disciplines Reliability, Availability and Maintainability. (See figure 7.1)

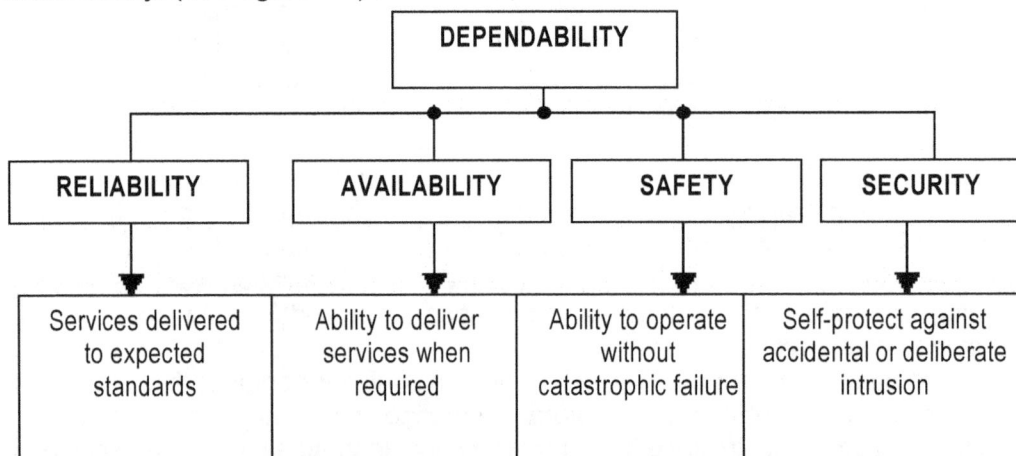

Figure 7.1. Four dimensions of dependability

Most authors refer to these as dimensions of dependability. Reliability focuses on the capability to function without interruption, Availability is the ability to operate when needed and Maintainability refers to how easy it is to repair or upgrade the product. To put this into practical context the European Space Agency (ESA) integrates the disciplines of dependability and safety covering satellites (hardware, software), as well as ground infrastructure and operations (human aspects). It encompasses many areas of expertise and scientific knowledge throughout the lifecycle phases of a space project. By integrating all these, overall measure of dependability can be obtained and this can help in risk assessment and also decisions whether a particular project is feasible under current conditions.

Space exploration is evidently a domain with many uncertainties and therefore dependability plays a significant part of any project. Nevertheless, in the more real world of software applications such as e-commerce, stock market trading, Inland Revenue Tax-returns etc. we find ourselves in a similar situation, that is we want to have dependable systems. Thus in order to quantify dependability we consider different aspects of a system within the four dimensions shown in figure 7.1. [46] Some real-world examples of these are included next. These are all form sourced from ACT Europe. [47]

Availability: Measures whether the system is able to deliver a service on request or not. For example: In 2004 there was a denial of service attack against GRC.com. It was reported that around 400 Windows 2000 servers running insecure versions of Microsoft IIS web server made a denial of service attack. The IIS was the apparent point of entry of the hacker into the system. The result as seen in figure 7.2 is a sudden drop in bandwidth down to virtually zero. [48] It took GRC 17 hours to recover from this attack, and apparently a 13-year old boy hacker, just having fun, perpetrated it.

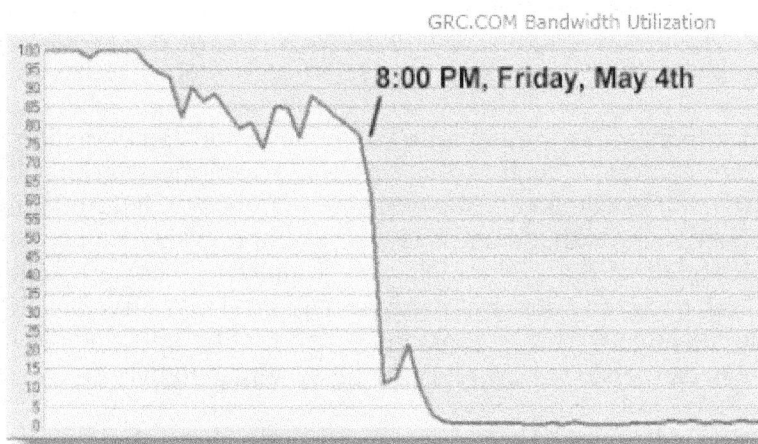

Figure 7.2. Denial of service attack

Reliability: Measures if the returned service is equivalent to the requested one (within system specification). Some examples of reliability issues are given next.

January 15, 1990: 9 hour nationwide telecom shutdown
1 month earlier ATT updated its software in 114 switching stations
• Cause: 1 misplaced "break" statement in a C program
January 2001: 230,000 units of new Internet-enabled mobile phones recalled
Users reported that their phones were freezing after accessing certain Web sites, and when they were powered back on, all stored information (addresses, e-mails, bookmarks, memos) had been lost
Matracom 6500 PABX (telephone switch)
Random phone messages are garbled, Long phone calls are cut
Windows 95/98/ME/2000 September 1997:
Propulsion system of the USS Yorktown ship failed
• Cause: Windows NT 4.0 crashed

Safety: Can using the system cause catastrophic results? Some examples of safety related failures are given next,

1986: Therac 25 radiation machine kills patients
- Cause: poor testing of the software

June 4, 1996: maiden flight of Ariane 5 failed: rocket destroyed
- Cause: Code from Ariane 4 guidance system reused in Ariane 5 but not tested. This is also discussed in Chapter 10 of this text

2000: Deadly accident in French highway
- Cause: Software malfunction in car braking system. Car manufacturer acknowledges responsibility

Security: Does the system have methods to protect it from intentional or accidental misuse? The following example shows how security can impact on dependability.

November 2, 1988 Internet Worm
A self-replicating program was accidentally released upon the Internet. This program (a worm) invaded VAX and Sun computers running versions of Berkeley UNIX, and used their resources to attack still more computers. Within hours this program had spread across the US, infecting thousands of computers and making many of them unusable due to the burden of its activity.
- Cause: undetected buffer overflow in C routine gets()

The above examples serve to show that software dependability can have a significant impact on corporations as well individual users. In the examples given above, much of the threat derives from malicious attacks on computers connected to the Internet. Additionally we often consider software in terms of the following attributes,

Maintainability: As the name implies this dimension considers how easy it is to maintain the software. Much of this has to do with the way that the product has been designed and documented. It expresses how easy it is to maintain a system in order to keep it running with the same level of dependability.

Survivability: Is the system still able to deliver its services after a failure of a component has occurred? Are the services still available after accidental misuse or after a deliberate attack? This dimension is important for security relevant systems. In some ways this can relate to how resilient the system is to failure.

7.3.   Effects of dependability

Costs

In software engineering projects it is generally accepted that costs rise exponentially when the dependability of a system is increased. [47] This is shown in figure 7.1. This is due to time and resource consuming development methods and due to the need of a longer testing and validation phase. It is further reported that company directors need to understand and appreciate the cost of outages. Which is to say that they need to know how the lack of dependability is costing their organisation. This will help them to decide how much they need to spend in order to have a dependable system. Procurement of software often focuses on cost and time scales to the detriment of dependability. More often than not, cheap software has hidden costs, for example, some have to be fixed with patches and the users have to live with the consequences. Hence, the total cost of development has to take into account the impact of failures as a result of potential short cuts made during the development process. [44]

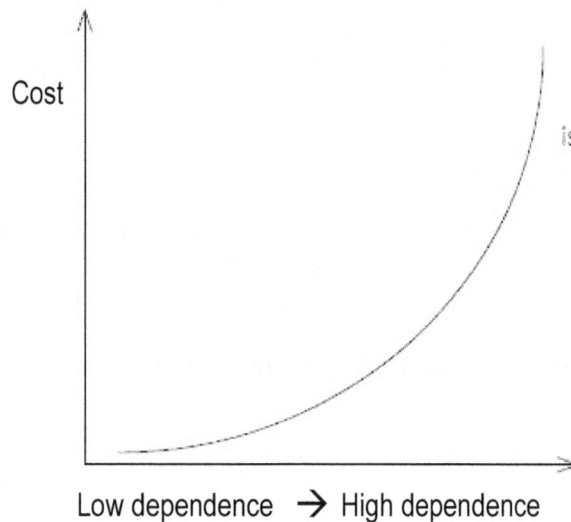

Figure 7.3. Cost Vs dependability

Performance

Performance may diminish due to system redundancies introduced in order to make a system dependable. This means that due to additional code, hard-disk drives or additional backup systems the performance of a system may fall below that of a less dependable system. However, it is difficult to implement software dependability after the system has been developed and so dependability should be considered during the early stages of development. It is also worth noting that not all users require the software they use to be dependable. Different user communities and different applications will have different thresholds of tolerance. This puts more emphasis on specifying dependability during the requirements phase of software development.

Example

An example for a dependable storage system would be a RAID based storage system with mirroring (or similar techniques). i.e. RAID levels 1, 5, 1+0.

In the case of a single HDD failure the other drives can still deliver the requested service without the loss of data. However, architecture like this requires additional storage capacities due to the fact that the data must be stored redundantly. This causes higher costs for additional drives, controllers and management.

7.4.   Failure protection

Fold avoidance: Special development methods to detect e.g. critical inputs before they cause a system fault.

Example: Sign test of input data before processing them in a system, which can only operate with positive values.

Fault detection and removal: Trying to detect and remove errors before the system is rolled out. This is done by methods of defect testing or similar methods.

Fault tolerance: The system has the possibility to detect a failure (after it has occurred) and prevent the failure causing an error. This can be done by runtime monitoring of variables.

Example: Kelvin temperature measurement, using a microcontroller. The result of any calculations or measurements must never be negative. Before any operations are made on a new measured number, a piece of code checks the carry flag. If the flag indicates that the temperature is negative a failure has occurred somewhere. Before any other operations are made, a system recovery is started to prevent a system failure. Failures might happen when the system operates with a negative temperature value. [47]

7.5. Safety and reliability

These terms are distinct but related. It is possible to have reliable systems that are unsafe. That is to say that they perform reliably to specification but the specification itself gives cause for safety concern. In general reliability and availability are necessary but not sufficient conditions for system safety. When considering safety we concern ourselves with the user and their environment.

Reliability	Safety
A measure of how well the system performs against its specification. Therefore when concerned with reliability we think of system specification.	Concerned with assuring that the system cannot cause damage to users and their environment irrespective of whether it conforms to its specification

Unsafe Reliable Systems:

Here the system is reliable but has the potential to become unsafe. For example, these can result from hardware failures generating spurious inputs. Also from context-sensitive commands; i.e. issuing the right command at the wrong time. Safety is compromised by any potentially hazardous event, which has not been identified within the specification. Thus it can be seen that safety and reliability have different impact on the system and consequently they have to be evaluated separately.

Safety Terminology

- **Accident or mishap:** An unplanned event, which results in human death or injury, damage to property or the environment. For example a computer controlled machine injuring an operator.
- **Hazard**: Is a condition with potential for causing or contributing to an accident e.g. failure of a sensor detecting an obstacle?
- **Damage**: Is a measure of the loss resulting from mishap? This can range from loss of life to minor injury.
- **Hazard probability:** The probability of events occurring which create a hazard.
- **Risk**: In very simple terms risk is measure of the probability that the system will cause an accident.

Example of reliability specifications

Functional reliability requirements

The system shall check all hard drive for bad blocks when it is initialised. A specified range for value that are input by the operator or otherwise, shall be defined and the system shall check that all the inputs fall into this pre-defined range.

Non-Functional reliability requirements

The requirement level of system reliability required should be expressed quantitatively i.e. 1 failure in 100,000 operations can be tolerated. Reliability is a dynamic system attribute and therefore we need to express the values quantitatively.

This is sometimes difficult since much of what non-functional requirements relate to is qualitative.

7.6. Reliability metrics

As previously mentioned metrics are used to provide a measure of characteristics that are qualitative. Some examples are given next.

- **Availability: (Avail)** This is a measure of the fraction of time that the system is available for use. Availability of 0.998 for example means that software is available for 998 out 1000 time units.
- **Probability Of Failure On Demand: (POFOD)** This metric is particularly useful when demands for service are intermittent and relatively infrequent. For example ABS system in a car or an air-bag system.
- **Rate Of Occurrence Of Failure: (ROCOF)** Numerical value giving an indication of the anticipated rate of failure occurrence. 0.002 means 2 failure in each, 1000 operational units. Relevant for operating systems, transaction-processing system where the system has to process a large number of similar requests which are relatively frequent.
- **Mean Time To Failure: (MTTF)** Measure of time between observed failures of the system. MTTF of 500 means that there are 500 units of time between failures.

These example metrics serve to show that it is possible to quantify aspects that relate to system reliability. It is possible to design and build highly reliable systems, but this comes at a cost, both in terms of development effort and system performance. Thus metrics can be used to make decisions on what levels of performance is to be expected from a system.

Failure classification

Failure is a very broad term and the impact on the system of any particular type of failure can vary. It is therefore useful to classify the types of failure that can occur in a system. Some of these are,

- **Transient:** This occurs at inputs that are within a certain range and at a particular time. (i.e. not occurring all the time)
- **Permanent**: This occurs with all inputs, all the time.
- **Recoverable:** Can be removed by the system without intervention.
- **Unrecoverable:** Operator intervention needed before we can recover from failure.
- **Non-corrupting:** failure does not corrupt system state or data.
- **Corrupting:** failure corrupts all data.

Example:

Question: Explain why ensuring system reliability is not a guarantee of system safety.

Solution:

System reliability and system safety are often related to each other but cover very different aspects of software development. System reliability is concerned with ensuring that a piece of software operates according to the specification and in a manner that is acceptable to the user. Software that has errors resulting in short term glitches, errors due to extreme conditions, or due to events that occur rarely, could be considered to be reliable as long as the errors did not result in program termination and the errors were not apparent to the user. Clearly if such software was used in a safety-critical situation where large sums of money were at stake (i.e. stock-market software) or people's lives were placed at risk then this would not be considered to be a safe implementation of the specification.

An example of a reliable system might be database software that passes information about a bank account balance across the Internet to be displayed on a customer's computer screen. If for example, the data received by the user was incomplete then the browser software could request for the information that is missing to be sent again. In this case the user would suffer a minor delay while the information is resent without the user being aware of what was going on. As long as the customer using the system received the correct information about their bank balance in say 90% of the time they tried to access this information they would consider the software to be reliable.

If on the other hand the software was responsible for transferring money electronically from one bank to another, the system would not be considered safe if part of the electronic data was lost and instead of £1000 appearing at the destination only £100 pounds appeared while the full amount was removed from the account at the transmitting end. Clearly if such a software based system had errors that resulted in 10% of customers transactions losing customers money it would be considered to be unsafe and an unsatisfactory implementation of the specification.

Safety is particularly important when the end result of errors is not the loss of money but the loss of life. For example, a software system could be designed for an airplane that was reliable and did not produce any errors throughout its working life, which could lead to major failures of the aircraft. If the only weakness of the software were that it would fail in the event of a lightening strike to the plane then we need to consider the likelihood of failure. On the one hand it could be expected for a software system to fail in such environmental conditions and at the same time this would be so rare as to be considered an act of God. On the other hand airplanes often fly through thunderstorms and are struck by lighting and it would not be acceptable to the industry if this resulted in just one aircraft falling out of the sky resulting in loss of life. Such a system is clearly not a safe system in the eyes of the user due to the severity of the failure and the damage the publicity of such an event would have on the aircraft company. Thus the safety argument needs to take into account the consequences of failure and to what extent these could be considered acceptable.

System reliability differs from system safety in that a system can be considered reliable as long as it does what the specifications says it should do and it will do this in a predictable manner for most of the time. System safety is not just concerned with the specification but also takes into account a much wider domain including failures in hardware, human error, and events outside the scope of the specification that can result in serious risk to human life, the environment or the loss of large sums of money. System safety is dependent on the users perception of what is safe and not the fact that the system is reliable and will do what it should do in most circumstances. What the purchaser of the system wants to know is that the software system will never do anything that could have serious repercussions in terms of cost of life or money.

For these reasons systems that are safety critical tend to incur much higher development costs as they have to be tested thoroughly and usually include redundancy in both the hardware and software so that a backup system can take over in the event of the primary system failure. Designers of safety critical system tend to include intelligent self-checking systems that can identify errors in the system long before they result in failure and take corrective action to avoid such failures.

7.7. Hazard and Risk Analysis

In all safety critical systems we need a method of analysing the risk and hazard that can lead to failure. Figure 7.4 shows the basic procedure for hazard risk analysis.

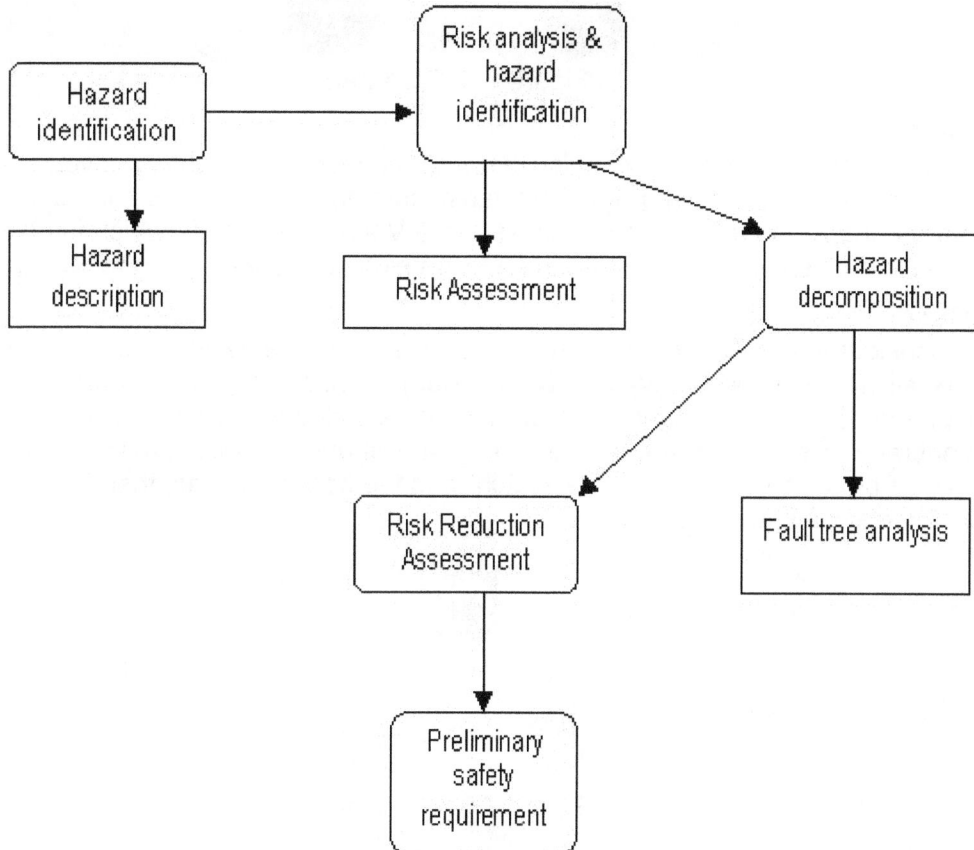

Figure 7.4. Hazard and risk analysis procedures

Fault-tree analysis

This is a method of hazard analysis, which begins with an identified fault and works backwards to the cause. It is a top down analysis method. However it can be modified to include bottom up methods to provide more accurate assessment.

A fault tree diagram follows a top-down structure and represents a graphical model of the pathways within a system that can lead to a failure. The pathways interconnect contributory events and conditions using standard logic symbols (AND, OR, etc.). The principle is quite straightforward since conditions that can lead to a fault are known in advance. Fault tree diagrams consist of gates and events connected with lines. The AND and OR gates are the two most commonly used gates in a fault tree. To illustrate the use of these gates, consider two events (called "input events") that can lead to another event (called the "output event"). If the occurrence of either input event causes the output event to occur, then these input events are connected using an OR gate. Alternatively, if both input events must occur in order for the output event to occur, then they are connected by an AND gate. Figure 7.5 shows a simple fault tree diagram in which either A or B must occur in order for the output event to occur. In this diagram, the two events are connected to an OR gate. If the output event is system failure and the two input events are component failures, then this fault tree indicates that the failure of A or B causes the system to fail. [49]

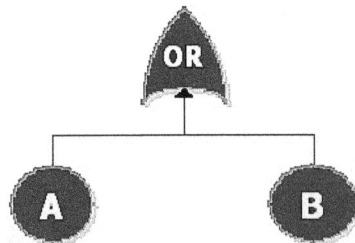
Figure 7.5. Fault tree

Basic Gates

Gates are the logic symbols that interconnect contributory events and conditions in a fault tree diagram. The most commonly used gates in fault tree analysis are the AND and OR gates, as well as a Voting OR gate in which the output event occurs if a certain number of the input events occur (i.e. k-out-of-n redundancy).

AND Gate

Consider a system with two components A and B. The system fails only if both A and B fail. This is shown in figure 7.6. For example, assume that you park your car on a slope and you put the handbrake on and you also leave the car in a low gear. If the handbrake fails the fact that the car is in gear will prevent it from rolling down the slope. But if both the gear system (i.e. clutch) and the handbrake fail, then the car will roll down the slope causing damage.

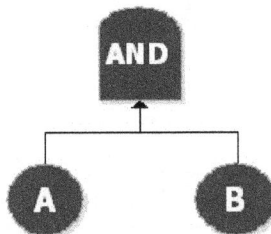
Figure 7.6 AND Gate

Voting OR Gate

In a voting OR gate, the output event occurs if one or more of the input events occur. In system reliability terms, this implies that if any k-out-of-n components fail (input) then the system will fail (output). Consider a fault tree diagram with a 2-out-of-4 Voting OR gate, as shown in Figure 7.7. In this diagram, the system will fail if any two of the blocks below fail.

In this configuration, the system will not fail if three out of four components are operating, but will fail if more than one fails. In other words, the fault tree looks at k-out-of-n failures for the system failure.

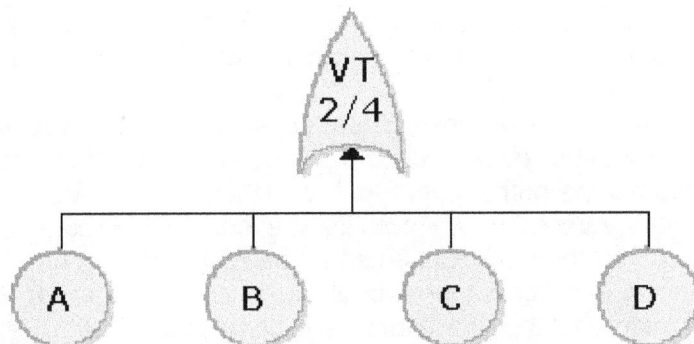
Figure 7.7. Voting OR gate

For example, in any one academic year a graduate student can be referred in up to 3 out of 8 units. If they fail more than 3 units, then they cannot be referred and have to repeat the year. It does not matter which units are failed, it is only the number of these that determines the outcome. In this case a 3/8 voting OR gate would be used to represent the system.

Combining Basic Gates

Fault tree analysis gates can be combined to create more complex representations. As an example, consider the fault tree diagram shown in Figure 7.8.

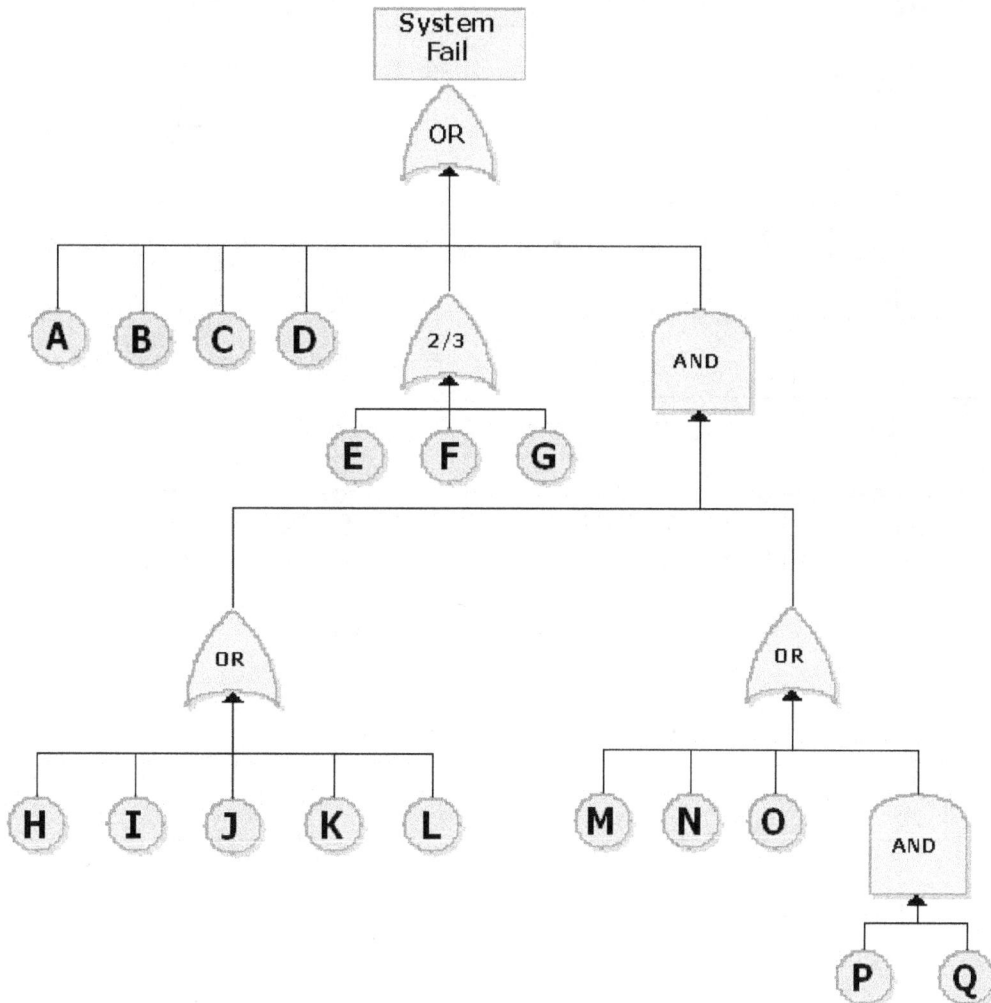

Figure 7.8. More complex fault-tree diagram

With reference to figure 7.8 we can analyse the conditions that can lead to failure. Thus if we start at the top of the tree we can see that the system will fail if any of the events A,B,C or D occurs. Furthermore, it will fail if 2/3 events E,F,G occur. Also it will fail if both inputs to the AND gate occur. That is to say if any of the events H,I,J,K,L occur at the same time as M,N,O or when P and Q occur at the same time. Clearly the worded explanation is quite complicated and the diagram provides a clearer view of events that can cause a fault. Typically fault trees are used to identify where additional measures are needed in order to prevent the occurrence of a fault.

Discussion of Basic Gates and Events

A fault tree diagram is always drawn in a top-down manner and with lowest item being a basic event block. Classical fault tree gates have no properties (i.e. they cannot fail). The fault tree indicates the different reasons, why a system might not perform the way specified. Example: Fault tree of a calculator is shown in figure 7.9.

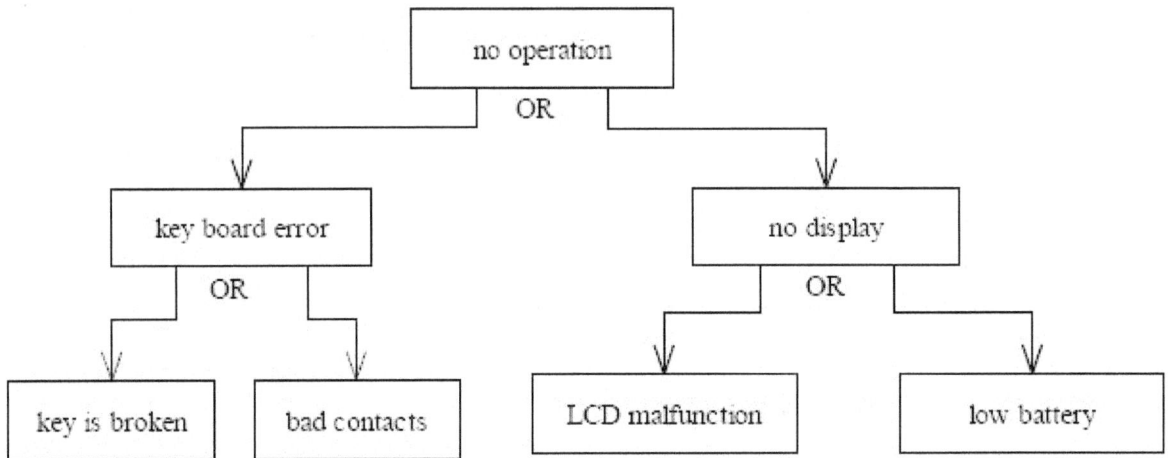

Figure 7.9. Fault tree analysis example

An example of hazard analysis using a fault tree is shown in figure 7.10. Here the hazard labelled "deleted data" is at the top of the tree and all the branches leading up to it are analysed. An example of fault tree analysis is presented next.

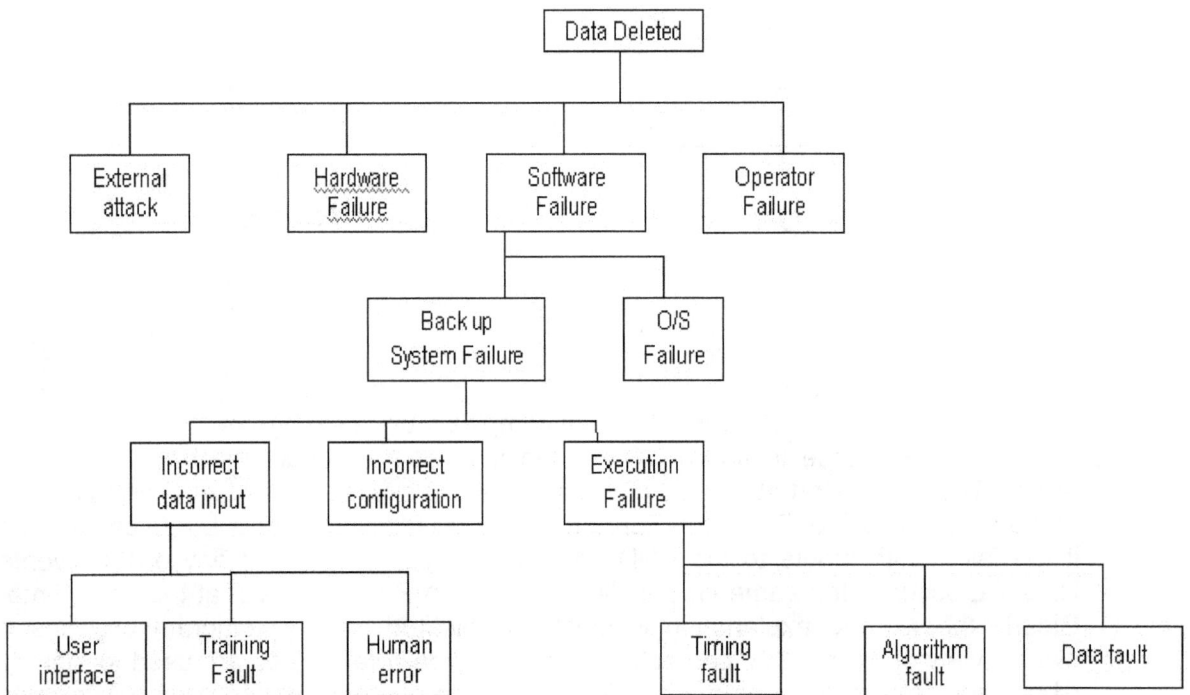

Figure 7.10. Hazard analysis

Example

A program design language (PDL) specification, of one component of a safety critical system is shown below. Here the system in question has radioactive components, which are considered a health hazard. This code identifies three conditions that can potentially lead to a hazard. The hazard occurs when the following conditions occur: the radiation level exceeds danger level and the radiation shield is not in place. By analysing the code listing and using fault tree analysis, develop a safety argument to determine that this code is potentially unsafe.

Figure (a) Question	Figure (b)Labels for the paths in the solution
| ```
{
      shieldStatus=Shield.getStatus();
      radiationLevel=RadSensor.get()

      if (radiationLevel<dangerLevel)
            state=safe;
      else
            state=unsafe;
      if (shieldStatus=Shield.inPlace())
            state=safe;
      if (state=safe)
            {
            Door.locked=false;
            Door.unlock();
            }
      else
      {
            Door.lock();
            Door.locked:=true;

      }
}
``` | ```
{
            shieldStatus = Shield.getStatus ( );
            radationLevel = RadSensor.get ( );
(1a)    if (radiationLevel < dangerLevel)
                 state = safe;
(1b)    else
                 state = unsafe;
(2)     if (shieldStatus == Shield.inPlace ( ) )
                 state = safe;
(3)     if (state == safe)
                 {
                 Door.locked = false;
                 Door.unlock ( );
                 }
           else
           {
                 Door.lock ( );
                 Door.locked = true;

           }
}
``` |

Figure 7.11. Hazard analysis question

Solution:

Stepping through the above PDL the program first considers the shield status and radiation level. The first test is for radiation level and a safe state is reached if this is below critical. Otherwise the state is unsafe. So far the program seems fine. Next consideration is given to shield position. If the shield is in place the state is safe. Notice that this happens after the result of the radiation level check. At this point the condition is tested if the `state =safe`. The status of `door.locked` is set to false and door is unlocked. Now, what the program is saying here is that if the state is safe, we can unlock the door and enter. Otherwise (else branch) we lock the door and no entry is possible.

The potential hazard should be relatively evident at the shield-status check stage. Here no action is specified if the shield is not in place. Thus the program must be modified to include an else statement declaring the system as unsafe if the shield is not in place.

Safety argument

A safety argument is a way of demonstrating that a program meets its safety obligations. The proof of a safety argument is not in proving that a program meets its specification but is instead in proving that the program execution cannot result in an unsafe state.

To do this we first assume that an unsafe state can be reached and we identify all the pre-conditions that can lead to this. Next we analyse the code in order to show that pre-conditions are contradicted by the post-conditions of all program paths leading to that state. Here the post-conditions are given in the code. If these conditions are met then the previous assumption of an unsafe state is incorrect. If this is repeated for all paths in the program then the software can be found to be safe. Conversely, if the post-conditions do not counter the pre-conditions, the system is shown to be unsafe.

Consider figure 7.11 as an example of a fault-tree for the system in question. From the initial specification and a quick step through the coding we can determine that the safety clause that leads to failure is as follows,

*(**Shields are not in place** AND **Radiation level > Danger value** AND **state is safe**)*

This is implied by the use of the variable state, which is either safe or unsafe. The pre-condition for the unsafe state is when the above clause is true. If we can demonstrate by analysing the code that the above clause cannot be true in any event then we have a valid safety argument. To do this we need to step through the software code and determine the paths that lead to the above clause. Thus we need to demonstrate that all program paths shown in figure 7.11 lead to a contradiction of this unsafe assertion. If this is true then the unsafe conditions cannot be true and the system is therefore safe.

In the program shown in figure 7.11 there are four paths that lead to IF statement 3, which decides if the door should be opened or closed, based on the pre-conditions. The four paths as unrealistic as they seem are as follows,

Path 1. The THEN branch of statement 1 is executed followed by the THEN branch of statement 2, which is executed. Code labels (1a)True-(2)True-(3)False

Path 2. The THEN branch of statement 1 is executed followed by NO result from statement 2, because it does not have an else statement. Code labels (1a)True-(2)False-(3)True

Path 3. The ELSE branch of statement 1 is executed followed by the THEN branch of statement 2, which is overwrites the state to safe. Code labels (1a)False-(2)True-(3)True

Path 4. The ELSE branch of statement 1 is executed followed by NO execution of statement 2, because it does not have an else statement. The therefore the state remains unsafe from (1b). Code labels (1a)False-(2)False-(3)False

By analysing the paths we can determine if the system is safe. Figure 7.11 indicates a fault tree diagram for this situation. According to the rules of contradiction it would appear that the system is safe since each path has a contradiction when compared with the safety clause above. In other words all paths lead to post-conditions that contradict the pre-conditions for the opening of the door.

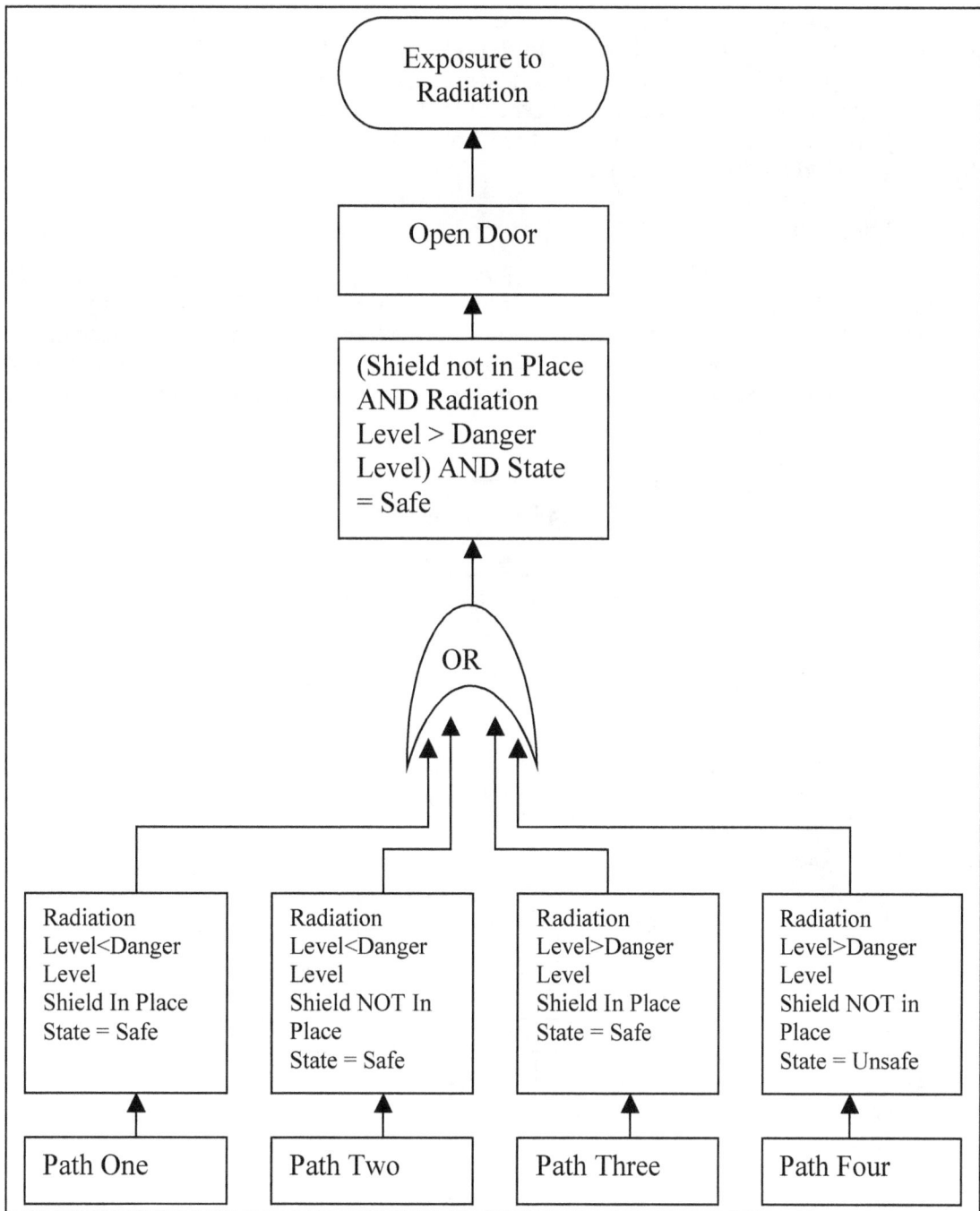

Figure 7.11. Fault-tree diagram for the example problem

Thus analysing the paths for contradiction is as follows,

- Path 1 has a post condition *"RadiationLevel<DangerLevel"* which contradicts the pre condition clause above.
- Path 2 has a post condition *"RadiationLevel<DangerLevel"* which contradicts the pre condition clause above.
- Path 3 has a post condition *"ShieldInPlace"* which contradicts the pre condition clause above.
- Path 4 has a post condition *"State=Unsafe"* which contradicts the pre condition clause above.

Thus it is demonstrated that each of the four paths is safe. The only area in the program where some ambiguity could be found is in the statement which checks if the shield is in place. This should really include a statement that says that the state is unsafe if the shield is not in place. In other words an Else statement is missing after label (2). This condition would indicate that the shield is not in place and consequently the state should be changed to unsafe.

Safety lifecycle

The safety lifecycle can be described as a sequence of phases as shown in figure 7.12. These phases cover design and development of safety features within a system, and at the end also describe how the system should be decommissioned. The basic concept in building software safety, i.e. safety features in software, is that safety characteristics and behaviour of the software and system must be specified and designed into the system.

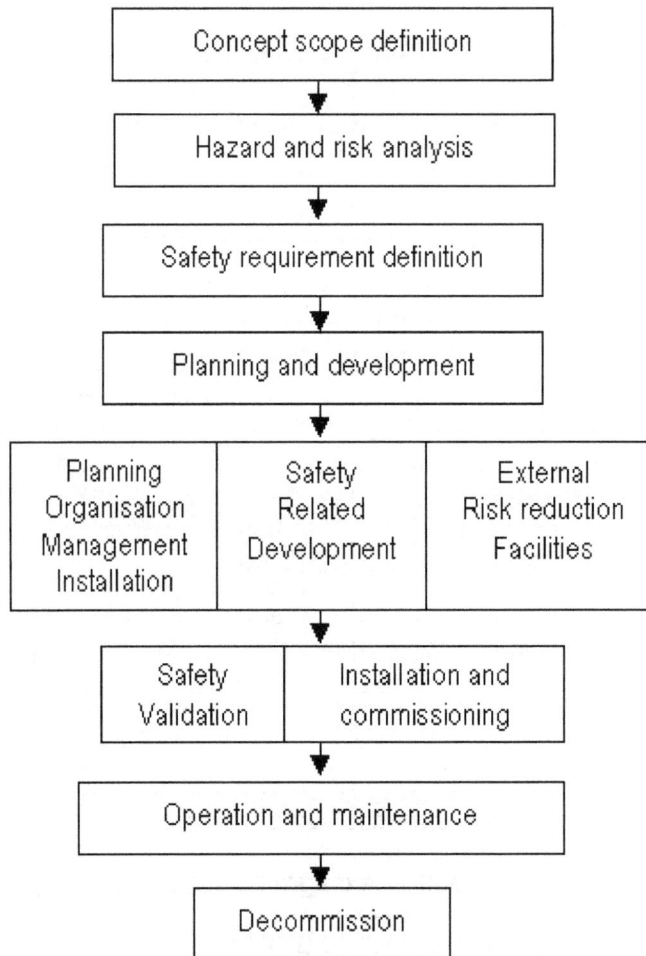

Figure 7.12. Safety lifecycle

The challenge for any systems designer lies in reducing the risk to an acceptable level and of course, the risk that can be tolerated will vary between applications. When a software application is to be used in a safety-critical system, then this must be taken into account at all stages in the software lifecycle.

The process of safety specification and assurance throughout the development and operational phases of a project is sometimes called the 'safety lifecycle'. The first stages of this lifecycle involve assessing the potential system hazards and estimating the risk that they pose. One method of doing this is fault tree analysis as presented in the previous section. (i.e. describe a clause for a fault to occur and prove by contradiction that the software will not allow that clause to be True).

Risk assessment

Assess the severity and probability of a hazard and also the probability that should a hazard occur, it will cause an accident. When designing safety critical systems we identify functional and non-functional requirements in the same way that we do for non-safety-critical systems. However we also determine more precisely the safety requirements. We use these to define error-checking and system-recovery features that are required in order to make the system safe. The results are used to assess safety implications and risk. Thus software project managers need to use risk-based assessment, which also take into account human factors. It is very important that appropriate teams carry out risk assessment. For example, in their analysis [44] BCS report that in some cases the wrong people carry out risk assessments. It is suggested that software designers must use a risk based analysis approach to their development work. Some participants thought that managers should probably use availability rather than reliability as a measure of software success. In other words a single very long outage may be worse than several very short outages. There is a real need to understand and agree with the client what the priorities are. Thus it seems that risk assessment concerns everyone involved in a safety-critical project.

The outcome of risk assessment is a statement of acceptability. Which is to say to what extent can we live with the risk of using the system. Figure 7.13 shows that the various levels of risk range from unacceptable (top) to increasing levels of acceptability (bottom). This figure shows an inverted triangle whose area represents the number of systems that fall within a category. At the top of the figure risk is not tolerated and down the figure the tolerance to risk progressively increases.

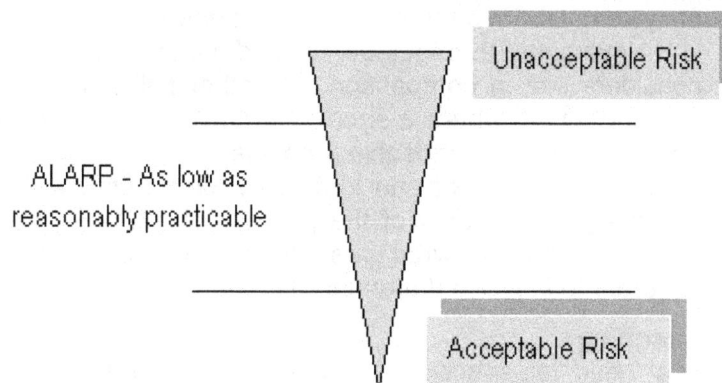

ALARP - As low as
reasonably practicable

Unacceptable Risk

Acceptable Risk

Figure 7.13. Risk of a hazard

Safety-critical systems are characterised by strict safety requirements and so figure 7.13 shows that a large number of these fall into the unacceptable risk category. (i.e. Top-part of down pointing triangle in figure 7.13). Making systems absolutely safe (i.e. risk-free) can lead to them not being functionally useful. For example, you can have a computer system that is risk-free of virus infection, but it would have no Internet connection and no external drives. Thus a compromise is required that minimises risk and maintains good functionality. Consequently the levels delimited by two horizontal lines in figure 7.13 describe the category ALARP. The majority of systems fall into this category. Perhaps it is expected in safety-critical systems that the lowest number of systems fall into acceptable risk systems, as shown in the bottom part of figure 7.13. The definition of risk in figure 7.13 is as follows,

Unacceptable (Intolerable): must never arise or result in an accident.

As low as reasonably practicable (ALARP): must minimise probability of hazard given cost and schedule constraints.

Acceptable: Consequences of hazard are acceptable and no extra cost should be incurred to reduce risk.

7.8.   Design recommendations for dependability

Referring once more to the a report produced by the British Computer Society [44] resulting from the 'Thought Leadership Debate' that was organised by BSC and which aimed at exploring issues surrounding the development of software and how it impacts on our everyday lives. I have to say that I found this article to be a very interesting read. It was prepared in 2006 and judging by the changes in the software marketplace it may be considered almost outdated, but some issues remain relevant and I thought of producing a modified version of the paper in this text. The following is my summary of their considerations regarding dependability.

The paper reports that many software engineering projects get cancelled and that most of those that do survive are over-budget and full of bugs. The US National Institute of Science and Technology has calculated that poor quality software costs the US economy nearly one per cent of GDP. Note however that the paper does not however consider the consequences of NOT developing software and the impact that this would have on GDP. Nevertheless, even though progress cannot be halted the consequences are that on average 1 in 3 software projects fail to complete, for example,

- US Internal Revenue Service Modernisation: US$4 Billion, dropped in early 1997.
- FBI Fingerprint system: US$500 million, project dropped.
- Bell Atlantic 411: November 1996, outage, backed out of upgrade.

The paper considers that in comparison with other fields of engineering, the software industry is years behind where it should be on the dependability issue. For this reason many projects still lead to unusable products.

The report further considers that due to its very nature software development does not readily enable a physical view of the process at the start; hence the end result frequently does not agree with what was intended. In their view, the following actions are needed in order to improve dependability,

Specification and planning

There is a real need for specifications and requirements to be agreed and documented before any software is developed. There is often a gap between customer expectations and actual deliverables. This could be minimised by having common base-specifications for software to ensure a certain level of dependability. Complacency, particularly with lack of planning, leads to increased costs, many of which are hidden.

Improved documentation is needed particularly in risk assessments, which should be done before software development begins. Smaller projects tend to be more successful than larger ones because these involve fewer people and so communication is better. One participant suggested that when a project becomes 'too big to fit in one person's head' That is when problems start to happen and failure becomes inevitable. For this reason documentation and planning have to be done meticulously.

Risk assessments

The approach to risk management must be formally introduced by managers so that it comes in early in the development process. It is hoped that software designers would adopt a risk-analysis approach to their development work but this is frequently not the case, with many opting to use availability (up–time) as a decisive factor rather than reliability. In some case this may be correct assessment of risk but in general there is a real need to understand and agree with the client what the priorities are so that appropriate levels of risk can be specified.

The appropriate model of software development

There was also some discussion of different models of software development. The 'waterfall model', for instance, requires a very formal process of defining the requirements and establishing the process of development, then implementing this step by step and often in a modular fashion. Problems can arise near the end of this process in integrating the modules together, testing the system and tracking down the bugs. Furthermore, there is often a missing link between policy-making and project decision-making, which can lead to considerable problems for the business.

Recently there have been trends towards interactive models of development, and so-called 'agile methods', in which the development is done in short time frames, and the team, meets frequently face-to-face to review progress. Thus, instead of having an unchanging specification, feedback during development can result in the goals changing and this is quite acceptable. (See Chapter 6)

The best language

It is suggested in the report that industry needs to go back to programming basics, with everyone utilising one language throughout. Good programmers will always write good code but as a result of an increase in the number of software engineering projects there is a growing shortage of skilled programmers. It would seem that industry trains its IT workers to use C++ or Java, however many participants believed that Praxis SPARK Ada is better.

In my own view Ada is a very elegant language and in many ways I can understand why a group of 45 selected experts in software would prefer it to C++ or Java. However not many universities teach Ada as do Java and C++ and therefore the marketplace is more abundant with Java and C++ trained programmers than those with Ada skills. Consequently, it is cheaper for software development companies to develop in C++ than in Ada. As a result there is never a real incentive to change the programming language to one, which might actually be better for the job in hand. Additionally there is often considerable pressure from software vendors to follow one popular route without considering what other options there might actually be. For example, Windows O/S is developed mainly in C++, consider that it would take for the Microsoft Corporation to change over to Ada? It is likely that using Ada would result in a better product but at what cost? Also, consider what the competition may be doing while Microsoft is re-developing the system in Ada?

Avoiding issues with Internet integration

A worrying trend, which was highlighted, is the movement to integrate software with the Internet, which by its very nature is an intrinsically anarchic environment, and one which seems to encourage software failure. In fact software development is becoming more of an issue as connectivity increases.

Unexpected developments are occurring as systems are connected where designers are unable to accurately predict the outcome of increased connectivity. For example interconnectivity could result in new properties being required of the system. This in turn can have significant impact on resources for the development. With a greater degree of interconnectivity no software is an island and asymmetry leads to greater design challenges. (i.e. small system connecting to a large system such as the Internet). In these systems security is a growing problem, with the only fool-proof way to avoid certain forms of contamination to run one PC completely separate from the Internet and have another connected online. Secure systems should, therefore, perhaps not connect to the Internet for safety reasons.

Less emphasis on cost

The report recommends that developers need to put more value on dependability of the system that they are developing. Although cost is important it should not be the only consideration, which often provides only a short-term benefit. Developing software on-the-cheap has hidden costs, for example, some systems have to be fixed with patches and users have to live with the consequences of updates. Hence, the total cost of development has to take into account the impact of failures as a result of potential shortcuts made during the development process. Change, however, will not happen unless costs are understood, whether they are hidden or otherwise.

Competence of users

It is estimated that the majority of projects fail because the users are not suitably trained. Or putting it in other words, because the systems engineering is inadequate for the user that it is designed to support. In fact the competence of the user is often over-looked and when the system fails blame is set in the designer who might have actually produced good software, which has been used incorrectly. However, focus on developing appropriate user interface as well as usability testing with talk-aloud protocols, could perhaps reveal problems at an earlier stage of development.

Briefly to clarify, a talk-aloud protocol is based on the simple idea that to get at someone's thought processes while they solve a problem, you get that person to talk aloud what they are thinking, which means to say everything that comes into their head, as they solve a problem. This assumes that as someone solves a problem, they retain a small amount of information (7 plus or minus items) in a volatile memory store, their Short Term Memory (STM). The validity of protocol analysis rests on the assumption that if you can get at the contents of someone's STM as they solve a problem, you learn a significant amount about their problem solving process. [50] Consequently, you can use this information to develop the software around the competence of the users.

Software designers treating customers fairly

As for customers, they often do not read the small print frequently enough, which they should do in order to make a judgement on risk. For example the risk of buying or ordering a product that is not exactly as required. It is also reported in the paper that software designers have a habit of influencing customers in the direction they want them to go, leaving people feeling manipulated and 'locked in' to a process. In the field of consumer-purchased mass-market software, it was noted that the software vendors' terms and conditions routinely deny that the user has any rights, and state that no warranty is expressed or implied. The implication here is that designers are not responsible for their product. It was thought by some participants that designers should be encouraged to use systems engineering tools so that their confidence in the product can be improved. Additionally everyone agreed that software should have more rigorous certification, whatever it might be used for.

Encourage professionalism

It was suggested that since parts of the civil service have no real idea about the nature of programming they are encouraging developers to move in the wrong direction and until we have more informed decisions made at the highest levels nothing significant will change. For example, government needs to encourage a more professional approach towards their commissioning of software projects by creating a framework, which will help to generate and maintain quality of the project. It was widely thought that industry knows what needs to be done but is averse to any change, which might inconvenience or add extra cost.

Questioning attitude

In software engineering it is important for designers to question systems as they are being developed and ask of themselves 'why' and 'what' might happen if they proceed down a particular path before they allow their system to connect to the Internet. They should also be asking themselves more frequently why they are doing what they are doing and for what reason as the requirements of the system and business will probably be constantly changing. Different countries have a different approach to software development. It was noted that India, for example, will supply as required, to the letter of the specifications originally sent, whereas Serbia will continue to ask questions throughout the development process, constantly asking for reasons why the project is headed in a particular direction. Note that outsourcing itself can create extra risks if not managed correctly, for example, we can lose control of safety properties when development is outsourced; hence a proper service model is important. In my own view this aspect is paramount. The minute that I lose control of any phase in software development of my product is the time that my confidence in my ability to market and support it begins to diminish. Thus, I would have to have a very close association with the outsourcing provision.

Feedback to individuals

As to whether professionalism and certification of individual practitioners would help to improve software quality, there was generally scepticism. Such schemes could make people victims of the narrow framework of whatever was considered to be important and flavour-of-the-month. And furthermore it is not clear who could be trusted to devise the syllabus? Several felt that a model based on feedback and reputation was more appropriate to the software industry.

One radical proposal put forward by a number of those at the debate was to set up a system whereby feedback on software would come from the developer's own peer group, creating a similar rating system to that seen on eBay such that a reputation system exists allowing people to read feedback on various developers and their products. It was suggested that BCS itself could host such a site as an independent organisation.

Certifications of companies

Others thought that the issue is not the professionalism and certification of individuals, but of the companies that undertake software development; mention was made of CMM, the Capability Maturity Model Methodology for refining the software development processes of an organisation, pioneered by the Software Engineering Institute at Carnegie Mellon University, Pittsburgh. Briefly, this approach provides for five levels of capability, and in Europe most organisations reach CMMI Level 3. It was said that CMM Level 5 is reached only by some organisations in the USA, Japan and India. To clarify, The Capability Maturity Model is an organisational model that describes 5 evolutionary stages (levels) in which an organisation manages its processes. The thought behind the Capability Maturity Model is that an organisation should be able to absorb and carry its software applications.

The model also provides specific steps and activities to get from one level to the next. The 5 stages of the Capability Maturity Model are:

1. **Initial** (processes are ad-hoc, chaotic, or actually few processes are defined)
2. **Repeatable** (basic processes are established and there is a level of discipline to attach to these processes)
3. **Defined** (all processes are defined, documented, standardised and integrated)
4. **Managed** (processes are measured by collecting detailed data on the processes and their quality)
5. **Optimising** (continuous process improvement is adopted and in place by quantitative feedback and from piloting new ideas ands technologies)

The Capability Maturity Model is useful not only for software development, but also for describing evolutionary levels of organisations in general and in order to describe the level of Value Based Management that an organisation has realised or is aiming for. [51]

Success stories

Games software has excellent specifications in comparison to most software used by businesses. Many developers could learn a lot from the games industry, which seems to have better standards and delivers more bug-free code. Ultimately, if a game gets a reputation for crashing the company which developed it can go bust. Nevertheless, there are many software systems that have been produced and do work well, for example software that runs chemical plants, pharmaceutical equipment, manufacture, finance applications etc. In fact there are many systems, which are sufficiently reliable most of the time and therefore are not flagged up as a problem. Disasters are frequently caused by human error or mechanical failure and not by software, as is often reported. Successes like the Oyster card system and London's congestion charging system are often overlooked and there is a need to celebrate these successes more, which organisations such as the BCS are endeavouring to do. [52]

7.9. Chapter summary

Dependability is a qualitative feature and so it is difficult to measure. When describing dependability many authors consider that it spans across a number of dimensions. In this chapter I cover the dimensions of dependability and provide a few examples of projects that failed as a result of a failing in these dimensions. The effects of implementing dependability are considered briefly and aspects such as failure and safety are considered. Reliability is a significant component of dependable systems and I briefly mention reliability metrics as a means of attempting to quantify it. Risk is a major factor and this is particularly important in safety-critical systems. I briefly consider hazard and safety analysis using fault-tree approach. This is not exhaustive, and should serve as a guide to explain the principles of application of the approach. In this chapter I also paraphrase a publication from BCS that reports on discussions concerning issues in software engineering that emerged when they hosted their event namely the 'Thought Leadership Debate' that was aimed at exploring issues surrounding the development of software and how it impacts on our everyday lives. The event was on 12 December 2006 at the Royal Society in London.

Exercises

7.1. Explain what you understand by the term dependable system.

7.2. Perform a literature survey to find out some system failures that were caused by software malfunction and try to consider what, if any impact dependability had in these cases.

7.3. Using examples as appropriate describe the four dimensions of dependability.

7.4. Imagine that you are the network administrator for a medium size corporation. You have the responsibility to ensure that the network of your corporation is working properly at all times. In terms of the dimensions of dependability given in Q7.3 classify the following failures and explain why you consider them to be in the selected category and also try to explain the possible effects of these failures.

7.5. For the following faults describe their relationship with the 4 dimensions of dependability. Also briefly explain what action could be taken to prevent them in the future.

    I) A domain controller on a corporate network was attacked externally by a denial of service attack from 20 servers on the Internet. The result was a complete loss of bandwidth on the network for 10 hours.

    II) A faulty network interface card on a local machine caused a significant drop in bandwidth by continually broadcasting on the network.

    III) A local PC on the network, which had a virus, infected a subnet. The router on the subnet was suitably configured to prevent the virus spreading beyond the subnet. The result was a 5-hour loss of subnet while machines were disinfected.

7.6. A program design language (PDL) specification, of one component of a safety critical system is shown below.

	This code identifies three conditions that can potentially lead to a hazard.

<pre>{
    shieldStatus=Shield.getStatus();
    radiationLevel=RadSensor.get()
 	
    if (radiationLevel<dangerLevel)
        state=safe;
    else
        state=unsafe;
    if (shieldStatus=Shield.inPlace())
        state=safe;
    if (state=safe)
        {
        Door.locked=false;
        Door.unlock();
        }
    else
    {
        Door.lock();
        Door.locked:=true;
    }
}</pre>
	i) The hazard occurs when the door is unlocked
	ii) the radiation level exceeds danger level
	iii) the shield is not in place
	
	Each of these in its own right is an unsafe condition, while a combination of these will lead to a hazard.
	
	You may make your own assumptions about the degree to which the system is potentially unsafe in each case.

By analysing the code listing and using fault tree analysis, develop a safety argument to determine that this code is potentially unsafe. Modify the code provided to make it safe

7.7. Discuss the implication of cost on dependability. How much are we prepared to pay to have dependable systems?

7.8. How would you go about including maintainability and survivability into your software development process? What impact do you think these will have on the overall dependability? Try to provide examples to justify your reasoning.

7.9. You are in charge of a major project to develop a system for monitoring student access to laboratories in a major London university. What dependability measures would you propose and why?

7.10. Describe the means that software project managers have at their disposal to provide fault protection.

7.11. Discuss safety and reliability and distinguish between the two giving suitable examples of each.

7.12. Describe the significance of hazard analysis in terms of overall system dependability.

7.13. What is fault-tree analysis? Provide examples to explain.

CHAPTER 8   SAFETY-CRITICAL SYSTEMS

8.1.   Introduction

Safety-critical systems are those systems whose mal-function can lead to fatal consequences such as injury to persons and possible loss of life. A significant number of software-based systems are used in areas where the overall system is considered to be safety critical. Consider for example a trip computer in a modern car. These computers enable the driver to set the driving parameters so that the car maintains a certain speed automatically, that is without driver involvement. The driver can over-ride this feature at any time, but while it is active, the speed of the car is under the control of the on-board computer. What happens if this on-board computer decides to malfunction, and the speed begins to increase out of control? On top of that, what happens if there is a fault in the system and this prevents the driver from over-riding the computer control? This situation may be a good scenario for a horror movie. Certainly, a car, which is out of control in this way, is a danger to persons inside as well as to anyone else on the same road at the same time. Could this happen in reality? Well the answer is probably not, because all cars that have this capability also have a built-in safe mode. This means that systems are made to be fail-safe, that is if the system fails, the car is safe. Nevertheless, I have to say that I had a car with such a computer on-board, it was not new when I bought it and guess what, I never dared to use the trip-computer option.

There are many other more obvious examples where safety is critical. All aircraft control systems whether on the airplane or on the ground, directing take-off and landing are safety critical. Looking at Heathrow airport for example, in 2007, there were 481,000 aircraft movements. These movements involved 68,066,028 passengers. Each landing or each take off is regarded as one movement. Therefore, for each day of 2007 there was an average of 1318 movements. This represents 659 landings and 659 take offs per day on average. Broken down even further this equates to 55 movements per hour or, almost one movement per minute all day and every day. This also equates to approximately 130 passengers taking off or landing every minute.

It goes without saying that systems, which are used to control take-offs and landings at Heathrow airport, are safety-critical. The design and development of these systems demands extra precautions with regard to safety. However this often comes at the expense of functionality. The safest aircraft would be those that never fly but this defeats the objective of aircraft. This means that safety has to take into account the element of risk. By introducing risk into systems design we can provide a degree of safety, which satisfies the acceptable level of risk. Thus safety-critical systems rely to a large extent on hazard and risk analysis. Some of these were covered briefly in chapter 7 of this text but we shall have another look at these from the safety-critical point of view.

8.2.   Hazard and Risk Analysis in safety-critical systems

In all safety critical systems we need a method to accurately identify the hazards that can lead to failure as well as a method of analysing the risk that a failure will occur. Hazard analysis is the process used to identify unacceptable risks and to select methods for eliminating them.

A hazard is defined in the Federal Aviation Administration document 'FAA Order 8040.4' [53] as a "Condition, event, or circumstance that could lead to or contribute to an unplanned or undesirable event." It is rare that a single hazard will cause an accident. More often, an accident occurs as the result of a sequence of causes. A hazard analysis will consider system state, for example operating environment, as well as failures or malfunctions.

As mentioned earlier, in most real situations a certain degree of risk must be accepted. Typically risk is assessed by combining the severity of consequence with the likelihood of occurrence. Risks that fall into the "unacceptable" category (e.g., high severity and high probability) must be controlled by some means so that they can be reduced. For example, in hazard analysis of airborne systems, when software is involved, the development of that software is often governed by standards documented in DO-178B, Software Considerations in Airborne Systems and Equipment Certification. [54] The failure conditions are categorised by their effects on the aircraft, crew, and passengers. These are,

- **Catastrophic** - Failure may cause a crash.
- **Hazardous** - Failure has a large negative impact on safety or performance, or reduces the ability of the crew to operate the aircraft due to physical distress or a higher workload, or causes serious or fatal injuries among the passengers.
- **Major** - Failure is significant, but has a lesser impact than a Hazardous failure (for example, leads to passenger discomfort rather than injuries).
- **Minor** - Failure is noticeable, but has a lesser impact than a Major failure (for example, causing passenger inconvenience or a routine flight plan change).
- **No Effect** - Failure has no impact on safety, aircraft operation, or crew workload.

In other safety critical systems alternative criteria are used, but in general the idea to safeguard the safety of individuals is a common feature in all standards. Some standard methodologies that are designed to identify potential failure modes for a product or process are the Failure Mode and Effects Analysis (FMEA) and Failure Modes, Effects and Criticality Analysis (FMECA). These are briefly covered next.

8.3.   Failure mode and effects analysis

A Failure mode and effects analysis (FMEA) is a procedure for analysing potential failure modes within a system. It is also used to classify these failure modes according to their severity or to determine the effect of the failure upon the system. It is widely used in the manufacturing industries in various phases of the product lifecycle. Causes of failure are considered to be any errors or defects in, process, design, or item, especially ones that affect the customer. Effects analysis refers to studying the consequences of those failures. [55]

History
The FMEA process was originally developed by the US military in 1949 to classify failures "according to their impact on mission success and personnel/equipment safety". FMEA has since been used on the 1960s Apollo space missions. In the 1980s it was used by the Ford Motor Company to reduce risks after one model of car, the Pinto, suffered a design flaw that failed to prevent the fuel tank from rupturing in a crash, leading to the possibility of the vehicle catching fire. There are two complementary types of FMEA called CONSTRUCTIONAL FMEA and PROCESS FMEA. The constructional FMEA is applied during the starting phase of product development to ensure that while planning and designing a product, foreseeable failures, their consequences, and correctional measures have been taken into consideration. The Process FMEA is applied during planning of product

manufacturing process to anticipate failures inherent to production technology and to production management. [56]

Basic terminology

Failure Mode and Effects Analysis (FMEA) and Failure Modes, Effects and Criticality Analysis (FMECA) are methodologies designed to identify potential failure modes for a product or process. They are also used to assess the risk associated with those failure modes, to rank the issues in terms of importance and to identify and carry out corrective actions to address the most serious concerns.

Although the purpose, terminology and other details can vary according to type (e.g. Process FMEA, Design FMEA, etc.), the basic methodology is similar for all. Following are definitions of the general terminology,

- **Failure mode:** The manner by which a failure is observed; it generally describes the way the failure occurs.
- **Failure effect:** The immediate consequences a failure has on the operation, function or functionality, or status of some item
- **Local effect:** The failure effect as it applies to the item under analysis.
- **Indenture levels:** An identifier for item complexity. Complexity increases, as the levels get closer to one. For example. The lowest indenture level is a single item and the highest level is the complete system.
- **Next higher-level effect:** The failure effect as it applies at the next higher indenture level.
- **End effect:** The failure effect at the highest indenture level or total system.
- **Failure cause:** Defects in design, process, quality, or item application, which are the underlying cause of the failure or which initiate a process that leads to failure.
- **Severity**: The consequences of a failure mode. Severity considers the worst potential consequence of a failure, determined by the degree of injury, property damage, or system damage that could ultimately occur.

8.4.   FMEA / FMECA Overview

In general, FMEA / FMECA requires the identification of the following basic information: [57]

- Item(s)
- Function(s)
- Failure(s)
- Effect(s) of Failure
- Cause(s) of Failure
- Current Control(s)
- Recommended Action(s)
- Plus other relevant details

Most analyses of this type also include some method to assess the risk associated with analysis and the two most common methods include:

- Risk Priority Numbers (RPNs)
- Criticality Analysis (FMEA with Criticality Analysis = FMECA)

Published Standards and Guidelines

There are a number of published guidelines and standards for the requirements and recommended reporting format of FMEAs and FMECAs. Some of the main published standards for this type of analysis include SAE J1739, AIAG FMEA-3 and MIL-STD-1629A. [58] In addition, many industries and companies have developed their own procedures to meet the specific requirements of their products/processes.

Basic analysis procedure for FMEA or FMECA

The basic steps for performing an FMEA/FMECA analysis include:
- Assemble the team.
- Establish the ground rules.
- Gather and review relevant information.
- Identify the items or processes to be analysed.
- Identify the functions, failures, effects, causes and controls for each item or process to be analysed.
- Evaluate the risk associated with the issues identified by the analysis.
- Prioritise and assign corrective actions.
- Perform corrective actions and re-evaluate risk.
- Distribute, review and update the analysis, as appropriate.

8.5.   Risk evaluation methods

A typical FMEA incorporates some method to evaluate the risk associated with the potential problems identified through the analysis. The two most common methods, *Risk Priority Numbers* and *Criticality Analysis*, are described next.

Risk priority numbers

To use the Risk Priority Number (RPN) method to assess risk, the analysis team must:
- Rate the severity of each effect of failure.
- Rate the likelihood of occurrence for each cause of failure.
- Rate the likelihood of prior detection for each cause of failure (i.e. the likelihood of detecting the problem before it reaches the end user or customer).
- Calculate the RPN by obtaining the product of the three ratings:

RPN = Severity x Occurrence x Detection

The RPN can then be used to compare issues within the analysis and to prioritise problems for corrective action.

Criticality analysis of risk

The MIL-STD-1629A document describes two types of criticality analysis: quantitative and qualitative. To use the quantitative criticality analysis method, the analysis team must:
- Define the reliability/unreliability for each item, at a given operating time.
- Identify the portion of the items unreliability that can be attributed to each potential failure mode.
- Rate the probability of loss (or severity) that will result from each failure mode that may occur.
- Calculate the criticality for each potential failure mode by obtaining the product of the three factors:

Mode Criticality = Item Unreliability x Mode Ratio of Unreliability x Probability of Loss
- Calculate the criticality for each item by obtaining the sum of the criticalities for each failure mode that has been identified for the item.

Item Criticality = SUM of Mode Criticalities

To use the qualitative criticality analysis method to evaluate risk and prioritise corrective actions, the analysis team must:
- Rate the severity of the potential effects of failure.

- Rate the likelihood of occurrence for each potential failure mode.
- Compare failure modes via a Criticality Matrix, which identifies severity on the horizontal axis and occurrence on the vertical axis.

8.6. Applications and benefits

The FMEA/FMECA analysis procedure is a tool that has been adapted in many different ways for many different purposes. It can contribute to improved designs for products and processes, resulting in higher reliability, better quality, increased safety, enhanced customer satisfaction and reduced costs. The tool can also be used to establish and optimise maintenance plans for repairable systems and/or contribute to control plans and other quality assurance procedures. It provides a knowledge-base of failure mode and corrective action information that can be used as a resource in future troubleshooting efforts and as a training tool for new engineers.

8.7. FMEA concept in software lifecycle management

The concept of FMEA, can be utilised to improve the reliability of the software production process resulting in higher product quality as well as in higher productivity. However there are some subtle differences between the production of software and the classical engineering production line where FEMA concepts were first applied.

In modern software production a software designer also needs to be a software developer, and vice versa, as against clearly distinct roles of e.g. product engineer, plant engineer and assembly plant worker in other kinds of industrial production. Thus modification is needed to the FMEA team in software production. Modification is also required in the workflow. In software projects it is not practicable to treat constructional FMEA and process FMEA as two tasks to be performed sequentially at different stages of the production. This is because the production of software is inherently different to the conventional manufacturing process in engineering. In software projects the main FMEA tasks to be performed by the team are the identification of:

1. The structure of the software product in terms of its subsystems, functions, external and internal interfaces and interdependencies;
2. The possible failure modes of the product and their causes;
3. The effects of the failures including calculation of gravity factors;
4. Possible measures to prevent and/or correct the failures;
5. Test plans to detect such failures during the software development phases;
6. Metric for the evaluation of the FMEA results.

Thus FMEA and FMEAC methodologies can be used in software engineering projects. However it is also necessary to have the existence of a working software lifecycle-process model. There are at least three aspects of FMEA leading to improvement in product quality. These are as follows,

- **Definition of a system model**: The task of defining a hierarchical model of all system functions, which is very often neglected or not done properly in software projects. This helps all members of the FMEA team to have a clear understanding of the user requirements.
- **Identification of potential failure modes**: This core task of FMEA performed at an early phase of the lifecycle helps to identify inadequate transformation of user requirements to system functions (design flaw), and also potential inadequacies during implementation of the functions (implementation flaw).
- **Bringing cohesion into the process** Making expert developers and testers work, as a team from the beginning of a project, pooling and documenting their

expertise systematically, is perhaps the chief success factor of FMEA, and definitely a very effective way of practicing preventive quality assurance. Additionally there are also at least three aspects of FMEA contributing to improvement in productivity by reducing production costs and improving of delivery times. These are as follows,

• **Effective realisation of preventive quality assurance:** The best way to reduce production cost and shorten delivery time is to prevent failures by using the method of "fore-checking". This means checking the system according to a procedure that involves the analysis of anticipated failure modes.

• **Defining corrective actions on a priority basis**; by using the RPN assessment method, the available resources (man-power, budget and time) can be suitably allocated to deal with issues.

• **Coordination of test planning with system design**: By coordinated planning of correctional actions and test cases before implementation, the effectiveness of testing can be enhanced. (See testing effectiveness assessment in Chapter 9)

8.8.   Hazard and Operability studies (HAZOP)

This is an alternative method to FMEA that was initially developed by ICI during the 1960s to analyse chemical process systems, but has later been extended to other types of systems and also to complex operations and to software systems. HAZOP is a qualitative technique based on guidewords and is carried out by a multi-disciplinary team during a set of meetings.

Trends in computer control cause modern plant to be increasingly more complex, and this means that traditional review approaches are likely to miss some critical points, which need to be considered at the design stage of a project. [59] HAZOPs are structured critical examinations of plant or processes, undertaken by an experienced team of company staff in order to identify all possible deviations from an intended design. A HAZOPs study process involves applying in a systematic way all relevant keyword combinations to the plant in question in an effort to uncover potential problems. The results are recorded in columnar format under the following headings:

• **Deviation:** The keyword combination being applied (e.g. Flow/No).

• **Cause:** Potential causes which would result in the deviation occurring. (e.g. "Strainer S1 blockage due to impurities in Dosing Tank T1" might be a cause of Flow/No).

• **Consequence:** This includes the consequences, which would arise, from the effect of the deviation (e.g. "Loss of pressure results in incomplete separation in V1"). And consequences from the cause itself (e.g. "Cavitation in Pump P1, with possible damage if prolonged").

• **Safeguards:** Any existing protective devices, which either prevent the cause or safeguard against the adverse consequences, would be recorded in this column. For example, you may consider recording "Local pressure gauge in discharge from pump might indicate problem was arising".

• **Action:** Where a credible cause results in a negative consequence, it must be decided whether some action should be taken. If it is deemed that the protective measures are adequate, then no action need be taken.

From the flow diagram of figure 8.1 it can be seen that HAZOPs it is very much an iterative process, applying in a structured and systematic way the relevant keyword combinations in order to identify potential problems.

```
                 ┌─────────────────────────────┐
                 │  Select a section of the plant │◄──────────┐
                 └─────────────────────────────┘           │
                               │                            │
                               ▼                            │
          ┌──────────────────────────────────────┐     ┌──────┐
     ┌───▶│ Have all relevant Primary Keywords for │────▶│ Yes  │
     │    │ this plant section been considered?    │     └──────┘
     │    └──────────────────────────────────────┘
     │                         │
     │                      ┌──────┐
     │                      │  No  │
     │                      └──────┘
     │                         ▼
     │    ┌──────────────────────────────────────┐
     │    │ Select a Primary Keyword not previously│
     │    │ considered (e.g. Pressure)             │
     │    └──────────────────────────────────────┘
     │                         │
  ┌──────┐                     ▼
  │ Yes  │◄───┌──────────────────────────────────────┐
  └──────┘    │ Have all relevant Secondary Keywords for│◄──────┐
              │ this Primary Keyword been considered?    │       │
              └──────────────────────────────────────┘       │
                               │                                │
                            ┌──────┐                            │
                            │  No  │                            │
                            └──────┘                            │
                               ▼                                │
              ┌──────────────────────────────────────┐       │
              │ Select a relevant Secondary Keyword not│       │
              │ previously considered (e.g. More)      │       │
              └──────────────────────────────────────┘       │
                               │                                │
                               ▼                                │
              ┌──────────────────────────────────────┐  ┌──────┐
              │ Are there any Causes for this deviation not│─▶│  No  │
              │ previously discussed and recorded?     │  └──────┘
              └──────────────────────────────────────┘
                               │
                            ┌──────┐
                            │ Yes  │
                            └──────┘
                               ▼
              ┌──────────────────────────────────────┐
              │         Record the new Cause            │
              └──────────────────────────────────────┘
                               │
                               ▼
              ┌──────────────────────────────────────┐  ┌──────┐
              │ Are associated consequences of any     │─▶│  No  │
              │ significance?                          │  └──────┘
              └──────────────────────────────────────┘
                               │
                            ┌──────┐
                            │ Yes  │
                            └──────┘
                               ▼
              ┌──────────────────────────────────────┐
              │       Record the Consequence/s          │
              └──────────────────────────────────────┘
                               │
                               ▼
              ┌──────────────────────────────────────┐
              │     Record any Safeguards identified    │
              └──────────────────────────────────────┘
                               │
                               ▼
              ┌──────────────────────────────────────┐  ┌──────┐
              │ Having regard to the Consequences and   │─▶│  No  │
              │ Safeguards, is an Action necessary?     │  └──────┘
              └──────────────────────────────────────┘
                               │
                            ┌──────┐
                            │ Yes  │
                            └──────┘
                               ▼
              ┌──────────────────────────────────────┐
              │        Record the agreed Action         │
              └──────────────────────────────────────┘
```

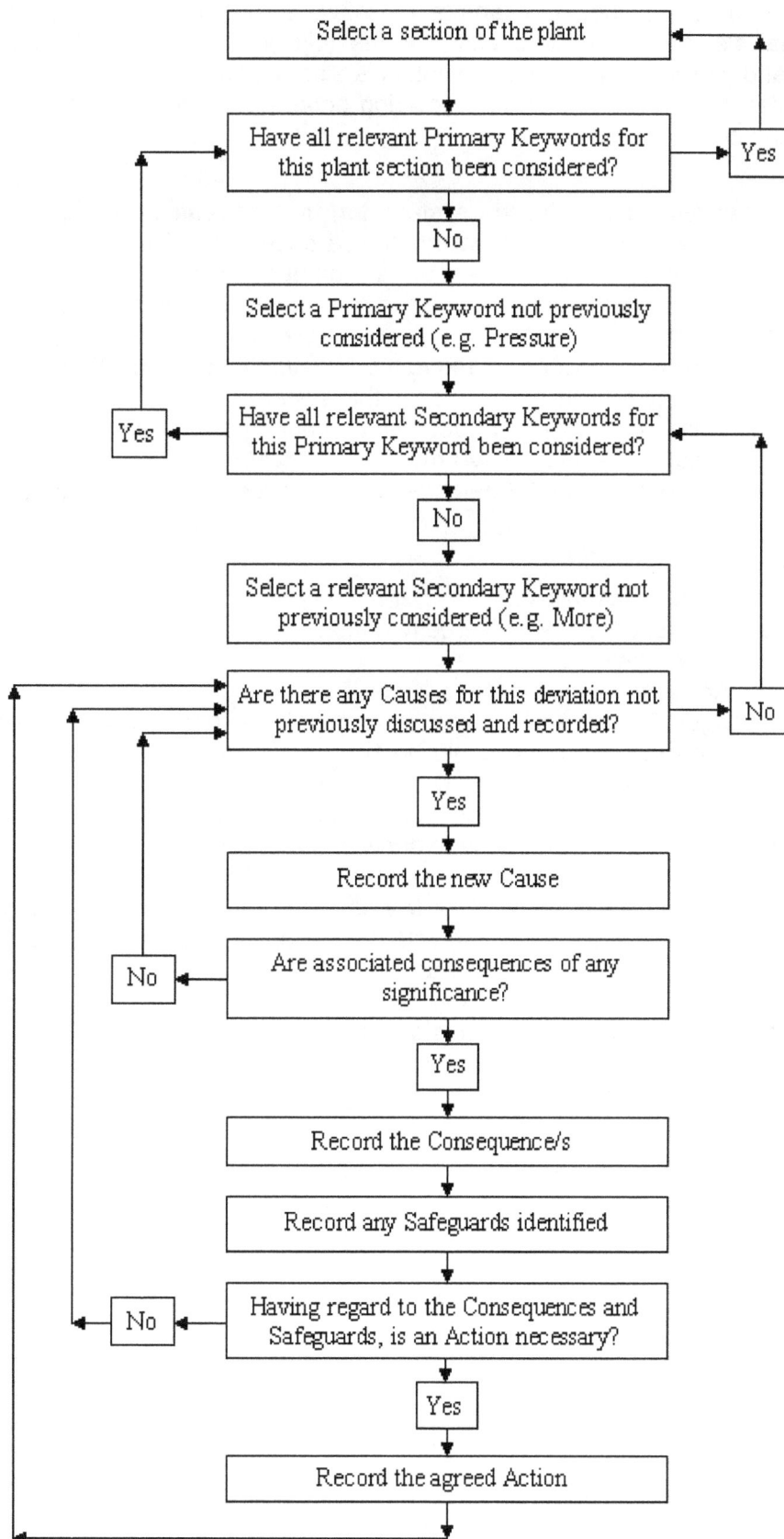

Figure 8.1. HAZOP flow diagram [60]

155

In order to provide an example in software engineering discipline of how hazard analysis may take place consider the following example. The example is simplified and you will notice that my solution is also not as thorough as it would need to be. Please note that I am simply providing some guidance as to how you could approach the problem.

Example

In a safety-critical software system for treating cancer patients, a linear accelerator machine is used to deliver controlled doses of radiation to tumour sites. The complete process is controlled by an embedded software system, which accesses a database to obtain details of the treatment given to each patient. The software ensures that the treatment requirements, which have been entered in this database, are automatically downloaded to the radiation therapy machine.

i) Identify three hazards that may arise in this system.
ii) For each hazard, suggest a defensive requirement, which will reduce the probability that these hazards will result in an accident.
iii) Explain why your suggested defence is likely to reduce the risk associated with the hazard.

Possible solution

Three hazards could be as follows,

      a) Incorrect dosage delivered to patient
      b) System misuse
      c) Accidental exposure to radiation

Incorrect dosage: To prevent incorrect dosages from incorrect calibration of the machine an electronic service log could be kept that ensures that maintenance and calibration tests are carried out regularly on the machine to ensure correct operation. The log could prevent the operator from using the machine until maintenance personnel have entered a unique code to show that the work has been carried out.

To make sure that the dosage was being administered to the correct site the system could provide visual feedback of the position of the radiation head in relation to the patient. This could be combined with the patient's records details to check for the correct positioning of the radiation source.

System abuse/misuse: Reasons for this could be:

- · Unauthorised access to patients details
- · Unauthorised operation of radiation machine
- · Opening of machinery to expose radiation source

Solutions to this problem could be:

Access to patient records and machine control system can only be accomplished by entering a user name and password. Machine has could also have a key operated switch that deactivates the system and the key is only provided to authorised personnel.

Security screws and keys could be used for all casing around radiation sources and safety critical systems to prevent unauthorised access to the internal workings of the machine. This could be complimented by an alarm activation system that sounds an alarm if the casing is opened without prior authorisation. Notification of any unauthorised access to the system could be provided via a computer screen to any personnel when they log onto the system.

Accidental exposure to radiation

Reasons for this occurring could be

- · Personnel being in the room when the radiation source is activated
- · Leakage of the radiation source from the machine
- · Exposure to source when carrying out maintenance

- · Exposure to contaminated materials

Solutions to this problem could be:

Audible and visual warnings could be used in the room to indicate that the radiation source has been turned on. The operators could wear protective clothing when working in the room where the radiation source is present. Radiation level indicators could be worn by personnel and meters placed in the room to indicate radiation levels within the room. Strict guidelines should be implemented for personnel responsible for maintenance of the machine to prevent exposure to radiation sources. Radiation sources should be mechanically protected to prevent leakage of the source outside of the machine. All materials that have been exposed to radiation should be disposed off according to guidelines on handling of contaminated waste materials.

8.9. Chapter summary

In this chapter I consider the implications in software development for safety-critical systems. Hazard and risk analysis constitute a major aspect of these types of systems and I provide a brief outline of hazard classification and failure mode analysis. Failure mode analysis tools such as Failure Mode and Effects Analysis (FMEA) and Failure Modes, Effects and Criticality Analysis (FMECA) are presented briefly. These tools were originally designed for the process industry and can be modified for use in software engineering. I provide some guidelines on the modifications that are required in this case. These methods are also used to assess the risk associated with failure modes and I offer a brief description of risk priority numbers and criticality analysis as a way off assessing risk. HAZOP is another method of hazard analysis that was first used in the chemical process industry and can be adapted in software engineering. I describe the essential features here only and leave it to the reader to find further application of these methods to software engineering projects. At the end of the chapter I provide a simple example of a hazard analysis problem in safety-critical systems.

Exercises

8.1. How would you define safety-critical systems? Give some examples of these.

8.2. Describe the categories of failure in safety-critical systems. Provide examples as appropriate.

8.3. Briefly describe the essential features of Failure Mode and Effects Analysis (FMEA) and Failure Modes; Effects and Criticality Analysis (FMECA) methodologies.

8.4. Describe how risk priority numbers can be used to assess risk. Use examples, as you feel appropriate.

8.5. How does criticality analysis help to assess risk in software engineering projects?

8.6. How suitable are FMEA methodologies for software engineering projects. Discuss any modifications that may be necessary.

8.7. Describe the main principle underlying HAZOP as a methodology for hazard analysis.

8.8. Given the flow diagram for HAZOP in figure 8.1, describe how the process can me used in software engineering projects.

8.9. Identify and briefly explain the four main stages of the iterative process of hazard and risk analysis in safety-critical systems.

8.10. In a regional airport the allocation of landing and take-off slots is provided by a safety-critical software system. You may assume that the airport gets quite busy during holiday times, and all slots are used-up and controlled by a scheduling algorithm. The complete process is controlled by a primary software system, with a back-up system running in the background for redundancy. The main and the back-up systems are synchronised at 10 millisecond intervals.

i) Identify three hazards that may arise in this system.

ii) For each hazard, suggest a defensive requirement, which will reduce the probability that these hazards will result in an accident.

iii) Explain why your suggested defence is likely to reduce the risk associated with the hazard.

CHAPTER 9 VALIDATION AND VERIFICATION

9.1. Introduction

During software development it is necessary to consider whether what is being developed corresponds to the requirements. Validation and verification are two distinct terms that are used to describe what is needed.

- Validation is the process of checking that, what has been specified is what the user actually wanted. This yields the first question; are we building the correct system?
- Verification is the checking to see if the system that was built conforms to and is consistent with the associated specification. Which yields the second question, are we building the system in the correct way?

In order to provide the answer to these two questions the system needs to be tested. Chapter 10 of this text deals with defect testing as a separate subject however in this chapter I intend to focus on the implications of validation and verification on software engineering project management.

9.2. Testing to validate the system

The reason for performing tests is to find out whether the system is behaving according to what we expect. During the development lifecycle there are a number of stages that can be tested. Figure 9.1 shows the typical testing stages. Here it can be seen that large systems are typically broken down and tested at subsystem level. At this level modules, procedures and functions are tested. When tests are complete the next stage is component testing and integration testing for larger systems. This leads onto the final stage which is the acceptance testing.

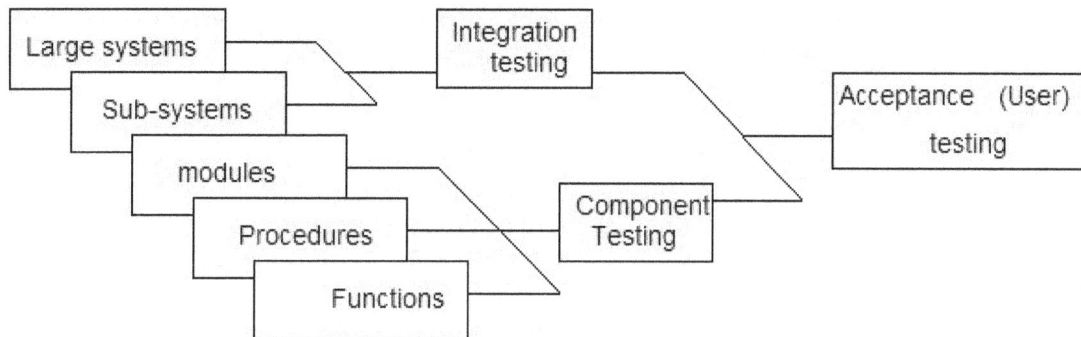

Figure 9.1. Testing stages

- Typically **dynamic** testing is used to establish that the product is functionally correct ⇒ **VALIDATION.**
- On the other hand **static** tests to verify specification, performed during the various stages in development ⇒ **VERIFICATION.**

Static analysis techniques

Perhaps the most important characteristic of static analysis techniques is that the testing as such does not require the execution of the program. Essential functions of static analysis are to check whether representations and descriptions of software are consistent, non-contradictory or ambiguous. It works with correct descriptions, specifications and representations of software systems and is therefore a precondition to any further testing exercise. In essence it can be compared to proofreading to ensure that mistakes are identified and corrected.

Static analysis covers the analysis of the program syntax and investigates and checks the structure and usage of individual statements. There are principally three different possibilities of static program testing,

i.   Look at the program internally, to check completeness and consistency.
ii.   Consider the pre-defined rules and check if they have been followed.
iii. Comparing the program with its specification or documentation for consistency.

Static analysis techniques can be performed automatically, i.e. with the aid of specific tools such as parsers, data flow analysers, syntax analysers and there are also manual techniques for testing that do not ask for an execution of the program. Figure 9.2 shows some of the commonly used static testing techniques.

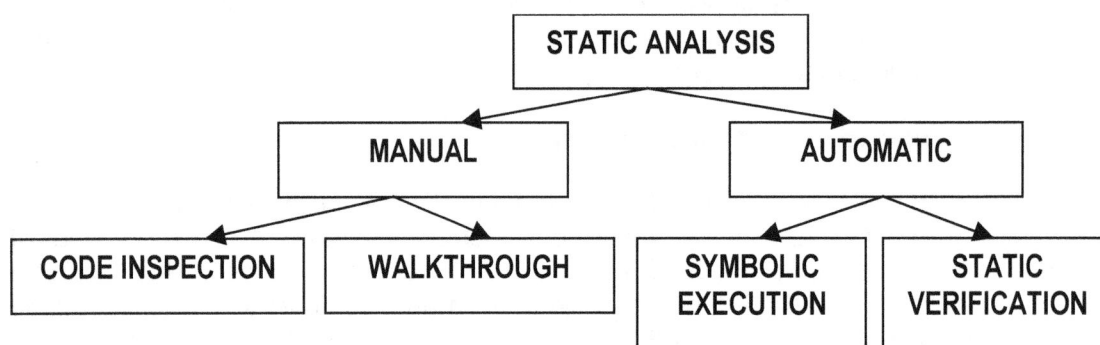

Figure 9.2 Static analysis options [61]

When a program is compared to its specification, the completeness and correctness of the program can be evaluated using static techniques. Thus it can be said that static verification aims to detect problems in the translation between specification and program implementation. This means that verification requires formal methods to specify the requirements. We must also specify the programming languages used as well as a method of algorithmic proving that the specifications are suited to these description means. I am not sure if this makes much sense to everyone reading, but what the last part of the sentence is saying is that you can use an algorithmic proof to show that formal methods used to write the specifications are appropriate.

Static verification compares the actual values provided by the program with the target values as pre-defined in the specification document. It does not, however, provide any means to check whether the program actually solves the given problems, i.e. whether the specification as such is correct. The result of automatic static verification procedures is described in Boolean terms, i.e. a statement is either true or false. The obvious advantage of static verification is that, being based on formal methods, it leads to objective and correct results. However, since it is both very difficult and time-consuming to elaborate the formal specifications, which are needed for static verification, it is mostly only performed for software that needs to be highly reliable.

Another technique, which is normally a part of static analysis, is called symbolic execution. This method analyses, in symbolic terms, what a program does along a given path. Symbolic execution is the process of computing the values of the variables in the program as a function is traced along a specific path through the program. Each function represents a sequence of operations carried out and these can be analysed symbolically without executing the program. Symbolic execution is most appropriate for the analysis of mathematical algorithms. Making use of symbolic values only, whole classes of values can be represented by a single interpretation, which leads to a very high coverage of test cases. The development of programs for symbolic execution is very expensive and therefore it is mainly used for testing numerical programs, where the cost can be justified by the benefits.

The most commonly used manual technique, which allows testing the program without running it, is software inspection. This method of inspection is a group review process that is used to detect and correct defects in a software product. It is an organised technical activity that is performed by the author of the software and a small peer group on a limited amount of material. It produces a formal, quantified report on the resources used and the results achieved'. During inspection the code and the design of the software is compared to a set of pre-established inspection rules. In this manner inspection is mostly performed with checklists, which cover typical aspects of software behaviour. Examining the software through reading, explaining, getting explanations and understanding of system descriptions, software specifications and programs carry out inspection of software.

Walkthroughs are similar peer review processes that involve the author of the program, the tester, a secretary and a moderator. The participants of a walkthrough create a small number of test cases by ``simulating" the computer. Its objective is to question the logic and basic assumptions behind the source code, particularly of program interfaces in embedded systems.

In its nature static inspection can be applied to any kind of document, e.g. specifications, test plans etc. A major advantage of static inspection processes is that any kind of problem can be detected and thus results can be delivered with respect to every software quality factor. However there is a catch in that most testing techniques are intimately related to the system attribute whose value they are designed to measure, and thus offer no information about other attributes. Thus if we overlook an attribute in the testing procedure, the test will fail to monitor it and so potentially the software could become unpredictable. This implies that testing should be meticulous.

Dynamic analysis techniques

While static analysis techniques do not require software programs to be executed, dynamic analysis involves running the system to test its behaviour. The characteristic feature of dynamic testing is the analysis of the behaviour of a software system before, during and after its execution. [62]

Dynamic analysis techniques involve the running of the program formally under controlled circumstances and identifying the specific results, which are expected. The result of such a test shows whether a system is correct in the system states examined. Dynamic analysers are software programs developed for testing the code. Typically the source code is modified to provide dynamic testing at prescribed stages of code execution. For example, they can be used to provide information on how often each statement in a program has been executed or the value of a particular variable during execution. The results are usually provided as a report through a report generator.

Among the most important dynamic analysis techniques are path and branch testing. Path testing involves the design of a test, which exercises as many as possible logical paths of a program during execution. Therefore it can be said that the quality attribute, which is measured by path testing, is program *complexity*.

Branch testing uses tests, which are designed so that every branch in a program is traversed at least once. The quality that attribute here is *completeness*.

More often than not it is the software development team that is in charge of developing the dynamic testing methods. It provides a way for them to monitor how the code is performing. They will be familiar with critical places in this code since they have designed it and so the tests that they will use will be tuned to test these aspects of the code. Figure 9.3 shows some features that dynamic analysers can be designed to test. More details are covered in defect testing in Chapter 10 of this text.

Type of Dynamic Analyser	Functionality of Tool
test coverage analysis	tests to which extent the code can be checked by glass box techniques
tracing	follows all paths used during program execution and provides e.g. values for all variables etc.
tuning	measures resources used during program execution
simulator	simulates parts of systems, if e.g. the actual code or hardware are not available
assertion checking	tests whether certain conditions are given in complex logical constructs

Figure 9.3 Dynamic analysis tools

9.3.   Testing Tools

Testing large and complex software systems requires dedicated tools that have been developed specifically to test the software. There are a number of different categories and a few of these are briefly covered next.

Test data generators: Test data generators are programs, which once supplied by the correct input syntax, automatically generate a large number of test inputs for some systems. The output is analysed and a report often generated automatically. Thus the selection and generation of test data is an important discipline. The most basic approach to test data generation is random testing, where a number of random input values are generated and the results noted. There are also two more sophisticated approaches to test data generation, i.e. structural testing and functional testing. Structural testing is an approach to testing in which the internal control structure of a program is used to guide the selection of test data. It is an attempt to take the internal functional properties of a program into account during test data generation and to avoid the limitations of black box functional testing. Chapter 10 covers black-box and white box testing, but for now it is sufficient to say that black-box deals with functional requirements and has no concern with the internal structure of the system. (i.e. system is treated like a black box). To some extent White-box is the opposite because it deals with the system structure.

Functional testing considers both functional requirements of the system and also those that are part of its design or implementation and which are not described in the requirements. In functional testing, a program is considered to be a function and is thought of in terms of input values and corresponding output values. Any intuitive functionality, not specifically addressed in the specifications, is also considered.

Tools for test data generation can be used in combination with specific programming languages. For example in embedded systems, tools for test data generation are very useful because they can be used to simulate a larger system environment providing input data for every possible system interface. In other words, if a system is not fully implemented or not linked to all relevant data sources, not all system interfaces can be tested, because no input values are given for non-implemented functions. Data Generation tools provide input values for all available system interfaces as if a real module was linked to it.

Oracles: An ORACLE is a program which, given a specification, can predict the results of the system test. The actual results are then compared with predicted ones and a report is generated.

Simulators: Are programs that imitate the actions of some system. These are widely used on real-time systems testing in order to assess system responses to conditions that cannot be tested on a real-time system.

Emulators: Emulate the performance of a system, usually embedded and are used as an aid towards final design.

Debugging: Involves locating and repairing program defects, the programmer usually does the repair and a debugging program is used to help with locating defects. The term bug is often used to refer to a problem or fault in a computer. There are software bugs and hardware bugs. Software testing should not be confused with debugging. Debugging is the process of analysing and locating bugs when software does not behave as expected. Although the identification of some bugs will be obvious from using the software, a methodical approach to software testing is a much more thorough means of identifying bugs. Debugging is therefore an activity, which supports testing, but cannot replace testing. However, no amount of testing can guarantee to discover all bugs.

Regression tests: Repairing program defects may introduce new defects and therefore testing should be repeated after a system has been modified. In practice it is not practical to test the system after every repair, so a test plan needs to be defined. As part of the test plan the various dependencies between parts of the system are identified. These can be used to determine which parts of the system need to be re-tested after modification.

9.4.   Testing Strategies

Whatever strategy is adopted the testing should be done incrementally. i.e., test complete units and after new units have been integrated test again.

Strategies:

i.   **Top-down:** Begins at the highest level with subsystems and modules represented by stubs at lower levels as shown in figure 9.3. Stubs are simple components that share a common interface with the system components at their level. After each level, testing proceeds to the next lower level.

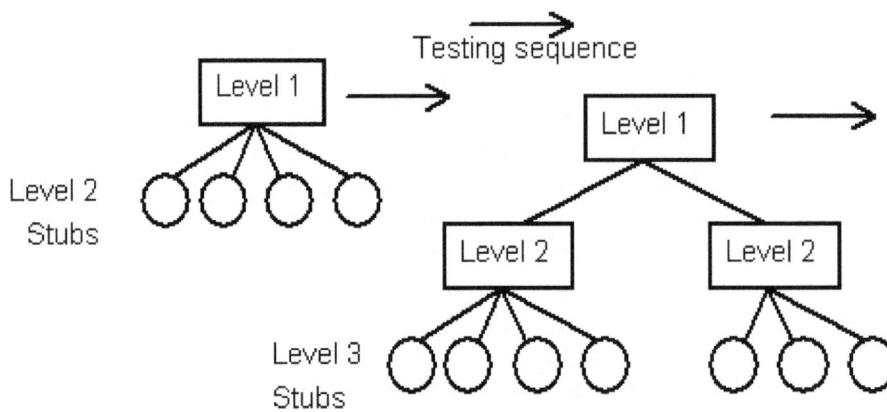

Figure 9.3 Top-down testing

ii.   **Bottom-up testing:** This is the reverse of top-down approach, i.e. begins with the low-level component testing where it is completed before moving to the next level.

iii.   **Thread testing:** Real-time systems are often made up of a number of co-operating processes that are interrupt-driven. The testing procedure therefore needs to be more controlled. Thread testing begins by testing each process individually, and once this is done to introduce or thread-in the next process. This yields a gradual build up of the testing. Clearly, with a large number of processes it cannot be suitable to test every sequence of interactions so some prescribed threads should be evaluated first.

iv.   **Stress testing:** Some systems are designed to handle a given load. For example a banking system may be designed to deal with 100 transactions/second. Tests need to be designed to check if these loads can be met. This usually means a gradual increase in loading up to and beyond the maximum. Response to failure (due to ultimate overload should be soft -rather than hard). These testing methods are particularly well suited to networks.

9.5.   Interface testing

Interface testing is one of the most important software tests in assuring the quality of software products. In a nutshell, human beings can only communicate with hardware through an interface.[63] This interface is actually software that consists of sets of messages, commands, images, and other features that allow communication between a device and a user. Various companies use this type of software testing to make sure that their customers will not encounter any problems when using a particular software product. In addition, developers usually want their products to be supported by more than one spoken language thus, their need to understand the interface. In this test, developers come up with changes or revisions and introduce these to a software application by taking note of the feedback from end-users. Usually, each end-user is assigned a specific task. During the course of this test, the program flow is checked and evaluated to determine if it matches the natural strategy of the user in navigating within the application. Moreover, this test determines which application areas are initially and usually accessed as well as its user-friendliness.

A moderator is often designated the task of performing this quality assurance test. Throughout the process, the moderator does not communicate anything to the end-user and instead observes and documents the reaction of users towards the application. At the end of the session the moderator interviews the end-users and endorses their feedback to the software developer. Developers can use this feedback to modify the interface. In this way, interface testing improves the overall acceptance level of the software and by implication the user experience. Factors like functionality, performance speed, the time needed to learn to use the program, the ease with which the user remembers how to use the program, user satisfaction, and the rate of user errors are the usual criteria that developers have for a well-designed user interface.

9.6. Levels of testing

The levels of software testing include component testing, system testing, acceptance testing, and release testing. Component testing requires testing all individual components of software design. System testing, on the other hand, involves testing the functional and non-functional requirements of application systems. Acceptance testing evaluates and compares the system against pre-set requirements. Lastly, release testing is conducted to determine if a new system is compatible to the current technical environment.

Our expectations from the system can be discerned from the requirements documents and also from our understanding of the structure that we are developing. This is to say that the requirements document will tell us the functional aspects of our system, what it needs to do and tests can be designed to determine if the system performs according to the specification. These types of tests fall into the category of so called 'Black box' tests or functional tests, because the internal structure is not considered and tests are simply carried out with inputs and outputs, treating the system as a black box, and hence the name. On the other hand tests that are based on the structure of the system are termed white box tests. Here the system structure is used to describe tests that will determine if the system is likely to fail. To facilitate white-box testing programmers have to write code, which is simpler to follow, better structured, and easier to maintain. These testing approaches will be covered in chapter 10 of this text.

9.7. Chapter summary

In this chapter we look at validation and verification of software products. To a large extent these are based on testing. Typically **dynamic** testing is used to establish that the product is functionally correct $\Rightarrow$ **VALIDATION.** On the other hand **static** tests verify specification, performed during the various stages in development $\Rightarrow$ **VERIFICATION.** The chapter briefly covers static and dynamic testing strategies and tools. Static techniques are generally slower and more expensive to implement largely because many of these cannot be done by automated systems. The chapter also covers some basic strategies for testing such as thread testing and stress testing but these should only serve as examples because the approach to testing is generally developed in-house and so most organisations will have their own testing procedures. The chapter also considers interface testing. This is a particular type of test to ensure that human beings are able to communicate with the system through the user interface. Finally we briefly introduce white box and black box testing strategies. These are discussed in more details in Chapter 10, and here we simply give them a mention to provide the reader with the basic features of these approaches to testing.

Exercises

9.1.   Explain the difference between verification and validation within the context of the software engineering phase of product development.

9.2.   How does testing help in the validation and verification stage of software development?

9.3.   What testing strategies are suitable for validation and what strategies are suitable for verification? Provide examples as appropriate.

9.4.   You are a software leader in a small software company producing computer games and teaching material. You are in charge of a project to develop a software application to run on a personal computer that will help to teach children aged 9-11 basic mathematics. You have a formal specification for the software development. What methods are you going to use for validation and verification on this project?

9.5.   Discuss the main differences between static and dynamic testing strategies. Use examples as appropriate.

9.6.   You are engaged on a project to design an embedded system to control the deployment of landing gear on small aircraft. You intend to use formal methods in the specification due to the safety-critical nature of the task. What analysis methods are you intending to use during validation and verification stages?

9.7.   Having spent a few years as a software developer you have decided to go-it-alone and have just started your own software development company. You have also brought with you a contract to develop and maintain a website for a medium size corporate client. You intend to expand your portfolio of clients and as a result you want to set-up a testing policy in your company. Explain how you would go about defining a testing policy for your software products.

9.8.   Why is interface testing important?

9.9.   In your opinion, what percentage of software development involves the design of a user interface?

9.10.   With respect to your answer to Q9.9 above, discuss the extent to which the user interface plays a part in overall product success. For example, developing Microsoft office application and the user interface and the impact that these two components have on the user. What percentage of the development effort went to the application and what percentage went to the interface? Relate this to the importance of the application running smoothly and the importance of the user interface.

CHAPTER 10   DEFECT TESTING

10.1.   Introduction

In the previous chapter we briefly considered the impact of testing on validation and verification stages in software development. However testing spans a broader range of activities within software development. This is to say that a large number of tests have to be performed long before we reach the validation and verification stages of development. Traditionally in software engineering projects, one of the tasks of the design team is to describe the exact nature of tests that are appropriate for evaluation of their software product. However, whereas software testing until recently was the sole domain of software developers, a gradual change in the underlying philosophy can now be perceived, giving the user more influence in the overall software development process. In other words the notion that software developers are not necessarily the best choice when it comes to testing their own programming product is gaining general acknowledgement.

Moreover, a new philosophy has emerged concerning the goals of testing: whereas so far the principal motivation for applying software tests was "... to look actively for problems so that these may be corrected thus improving the software", the evaluation and comparison of existing software products is gaining more and more importance. [64]

Main approaches to testing

There are a large number of tests and we have already considered some that relate to validation and verification in the previous chapter. In this section I shall focus on describing white-box (structural) testing and black box (functional) testing. Both black box and structural testing are used in the process of defect testing of the software product. The purpose of defect testing is to expose latent defects in a software system before the system is delivered. Defect testing is in contrast to traditional testing, which is used to show that the system works without faults occurring. Thus a successful defect test will cause the system to perform incorrectly thus exposing defects within the system.

In general a defects testing procedure is based on the generation of test cases that are used to produce test data to be fed into the software. The results produced from the software for the given test data are then compared with the test case to see if any faults have occurred. The type of test cases generated tends to be based on the test engineer's experience of program operation rather than the testing of all possible operational scenarios, as this would prove difficult and time consuming to implement. For this reason the test engineer will usually pick a range of test cases and data that they would expect to highlight potential errors in the system.

Black box testing treats the software system as a series of inputs and outputs and does not concern itself with the internal operation of the program (hence black-box). Instead the black-box method studies the behaviour of the whole system and is concerned with the functionality of the software and not how the software was implemented.

White box or structural testing is based on the principle that the tester has knowledge of the software structure and implementation. Structural testing is carried out on the program routines or objects to check for correct operation based on knowledge of how these smaller units are constructed. Test cases and data are generated from this understanding of code execution so that all of the subroutines or objects are tested at least once on an individual basis. As a general comparison table 10.1 summarises the main features of white-box and black box approaches to testing.

Using black box and structural testing together allows the program to be fully tested throughout the development process. Structural testing allows different program writers to work on different sections of the program at the same time and test these smaller objects and routines to make sure they are free of bugs without the need to consult other groups working on other modules. This helps to speed up the development process and ensure that each program module is reliable and robust in its own right. Using black box testing would allow the test team to check that all the individual modules work together in the correct way to produce the overall objectives of the software.

Table 10.1 Black box and White box testing features

Black box Testing	White box testing
Based on how the whole system works.	Based on testing how individual bits of the system work.
Does not require understanding of code implementation.	Requires knowledge of individual routines and code implementation.
Usually uses equivalence partitioning to test common input characteristics such as positive/negative numbers, strings etc.	Uses equivalence partitioning with knowledge of program execution to derive test data that will test all routines used within the smaller units of the program.
Test data set is based on worst-case scenarios, valid and invalid input ranges derived from previous testing experience.	Test data derived from knowledge of the program structure and how the program will use the data.
Test team can be independent of the design team. Thus they require no knowledge of the program but instead understand the domain in which the program will operate.	Some or even all of the test team will be the designers of the tests because of their knowledge of the program design and execution.
Use on large scale programs requiring shorter testing period.	Used on small-scale objects and modules of program and test units of program execution thoroughly. This requires longer time span to test whole program.
Usually has to be carried out after the final program has been written resulting in bigger problems to solve major errors in the program execution.	Can be carried out at all stages of the program development thus reducing likelihood of major modifications at later stages, which can be expensive.

Typically, black box testing would highlight errors in the whole program and this information could then be passed on to the programmers responsible for the individual modules so they can correct the code to fix the problem. This method of working facilitates more rapid development and ensures reliability of safety critical sections of code. It also helps to reduce the need for major redesign to be carried out at later stages of the development cycle. Since the black box testers control how they believe the system as a whole should operate there are fewer disagreements about which modules need to be changed. This is because the decision lies with the black box test team who are looking at the behaviour of the overall product and not with the module design team who have a low level view of the system.

10.2. White box or structural Testing

For a long time, the majority of the programmers believed that programs are only written so that a computer can read them. It was also their opinion that the only way to test a program is to execute it on the machine for which it was designed. This attitude often led towards badly structured, illegible, and nearly unchangeable programs.

But consider the implications on software coding if programmers knew that they would have to present their code to other professionals? How would a programmer approach testing before releasing the code? The programmer would instinctively write programs that are simpler to read, better structured, and easier to maintain. During a presentation the internal structure of a program is disclosed with the main goal to detect faults, which are otherwise hard to find, resulting in a strong psychological influence on the programmer. Therefore such a procedure is in general called a "White Box Test".

In addition to those tests done in teams, other white box tests have been derived from one of the oldest tests, namely the desk-test where programmers check their work at their desk. In the following some of the most common white box tests from both of these fields are considered.

White Box tests done in teams

Code-inspections and walk-troughs

This testing strategy was presented previously in the context of static testing. However, here we are considering the process rather than the actual detail of the tests. Typically white box tests are static test methods, which can be used in very early phases of the development process. This makes it possible to detect faults early when they can be removed without causing much disruption and cost. To provide a clearer picture, the common order of events for these tests will be given next.

First, the team is assigned. Each member gets enough information to be able to prepare when the team meets for the first time a couple of weeks later. During this meeting, which lasts approximately two hours and should not be interrupted, an exact list of all faults found is produced. It is important that the group does not start to look for solutions, because this would require too much time and it would distract them from their aim, which is to identify faults. They are only supposed to find the bugs not to fix them. There is some controversy in the literature concerning the ideal size of this team and who should be in charge. This is to ask, should the person who was instrumental in creating the software be the team leader? Or should a software engineer who had nothing to do with the product be in charge of testing it? Typically the team would have about five members and the structure would be as follows,

- **Team manager** is the organiser, chairman, and ultimately responsible for the whole enterprise. It is absolutely mandatory that team members acknowledge the authority of the team leader.
- **The design engineer** who has to contribute know-how about the design to the group. The test design engineer should not be one of those who designed the program, which is being tested; but only has to have specialised knowledge about designing such a product.
- **The programmer** who has to contribute expertise in the programming language used. Like the engineer the programmer needs to have expertise but must not be the one who coded the program being tested.
- **The tester** who has to be an expert on testing procedures. In this capacity the tester has to control the process in a way that is more likely to detect faults.

• **Administrator** The keeper of the minutes who should relieve the manager from administrative duties and who should make sure that everything done gets recorded.

• **The author** who wrote the program that the group is testing.

• **The user** who should maintain the connection between testing and the "outside world". The user may spend hours without understanding anything the experts are talking about, but if he is able to find one single fault, it would have been worthwhile. User input is also important in product quality in order to determine if the final product is meets with expectations of users.

White Box tests which are not team oriented

Most programmers have had the experience that it is sometimes more efficient to leave the computer, sit down at a desk, take a sheet of paper, and think about the actual problem. As mentioned before, this is the idea of one of the oldest tests -- the desk tests. The tester who should not be the author takes a listing of the module he is going to analyse and tries to read it -- again with the goal to find bugs. Three types of analysis can be identified and these are path, loop and domain testing, which are briefly described next.

Path testing

Path testing was mentioned earlier and it is one of the oldest test methods, and even though it is a typical white box test, nowadays it is also used in black box tests. The procedure starts by selecting a path through the program. For this path the possible inputs and the correct outputs are written down. Then the program is executed by hand, and the result is compared to the expected result. If a fault is detected then this is recorded so that it can be corrected.

Choice of path is at the discretion of the test team but there are strategies that can help. In an ideal situation all paths would be tested, but this can be time consuming and expensive. Thus choice of path is made based on the general understanding of the program flow. For example, assume that a short program consists of a loop that is executed twenty times. Inside this loop are a number of decision instructions, which allow ten different routes. The total number of paths trough this program would be 1020. Many of these paths would be repetitive and so concentration could be a problem for the tester. To make testing more manageable therefore it is necessary to reduce the number of paths. There is no ideal solution to this problem, and the following considerations may be used to point the way forward,

- When in doubt prefer the shorter way out.
- Choose a path, which involves fewest variables first.
- Be sure to use each instruction at least once.
- Do not ignore the important paths -- even if they seem complex.
- Do not look over parts, which seem to be difficult to understand.
- Trust your intuition.

It is also important to keep in mind that, due to the fact that conditions in a program are normally not completely independent of each other, not all paths are possible. For instance, there are only two different routes through the following program:

```
if (C) {
    instruction block A1
} else {
    instruction block A2
}
if (C) {
    instruction block B1
} else {
    instruction block B2
}
```

Assuming that the instruction blocks A1 and A2 do not influence the condition C then, regardless of whether the condition C is true or false, the paths A1-B2 and A2-B1 will never be used. That is to say value of C will exclude these combinations at all times.

Loop testing

In the majority of programming languages, loops present typical spots for a bugs to be created. They make path testing difficult because loops significantly increase the number of possible paths, and they often contain bugs within a condition in the loop, which are hard to find. An even bigger threat is within nested loops. All this justifies extra inspection of loops within a program. For example consider the following program. The syntax is in Perl but it should be fairly easy to interpret by anyone familiar with C.

```
#!/usr/local/bin/perl -w

open(DB, "filename");

$to_work_with = <DB>;

while (!eof(DB)) {

    print "$to_work_with";

    $to_work_with = <DB>;

}
```

The program opens a certain file, reads it line by line, and processes this input. The problem is that the last line read is never used. It may appear that most loops can be tested with two checks, but a lot of bugs are not found this way. The condition of a loop has to be checked at least three different times: when the loop is entered, during its execution, and when the loop is left. The two borders are of special interest. Consider next an example of a nested loop. Note that even more dangerous are partly nested loops:

```
label1:

    instruction block A1

label2:

    if C1 then goto label1:

    instruction block A2

    if C2 then goto label2:

close DB;
```

If C1 is TRUE then program loops to label1. This is fine and so long as C1 is TRUE the program will loop and maintain A1 blocked.
If C1 is FALSE then instruction is to block A2 and check if C2 is TRUE.
If C2 is TRUE then program loops to label2 which is an illegal operation because it crosses into the first loop.

Constructions of this kind normally only appear when the command `goto` or a similar instruction is used, but in low level programming languages like assembly it is almost impossible to avoid those commands. Therefore it is particularly important to check those programs for constructions of this kind.

Domain testing

The goal of domain testing is to check values taken by a variable, a condition, or an index, and to prove that they are outside the specified or valid range. It also checks that the program accepts only valid inputs. The following points need to be taken into account for domain testing,

- Have all variables used been initialised correctly?
- Are all indices used to access an array within the prescribed array dimensions?
- Are all those indices integers?
- Are all arguments that are used in a comparison of the same type?
- Are all Boolean expressions correct? Check logical operands like AND, and OR, and their priorities.
- Are there any "off by one" situations, like a loop which is executed once too often, or a field index of an array which is inadvertently increased by one?

This list is not complete by far, but it should provide an idea of where to look for possible faults. It is known from experience that, if programs pass the majority of these tests, then the number of bugs found by other tests is, significantly reduced. [65]

10.3.　Black Box or functional testing

All white box tests have the disadvantage that the program source code is needed to run the tests. Functional or black box testing, however, aims to test behaviour of a given program against its specification without making any reference to the internal structures of the program or the algorithms used.

Black box testing implies that the selection of test data as well as the interpretation of test results are performed on the basis of the functional properties of a piece of software. It is recommended that the author of the program who knows too much about the program internals should not perform black box testing. In new testing approaches, software systems are given a third external party for black box testing after having successfully completing the internal white box testing exercises.

Although it is focused on the knowledge of user requirements, black box tests do not necessarily involve the participation of users. Among the most important black box tests that do not involve users are functionality testing, volume tests, stress tests, recovery testing, and benchmarks. Additionally, there are two types of black box test that involve users, i.e. field and laboratory tests. In the following the most important aspects of these black box tests will be described briefly.

Black box testing without user involvement

The primary objective of black box testing is to assess whether the program does what it is supposed to do, i.e. what is specified in the requirements. There are different approaches to black box testing. One is the testing of each program feature or function in sequence. The other is to test module by module, i.e. each function is tested where it is called first.

Volume tests

The objective of volume tests is to find the limitations of the software by processing a huge amount of data. A volume test can uncover problems that are related to the efficiency of a system, e.g. incorrect buffer sizes, a consumption of too much memory space, or only show that an error message would be needed telling the user that the system cannot process the given amount of data.

Stress tests

During a stress test, the system has to process a huge amount of data or perform many function calls within a short period of time. A typical example could be to perform the same function from all workstations connected in a LAN within a short period of time (e.g. sending e-mails, or to modify a particular variable via different terminals simultaneously).

Recovery tests

The aim of recovery testing is to determine to which extent data can be recovered after a system breakdown. Does the system provide possibilities to recover all of the data or part of it? How much can be recovered and how? Is the recovered data still correct and consistent? Thus recovery testing is particularly important for software that needs high reliability standards.

Benchmark tests

The notion of benchmark tests involves the testing of program efficiency. Efficiency of a piece of software strongly depends on the hardware environment and therefore benchmark tests always consider the software/hardware combination. Most software engineers consider benchmark tests to be concerned with quantitative measurement of specific operations. However they can also be user driven tests used to compare the efficiency of different software systems. (i.e. to establish a performance benchmark)

Black box testing with user involvement

For tests involving users, methodological considerations are rare in software engineering literature. Rather, one may find practical test reports that can be broadly classified as field and laboratory tests. In the following a brief description of field and laboratory tests will be given.

Field tests

In field tests users are observed while using the software system at their normal working place. Apart from general aspects related to usability, field tests are particularly useful for assessing the interoperability of the software system, i.e. how the technical integration of the system works. Moreover, field tests are the only real means to identify problems resulting from integration of the software system into existing procedures. For example, consider the organisational problem of implementing a language translation service of a big automobile manufacturer. Here the major implementation problem is not the technical environment, but the fact that many clients still submit their orders as print-out, that neither source texts nor target texts are properly organised and stored and furthermore individual translators are not too motivated to change their working habits. In the event that a software system is introduced to automate the process it should be clear that field tests would be required in order to ensure that a smooth transition to the software system is achieved.

Laboratory tests

Laboratory tests are mostly performed to assess the general usability of the system. Due to the high laboratory equipment costs laboratory tests are mostly only performed at big software houses such as IBM or Microsoft. Since laboratory tests provide testers with many technical possibilities, data collection and analysis are easier than for field tests.

To conclude, apart from the above-described analytical methods of both white box and black box testing, there are further constructive means to guarantee high quality software end products. Among the most important constructive means is the usage of object-oriented programming tools, the integration of CASE tools, rapid prototyping, and also the involvement of users in both software development and testing procedures. [66]

Advantages and Disadvantages of Black Box Testing [67]

Advantages of black box testing	Disadvantages of black box testing
Black box tests are reproducible.	The results are often overestimated.
The environment the program is running is also tested.	Not all properties of a software product can be tested.
The invested effort can be used multiple times.	The reason for a failure is not found.

Equivalence partitioning and boundary value analysis

Function testing is usually the first black box test. The main goal here is to find if the specification agrees with the behaviour of the program from the users point of view. This is often done in the following way:

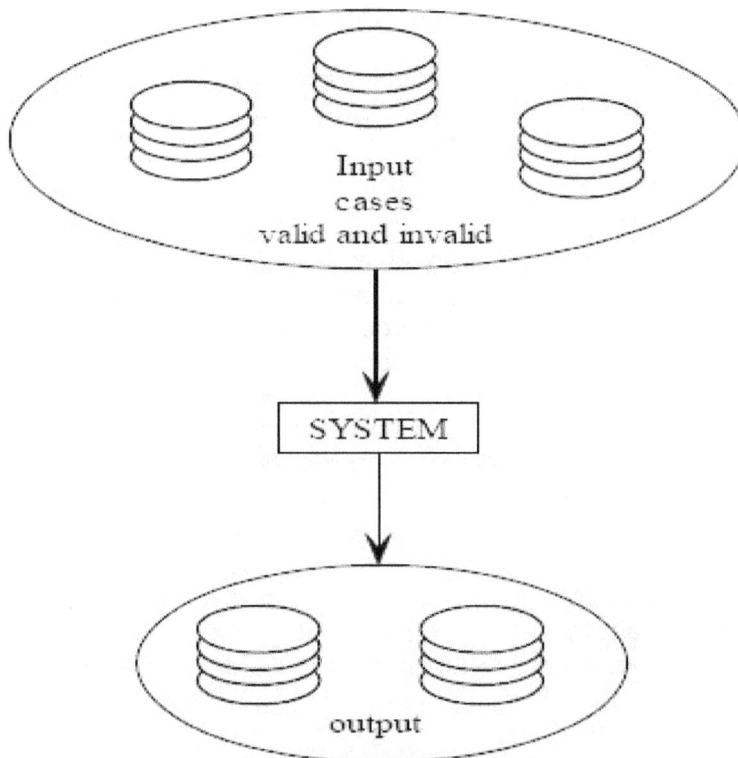

Figure 10.1. Equivalence partitioning

In function testing for each of the input fields in the program, the allowed inputs are written down. It is useful to try to divide the possible inputs into the so-called equivalence classes to reduce the number of possible inputs, which should be tested. Another approach is to consider boundary value analysis. With equivalence partitioning, input data fall into different classes, which have common characteristics, e.g. numbers, strings etc. Programs normally behave in similar ways for all members of a Class, this is equivalence behaviour and testing on this basis is called equivalence partitioning. Suitable partitions are chosen followed by a choice of test case data, i.e. at boundaries, in the middle, atypical and typical values etc. This is shown in figure 10.1

With boundary value analysis, it is considered that programs often fail at the boundaries of functional domains, i.e. null strings, zero iterations, empty files or out of range values. Values on either side of the boundaries are identified and their effects analysed. Therefore these boundaries are productive testing areas. For example a program, which decides if a number, is in the region between 50000 and 99999. It gets five input digits. Equivalence partitions are: Numbers, which have five digits. Test: 5 digits. Another is, numbers, which have more or fewer digits than five. Test: 0,4,6 digit inputs. Two other equivalence partitions are numbers between 50000 and 99999, and other numbers with five digits. Tests: 50000,50001,99998,99999. Tests: 00000, 49999.

Equivalence Partitioning Example: On-line shoe store software

Consider a software application for an on-line retail store selling footwear. The programme is intended to accept the name of an item and a list of the different sizes the item comes in, specified in UK shoe sizes. The specifications state that the item name is to be alphabetic characters 2 to 15 characters in length. Each size may be a value in the range of 4 to 13, whole numbers only. The sizes are to be entered in ascending order (smaller sizes first). A maximum of five sizes may be entered for each item. The item name is to be entered first, followed by a comma, then followed by a list of sizes. A comma will be used to separate each size. Spaces (blanks) are to be ignored anywhere in the input.

Solution:

From the above specification the following Equivalence Classes can be derived. I shall number these classes so that I can refer to them during testing.

1. Item name is alphabetic (valid)
2. Item name is not alphabetic (invalid)
3. Item name is less than 2 characters in length (invalid)
4. Item name is 2 to 15 characters in length (valid)
5. Item name is greater than 15 characters in length (invalid)
6. Size value is less than 4 (invalid)
7. Size value is in the range 4 to 13 (valid)
8. Size value is greater than 13 (invalid)
9. Size value is a whole number (valid)
10. Size value is a decimal (invalid)
11. Size value is numeric (valid)
12. Size value includes nonnumeric characters (invalid)
13. Size values entered in ascending order (valid)
14. Size values entered in non-ascending order (invalid)
15. No size values entered (invalid)
16. One to five size values entered (valid)
17. More than five sizes entered (invalid)
18. Item name is first (valid)
19. Item name is not first (invalid)
20. A single comma separates each entry in list (valid)
21. A comma does not separate two or more entries in the list (invalid)
22. The entry contains no blanks
23. The entry contains blanks

For the above equivalence classes we can describe the following tests. Each test lists the expected outcome and also indicates the classes involved in the test. (i.e. Class number as above). The process should be fairly intuitive. You simply select test data within a particular equivalence class. You compare the actual outcome with that which you expect. Table 10.2 shows the equivalence partitions and the corresponding tests with expected outcomes.

Table 10.2

Number	Test Data	Expected Outcome	Classes Covered
1	xy,4	T	1,4,7,9,11,13,16,18,20,22
2	AbcDefghijklmno,4,5,..13	T	1,4,7,9,11,13,16,18,20,23
3	A2x,4	F	2
4	A,4	F	3
5	abcdefghijklmnop	F	5
6	Xy,0	F	6
7	XY,49	F	8
8	Xy,2.5	F	10
9	xy,2,1,3,4,5	F	14
10	Xy	F	15
11	XY,1,2,3,4,5,6	F	17
12	1,Xy,2,3,4,5	F	19
13	XY2,3,4,5,6	F	21
14	AB,2#7	F	12

10.4. Assessing the effectiveness of testing

"Trying to improve quality by increasing testing is like trying to lose weight by weighing yourself more often." McConnell, S., Code Complete, Microsoft Press, 1993".

Testing the effectiveness of a testing procedure can determine whether the testing effort is justified. It is suspected that many organisations invest a lot of effort into testing software in their products. In many cases, test suites evolve over time and often include dozens or even hundreds of "non-productive" tests. These tests are often looking for problems in areas where there are no problems. Even worse, there can be several areas that have inadequate or non-existent test coverage.

As an organisation it is important to realise what testing is intended to do. Testing intends to provide, information about potential defects in the product. It is also geared towards building confidence that requirements are being met and that changes to software have not introduced new defects.

Testing requires a significant investment in both time and effort. The return on this investment is measured in terms of information and confidence gained compared to the effort required. As a result of increasing the effectiveness of testing, critical information will be identified sooner and a higher confidence level will be achieved.

Points to consider for testing

Tailored training for testers can be provided to help improve skills in areas such as:
- Test planning
- Act like a customer testing
- Identifying equivalence classes
- Data-flow testing
- Boundary analysis
- Requirements management
- Test automation

Once this process is correctly completed, the resulting test suite will contain a more meaningful collection of tests that will have a higher probability of finding defects. The net result will be a significant increase in return on investment for the testing activity.

Procedure for assessing the effectiveness of testing

Every organisation will have their own policy on testing and it will be in their interest to improve the testing activity. Assessing the effectiveness of testing which includes the following four steps can do this.

Step 1. Test the requirements

Tests can only be as good as the requirements they are intended to test. If requirements are vague and ambiguous, the tests will not be very effective. Therefore, the first step in the assessment process is a thorough review of the requirements. Based on this review, a requirements test may be necessary. A report listing the requirements that need to be cleared up is prepared. (i.e. list of omissions, ambiguities and conflicts).

Step 2. Update the requirements trace matrix (RTM)

Once the requirements have been reviewed, the next step is to update the RTM. The RTM is an extremely important document. In its simplest form, it provides a way to determine if all requirements are tested. Table 10.3 provides an example of a requirements trace matrix. However, the RTM can do much more. Consider the following example.

Table 10.3.

Requirement	Estimated Tests Req'd	Type of Tests	Automated or Manual?	Re-use Existing Tests?
4.1.2 User Interface	22	10 Functional 3 Positive 4 Negative 5 Boundary	7 Auto 5 Manual	T0167 T0045
4.1.4 Calculation Precision	5	2 Functional 3 Boundary	5 Manual	T0056 T6069
...		...		
...		...		
Total Estimated Tests	150	90-A 60-M	50	

In this example, the RTM is used as a test planning tool to help determine how many tests are required, what types of tests are required, whether tests can be automated or manual, and if any existing tests can be re-used. Using the RTM in this way helps ensure that the resulting tests are most effective.

The RTM can serve many purposes over the course of a development project. Initially, it can be used as a planning tool (as mentioned above). Once the tests are developed and validation testing has begun, the RTM can be used to help determine the extent of testing that is required. This is based on the relationship between the requirements, design, code, and specified tests. Table 10.4 shows an example template that can be used to show these relationships.

Table 10.4.

Requirements Use-cases	Functional Requirements	Design Elements	Code	Test Case
UC-28	catalog.query.sort	Class catalog	Catalog.sort()	search.7 search.8
UC-29	catalog.query.import	Class catalog	Catalog.import() catalog.validate()	search.11 search.13 search.14

The RTM can be created by using automated tools or using simple tools like spreadsheets and tables and is often included as part of the validation test plan. When it becomes necessary to perform testing, the accurate information included in the RTM will be invaluable in helping to select a reasonable set of tests to run. Other information that can be included in the validation test plan includes:

- Test estimates: This considers what is expected of the tests?
- Resource requirements: What additional resources are needed to perform testing?
- Validation readiness review criteria: How appropriate are test results to give us an idea of what is required to improve the system?
- Validation completion criteria: How suitable are the results to be able to complte testing?

The output from this step of the assessment process is a revised RTM. Please note that this is only an example of how tests can be used in validation. It is likely that particular organisations will develop their own approaches, but the points identified above should provide useful guidelines.

Step 3. Analyse the existing test suite

The RTM can also be used to help analyse the existing test suite to determine whether or not it is appropriate for its intended system. For example, RTM can be used to analyse different test types in order to determine how many test types are associated with each requirement. Some examples of this are shown in Table 10.5.

Table 10.5.

Some Examples of Test Types	
• Functional • Algorithmic • Positive • Negative • Usability • Boundary • Startup & Shutdown • Configuration • Platform • Load/Stress • Security	• Performance • Safety-related • Compatibility • Documentation • Timing • Error Checking • Power Failure • Resources • Installation • Upgradeability • Volume scalability • Throughput

Data Flow tests

Data flow tests are based on known patterns of data usage and data flow and consequently they are often derived from data flow diagrams. These tests are relatively easy to implement because DFDs are clear about the sources and sinks of data. However, structural faults in the DFD diagram are not easy to identify and consequently data flow tests are often used in conjunction with other tests.

Equivalence Classes

A group of tests can form an equivalence Class if:
- They all test the same thing
- If one test passes, all tests will likely pass
- If one test fails, all tests will likely fail

Identifying potential equivalence classes allows redundant, ineffective tests to be identified.

Boundary Analysis

By identifying ranges and boundaries, tests can be created that are:
- Well within boundary or range
- One less than boundary
- Equal to boundary
- One greater than boundary
- Well beyond boundary

Boundary analysis helps ensure that all boundary conditions are covered in the test suite. This means that problems related to boundaries will be more likely found through testing.

Workflow Tests

Workflow tests are based on how users actually use your product need to be created. These workflow tests are critical in helping to uncover the kinds of defects that users are likely to encounter. Workflow tests are based on the principle of Act Like A Customer Testing, illustrated in figure 10.2.

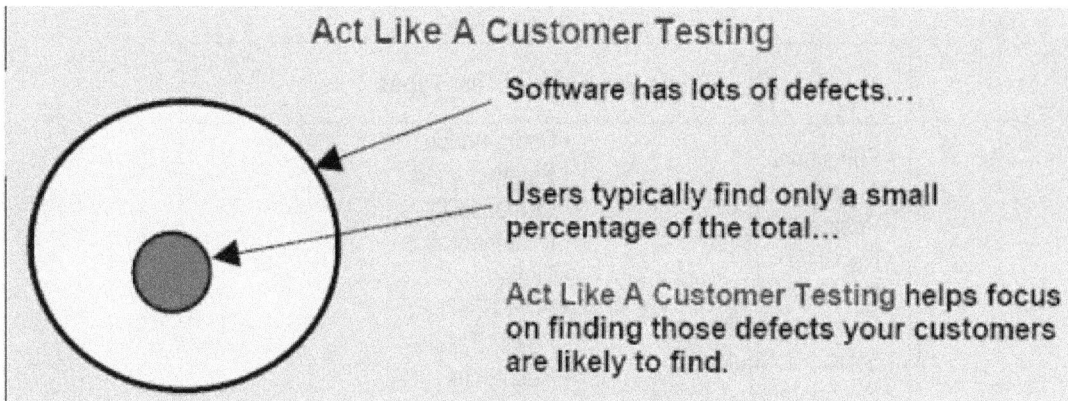

Act Like A Customer Testing

Software has lots of defects...

Users typically find only a small percentage of the total...

Act Like A Customer Testing helps focus on finding those defects your customers are likely to find.

Figure 10.2. Workflow testing

Using knowledge of how customers use your product creates workflow tests. Workflow tests can also be easily created from Use-case/Workflow diagrams.

Step 4. Clean-up the existing test suite

The last step in the process is to remove redundant, unnecessary tests from the test suite. A report identifying the test cases removed from the test suite and why they were removed is provided.

10.5. Chapter summary

This chapter covers testing from a software development point of view. This means that all stages of development are considered and suitable tests discussed. The subject area is very broad indeed and what has been presented can be considered as an overview rather than a prescribed approach to testing. It is accepted that most organisations will define their own testing procedures, and these will embody some of the aspects described in this text. Thus we cover white box and black box testing with some emphasis placed on the procedures during testing. Equivalence partitioning is used as an example of white box testing to demonstrate how test data can be used to examine behaviour around the equivalence classes and the boundaries of their definition. Finally testing effectiveness assessment is mentioned because often testing paranoia may settle in and the organisation is not aware that they may be over-testing or indeed not using the appropriate testing methods.

Exercises

10.1. Describe why it is necessary to perform testing as part of the software engineering process. Additionally, distinguish between black box and white box testing, clearly identifying their respective merits and shortcomings.

10.2. Discuss the differences between black box and structural testing and suggest how they can be used together in a defect testing process.

10.3. Figure Q10.3 below shows the components of a typical testing workbench. Assuming that you are testing a weather station system, and that the system to be tested is made up of three stages, namely Communications Controller, Weather Station and Weather Data, use the components shown in the diagram to explain how the testing could be performed. In your answer include a testing sequence diagram and also discuss any issues that you consider relevant to testing of your system. (You may assume a system other than a weather station as your example)

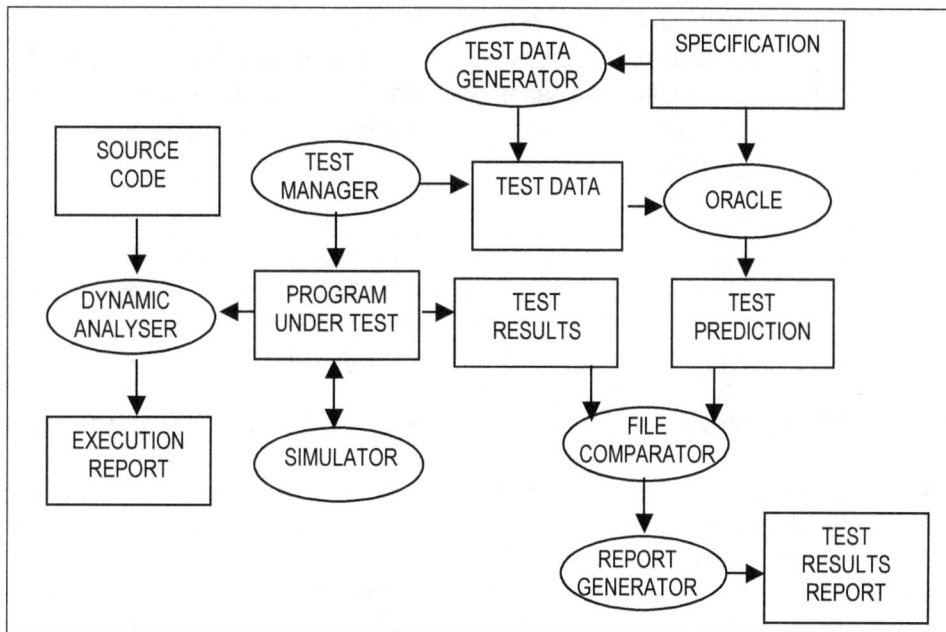

Figure Q10.3 Components of a testing workbench

10.4. You are in charge of a software development project where the client is particularly concerned with system reliability. You need to design tests that will convince the client that suitable testing is embedded into the software development. The client has hired a consultant on the project who has drawn up the following specification.

> *procedure*: insertElement
> *inputs*: list: an array containing elements in ascending order
> length: integer (range 0..maxLength) - the length of list, maxLength is declared as a constant.
> *e*: element – an element to be added to list
> *outputs*: newList: an array containing elements in ascending order
> *newLength*: integer - the length of newList
> *function*: e is placed in list in such a way as to maintain the relative ordering of the original elements in list. The new value of list is returned in newList. newLength = 1 + length.
> *exceptions*: length = maxLength: in this case e is not inserted into list i.e. the value returned by newList is the same as list and the value of newLength is the same as length. The message "Exception: Unable to add element to list - list full" is displayed on the screen.
> *side effects:* none.

i) Describe how you would convince the client that the equivalence partitioning and boundary value analysis techniques for defect testing software would be suitable for this project.

ii) Use equivalence partitioning to derive test cases for software written to satisfy the above specification.

iii) Identify any omissions from, or ambiguities in, the specification.

10.5. Describe the four stages that are used as part of the testing effectiveness Assessment during testing of a software engineering project. In your answer clearly identify the approach to each stage.

10.6. You are a leader of a software engineering project for a grocery store. Your team has developed a software module that is intended to accept the name of a grocery item and a list of the different sizes the item comes in, specified in kilograms. The requirements specifications state that the item name is to be alphabetic characters 2 to 15 characters in length. Each size may be a value in the range of 1 to 48, whole numbers only. The sizes are to be entered in ascending order (smaller sizes first). A maximum of five sizes may be entered for each item. The item name is to be entered first, followed by a comma, and then followed by a list of sizes. A comma will be used to separate each size. Spaces (blanks) are to be ignored anywhere in the input. Use equivalence partitioning to produce equivalence classes and also derive the corresponding test cases for software written to satisfy these requirements specifications.

CHAPTER 11 SOFTWARE QUALITY

11.1. Introduction

Software quality is as a concept can be considered from many aspects. Basically the question is how good is our software? Developers may give us one answer and users another, but what we are looking for is a generalised approach that most will accept as a useful measure of quality. Two leading firms that have placed a great deal of importance on software quality are IBM and Hewlett-Packard. IBM has defined eight dimensions for measuring quality as well as overall user satisfaction: These are shown in figure 11.1.

	Capability	Usability	Performance	Reliability	Instability	Maintainability	Documentation	Availability
Capability								
Usability								
Performance	●	●						
Reliability	●	○	●					
Instability		○	○	○				
Maintainability	●	○	●	○				
Documentation	●	○				○		
Availability	●	○	○	○	○	○		

●: Conflict One Another

○: Support One Another

Blank: Not Related

Figure 11.1. IBM's Measures of user satisfaction

It can be seen form figure 11.1 that some of these factors conflict with each other, and some support each other. For example, usability and performance may conflict, as may reliability and capability or performance and capability. IBM has user evaluations down to a science.

Similarly, Hewlett-Packard uses five quality parameters: functionality, usability, reliability, performance, and serviceability. Other computer and software vendor firms may use more or fewer quality parameters and may even weight them differently for different kinds of software or for the same software in different vertical markets. Also, some firms focus on process quality rather than product quality. [68]

Total Quality Management

In the 1980s and '90s, Total Quality Management (TQM) emerged as a buzzword and a large number of organisations adopted specific methods for achieving it. In fact the ISO 9000 standards is testimony to the TQM movement. In the software engineering field the main standard on quality is probably the Capability Maturity Model (CMM) developed by the Software Engineering Institute (SEI). This was briefly mentioned in chapter 7 of this text, In 2000, the SW-CMM was upgraded to Capability Maturity Model Integration (CMMI). [70]

Implementation of TQM has many varieties, but the four essential characteristics of the TQM approach are as follows:

- **Customer focus:** The objective is to achieve total customer satisfaction—to "delight the customer." Customer focus includes studying customer needs and wants, gathering customer requirements, and measuring customer satisfaction.
- **Process improvement:** The objective is to reduce process variation and to achieve continuous process improvement of both business and product development processes.
- **Quality culture:** The objective is to create an organisation-wide quality culture, including leadership, management commitment, total staff participation, and employee empowerment.
- **Measurement and analysis:** The objective is to drive continuous improvement in all quality parameters by a goal-oriented measurement system.

11.2. Generic software quality measures

Software metrics

In 1993 the IEEE published a standard for software quality metrics methodology that has since defined and led development in the field. This standard was intended as a more systematic approach for establishing quality requirements and identifying, implementing, analysing, and validating software quality metrics for software system development. It spans the development cycle in five steps, as shown in figure 11.2.

Software Quality Activity	Development Cycle Phasing
Establish software quality requirements	___
Identify software quality metrics	___
Implement software quality metrics	_____
Analyze results of these metrics	_____
Validate the metrics	___

Figure 11.2. IEEE Software Quality Metrics Methodology

Step 1: The first step in the IEEE recommended methodology is to establish direct metrics with values as numerical targets to be met in the final product. The factors to be measured may vary from product to product, but it is critical to rank the factors by priority and assign a direct metric value as a quantitative requirement for that factor. There is no mystery at this point, because Voice of the Customer (VOC) and Quality Function Deployment (QFD) are the means available not only to determine the metrics and their target values, but also to prioritise them.

Step 2: The second step is to identify the software quality metrics by decomposing each factor into sub-factors and those further into the metrics. For example, a direct final metric for the factor reliability could be faults per 1,000 lines of code (KLOC) with a target value—say, one fault per 1,000 lines of code (LOC). For each validated metric a value should be assigned that will be achieved during development. Figure 11.3 gives the IEEE's suggested paradigm for a description of the metrics set. [71]

Step 3: To implement the metrics in the metric set chosen for the project under design, the data to be collected must be determined, and assumptions about the flow of data must be clarified. Any tools to be employed are defined, and any organisations to be involved are described, as are any necessary training. It is also wise at this point to test the metrics on some known software to refine their use, sensitivity, accuracy, and the cost of employing them.

Term	Description
Name	Name of the metric
Metric	Mathematical function to compute the metric
Cost	Cost of using the metric
Benefit	Benefit of using the metric
Impact	Can the metric be used to alter or stop the project?
Target value	Numerical value to be achieved to meet the requirement
Factors	Factors related to the metric
Tools	Tools to gather data, calculate the metric, and analyze the results
Application	How the metric is to be used
Data items	Input values needed to compute the metric
Computation	Steps involved in the computation
Interpretation	How to interpret the results of the computation
Considerations	Metric assumptions and appropriateness
Training	Training required to apply the metric
Example	An example of applying the metric
History	Projects that have used this metric and its validation history
References	List of projects used, project details, and so on

Figure 11.3. IEEE Metric Set Description Paradigm

Step 4: Analysing the metrics can help you identify any components of the developing system that appear to have unacceptable quality or that present development bottlenecks. Any components whose measured values deviate from their target values are considered to be noncompliant.

Step 5: Validation of the metrics is a continuous process spanning multiple projects. If the metrics employed are to be useful, they must accurately indicate whether quality requirements have been achieved or are likely to be achieved during development. Furthermore, a metric must be revalidated every time it is used. Confidence in a metric will improve over time as further usage experience is gained.

11.3. Current metrics and models technology

A very good treatment of current software metrics and models can be found in the title "Software Measurement: A Visualization Toolkit for Project Control and Process Measurement". [72] It comes with a CD-ROM that contains the Project Attribute Monitoring and Prediction Associate (PAMPA) measurement and analysis software tools. The book traces software metrics from 1977 and then brings the field up to date to 1997, technologically updating the metrics and models by including later research and experience. The updated metrics are grouped by size, effort, development time, productivity, quality, reliability, verification, and usability. [68] Precise treatment of metrics is beyond the scope of this text and only a brief overview will be presented.

In all engineered products, quality is an issue that can impact on profit. Generally good quality products are favoured above poor quality even taking into account the cost differential. For this reason software houses are investing into measures that will ensure that their product meets the quality standards that are prescribed. Figure 11.4 shows the effect that quality has on profit.

Example:

A recent version of a popular PC spreadsheet application reached the market over a year behind schedule. The program was implemented in 400 000 lines of code, required 263 staff years of effort and cost $22 million, $15 million of which was invested in quality control activities.

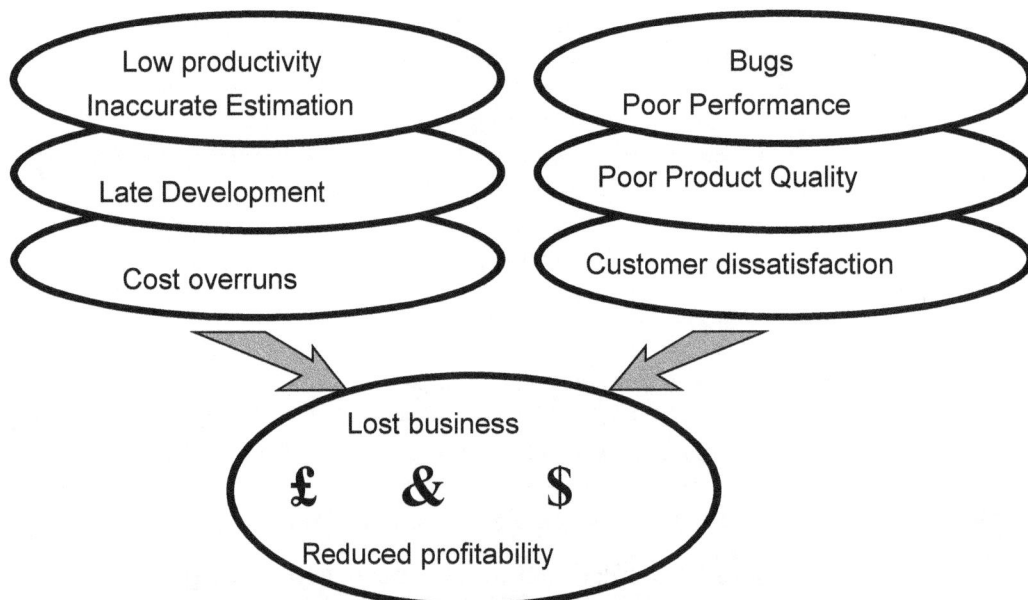

Figure 11.4. Metrics and their effect on profit

In table 11.1 I show a rough guide to the cost of a software development project in relation to the type of development and the millions of lines of code (MLOC) parameter. It is evident from this that software projects are substantial and comparable in cost and effort to other engineering disciplines such as construction for example.

Table 11.1

Product Application	Size (MLOC)	Cost (£M)
Operating System, Large communications system	2-5	150-350
Mid-sized communications system	1-2	50-100
Data Base system, Compiler	0.4-1	9-22
Transaction monitor	0.2-0.4	5-10
Monitoring system (Medical)	0.2-0.4	4-8

The difficulty in software engineering (unlike in construction engineering) is that we do not have a long history of experience to rely on. Therefore during all stages of development we are working with a large number of unknowns. In the previous chapters on dependability (Chapter 7) and validation (Chapter 9) we discussed aspects that are being considered to improve quality during design and implementation stages. Nevertheless we do have to bear in mind that this is still a relatively new industry and therefore we need to be very vigil with monitoring quality issues. In general the following points should be considered in relation to quality in software engineering projects,

- There is a need for the ability for accurate estimation of the development time for software products.
- It is also desirable to decrease the elapsed time from product conception to customer delivery.
- Improving software quality and productivity by the application of quantitative methods or 'metrics'
- The application of software metrics is a tool for effectively managing the software development and maintenance process.

Metrics application

A large number of specific metrics can be defined, but for classification purposes we identify three main categories,

- **Global Objective metrics**: These include program size measured in function point counts, lines of code, effort, schedule, number of faults, cost and others.

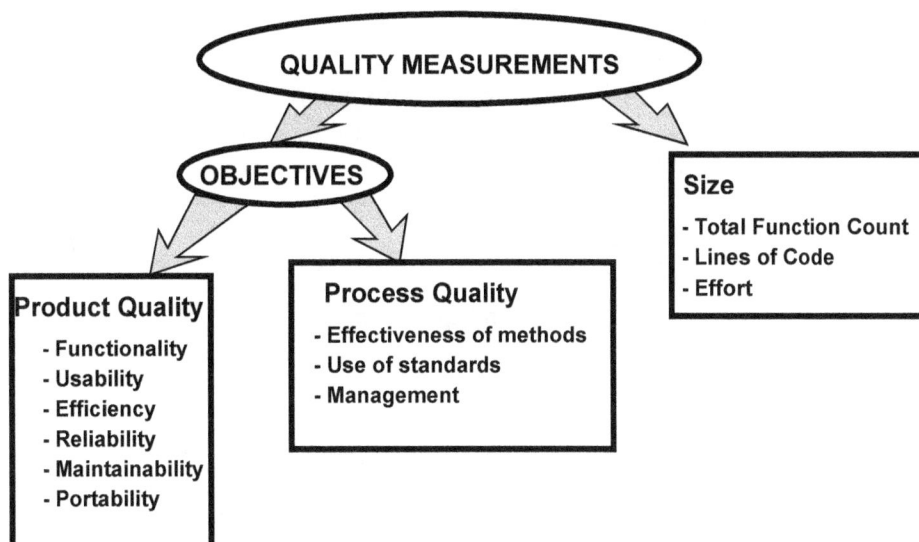

Figure 11.5. Quality measurement using metrics

- **Global Subjective metrics**: These relate to customer satisfaction. Data is often obtainable from interviews and surveys. They include product quality and process quality measurement: i.e. number of faults detected and counted during System Test and the number of Customer Change Requests. They can also be used to characterise the environment within which software is being developed, as shown in figure 11.5. i.e. Management of development team productivity.

- **Global/Phase metrics:** Global metrics are tools for software product management of primary interest to software engineers. They provide insights for management concerning project status on size, product quality and process quality. Phase metrics are metrics that are indicators for a specific phase of the software development.

The relationship of these metrics to software development is shown in figure 11.6. Here it is seen that phase metrics are confined to the coding stage while global metrics apply throughout development.

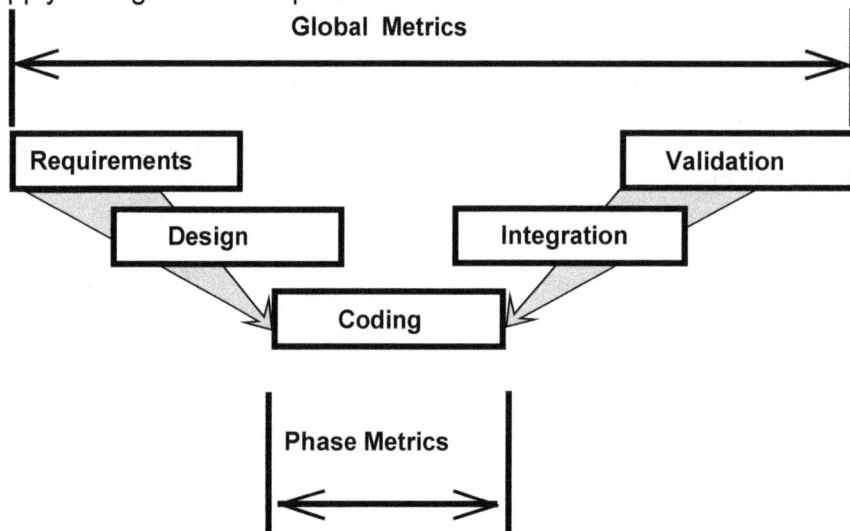

Figure 11.6. Global and phase metrics to overall software development

Feedback and process improvement

The software development process is dynamic in that the metrics provide an indicator as to which process steps can be improved. Figure 11.7 shows how metrics fit into the overall software development process.

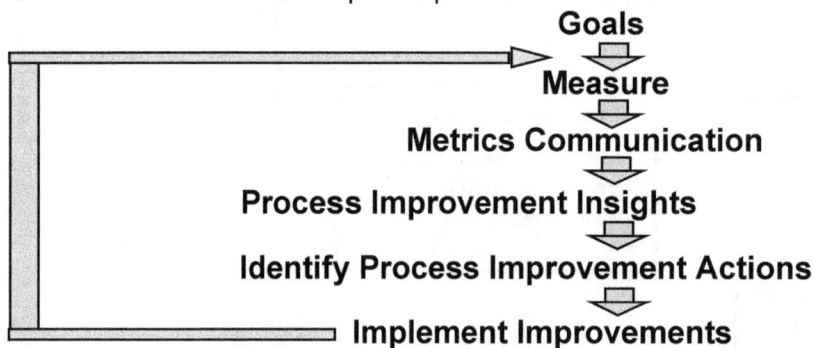

Figure 11.7. Metrics in software development

11.4. Metrics characteristics

As mentioned earlier a large number of metrics can be defined, and quite often an organisation will select those that are most appropriate for their development. The following are a few example metrics,

- **Lines of Code:** This metric is defined as the count of program line of code excluding comment or blank lines. This metric is typically given in units of thousands lines of code. (KLOC)
- **System Test Faults:** This metric is calculated by dividing the total number of software faults reported during System Test by the number of thousand lines of code for each product and for each release. This is used as an indicator of the software quality and also of the testing effectiveness of the software engineering process.
- **Customer Change Requests:** This metric is calculated by dividing the number of unique change requests, due to faults, made by the customers for the first year of field use of a given release by the number of thousand lines of code for that release.

As development proceeds, these metrics are used to improve the overall quality of the product. Figure 11.8 shows the graph that can be expected from the use of metrics during development. It is seen from the figure that as a direct result of applying metrics, the number of faults is gradually reducing during the development stages.

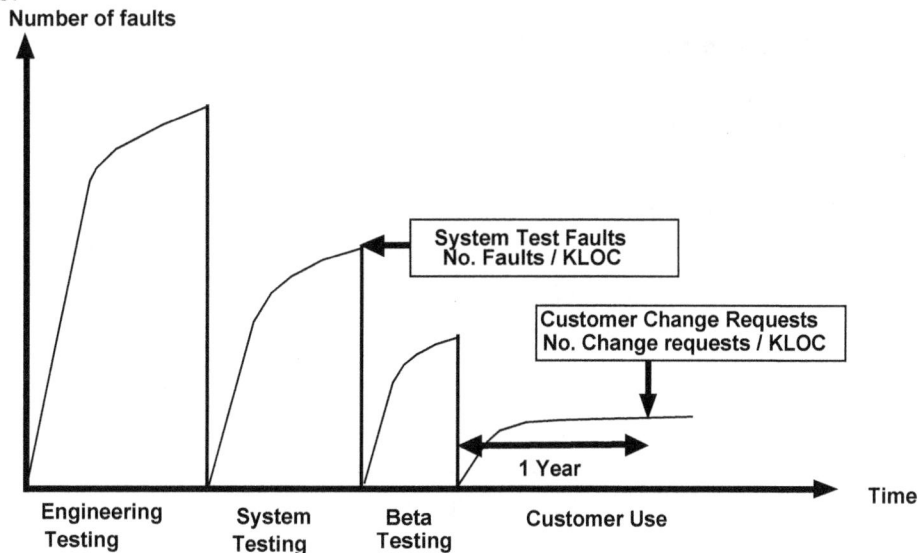

Example Product Quality Metrics
Figure 11.8 Example product metrics

11.5. Impact of metrics on modern software engineering

With increasing complexity from technology, software quality has become a paramount issue in many cases. Companies and institutions use metrics in order to get a quantitative view of performance. Software metrics are a quantitative guide to some performance criteria of a certain piece of software. They have been established upon the concept that before something can be measured or quantified, it needs to be translated into numbers. [73] There are several areas where software metrics are found to be of particular use. For example some areas where software metrics are necessary are,

- In determining how many programmers are needed to finish a module in a week or month.
- Knowing the timeframe for patching certain bugs in the program.
- Knowing the number of bugs per line of codes written by each programmer.

Thus the management of a company can use metrics be improve software quality. For example, in UK alone it is estimated that £1,000,000 per hour of effort is lost as a result of poor quality software. A recent survey produced a study, which described security, quality, code integrity, and business relevance as the most important factors on which to focus for software development. [74]

When asked how many organisations found serious problems during post release code review, 25.5% said "very often" or "all the time," and 41% said they had issues with defects found after review. Figure 11.9 shows the results of the survey when the following question was asked,

"On average, how many critical bugs requiring patches are discovered in the 12-month period following release of the software into production?"

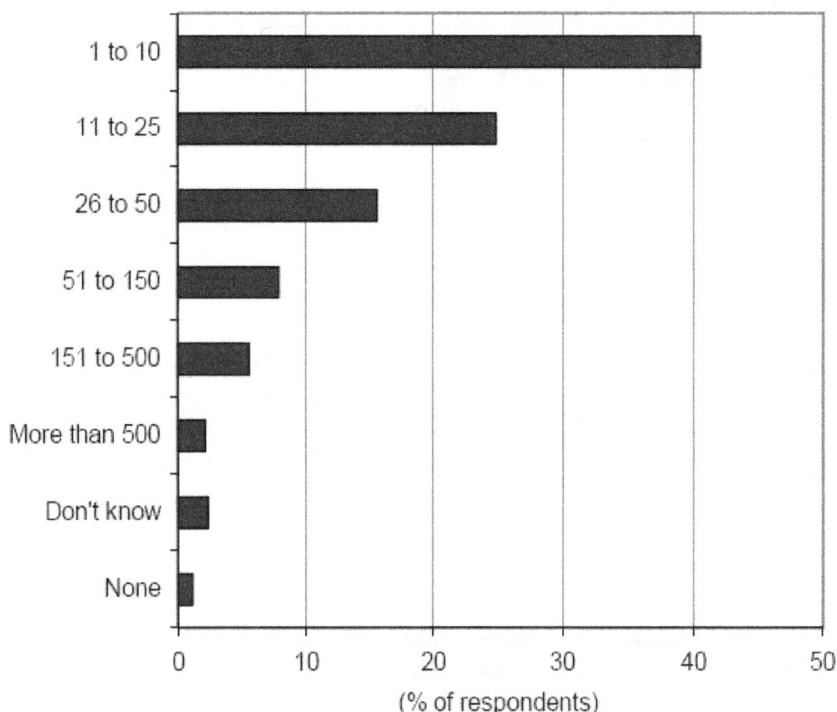

(% of respondents)

Figure 11.9. Number of critical bugs found within one year after release. [75]

The results show that 40% of tests reveal at least 10 serious bugs after the product has been released, and about 15% find up to 59 bugs. This reduces in number but nevertheless the quality aspect should be better. The review concludes that current, typical quality approaches are inadequate to deal with code defect costs and issues. This means that they find problems after QA and spend significant amounts of effort and time to repair defects.

It is accepted that new approaches to software development and coordination across software lifecycle areas improves quality. It is helpful to consider specific quality areas that can augment existing approaches to improve code quality and decrease defects. Surveys suggest that 69% of analysts use manual code reviews to find bugs, while 60% use static analysis and 57% use dynamic analysis tools. (See chapter 10 of this text on testing) A combination of static and dynamic tests is seen as the best way to improve quality. For instance, static analysis tools provide code analysis without requiring the developer to produce complex unit test suites. White-box testing of this kind is available via automated source code analysis. In addition, the developer can perform this test before the coding is completed.

Static analysis tools enable developers to test incomplete code, without executables. Also different types of quality defects can be identified with static analysis. Given the code coverage and analysis provided, these tools are able to uncover defect types such as security vulnerabilities, memory leaks, boundary conditions, and crash-causing code constructs that might be missed using other testing methods that depend on human beings to establish operational parameters.

Most development organisations agree that costs of debugging are significant. To some extent this is the fault of the industry as a whole, because debugging is a part of the development process, whereas many consider it to be just a bug-fixing phase, and since there should be no bugs in the system, this stage should be redundant. But this is not the reality in software development. The debugging phase is very much a part of development because the system cannot be completed without it.

In order to put this into perspective consider for example the cost of repairing defects. Assuming the average cost of one developer per hour is (£50) and further assuming 30 hours to find and repair one defect in production. The resulting cost of a single fault is £1500. As is clear from the survey results (see Figures 11.9 and 11.10), significant numbers of respondents experienced 11.25+ bugs annually that require multiple developers and multiple hourly cycles to discover and to repair.

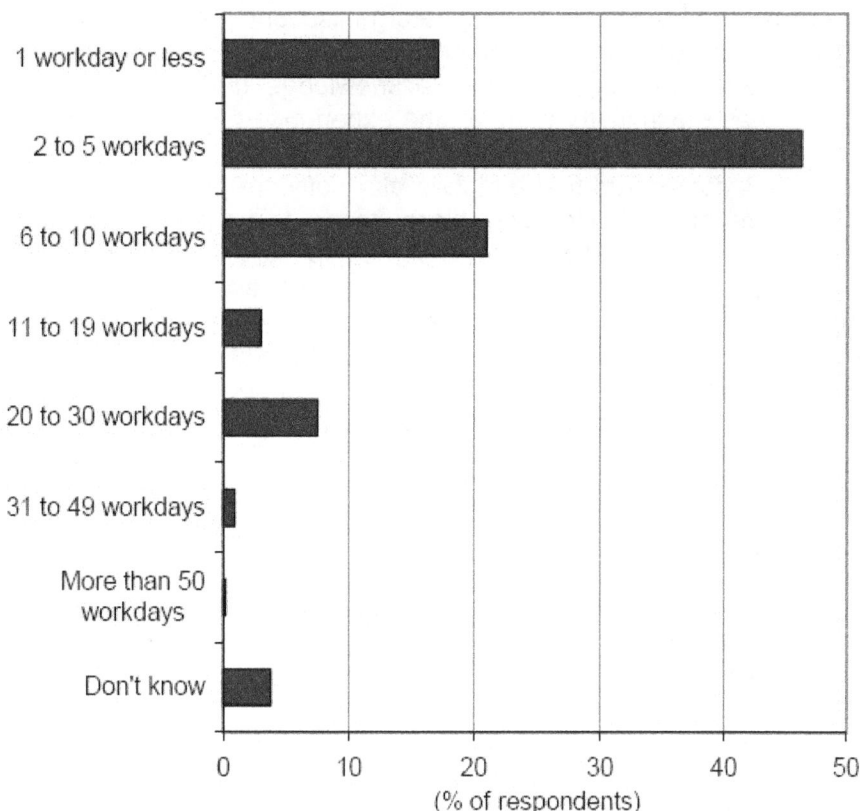

Figure 11.10. Number of days required for correcting a field defect

While the scope of this survey focused on development teams, there are other, additional costs to consider; such as QA cycles, support calls, and the time it takes engineers to find the root cause of errors, all of which can significantly increase cost.

These financial penalties are significant and generally they do not take into consideration the additional business costs for downtime of critical applications. Additionally and quite significantly, costs can include damage to corporate brand and reputation, product recalls, and significant revenue loss when related to transactional applications.

With complex system, experience shows that repairing field defects is complex. From figure 11.10 it is seen that the majority of respondents (67%) estimate that 2 to 10 workdays are needed to repair field defects and 11% said that it takes from 11 to 30 days. From the same graph it is seen that 37% of developer time is spent debugging for large organisations that do internal software development. The annual cost for this effort in debugging can range from £3.5 million (based on a midpoint median 100 developers per organisation) to £15 million (based on a midpoint-mean of 416 developers per organisation). From these data it is estimated that if 100% of defects were addressed and corrected prior to production, they would experience a 32% cost savings. This percentage is large enough to justify the effort to improve product quality and remove defects as early as possible in the development cycle.

11.6. Corporate attitude to software quality

Despite a general awareness of the need to maintain quality in their products many software houses tend to have an overly optimistic view about consequences of defective software. This could be related to the general drive to present their quality success as better than it is, particularly given the competitive pressure of outsourcing. And it may also be related to the typical, human tendency to view one's own work as better than it actually is. For this reason some organisations prefer to have a separate quality assurance (QA) department that only deals with quality issues and has no input to development. Most organisations acknowledge that they are still on the learning curve and as the industry matures the experience gained will tend to reduce the cost of maintaining quality.

It is generally considered that a high-quality software process should lead to a high-quality software product. However there needs to be a correct approach to quality assurance in order for this to be true. Some aspects are considered next.

The concept of a high quality software process is derived from the manufacturing industry where a product is designed to be of a particular standard. By auditing the processes that are used to produce a final product it is possible to identify weaknesses and omissions in these, which could lead to poor design of products that are of a low standard and would not be acceptable to the customer. There are three main activities associated with software quality management. These are quality assurance, planning and control and I provide a brief description next.

Quality assurance.

This is a framework that is put in place so that all personnel involved in the software design process know the steps that they should follow in order to carry out their particular task within the global objective of producing a quality product. This framework usually takes the form of documentation manuals, which describe two areas of the software design process. The two areas are the product and the process.

- **Product standards.** These standards specify how areas like program code should be structured, formats used, and the layout of design diagrams such as flow charts and Class diagrams etc. The reasons for using standards is so that everybody within a company is working from the same format which means that there is no confusion about how different types of documentation are interpreted.

- **Process standards.** This is the standard used to define the processes that should be followed during the different stages of software development. This would include stages such as specification, design, validation etc and the documentation that should be produced to show that these stages have been implemented.

Standards are important in the software design process because they describe best practices gained from years of experience thus preventing the repetition of previous mistakes. They provide a means by which to carry out the quality assurance process from the resulting documentation. Standards allow previous knowledge to be retained and passed on thus preventing the loss of valuable know-how when key members of staff leave the company.

Quality planning

The quality planning process involves selection of suitable standards for to be used on a particular project. This may involve creation of new standards to meet the requirements of new projects where there has been no previous work carried out. A plan is usually drawn up that outlines the desired product qualities for a particular project and how these qualities can be achieved. This usually includes the following section,

- **Product introduction.** Giving a description of the intended market and quality expectations.
- **Product plans.** These outline important dates, responsibilities etc
- **Process descriptions**. Here focus is to provide a clear description of processes to be followed throughout the product development.
- **Quality goals.** These describe the quality attributes of the product
- **Risks.** Risk analysis and how this impacts on product quality.

Quality control

This is the process by which the whole design process is checked to make sure that everyone is adhering to the correct standards and following the correct processes to ensure that a quality product is being produced from start to finish. This is achieved by the use of quality reviews and automated software assessment where all documentation produced throughout the design process is checked to make sure that the right format has been produced and that a common working process is followed across the full range of projects that a company is involved in.

By using these three activities of quality assurance, planning and control the software process should become refined over time by constantly reviewing the methods employed and standards used until the processes of carrying out a project becomes as efficient and predictable as possible. This allows the software design company to produce consistent quality for each project, bring projects in on time, according to specification, and within budget.

Because the notion of what a quality product cannot be easily defined it is usually determined by the purchaser of the product. Many of the factors considered previously will be part of their decision as to whether the product is of sufficient quality. The use of quality software processes allows the software engineer to try to anticipate what factors the customer will find most important when considering if a product is of a high quality and base the software design process around these factors. But there are other factors to consider. For example consider a software system that meets the specifications but costs twice the price of similar products on the market and it took three times as long to produce. Does this make the product a quality product? Does it offer value for money? Is the user getting what they want?

Thus it can be seen that there are a number of problems with delivering quality products to customers.

One major issue is that the quality process is derived from the manufacturing industry and there are a lot of areas that do not translate easily from one industry to the other. This leads to many grey areas, as the software industry does not always work in the same way as the manufacturing industry. These grey areas tend to lead to different companies having different interpretations of the way quality is built into the software design process. This can lead to difficulties during the auditing process for the purpose of checking the quality processes carried out within a company. Additionally many companies implement quality processes in order to gain accreditation for different quality standards. Consequently they tend to see the quality process as an exercise in documenting all areas of the project lifecycle. This in turn leads to mountains of paperwork and increased workloads when the real purpose of quality processes is to make the project lifecycle as efficient as possible by refining the process until a lean process is developed. The mountains of paperwork developed when this approach is used usually leads to staff looking for shortcuts that are not documented so they can avoid the form filling that can be associated with the quality assurance process. Therefore, although much effort has gone into documenting the process quality of the product is not accurately established.

Quality processes should be capable of evolving all the time as the outside world is changing but invariably upper management have a tendency to see the quality process as a way of setting out rigid guidelines to be followed to ensure that they are producing the right product. This leads to companies that become inflexible to change and ultimately extinction as they are unable to keep up with the rapid developments that take place in the industry. Many companies see other companies using a quality process and succeeding in improving their business and profitability. They then decide that they will use this quality process within their own company because it worked so well for their competitor. They have not taken into account the different company structure of their competitor and as a result end up pulling their own company apart in order to fit the new quality process model, which results in failure and sometimes bankruptcy.

The software design process often involves the implementation of new ideas and the standards used are constantly changing. This can make it difficult to stick to common standards as new technologies have to be used all the time in order to keep up with competitors and this makes it difficult to keep the documentation up to date as the lifespan of standards gets shorter.

11.7. Chapter summary

In this chapter I briefly cover quality in software engineering projects. This is a very important and also broad field in engineering, which makes it difficult to cover all the important aspects. I consider some general points regarding quality and relate these to metrics, which are used to provide a measure of quality. I cover some generic software measures that were first introduced by IBM and HP and which are still valid. I provide example metrics and also try to explain where these fit in the overall software development cycle. I follow this by examples of a more modern approach and provide an indication through a survey that was carried out to establish corporate attitude to software quality. Here I briefly cover quality assurance planning and control and consider any potential pit-falls in quality assurance.

Exercises

11.1. Why are metrics used in software engineering projects?

11.2. Discuss using examples why good quality software is hard to achieve in practice.

11.3. What is TQM? Do some research to identify how the TQM movement in the 1990s impacted on software engineering industry?

11.4. Explain the 5 steps identified in the metrics methodology. How realistic are these in your view, when applied to medium size software projects? Use examples, as you consider necessary.

11.5. Describe five types of static product metrics, which are used for assessing quality attributes of software.

11.6. You are a senior software manager for a games developer and you have to prepare the release of a new game that your organisation has developed. The game is played for free by on-line users under a browser (Internet Explorer or Mozilla Firefox). Revenue is generated by hosting banners of advertisers on the game website and the fees for this are proportional to the number of users playing the game. From this brief explanation, stating any assumptions that you consider relevant, discuss the quality issues that you would recommend in order to increase the chances of success of the launch of your new game. Discuss how usability of the system is affected by security measures.

11.7. Explain quality assurance, quality planning and quality control and suggest how software metrics can be utilised to ensure that a high-quality software process should lead to a high-quality software product. Discuss the possible problems with this system of quality management.

CHAPTER 12 SOFTWARE COSTING

12.1. Introduction

In all engineering projects one of the driving factors is cost. We have discussed quality issues and other aspects such as dependability and all those features are influenced by cost. On the other side of the cost equation considers the value of the product and how much profit the organisation will make. If you make a reliable product that everyone loves and you lose money when you sell it the product will not have a future in the marketplace. In other words the economics of production play a significant role in software engineering projects. In the previous chapter on metrics, we mentioned that the cost of repairing defects could be significant. Very often we cannot predict what defects our product will develop or have at the time of testing, and so it can be difficult to estimate how much time and effort is needed to get the product right. Apart form the testing and quality issues, the actual product design and development takes time and effort and therefore costs money. Thus we need a reasonably accurate means of estimating how much a development project will cost?

Example

Consider the following scenario,

You are a consultant on a project for a small software company producing computer games and teaching material. The client is asking you to design a software application to run on a personal computer, which will help to teach children aged 9-11 basic mathematics. You have arranged the first meeting with the client where you are determined to obtain all the information that is necessary for you to prepare a formal specification for the software development. During this meeting your client wants to know how much he should be expecting to pay for this. You need to provide a guideline price that will ensure that you and your software development team will make a profit and also that your client will be satisfied with your fees for the job.

How would you go about pricing your work?

I am pretty sure that most of us could hazard a guess, but in business whenever possible blind guessing should be avoided. We therefore need a method that will guide us in terms of how to provide a realistic estimate for the cost of software development.

As a first reaction I would say that the cost would depend on the effort. If I measure effort as my cost per hour, then I can estimate cost. But there are other factors to consider, such as, do I have experience in this work? If, so I can probably do it all more efficiently and more quickly, so I could reduce the price and become more competitive. Thus it can be seen that many parameters can influence the decision on cost. A very useful cost estimation-modelling tool was initially developed by Boehm and has since been manipulated and modified by various organisations. It is used to estimate the cost of software development projects. [76]

The original model described cost as a function of a metric, which typically would relate to effort.

$$\text{For example: } cost = A(\mathit{effort\_metric})^B$$

As a model this expression is very useful because it has a linear coefficient A and an exponential coefficient B. Remember that we are in charge of the values here and if we decide to keep A=1 and B=1 then the cost will be directly proportional to effort. Note that any change in the coefficient A will affect the cost as a linear multiplier. For example keeping B=1 and changing A=2 will double the price. On the other hand, keeping A=1 and changing B=2, will increase the price exponentially. The general behaviour of this function is shown in figure 12.1.

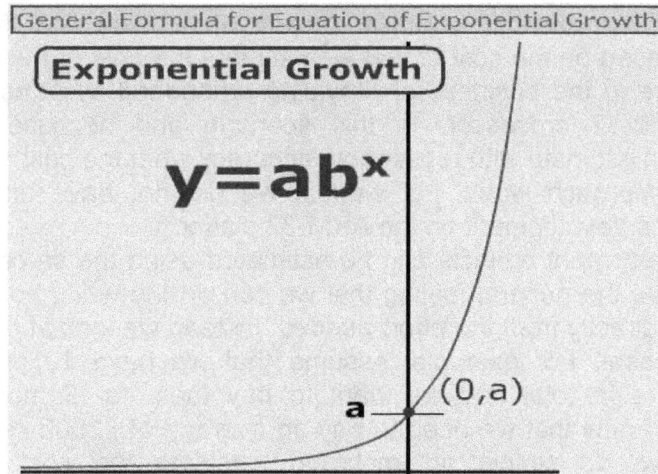

General Formula for Equation of Exponential Growth

Exponential Growth

$$y = ab^x$$

a   (0,a)

Figure 12.1. Exponential growth function

Thus the exponential model is useful because we can change the values of A and B to suit the task for which we are trying to estimate cost. This means that if the effort is strenuous we can increase the value of A and therefore adjust for the cost in that way. On the other hand if the effort is such that we have to deal with a very complex issues, which require a lot of effort, then we may choose to increase the exponential coefficient B.

In order to help with choosing the appropriate model Boehm described three types of models and differentiated between these by allocating different coefficients for A and B. A summary of these is given next.

Summary Extracted from: Software Engineering Economics
Boehm, BW, Prentice-Hall, 1981
Note: In the following models KDSI = Kilo Delivered Source Instructions

Boehm's basic Model:

$$Effort = 2.4(KDSI)^{1.05}$$

$$Time = 2.5(Effort)^{0.38}$$

Three varieties of the basic model:

Organic

$$Effort = 2.4(KDSI)^{1.05}$$

$$Time = 2.5(Effort)^{0.38}$$

Semi-detached

$$Effort = 3.0(KDSI)^{1.12}$$

$$Time = 2.5(Effort)^{0.35}$$

Embedded

$$Effort = 3.6(KDSI)^{1.20}$$

$$Time = 2.5(Effort)^{0.32}$$

Boehm's approach was algorithmic, which is to say he developed a mathematical model that can be modified in order to fit different projects. There are however other ways of estimating how much a project would cost. The most obvious way to estimate cost is to ask an expert who has done this before to help with the estimate. The initial cost is a consultancy fee and it would be considerably less that the consequence of getting the estimate wrong. Another method would be to estimate by analogy, here we consider a similar project or at least one that we consider analogous, and based on the cost of that we estimate the cost of the new project. For example, if we are in the business of providing embedded systems solutions using primarily the ARM-32 processor. In this scenario and because we are highly specialised we can estimate with reasonable accuracy what the cost of a development would be. This approach would not work if we did not have any experience in embedded systems development on the ARM-32 platform.

Some development projects can be estimated using the so-called Parkinson's Law. Here we have the general feeling that we can do the work, however we do not estimate the cost directly from the effort needed. Instead we look at resources that we have at our disposal. For example, assume that we have 10 programmers and software engineers in total and we want to pay them for 3 months out of this development. We know that we need to pay an average of £2000 per month to each employee and we do simple arithmetic to calculate the cost of this project. Accordingly, this project would cost £60,000. If you think this is too high or too low, you can tweak it, but the ball-part figure is there.

Pricing to win is an approach where you set the price according to what you consider the customer is willing to pay. It does not necessarily reflect the cost of development, rather it considers that some clients will be able to pay more than others and on average if you do a few projects, you will be profitable even if in some cases the profit margin was not significant. Also, sometimes it is better to break even and continue in business than to close shop because you are not making a profit.

These last two methods are not scientific at all, but they are equally valid. Very often in business you may be stuck for revenue, and you will try to undercut competition and even take a temporary loss in order to stay in business. These decisions are really management and business decisions and I shall not delve into them any more. I shall move onto the more established costing procedures supplied by Boehm in the shape of the COCOMO model. Table 12.1 summarises the basic techniques that can be used to estimate cost.

We will discuss Boehm's models in more detail but the above serve to show that cost can be modelled using linear and exponential coefficients. Note that when linear coefficients halve, the equation result is halved. However when the power is taken to 0.5 than the result is square rooted. (i.e. it is taken to the power of 0.5, which means square root). With this type of equation it is possible to model a large number of systems and cost in software engineering projects is one of them. To obtain the actual figure of cost there are more multipliers but the essential model remains the same. We will consider some aspects of the COCOMO model next.

Table 12.1 Cost estimation methods

Technique	Description
Algorithmic cost modelling	A model is developed using historical cost estimation that relates some software metric to the project cost. An estimate is made of that metric and the model predicts the effort required. Boehm's Three varieties of the basic model: Organic $Effort = 2.4(KDSI)^{1.05}$ $Time = 2.5(Effort)^{0.38}$ Semi-detached $Effort = 3.0(KDSI)^{1.12}$ $Time = 2.5(Effort)^{0.35}$ Embedded $Effort = 3.6(KDSI)^{1.20}$ $Time = 2.5(Effort)^{0.32}$
Expert Judgement	Several experts on the proposed software development techniques and the application domain are consulted. They each estimate the project cost. These estimates are compared and discussed. The estimation process is iterated until an agreed estimate is reached.
Estimation by analogy	This technique is applicable when other projects in the same application domain have been completed. The cost of a new project is estimated by analogy with these completed projects.
Parkinson's law	Parkinson's law states that the work expands to fill the time available. The cost is determined by available resources rather than by objective assessment. If software has to be delivered in 12 months and five people are available the effort required is estimated at 60 person months.
Pricing to win	The software cost is estimated to be whatever the customer has available to spend on the project. The estimated effort depends on the customer's budget and not on the cost of development to provide the required functionality.

12.2. COCOMO cost estimation model

The COnstructive COst MOdel (COCOMO) is an example of statistical models used for estimating software cost and effort. These methods use a basic formula with parameters that are determined empirically from a historical database and current project characteristics. The COCOMO cost estimation model is used by thousands of software project managers, and is based on a study of hundreds of software projects. Unlike other cost estimation models, COCOMO is an open model, so all of the details are published.

Software cost estimation is used to determine how much effort and time a software project requires. It establishes a firm, reliable budget for a project, which can help with making competitive contract bids or deciding which project is most cost effective for the organisation. Without a reasonably accurate cost-estimation capability, software projects often experience the following problems: [77]

• Software project personnel have no firm basis for telling a manager, customer, or salesperson that their proposed budget and schedule are unrealistic. This leads to optimistic over-promising on software development, lowering cost on competitive software contract bids, and the inevitable overruns and performance compromises as a consequence.

• Software analysts have no firm basis for making realistic hardware-software trade-off analysis during the system design phase. This often leads to a design in which the hardware cost is decreased at the expense of an even larger increase in software cost.

- Project managers have no firm basis for determining how much time and effort each software phase and activity should take. This leaves managers with no way to tell whether or not the software is proceeding according to plan. That basically means that the software portion of the project is out of control from the beginning.

Estimation model development procedure

Interests of a software organisation are best served when it develops its own cost estimation models. To develop an estimation model we have to follow these steps:
- Determine a list of potential / most important effort cost drivers.
- Determine a scaling model for each effort and cost driver.
- Select initial estimation model.
- Measure and estimate projects and compare.
- Evaluate quality of estimation as part of project post-mortem.
- Update and validate model at appropriate intervals.

Cost Drivers

Cost drivers are those variables, which influence the actual amount of money spent on any given project. The cost drivers can vary from project to project. In addition, the model employed to estimate the cost can influence cost drivers. One of the major cost drivers in many estimation models is the size of the software product. The size of the software product:
- Is one of the major cost drivers in software development projects?
- Is also the weakest link in the estimation process?
- Needs extra attention if an organisation is developing its own model.

Size estimation

Function Points (FP) is one method that has been developed from empirical evidence. Many projects were examined with respect to their different characteristics and the size of the final products examined, and finally a model produced to fit the data. The FP method works best with applications that process business type information, since those are the projects that were examined to produce the model. It is also not as widely known, used or trusted for estimating SIZE as COCOMO is for estimating EFFORT. There are five items shown in table below, which determine the ultimate complexity of an application.

Characteristic	Weight
Number of Inputs	4
Number of Outputs	5
Number of Enquiries	4
Number of Files	10
Number of Interfaces	7

The process used is to take the weighted sum of these counts to get the number of function points (FP) in a system. Once the number of function points (FP) is calculated (from requirements), other data is used to estimate module/system SIZE. For various programming languages, data can be obtained to determine how many lines of code are usually needed to implement one function point.

Example

Suppose that Ada program needs 70 LOC per FP. A system with, 10 inputs, 10 outputs, 5 Enquiries, 4 Files and 2 Interfaces would have an FP equal to:

$$FP = (10 * 4) + (10 * 5) + (5 * 4) + (4 * 10) + (2 * 7) = 164$$

And the estimated Size would be equal to:

$$Size = FP * 70 = 164 * 70 = 11480\ LOC$$

Software cost-modelling accuracy

Software cost and effort estimation will never be an exact science. Too many parameters such as technical, environmental, personal or political can affect the final cost of software and the effort required to develop it. It is important to recognise that we cannot estimate the cost of producing 100,000 source instructions of software as accurately as we can estimate the cost of producing 100,000 transistor radios. There are many reasons for this; some of the main ones are:

• Source instructions are not a uniform commodity, nor are they the essence of the desired product.

• Software requires the creativity and co-operation of human beings, whose individual and group behaviour is generally hard to predict.

• Software has a much smaller base of relevant quantitative historical experience and it is hard to add to the base by performing small controlled experiments.

By current standards a software cost estimation model is doing well if it can estimate software development costs within 20% of the actual costs, 70% of the time, within the Class of projects to which it is calibrated. Currently the Intermediate and Detailed COCOMO models perform close to this level (within 20% of the actual costs, 68 to 70% of the time) over a fairly wide range of applications.

12.3. Estimation models

Estimation models are produced by reference to past, successful projects and from these measuring certain properties and characteristics (duration, cost, team size, disk usage, etc.) in order to estimate cost of a new development project. Curve-fitting methods are used on data points to get descriptive equations, which are the models that will be used to predict cost. There is no real guarantee that the resulting estimates will be correct however the fact that they came from measurements of past projects provides a degree of confidence.

Small projects

Measurements of small to moderate projects resulted in a model of the following form,

$$EFFORT = a * SIZE + b$$

Here, the magnitude of the effort is a linear function of the size of the project (Number of Lines of Code, usually). This model holds up until a certain point, usually for projects that can be reasonably accomplished by small teams of two or three people. By increasing the size of the project, the above model becomes less and less accurate and the need for a new model increases.

Large projects

Projects requiring teams of more than three or so people tend to behave in the following way:

$$EFFORT = a * SIZE^{\,b}$$

Here, the size of the project is scaled exponentially; therefore as a product increases in size, the effort to produce the product grows more than linearly (for $b >= 1$). It means that if we try to develop a larger product, our productivity ($EFFORT/SIZE$) decreases. This decrease in productivity on larger projects is sometimes referred to as a **diseconomy** of scale. The main reasons why larger software products incur diseconomies of scale are the following,

- Relatively more product design is required to develop and support the parallel activity of a larger number of programmers.
- More effort is required to verify and validate the larger requirements and design specifications.
- Even with a thoroughly defined specification, programmers on a large project will spend relatively more time communicating and resolving interface issues.
- More integration activity is required to put the units together.
- In general, more extensive testing is required to verify and validate the software product.
- Relatively more effort will be required to manage the project.

12.4. COCOMO model types

The COCOMO Model is the most widely used and accepted of the cost/effort estimation models. This model as a size-driven model is highly dependent upon the ability to estimate the size of the software product at an early stage. For this reason this method is generally used in conjunction with one of the size estimation models such as function points. Three basic types of COCOMO models are in use and these are the Basic, Intermediate and Detailed models. Briefly these are described next, the main reference for this is work by Boehm, 1981.

- **Basic** COCOMO is applicable to the large majority of software projects: small to medium products developed in a familiar in-house software development environment. It is good for quick, early, rough order of magnitude estimates of software costs, but its accuracy is necessarily limited because of its lack of factors to account for difference in hardware constraints, personnel quality and experience, use of modern tools and techniques, and other project attributes known to have a significant influence on software costs.
- **Intermediate** COCOMO includes these factors (i.e. missing from the basic model) in terms of their aggregate impact on overall project costs. The Intermediate COCOMO is an extension of the basic COCOMO model. Here we use the same basic equation for the model but coefficients are slightly different for the effort equation
- **Detailed** COCOMO accounts for the influence of these additional factors on individual project phases. The detailed model differs from the Intermediate model in only one major aspect: the detailed model uses different Effort Multipliers for each phase of a project. These (phase dependent) Effort Multipliers yield better estimates than the Intermediate model. The six phases COCOMO defines are: Requirements, Product Design, Detailed Design, Code & Unit Test, Integrate & Test, and Maintenance.

The basic COCOMO model

The Basic Model makes its estimates of required effort (measured in Person-Months PM) based primarily on your estimate of the size (as measured in thousands of Delivered Source Instructions KDSI) of the software project,

$$PM = a\,(KDSI)^{\,b}$$

The Basic model also presents an equation for estimating the development schedule (Time of Develop TDEV) of the project in months:

$$TDEV = c\ (PM)^d$$

Before we can put these equations to practical use, we need to resolve a number of significant definitional issues, such as:

- Which instructions count as delivered source instructions?
- Which Person-Months are included in the estimate?
- Which phases are included in "development"?
- What classes of projects are covered by the estimating equations?

Basic definitions

Below are some additional definitions and assumptions underlying the use of COCOMO.

- The primary cost driver is the number of delivered source instructions (DSI) developed by the project. DSI is defined such that:
  (i)   Only source lines that are *DELIVERED* as part of the product are included. Therefore test drivers and other support software are excluded.
  (ii) *SOURCE* codes, created by project staff and processed into machine code by some combination of pre-processors, compilers, and assemblers. Code created by applications generators is excluded.
  (iii) *INSTRUCTIONS* are defined as lines of code. Declarations are counted as instructions but comments are excluded.
- The COCOMO cost estimates only cover the period between beginning of the design phase and end of the integration and test phase. Costs and schedules of other phases (like requirement phase) are estimated separately.
- A COCOMO Person-Month (PM) consists of 152 hours of working time. This has been found to be consistent with practical experience with the average monthly time due to holidays, vacation and sick leaves. COCOMO avoids estimating labour costs in currencies because of the large variations between organisations in what is included in labour costs and therefore PM is considered to be a more stable unit. After estimating the effort in PM we convert it into cash estimate by applying different average cost per Person-Month figure for each major phase, to account for inflation and the difference in salary level of the people required for each phase. For example, senior staff (with high salary) are heavily involved in the requirement and early design phases while junior staff (less salary) are more involved in later phases (detailed design, code and test phases). Therefore the average PM is higher for early phases.
- COCOMO estimates assume that the project will enjoy good management by both the developer and the customer.
- COCOMO assumes that the requirement specification is not substantially changed after the plans and requirement phase. Any significant modification should be covered by a revised cost estimate.

The detailed COCOMO model assumes that the influence of the software cost drivers is phase dependent. Basic COCOMO and Intermediate COCOMO do not, except for distinguishing between development and maintenance.

12.5. Development modes for software costing

There are several modes of software development. These different software development modes have cost-estimating relationships which are similar in form, but which yield significantly different cost estimates for software products of the same size. In the COCOMO Model, one of the most important factors contributing to the

duration of the project and cost is the development mode. Every project is considered to be developed in one of three modes:
- Organic Mode.
- Semidetached Mode
- Embedded Mode

To estimate the effort and development time, COCOMO models use the same equations but with different coefficients (a, b, c, d in the effort and schedule equations) for each development mode. Therefore before using the COCOMO model we must be able to recognise the development mode of our project. Basic definitions of these modes are given next.

Organic mode

In the organic mode the project is developed in a familiar, stable environment and the product is similar to previously developed products. The product is relatively small, and requires little innovation. Most people connected with the project have extensive experience in working with related systems within the organisation and therefore can usefully contribute to the project in its early stages, without generating a great deal of project communication overhead. An organic mode project is relatively relaxed about the way the software meets its requirements and interface specifications. If a situation arises where an exact correspondence of the software product to the original requirements would cause an extensive rework, the project team can generally negotiate a modification of the specifications that can be developed more easily. The Basic COCOMO Effort and schedule equations for organic mode software projects are:

$$PM = 2.4 * (KDSI)^{1.05}$$

$$TDEV = 2.50 * (PM)^{0.38}$$

Semidetached mode

In this mode project's characteristics are intermediate between Organic and Embedded. "Intermediate" may mean either of two things:
- An intermediate level of project characteristics.
- A mixture of the organic and embedded mode characteristics.

Therefore in an Semidetached mode project, it is possible that:
- The team members all have an intermediate level of experience with related systems.
- The team has a wide mixture of experienced and inexperienced people.
- The team members have experience related to some aspects of the system under development, but not others.

The size of a Semidetached mode product generally extends up to 300 KDSI.

The Basic COCOMO Effort and schedule equations for semi-detached mode software projects are:

$$PM = 3.0 * (KDSI)^{1.12}$$

$$TDEV = 2.50 * (PM)^{0.35}$$

Embedded mode

In this development mode Project is characterised by tight, fairly rigid constraints and interface requirements. The product must operate within a strongly coupled and complex combination of hardware, software, regulations, and operational procedures. The embedded-mode project does not generally have the option of negotiating easier software changes by modifying the requirements and interface specifications. The project therefore needs more effort to accommodate these when required. The embedded mode project is generally charting its way through unknown territory to a greater extent than the organic mode project. Thus the project may use a smaller team of analysts in the early stages, as a large number of people would get swamped in communication overhead.

Once the embedded mode project has completed its product design, its best strategy is to bring on a very large team of programmers to perform detailed design, coding and unit testing in parallel. Otherwise the project would take much longer to complete. This strategy leads to the higher demands of the personnel in embedded-mode projects, and to the greater amount of effort consumed compared to an organic mode project working to the same total development schedule.

The Basic COCOMO Effort and schedule equations for embedded mode software projects are:

$$PM = 3.6 * (KDSI)^{1.20}$$
$$TDEV = 2.50 * (PM)^{0.32}$$

Example

A large chemical products company is planning to develop a new computer program to keep track of raw materials. An in-house team of programmers and analysts who have been developing similar programs for several years will develop it. An initial study has determined that the size of the program will be roughly 32,000 delivered source instructions. (DSI) [78]

This project is a good example of an organic-mode software project. Using the Basic COCOMO equations for this development mode we have:

Effort: PM = 2.4*(32)$^{1.05}$ = 91 Person-Months

Productivity: 32000DSI / 91 PM = 352 DSI / PM

Duration and staffing:

Once an estimate is obtained for effort (Person-Month) a manager must determine how many persons to put on the job. This will ultimately determine the calendar duration of the project. It is very important to note that more staff does not mean proportionately less calendar time. For example, more staff complicates communications and this complexity translates into a project slowdown.

The second equation of the COCOMO model uses the estimated effort of the project (PM) to suggest the optimum calendar duration of the project. For the example above with estimated effort of 91 PM we have:

Schedule:

TDEM = 2.5 * (91)$^{0.38}$ = 14 months

After estimating the duration of the project the manager can determine how many persons in the average must be put on the project:

Average Staffing:
91 staff-months / *14* months = *6.5* FSP (*Full Time Equivalent Software Personnel*)

Phase distribution of effort and schedule for organic mode projects

After estimating the effort and schedule of a project we need to determine how to distribute them among different phases of the project. This distribution varies as a function of the size of the product. Larger software projects require relatively more time and effort to perform integration and test activities. However they are able to compress the programming portion by having larger number of teams programming components in parallel. Smaller software projects have a more uniform, flat distribution of labour throughout the development cycle, and have relatively more resources devoted to the phases other than integration and test. Table 12.2 and Table 12.3 present the percentage distribution of the basic software effort and schedule within the development phases of an organic mode product:

Table 12.2 - Phase Distribution of **Effort**: Organic Mode

Phase	Small (2 KDSI)	Intermediate (8 KDSI)	Medium (32 KDSI)	Large (128 KDSI)
Plans & Requirements	6%	6%	6%	6%
Product Design	16%	16%	16%	16%
Detailed Design	26%	25%	24%	23%
Code & Unit Test	42%	40%	38%	36%
Integration & Test	16%	19%	22%	25%
Total:	**100%**	**100%**	**100%**	**100%**

Table 12.3 - Phase Distribution of **Schedule**: Organic Mode

Phase	Small (2 KDSI)	Intermediate (8 KDSI)	Medium (32 KDSI)	Large (128 KDSI)
Plans & Requirements	10%	11%	12%	13%
Product Design	19%	19%	19%	19%
Detailed Design & **Code & Unit Test**	63%	59%	55%	51%
Integration & Test	18%	22%	26%	30%
Total:	**100%**	**100%**	**100%**	**100%**

Example

Using table 12.2 and table 12.3 we can calculate the number of staff needed for programming (Detailed design and code and unit test) phase of the previous example:

Programming effort:

$$(0.62)\ (91\ PM) = 56\ \text{Person-Months}$$

Programming Schedule:

$$(0.55)\ (14) = 7.7 \text{ months}$$

Average Staffing:

56 staff-months / *7.7* months = *7.3* FSP (Full *Time Equivalent Software Personnel*)

Phase Distribution of Effort and Schedule for Other Modes:
Table 12.4 and Table 12.5 present the percentage distribution of the basic software effort and schedule within the development phases of a semidetached mode product:

Table 12.4 - Phase Distribution of Effort: Semidetached Mode

Phase	Small (2 KDSI)	Intermediate (8 KDSI)	Medium (32 KDSI)	Large (128 KDSI)
Plans & Requirements	7%	7%	7%	7%
Product Design	17%	17%	17%	17%
Detailed Design	27%	26%	25%	24%
Code & Unit Test	37%	35%	33%	31%
Integration & Test	19%	22%	25%	28%
Total:	**100**%	**100**%	**100**%	**100**%

Table 12.5 - Phase Distribution of Schedule: Semidetached Mode

Phase	Small (2 KDSI)	Intermediate (8 KDSI)	Medium (32 KDSI)	Large (128 KDSI)
Plans & Requirements	16%	18%	20%	22%
Product Design	24%	25%	26%	27%
Detailed Design & Code & Unit Test	56%	52%	48%	44%
Integration & Test	20%	23%	26%	29%
Total:	**100**%	**100**%	**100**%	**100**%

Table 12.6 and Table 12.7 present the percentage distribution of the basic software effort and schedule within the development phases of an embedded mode product:

Table 12.6- Phase Distribution of Effort: Embedded Mode

Phase	Small (2 KDSI)	Intermediate (8 KDSI)	Medium (32 KDSI)	Large (128 KDSI)
Plans & Requirements	8%	8%	8%	8%
Product Design	18%	18%	18%	18%
Detailed Design	28%	27%	26%	25%
Code & Unit Test	32%	30%	28%	26%
Integration & Test	22%	25%	28%	31%
Total:	**100%**	**100%**	**100%**	**100%**

Table 12.7 - Phase Distribution of Schedule: Embedded Mode

Phase	Small (2 KDSI)	Intermediate (8 KDSI)	Medium (32 KDSI)	Large (128 KDSI)
Plans & Requirements	24%	28%	32%	36%
Product Design	30%	32%	34%	36%
Detailed Design & Code & Unit Test	48%	44%	40%	36%
Integration & Test	22%	24%	26%	28%
Total:	**100%**	**100%**	**100%**	**100%**

By comparing tables 12.2 through 12.7 we can see some differences between the effort and schedule distribution of the products developed in different modes.
The main differences are:
- The embedded-mode project consumes considerably more effort in the integration and test phase. This results from the need to follow and verify software requirements and interface specifications more carefully in the embedded and semidetached mode.
- The embedded-mode project consumes proportionally less effort in the code and unit test phase. This is the result of proportionally higher effort required for the other development phases.
- The embedded-mode project consumes considerably more schedule in both the plans and requirement phase and the product design phase. This is because of the need for more thorough, validated requirements and design specifications, and the greater need to perform these phases with a relatively small number of people.
- The embedded-mode project consumes considerably less schedule in the programming phase. This results from the strategy of employing a many teams of people programming in parallel, in order to reduce the project's overall schedule.

Intermediate COCOMO Model

The Intermediate COCOMO is an extension of the basic COCOMO model. Here we use the same basic equation for the model. But coefficients are slightly different for the effort equation. Also in addition to the size as the basic cost driver we use 15 more predictor variables. These added cost drivers help to estimate effort and cost with more accuracy. The person responsible for estimating cost looks closely at many factors of a project such as amount of external storage required, execution speed constraints, experience of the programmers on the team, experience with the implementation language, use of software tools, etc. For each characteristic, the estimator decides where it is on the importance scale of "very low", " low", " Nominal", "High", "Very High" and "High". Each characteristic gives an adjustment factor (from table 12.8) and all factors are multiplied together to give an Effort Adjustment Factor (EAF).

If a project is judged normal in some characteristic the adjustment factor will be 1 for that characteristic (Nominal column in Table 7), which means that this factor has no effect on overall EAF. The effort equation for the intermediate model has the form of:

$$PM = EAF * a * (KDSI)\ b$$

If we assume that the project is "Nominal" in every aspect then all adjustment factors would be 1, which results in EAF=1, and the effort equation would have the same form as the Basic mode. In addition to the EAF the model parameter "a" is slightly different in Intermediate COCOMO, but the "b" parameter is the same. The effort equation for different modes of Intermediate COCOMO is given in the following table:

Development Mode	Intermediate Effort Equation
Organic:	$PM = EAF * 3.2 * (KDSI)^{1.05}$
Semidetached	$PM = EAF * 3.0* (KDSI)^{1.12}$
Embedded	$PM = EAF * 2.8* (KDSI)^{1.20}$

Boehm in *Software Engineering Economics* defines each of the cost drivers, and defines the Effort Multiplier associated with each rating (Table 12.8).

Example: If your project is rated Very High for Complexity (Effort Multiplier of 1.30), and Low for Tools Use (Effort Multiplier of 1.10), and all of the other cost drivers are rated to be Nominal, these Effort Multipliers are used to calculate the Effort Adjustment Factor, which is used in the effort equation:

$$EAF = 1.30 * 1.10 = 1.43$$
$$Effort = EAF * 3.2 * 31.05 = 14.5\ PM$$
$$TDEV = 2.5 * 14.50.38 = 6.9\ Months$$
$$Average\ staffing:\ 14.5 / 6.9 = 2.1\ people$$

There are two reasons why Intermediate model produces better results than the Basic Model. First, it considers the effect of more cost drivers. Second, in the Intermediate model the system can be divided into "components". DSI value and Cost Drivers can be chosen for individual components, instead of for the system as a whole. COCOMO can estimate the staffing, cost, and duration of each of the components--allowing you to experiment with different development strategies, to find the plan that best suits your needs and resources.

Table 12.8 - Project Characteristic Table

Cost Driver	Very Low	Low	Nominal	High	Very High	Extra High
ACAP Analyst Capability	1.46	1.19	1.00	0.86	0.71	--
AEXP Application Experience	1.29	1.13	1.00	0.91	0.82	--
CPLX Product Complexity	0.70	0.85	1.00	1.15	1.30	1.65
DATA Database Size	--	0.94	1.00	1.08	1.16	--
LEXP Language Experience	1.14	1.07	1.00	0.95	--	--
MODP Modem Programming Practices	1.24	1.10	1.00	0.91	0.82	--
PCAP Programmer Capability	1.42	1.17	1.00	0.86	0.70	--
RELY Required Software Reliability	0.75	0.88	1.00	1.15	1.40	--
SCED Required Development Schedule	1.23	1.08	1.00	1.04	1.10	--
STOR Main Storage Constraint	--	--	1.00	1.06	1.21	1.56
TIME Execution Time Constraint	--	--	1.00	1.11	1.30	1.66
TOOL Use of Software Tools	1.24	1.10	1.00	0.91	0.83	--
TURN Computer Turnaround Time	--	0.87	1.00	1.07	1.15	--
VEXP Virtual Machine Experience	1.21	1.10	1.00	0.90	--	--
VIRT Virtual Machine Volatility	--	0.87	1.00	1.15	1.30	--

The detailed COCOMO model

The detailed model differs from the Intermediate model in only one major aspect; the detailed model uses different Effort Multipliers for each phase of a project. These, phase dependent Effort Multipliers yield better estimates than the Intermediate model. The six phases COCOMO defines are:

Abbreviation	Phase
RQ	Requirements
PD	Product Design
DD	Detailed Design
CT	Code & Unit Test
IT	Integrate & Test
MN	Maintenance

The phases from Product Design through Integrate & Test are called the Development phases. Estimates for the Requirements phase and for the Maintenance phase are performed in a different way than estimates for the four Development phases.

The Programmer Capability cost driver is a good example of a phase dependent cost driver. The Very High rating for the Programmer Capability Cost Driver corresponds to an Effort Multiplier of 1.00 (no influence) for the Product Design phase of a project, but an Effort Multiplier of 0.65 is used for the Detailed Design phase. These ratings indicate that good programmers can save time and money on the later phases of the project, but they do not have an impact on the Product Design phase because they are not involved in it.

12.6. COCOMO II software cost estimation model

COCOMO II is tuned to modern software lifecycles. The original COCOMO model has been very successful, but it does not take into account the newer software development practices. COCOMO II targets the software projects of the 1990s and 2000s, and will continue to evolve over the next few years. In reality COCOMO II consists of three different models, These are briefly described next,

The Application Composition Model: This model is suitable for projects built with modern GUI-builder tools. Based on new Object Points.

The Early Design Model: You can use this model to get rough estimates of a cost and duration of the project before theproject entire architecture is known. It uses a small set of new Cost Drivers, and new estimating equations. It is based on Unadjusted Function Points or KSLOC.

The Post-Architecture Model: This is the most detailed COCOMO II model. It is used after the overall architecture for the project has been developed. It has new cost drivers, new line counting rules, and new equations. [79] In the COCOMO II model, some of the most important factors contributing to duration and cost of the project are the Scale Drivers. You set each scale driver to the exponent used in the effort equation. The 5 Scale Drivers are:
- Precedentedness (is there a precedent?)
- Development Flexibility
- Architecture / Risk Resolution
- Team Cohesion
- Process Maturity

Note that the Scale Drivers have replaced the Development Mode of COCOMO 81. The first two Scale Drivers, Precedentedness and Development Flexibility actually describe much the same influences that the original Development Mode did.

Cost Drivers

COCOMO II has 17 cost drivers that are based on the assessment of the project, development environment, and team to set each cost driver. These cost drivers are multipliers that determine the effort required to complete a software project. For example, if your project will develop software that controls an the flight of an airplane, you would set the Required Software Reliability (RELY) cost driver to Very High. That rating corresponds to an effort multiplier of 1.26, meaning that your project will require 26% more effort than a typical software project.

COCOMO II effort equation

The COCOMO II model estimates the required effort (measured in Person-Months – PM) based primarily on the estimate of the size of software project. (as measured in thousands of SLOC, KSLOC)):

$$Effort = 2.94 * EAF * (KSLOC)E$$

Where,

EAF: Is the Effort Adjustment Factor derived from the Cost Drivers

E: Is an exponent derived from the five Scale Drivers

As an example, a project with all Nominal Cost Drivers and Scale Drivers would have an EAF of 1.00 and exponent, E, of 1.0997. Assuming that the project is projected to consist of 8,000 source lines of code, COCOMO II estimates that 28.9 Person-Months of effort is required to complete it:

$$Effort = 2.94 * (1.0) * (8)1.0997 = 28.9 Person-Months$$

Effort adjustment factor

The Effort Adjustment Factor in the effort equation is simply the product of the effort multipliers corresponding to each of the cost drivers for the project. For example, if the project is rated Very High for Complexity (effort multiplier of 1.34), and Low for Language & Tools Experience (effort multiplier of 1.09), and all of the other cost drivers are rated to be Nominal (effort multiplier of 1.00), the EAF is the product of 1.34 and 1.09.

$$Effort Adjustment Factor = EAF = 1.34 * 1.09 = 1.46$$

$$Effort = 2.94 * (1.46) * (8)1.0997 = 42.3 Person-Months$$

COCOMO II schedule equation

The COCOMO II schedule equation predicts the number of months required to complete the software project. The duration of a project is based on the effort predicted by the effort equation:

$$Duration = 3.67 * (Effort)SE$$

Where,

Effort: Is the effort from the COCOMO II effort equation

SE: Is the schedule equation exponent derived from the five Scale

Drivers

Continuing the example, and substituting the exponent of 0.3179 that is calculated from the scale drivers, yields an estimate of just over a year, and an average staffing of between 3 and 4 people:

$$Duration = 3.67 * (42.3)0.3179 = 12.1 months$$
$$Average staffing = (42.3 Person-Months) / (12.1 Months) = 3.5 people$$

The SCED cost driver

The COCOMO cost driver for Required Development Schedule (SCED) is unique, and requires a special explanation. The SCED cost driver is used to account for the observation that a project developed on an accelerated schedule will require more effort than a project developed on its optimum schedule. A SCED rating of Very Low corresponds to an Effort Multiplier of 1.43 (in the COCOMO II.2000 model) and means that you intend to finish the project in 75% of the optimum schedule (as determined by a previous COCOMO estimate). Continuing the example used earlier, but assuming that SCED has a rating of Very Low, COCOMO produces these estimates:

*Duration = 75% * 12.1 Months = 9.1 Months*
*Effort Adjustment Factor = EAF = 1.34 * 1.09 * 1.43 = 2.09*
*Effort = 2.94 * (2.09) * (8)1.0997 = 60.4 Person-Months*
Average staffing = (60.4 Person-Months) / (9.1 Months) = 6.7 people

Notice that the calculation of duration is not based directly on the effort (number of Person-Months) – instead it uses the schedule that would have been required for the project assuming it had been developed on the nominal schedule. Remember that the SCED cost driver means "accelerated from the nominal schedule". [80] Dr. Barry Boehm and his students are developing COCOMO II at USC. [81]

12.7. Chapter summary

In this chapter I cover cost estimation of software engineering projects. This is a very challenging task if we aim to do it accurately. A large number of factors can impact on the cost of a project and Boehm's COCOMO model provides a good starting point for estimating cost. I describe the basic model type and then proceed to give some application details. COCOMO has been used in software engineering for a reasonably long time and we now have more information about successful and not-so successful projects. Consequently the cost drivers of the basic COCOMO model can be enhanced. The result is COCOMO II and I briefly cover the basic features of this evolved model. As with the rest of this textbook, I emphasise that the main aim is to provide the reader with insight into a subject area, rather than going into details. For further reading the references given corresponding to each chapter are a good starting point.

Exercises

12.1. Discuss why it is generally difficult to estimate the cost of software engineering projects.
12.2. Statistical models have been used to describe behaviour between variables. Explain how Boehm's basic equation fits in with costing software engineering projects.
12.3. Do some research into statistical modelling and try to find out if there are other models that would be applicable.
12.4. Describe the basic procedure for cost estimation. Use examples, as you consider appropriate.
12.5. Describe the main methods for estimating the size of a software project.
12.6. You are using Floating-point counts to estimate software size. Suppose that a C program needs 80 LOC per FP. A system with, 15 inputs, 15 outputs, 10 Enquiries, 5 Files and 3 Interfaces. What is the FP? What is the estimated program size?
12.7. Explain the basic approach of the estimation models for small projects and large projects. Discuss why the modelling equations are different.
12.8. Giving examples of each, discuss the three types of COCOMO (i.e. basic, Intermediate and detailed)

12.9. There are three distinct development modes in COCOMO (Organic, Semidetached, Embedded) for each of these, discuss the main features and how they reflect on cost.

12.10. For the following list of projects suggest which type of development mode you would recommend, (You may make assumptions as you see fit)

a. Developing Control Unit software for a new Jaguar sports car. The software will control the engine management system and all the associated sub-systems.

b. New software to maintain student records in a typical university. The university has 10,000 students and you need to monitor all records including their study records, fees as well as personal information.

c. Inland revenue is developing a new system to enable individuals and companies to file all the tax returns on-line.

12.11. Briefly describe the different methods that can be used to estimate the cost of software development. Include in your answer a brief description of the COCOMO model and three variations thereof as a means of obtaining a cost estimate for a software engineering project.

12.12. You are a software engineering consultant invited to produce a cost estimate for a software engineering project and you are given the following information:

> MIG Consulting Ltd, a software house, has been approached to develop and install a system for the control of production in a large manufacturing plant. The solution is likely to involve a large number of dedicated, distributed microprocessors and a large central machine for overall monitoring, control and data collection and analysis. The software, which is expected to contain approximately 60 KDSI, is likely to be highly complex and to use a database of approximately 15 mega bytes.
>
> The company has seven years' experience in developing and installing systems of this type, but is unfamiliar with the new operating system and programming language specified for the project. However, these were chosen for the good tool support and interactive development environment that they provide.
>
> About 40% of the company employees that are available for this project have analysis experience and they use reliable methods for engineering software.

i) Which of Boehm's COCOMO models should be used for the estimation of effort and development time of this project? Justify your answer.

(ii) Identify the cost drivers and effort multipliers associated with this project. List any assumptions you have made.

(iii) Use the COCOMO intermediate model to obtain estimates of the effort required and the development time for the project.

(iv) Estimate the distribution of effort and time throughout the development lifecycle. Hence, estimate the personnel requirements for each phase.

(v) Assuming that MIG Consulting Ltd calculates its estimates of price on the basis of £5000 per person per month (£4000 for salary and overheads + £1000 'profit'), estimate the price quoted for the project.

12.13. Explain how COCOMO II differs form the first COCOMO model. Do you think that other COCOMO versions will evolve over time? If so why?

References

Please note: All web pages accessed between March 2009 and December 2009.

Chapter 1

1. [ieeexplore.ieee.org/book/076950874X.excerpt.pdf]
2. http://www.builderau.com.au/program/python/soa/Using-Google-as-an-application-platform/0,2000064084,339290251,00.htm
3. http://www.adobe.com/devnet/flashplatform/articles/flashplatform_overview.html
4. http://www.smalltalk.org/versions
5. http://en.wikipedia.org/wiki/Exploratory_programming
6. http://www.rspa.com/spi/formal-methods.html
7. M. P. Ward, Program Analysis by Formal Transformation, The Computer Journal 1996 39(7):598-618; doi:10.1093/comjnl/39.7.598, © 1996 by British Computer Society
8. http://www.researchportal.be/en/organisation/formal-techniques-in-software-engineering-fots--(UA_21016)/
9. http://www.fmeurope.org
10. http://en.wikipedia.org/wiki/Code_reuse
11. http://en.wikipedia.org/wiki/Programming_paradigm
12. http://en.wikipedia.org/wiki/Procedural_programming
13. John R. Cameron, The Jackson Approach to Software Development IEEE Computer Society Press,U.S.; 2 edition (May 1989)
14. G. Bezanov, LTL Ltd, Procedural Programming Languages, An overview series publication, 2004, LTL PPL book
15. www.rational.com/uml

Chapter 2

16. Hubert Zimmermann. OSI Reference Model - The ISO Model of Architecture for Open Systems Interconnection. IEEE Transactions on Communication, 28(4):425-432, April, 1980
17. Windows NT 2000 Kernel Architecture
18. Philippe Kruchten, Architectural Blueprints—The "4+1" View Model of Software Architecture, Rational Software Corp. published in IEEE Software 12 (6), November 1995, pp. 42-50

Chapter 3

19. John Hunt (2000). *The Unified Process for Practitioners: Object-oriented Design, UML and Java.* Springer, 2000. ISBN 1852332751. p.5.door
20. http://en.wikipedia.org/wiki/Unified_Modeling_Language#Modeling
21. http://www.tutorialspoint.com/uml/index.htm
22. http://www.agilemodeling.com/essays/umlDiagrams.htm

Chapter 4

23. Dennis D.L., Dennis L.B., Management Science, West Publishing Company, 1991
24. http://www.businessballs.com/project.htm39 rpm book
25. Method 123 website,
26. http://www.method123.com/free-risk-management.php?gclid=CJWjoo7FIJACFQJCMAodgD-_kQ
27. www.ieee.org
28. http://www.aldex.co.uk/reqspec.html
29. Robert Japenga, Software requirements Specification, How to write a software requirements specification
http://eent3.sbu.ac.uk/units/softwareengineering/speed/How%20to%20write%20a%20software%20requirements%20specification.htm
30. Somerville, Ian, Software Engineering, Fourth Edition, Addison-Wesley Publishing Company, Wokingham, England, 1992
31. http://en.wikipedia.org/wiki/Metrics

32.   Winston, W.L., Operations research: Applications and Algorithms, Duxbury Press, Boston, 1987.

33.   http://ieeexplore.ieee.org/xpl/freeabs_all.jsp?arnumber=824376 Object-oriented natural language requirements specification

Bryant, B.R.   Dept. of Comput. & Inf. Sci., Alabama Univ., Birmingham, AL

34.   http://www.gamedev.net/reference/articles/article1384.asp

35.   http://users.csc.calpoly.edu/~jdalbey/SWE/pdl_std.html

Chapter 5

36.   http://en.wikipedia.org/wiki/Computing

37.   http://en.wikipedia.org/wiki/Software_quality

38.   http://www.sei.cmu.edu/library/abstracts/reports/89cm021.cfm

39.   www.hindawi.com/journals/ES/si/0022008003.pdf

Chapter 6

40.   Scott G. Bieman J.M, Reported effects of rapid prototyping on industrial software quality, Software Quality Journal 2, 93-108 (1993)

41.   http://en.wikipedia.org/wiki/Software_prototyping

42.   http://en.wikipedia.org/wiki/Extreme_Programming

43.   http://martinfowler.com/articles/newMethodology.html#FromNothingToMonumentalToAgile

Chapter 7

44.   http://www.bcs.org/server.php?show=nav.5651

45.   http://www.esa.int/SPECIALS/Space_Engineering/SEM0LDLXOWF_0.html

46.   I. Sommerville, Software Engineering, seventh ed., Addison-Wesley, 2005

47.   ACT Europe under the GNU Free Documentation License
http://libre.adacore.com/libre

48.   www.crime-research.org/library/grcdos.pdf

49.   http://www.weibull.com/SystemRelWeb/fault_tree_analysis_and_reliability_block_diagrams.htm

50.   http://www.sinc.sunysb.edu/Class/est571go/ta.html

51.   http://www.sei.cmu.edu/cmmi/start/faq/related-faq.cfm

52.   http://www.bcs.org/server.php?show=conWebDoc.9933

Chapter 8

53.   http://docs.google.com/viewer?a=v&q=cache:FEdz-E42o8UJ:www.faa.gov/documentLibrary/media/Order/ND/8040.1C.pdf+FAA+Order+8040.&hl=en&gl=uk&sig=AHIEtbR-ARb7I0uAdkg6aaInsmhTvIpMXA

54.   http://en.wikipedia.org/wiki/DO-178B

55.   http://en.wikipedia.org/wiki/Failure_mode_and_effects_analysis

56.   Utilization of FMEA concept in software, lifecycle management, N. Banerjee, Transactions on Information and Communications Technologies vol 11, © 1995 WIT Press, www.witpress.com, ISSN 1743-3517, 220 Software Quality Management

57.   http://www.weibull.com/hotwire/issue46/relbasics46.htm

58.   http://engineers.ihs.com/document/abstract/YTAFABAAAAAAAAAA

59.   http://www.theprocessengineer.com/hazop-chairman.html

60.   http://www.lihoutech.com/hzp1frm.htm

Chapter 9

61.   http://www.issco.unige.ch/en/research/projects/ewg96/node81.html

62.   Hausen, H. (1984). Comments on practical constraints of software validation techniques, Proceedings of symposium on software validation., pp. 323-333

63.   http://ezinearticles.com/?Software-Interface-Testing-and-Other-Types-of-Software-Testing&id=1241042

Chapter 10

64.   http://www.issco.unige.ch/en/research/projects/ewg96/node79.html

65. Krüger90   Michael Krüger: Testen von Software als analytische Maß nahme der Software-Qualitätssicherung, (Testing Software as an Analytic Step to Software Quality Assuring) Dissertation at the University of Ulm, 1990

66. http://www.issco.unige.ch/en/research/projects/ewg96/node82.html#SECTION00732 000000000000000

67. http://www.mathematik.uni-ulm.de/~melzer/thesis/node1.html

Chapter 11

68. http://www.developer.com/tech/article.php/10923_3644656_1/Software-Quality-Metrics.htm

69. S. H. Kan, Metrics and Models in Software Quality Engineering (Singapore: Pearson Education, 2003), p. 7

70. P. C. Patton and L. May, "Making Connections: A five-year plan for information systems and computing," ISC, University of Pennsylvania, 1993.]

71. IEEE, Standard for a Software Quality Metrics Methodology (New York: IEEE, Inc., 1993).

72. D. B. Simmons, N. C. Ellis, H. Fujihara, W. Kuo, *Software Measurement: A Visualization Toolkit for Project Control and Process Measurement* (New Jersey: Prentice-Hall, 1998)]

73. http://ezinearticles.com/?Areas-Of-Use-For-Software-Metrics&id=905054

74. http://www.coverity.com/library/pdf/IDC_Improving_Software_Quality_June_2008.pdf

75. Source: [7] IDC's Software Quality Survey, 2008

Chapter 12

76. Boehm, BW, Prentice-Hall, 1981

77. http://enel.ucalgary.ca/People/Smith/619.94/prev689/1997.94/reports/farshad.htm

78. http://enel.ucalgary.ca/People/Smith/619.94/prev689/1997.94/reports/farshad.htm

79. http://www.softstarsystems.com/overview.htm

80. http://www.softstarsystems.com/overview.htm

81. Main Reference: Software Engineering Economics, Barry Boehm, Prentice Hall, 1981

APPENDIX I   SRS Template

Software Requirements Specification
For
<Project>
Version <x.x> approved
Prepared by <author>
<organisation>
<date created>

Table of Contents

Table of Contents
Revision History
1.   Introduction
1.1 Purpose   1
1.2 Document Conventions
1.3 Intended Audience and Reading Suggestions
1.4 Project Scope
1.5 References
2.   Overall Description
2.1 Product Perspective
2.2 Product Features
2.3 User Classes and Characteristics
2.4 Operating Environment
2.5 Design and Implementation Constraints

2.6 User Documentation
2.7 Assumptions and Dependencies

3.   System Features
3.1 System Feature 1
3.2 System Feature 2 (and so on)
4.   External Interface Requirements
4.1 User Interfaces
4.2 Hardware Interfaces
4.3 Software Interfaces
4.4 Communications Interfaces
5.   Other Nonfunctional Requirements
5.1 Performance Requirements
5.2 Safety Requirements
5.3 Security Requirements
5.4 Software Quality Attributes
6.   Other Requirements

Appendix A: Glossary
Appendix B: Analysis Models
Appendix C: Issues List

Revision History

Name	Date	Reason For Changes	Version

1   Introduction

Purpose

<Identify the product whose software requirements are specified in this document, including the revision or release number. Describe the scope of the product that is covered by this SRS, particularly if this SRS describes only part of the system or a single subsystem. >

Document Conventions

<Describe any standards or typographical conventions that were followed when writing this SRS, such as fonts or highlighting that have special significance. For example, state whether priorities for higher-level requirements are assumed to be inherited by detailed requirements, or whether every requirement statement is to have its own priority. >

Intended Audience and Reading Suggestions

<Describe the different types of reader that the document is intended for, such as developers, project managers, marketing staff, users, testers, and documentation writers. Describe what the rest of this SRS contains and how it is organised. Suggest a sequence for reading the document, beginning with the overview sections and proceeding through the sections that are most pertinent to each reader type. >

Project Scope

<Provide a short description of the software being specified and its purpose, including relevant benefits, objectives, and goals. Relate the software to corporate goals or business strategies. If a separate vision and scope document is available, refer to it rather than duplicating its contents here. An SRS that specifies the next release of an evolving product should contain its own scope statement as a subset of the long-term strategic product vision. >

References

<List any other documents or Web addresses to which this SRS refers. These may include user interface style guides, contracts, standards, system requirements specifications, use-case documents, or a vision and scope document. Provide enough information so that the reader could access a copy of each reference, including title, author, version number, date, and source or location. >

2   Overall Description

Product Perspective

<Describe the context and origin of the product being specified in this SRS. For example, state whether this product is a follow-on member of a product family, a replacement for certain existing systems, or a new, self-contained product. If the SRS defines a component of a larger system, relate the requirements of the larger system to the functionality of this software and identify interfaces between the two. A simple diagram that shows the major components of the overall system, subsystem interconnections, and external interfaces can be helpful. >

Product Features

<Summarise the major features the product contains or the significant functions that it performs or lets the user perform. Details will be provided in Section 3, so only a high level summary is needed here. Organise the functions to make them understandable to any reader of the SRS. A picture of the major groups of related requirements and how they relate, such as a top level data flow diagram or a Class diagram, is often effective. >

User Classes and Characteristics

<Identify the various user classes that you anticipate will use this product. User classes may be differentiated based on frequency of use, subset of product functions used, technical expertise, security or privilege levels, educational level, or experience. Describe the pertinent characteristics of each user Class. Certain requirements may pertain only to certain user classes. Distinguish the favoured user classes from those who are less important to satisfy. >

Operating Environment

<Describe the environment in which the software will operate, including the hardware platform, operating system and versions, and any other software components or applications with which it must peacefully coexist. >

Design and Implementation Constraints

<Describe any items or issues that will limit the options available to the developers. These might include: corporate or regulatory policies; hardware limitations (timing requirements, memory requirements); interfaces to other applications; specific technologies, tools, and databases to be used; parallel operations; language requirements; communications protocols; security considerations; design conventions or programming standards (for example, if the customer's organisation will be responsible for maintaining the delivered software). >

User Documentation

<List the user documentation components (such as user manuals, on-line help, and tutorials) that will be delivered along with the software. Identify any known user documentation delivery formats or standards. >

Assumptions and Dependencies

<List any assumed factors (as opposed to known facts) that could affect the requirements stated in the SRS. These could include third-party or commercial components that you plan to use, issues around the

development or operating environment, or constraints. The project could be affected if these assumptions are incorrect, are not shared, or change. Also identify any dependencies the project has on external factors, such as software components that you intend to reuse from another project, unless they are already documented elsewhere (for example, in the scope document or the project plan). >

3   System Features

<This template illustrates organising the functional requirements for the product by system features, the major services provided by the product. You may prefer to organise this section by use-case, mode of operation, user Class, object Class, functional hierarchy, or combinations of these, whatever makes the most logical sense for your product. >

System Feature 1

<Don't really say "System Feature 1." State the feature name in just a few words. >

Description and Priority

<Provide a short description of the feature and indicate whether it is of High, Medium, or Low priority. You could also include specific priority component ratings, such as benefit, penalty, cost, and risk (each rated on a relative scale from a low of 1 to a high of 9).>

Stimulus/Response Sequences

<List the sequences of user actions and system responses that stimulate the behaviour defined for this feature. These will correspond to the dialogue elements associated with use-cases. >

Functional Requirements

<Itemise the detailed functional requirements associated with this feature. These are the software capabilities that must be present in order for the user to carry out the services provided by the feature, or to execute the use-case. Include how the product should respond to anticipated error conditions or invalid inputs. Requirements should be concise, complete, unambiguous, verifiable, and necessary. Use "TBD" as a placeholder to indicate when necessary information is not yet available. >

<Each requirement should be uniquely identified with a sequence number or a meaningful tag of some kind.>

REQ-1:

REQ-2:

System Feature 2 (and so on)

4   External Interface Requirements

User Interfaces

<Describe the logical characteristics of each interface between the software product and the users. This may include sample screen images, any GUI standards or product family style guides that are to be followed, screen layout constraints, standard buttons and functions (e.g., help) that will appear on every screen, keyboard shortcuts, error message display standards, and so on. Define the software components for which a user interface is needed. Details of the user interface design should be documented in a separate user interface specification. >

Hardware Interfaces

<Describe the logical and physical characteristics of each interface between the software product and the hardware components of the system. This may include the supported device types, the nature of the data and control interactions between the software and the hardware, and communication protocols to be used.>

Software Interfaces

<Describe the connections between this product and other specific software components (name and version), including databases, operating systems, tools, libraries, and integrated commercial components. Identify the data items or messages coming into the system and going out and describe the purpose of each. Describe the services needed and the nature of communications. Refer to documents that describe detailed application programming interface protocols. Identify data that will be shared across software components. If the data sharing mechanism must be implemented in a specific way (for example, use of a global data area in a multitasking operating system), specify this as an implementation constraint. >

Communications Interfaces

<Describe the requirements associated with any communications functions required by this product, including e-mail, web browser, network server communications protocols, electronic forms, and so on. Define any pertinent message formatting. Identify any communication standards that will be used, such as FTP or HTTP. Specify any communication security or encryption issues, data transfer rates, and synchronization mechanisms. >

5   Other Nonfunctional Requirements

Performance Requirements

<If there are performance requirements for the product under various circumstances, state them here and explain their rationale, to help the developers understand the intent and make suitable design choices. Specify the timing relationships for real time systems. Make such requirements as specific as possible. You may need to state performance requirements for individual functional requirements or features.>

Safety Requirements

<Specify those requirements that are concerned with possible loss, damage, or harm that could result from the use of the product. Define any safeguards or actions that must be taken, as well as actions that must be prevented. Refer to any external policies or regulations that state safety issues that affect the product's design or use. Define any safety certifications that must be satisfied. >

Security Requirements

<Specify any requirements regarding security or privacy issues surrounding use of the product or protection of the data used or created by the product. Define any user identity authentication requirements. Refer to any external policies or regulations containing security issues that affect the product. Define any security or privacy certifications that must be satisfied.>

Software Quality Attributes

<Specify any additional quality characteristics for the product that will be important to either the customers or the developers. Some to consider are: adaptability, availability, correctness, flexibility, interoperability, maintainability, portability, reliability, reusability, robustness, testability, and usability. Write these to be specific, quantitative, and verifiable when possible. At the least, clarify the relative preferences for various attributes, such as ease of use over ease of learning.>

6   Other Requirements

<Define any other requirements not covered elsewhere in the SRS. This might include database requirements, internationalisation requirements, legal requirements, reuse objectives for the project, and so on. Add any new sections that are pertinent to the project.>

Appendix A: Glossary

<Define all the terms necessary to properly interpret the SRS, including acronyms and abbreviations. You may wish to build a separate glossary that spans multiple projects or the entire organisation, and just include terms specific to a single project in each SRS. >

Appendix B: Analysis Models

<Optionally, include any pertinent analysis models, such as data flow diagrams, Class diagrams, state-transition diagrams, or entity-relationship diagrams.>

Appendix C: Issues List

< This is a dynamic list of the open requirements issues that remain to be resolved, including pending decisions, information that is needed, conflicts awaiting resolution, and the like.>

APPENDIX II   Program Design Language (PDL)

Program Design Language description was downloaded from the following URL on 29/11/2009. [http://users.csc.calpoly.edu/~jdalbey/SWE/pdl_std.html]

PDL STANDARD

PDL is a kind of structured English for describing algorithms. It allows the designer to focus on the logic of the algorithm without being distracted by details of language syntax. At the same time, the PDL needs to be complete. It describes the entire logic of the algorithm so that implementation becomes a rote mechanical task of translating line by line into source code. In general the vocabulary used in the PDL should be the vocabulary of the problem domain, not of the implementation domain. The PDL is a narrative intended for someone who knows the requirements (problem domain) and is trying to learn how the solution is organised. The following are three examples of good and poor usage of PDL statements,

```
Extract the next word from the line (good)
set word to get next token (poor)
Append the file extension to the name (good)
name = name + extension (poor)
FOR all the characters in the name (good)
FOR character = first to last (ok)
```

Note that in PDL the aim is to decompose the logic to the level of a single loop or decision. Thus "Search the list and find the customer with highest balance" is too vague because it takes a loop AND a nested decision to implement it. It is fine to use "Find" or "Lookup" if there's a predefined function for it such as String.indexOf().

Each textbook and each individual designer may have their own personal style of PDL. PDL is not a rigorous notation, since other people read it (not a computer). There is no universal "standard" for the industry, but for instructional purposes it is helpful if we all follow a similar style. The format below is intended as an example only.

The "structured" part of PDL is a notation for representing six specific structured programming constructs: SEQUENCE, WHILE, IF-THEN-ELSE, REPEAT-UNTIL, FOR, and CASE. Each of these constructs can be embedded inside any other construct. These constructs represent the logic, or flow of control in an algorithm.

It can be shown that three basic constructs for flow of control are sufficient to implement any "proper" algorithm. (Refer to chapter 1 sequence, iteration and decision components)

SEQUENCE is a linear progression where one task is performed sequentially after another.

WHILE is a loop (repetition) with a simple conditional test at its beginning.

IF-THEN-ELSE is a decision (selection) in which a choice is made between two alternative courses of action.

Although these constructs are sufficient, it is often useful to include three more constructs:

REPEAT-UNTIL is a loop with a simple conditional test at the bottom.

CASE is a multi-way branch (decision) based on the value of an expression.

CASE is a generalisation of IF-THEN-ELSE.

FOR is a "counting" loop.

SEQUENCE

Sequential control is described by writing one action after another, each action on a line by itself, and all actions aligned with the same indent. The actions are performed in the sequence (top to bottom) that they are written.

Example (non-computer)

Brush teeth
Wash face
Comb hair
Smile in mirror
Example
READ height of rectangle
READ width of rectangle
COMPUTE area as height times width

Common Action Keywords
Several keywords are often used to indicate common input, output, and processing operations.

> Input:: READ, OBTAIN, GET
> Output:: PRINT, DISPLAY, SHOW
> Compute: COMPUTE, CALCULATE, DETERMINE
> Initialise: SET, INIT
> Add one: INCREMENT

IF-THEN-ELSE
Binary choice on a given Boolean condition is indicated by the use of four keywords: IF, THEN, ELSE, and ENDIF. The general form is:

```
IF condition THEN
        sequence 1
ELSE
        sequence 2
ENDIF
```

The ELSE keyword and "sequence 2" are optional. If the condition is true, sequence 1 is performed, otherwise sequence 2 is performed.
Example

```
IF HoursWorked > NormalMax THEN
  Display overtime message
ELSE
  Display regular time message
ENDIF
```

WHILE
The WHILE construct is used to specify a loop with a test at the top. The beginning and ending of the loop are indicated by two keywords WHILE and ENDWHILE. The general form is:

```
WHILE condition
   sequence
ENDWHILE
```

The loop is entered only if the condition is true. The "sequence" is performed for every iteration. At the conclusion of every iteration, the condition is evaluated and the loop continues as long as the condition is true.
Example

```
WHILE Population < Limit
Compute Population as Population + Births - Deaths
ENDWHILE
Example
WHILE employee.type NOT EQUAL manager AND personCount <
numEmployees
INCREMENT personCount
CALL employeeList.getPerson with personCount RETURNING employee
ENDWHILE
```

CASE
A CASE construct indicates a multiway branch based on conditions that are mutually exclusive. Four keywords, CASE, OF, OTHERS, and ENDCASE, and conditions are used to indicate the various alternatives. The general form is:

```
CASE expression OF
condition 1 : sequence 1
condition 2 : sequence 2
...
condition n : sequence n
OTHERS:
default sequence
ENDCASE
```

The OTHERS clause with its default sequence is optional. Conditions are normally numbers or characters

Indicating the value of "expression", but they can be English statements or some other notation that specifies the condition under which the given sequence is to be performed. A certain sequence may be associated with more than one condition.

Example

```
CASE Title OF
Mr : Print "Mister"
Mrs : Print "Missus"
Miss : Print "Miss"
Ms : Print "Mizz"
Dr : Print "Doctor"
ENDCASE
```

Example

```
CASE grade OF
A : points = 4
B : points = 3
C : points = 2
D : points = 1
F : points = 0
ENDCASE
```

REPEAT-UNTIL

This loop is similar to the WHILE loop except that the test is performed at the bottom of the loop instead of at the top. Two keywords, REPEAT and UNTIL are used. The general form is:

```
REPEAT
sequence
UNTIL condition
```

The "sequence" in this type of loop is always performed at least once, because the test is performed after the sequence is executed. At the conclusion of each iteration, the condition is evaluated, and the loop repeats if the condition is false. The loop terminates when the condition becomes true.

FOR

This loop is a specialised construct for iterating a specific number of times, often called a "counting" loop. Two keywords, FOR and ENDFOR are used. The general form is:

```
FOR iteration bounds
sequence
ENDFOR
```

In cases where the loop constraints can be obviously inferred it is best to describe the loop using problem domain vocabulary.

Example

```
FOR each month of the year (good)
FOR month = 1 to 12 (ok)
FOR each employee in the list (good)
FOR empno = 1 to listsize (ok)
```

NESTED CONSTRUCTS

The constructs can be embedded within each other, and this is made clear by use of indenting. Nested constructs should be clearly indented from their surrounding constructs.

Example

```
SET total to zero
REPEAT
      READ Temperature
      IF Temperature > Freezing THEN
       INCREMENT total
      END IF
UNTIL Temperature < zero
Print total
```

In the above example, the IF construct is nested within the REPEAT construct, and therefore is indented.

INVOKING SUBPROCEDURES
Use the CALL keyword. For example:

```
CALL AvgAge with StudentAges
CALL Swap with CurrentItem and TargetItem
CALL Account.debit with CheckAmount
CALL getBalance RETURNING aBalance
CALL SquareRoot with orbitHeight RETURNING
nominalOrbit
```

EXCEPTION HANDLING

```
BEGIN
statements
EXCEPTION
WHEN exception type
statements to handle exception
WHEN another exception type
statements to handle exception
END
```

Sample PDL
Adequate

```
FOR X = 1 to 10
 FOR Y = 1 to 10
 IF gameBoard[X][Y] = 0
 Do nothing
 ELSE
 CALL theCall(X, Y) (recursive method)
 increment counter
 END IF
 END FOR
END FOR
```

Better

```
Set moveCount to 1
FOR each row on the board
 FOR each column on the board
 IF gameBoard position (row, column) is occupied THEN
 CALL findAdjacentTiles with row, column
 INCREMENT moveCount
 END IF
 END FOR
END FOR
```

(Note: the logic is restructured to omit the "do nothing" clause)

Not so good

```
FOR all the number at the back of the array
 SET Temp equal the addition of each number
 IF > 9 THEN
 get the remainder of the number divided by 10 to that index
 and carry the "1"
 Decrement one
Do it again for numbers before the decimal
```

Good enough (but not perfect)

```
SET Carry to 0
FOR each DigitPosition in Number from least significant to
most significant
 COMPUTE Total as sum of FirstNum[DigitPosition] and
SecondNum[DigitPosition] and Carry
```

```
IF Total > 10 THEN
SET Carry to 1
SUBTRACT 10 from Total
ELSE
SET Carry to 0
END IF
STORE Total in Result[DigitPosition]
END LOOP
IF Carry = 1 THEN
 RAISE Overflow exception
END IF
```

Another example

The following example shows how PDL is written as comments in the source file. Please note that the double slashes are indented.

```
public boolean moveRobot (Robot aRobot)
{
    //IF robot has no obstacle in front THEN
        // Call Move robot
        // Add the move command to the command history
        // RETURN true
    //ELSE
        // RETURN false without moving the robot
    //END IF
}
```

Example Java Implementation

- Source code statements are interleaved with PDL.
- Comments that correspond exactly to source code are removed during coding.

```
public boolean moveRobot (Robot aRobot)
{
    //IF robot has no obstacle in front
THEN
    if (aRobot.isFrontClear())
    {
        // Call Move robot
        aRobot.move();
        // Add the move command to the
command history
        cmdHistory.add(RobotAction.MOVE);
        return true;
    }
    else // don't move the robot
    {
        return false;
    }//END IF
}
```

APPENDIX III   User Interface Guidelines

User Interface design guidelines document was downloaded from the following URL on 29/11/2009. http://www.classicsys.com/css06/cfm/article.cfm?articleid=20

Guidelines for user interface design

We have used the principles offered here for work with our own customers and have taught more than 20,000 GUI-design students nationally and internationally. These principles should help you as well.

Design Principle 1: Understand People Applications must reflect the perspectives and behaviours of their users. To understand users fully, developers must first understand people because we all share common characteristics. People learn more easily by recognition than by recall. Always attempt to provide a list of data values from which the user can select, rather than having the user key in values from memory. The average person can recall about 2,000 to 3,000 words; yet can recognise more than 50,000 words.

Design Principle 2: Be Careful of Different Perspectives Many designers unwittingly fall into the perspective trap when it comes to icon design or the overall behaviour of the application. I recently saw an icon designed to signify "Rolled Up" totals for an accounting system. To show this function, the designer put a lot of artistic effort into creating an icon resembling a cinnamon roll. Unfortunately, the users of the system had no idea what metaphor the icon was supposed to represent even though it was perfectly intuitive from the designer's perspective. A reserved icons table containing standard approved icons, such as the one shown in Figure 1, will help eliminate these problems.

Figure 1 - **Reserved Icons**

Meaning and Behaviour	Used to Identify an Application	Used to Identify a Function	Reserved Word Text Label
Information message	No	Yes (identifies an information message box)	None
Warning message	No	Yes (identifies a warning message box)	None
Question message	No	Yes (identifies a question message box)	None
Error message	No	Yes (identifies an error message box)	None

Design Principle 3: Design for Clarity GUI applications often are not clear to end-users. One effective way to increase the clarity of an application is to develop and use a list of reserved words. A common complaint among users is that certain terms are not clear or consistent. I often see developers engaging in spirited debates over the appropriate term for a button or menu item, only to see this same debate occurring in an adjacent building with a different set of developers. When the application is released, one screen may say "Item," while the next screen says "Product," and a third says, "Merchandise", when all three terms denote the same thing. This lack of consistency ultimately leads to confusion and frustration for users.

Figure 2 gives an example of a list of reserved words. An application development group might complete and expand the table with additional reserved words.

Figure 2 - **List of Reserved Words**

Text	Meaning And Behaviour	Appears on Button	Appears on Menu	Mnemonic Keystrokes	Shortcut Keystrokes
OK	Accept the data entered or acknowledge the information presented and remove the window	Yes	No	None	Return or Enter
Cancel	Do not accept the data entered and remove the window	Yes	No	None	Esc
Close	Close the current task and continue working with the application; close the view of the data	Yes	Yes	Alt+C	None
Exit	Quit the application	No	Yes	Alt+X	Alt+F4
Help	Invoke the application's help facility	Yes	Yes	Alt+H	F1
Save	Save the data entered and stay in the current window	Yes	Yes	Alt+S	Shift+F12
Save As	Save the data with a new name	No	Yes	Alt+A	F12
Undo	Undo the latest action	No	Yes	Alt+U	Ctrl+Z
Cut	Cut the highlighted information	No	Yes	Alt+T	Ctrl+X
Copy	Copy highlighted information	No	Yes	Alt+C	Ctrl+C
Paste	Paste the copied or cut information at the insertion point	No	Yes	Alt+P	Ctrl+V

Design Principle 4: Design for Consistency Good GUIs use consistent behaviours throughout the application and build upon a user's prior knowledge of other successful applications. When writing software for business applications, provide the user with as many consistent behaviours as possible. For example, both the Embassy Suites and Courtyard Marriot hotel chains are growing rapidly due to their popularity among business travellers who know that they will be provided with a familiar room and a consistent set of amenities. The bottom line is that business travellers are not looking for a new and exciting experience in each new city. Business users of your software have similar needs. Each new and exciting experience you provide in the software can become an anxiety-inducing experience or an expensive call to your help desk.

Design Principle 5: Provide Visual Feedback If you've ever found yourself mindlessly staring at the hourglass on your terminal while waiting for an operation to finish, you know the frustration of poor visual feedback. Your users will greatly appreciate knowing how much longer a given operation will take before they can enjoy the fruits of their patience. As a general rule, most users like to have a message dialogue box with a progress indicator displayed when operations are going to take longer than seven to ten seconds. This number is highly variable based on the type of user and overall characteristics of the application.

Design Principle 6: Be Careful With Audible Feedback Last week, I had the opportunity to ride in elevators in which a pleasant voice informed riders which floor they were on. The building was fairly new, and at first, employees thought the voice was cute. After six months of travelling floor to floor, employees are sure to ignore the voice and see it as more of an annoyance than help. The same thing can happen with your GUIs, except the annoying sounds are not contained within the walls of an elevator, but instead are available to everyone within earshot of the worker's cubicle. Put sound on a few hundred workstations and a cacophony emerges in the open-air cubicle environment. However, audible feedback can be useful in cases where you need to warn the user of an impending serious problem, such as one in which proceeding further could cause loss of data or software. Allow users to disable audio feedback, except in cases when an error must be addressed.

Design Principle 7: Keep Text Clear Developers often try to make textual feedback clear by adding a lot of words. However, they ultimately make the message less clear. Concise wording of text labels, user error messages, and one-line help messages is challenging. Textual feedback can be handled most effectively by assigning these tasks to experienced technical writers.

Design Principle 8: Provide Traceable Paths If your users ever say something akin to, "I don't know how I got to this window, and now that I'm here, I don't know how to get out," then you have not provided a traceable (or, in this case, retraceable) path. Providing a traceable path is harder than it sounds. It starts with an intuitive menu structure from which to launch your specific features.

You must also identify areas where you can flatten the menu structure and avoid more than two levels of cascading menus. Providing a descriptive title bar within each dialogue box greatly helps to remind users what menu items or buttons were pressed to bring them to the window now in focus.

Design Principle 9: Provide Keyboard Support Keyboards are a common fixture on users' desktops and provide an efficient means to enter text and data. With the introduction of GUI applications, we often assume users will embrace a mouse as the primary interactive device. Using a mouse can become time-consuming and inefficient for the touch typist or frequent users of an application.

Keyboard accelerators can provide an efficient way for users to access specific menu items or controls in a window. The accelerators used should be easy to access and limited to one or two keys (such as F3 or Ctrl-P). Keyboards have limitations in the GUI world, such as when trying to implement direct-manipulation tasks like drag and drop, pointing, and re-sizing.

In contrast, you will always find a smaller set of users who are not touch typists and hence embrace the mouse as a point-and-click nirvana. The result is that you need to provide complete and equal keyboard and mouse support for all menu and window operations.

Design Principle 10: Watch the Presentation Model A critical aspect that ties all these facets of the interface together is the interface's look and feel. The look and feel must be consistent. On the basis of users' experiences with one screen or one dialogue box, they should have some sense of how to interact with the next screen or control.

Searching the interface model for good design and continuity is very important. The model should involve careful decisions, such as whether the application has a single or multiple document interface. The model also will validate how users perform the main tasks within the application.

Identifying the appropriate presentation for the application greatly facilitates the subsequent windows being developed since they will have a common framework in which to reside. On the other hand, if you do not define the presentation model early in the design of your GUI, late changes to the look and feel of the application will be much more costly and time-consuming because nearly every window may be affected.

Design Principle 11: Use Modal vs. Modeless Dialogues Appropriately When we need input from the user, we often use a modal dialogue box. Using modal dialogues has long been shunned by many developers as too constraining on the user. However, modal dialogues do have many uses in complex applications since most people only work on one window at a time. Try to use modal dialogues when a finite task exists. For tasks with no fixed duration, modeless dialogues are normally the preferable choice with a major caveat: Try to keep the user working in no more than three modeless windows at any one time. Go beyond this magical number and the support-desk phones will start ringing, as users spend their time managing the open windows rather than concentrating on their tasks. Use the table in Figure 3 to determine the appropriate use of dialogue boxes and windows.

Figure 3 - **When to Use Dialogue Boxes or Windows**

Type	Description	Use	Example
Modal	Dialogue box	Presentation of a finite task	File Open dialogue box, Save As dialogue box
Modeless	Dialogue box	Presentation of an ongoing task	Search dialogue box, History List dialogue box, Task List dialogue box
Application window	Window frame with document (child) windows contained within	Presentation of multiple instances of an object, Comparison of data within two or more windows	Word processor, Spreadsheet
Document window	Modeless dialogue box or document window contained within and managed by the application window	Presentation of multiple parts of an application	Multiple views of data (sheets)
Secondary window	Primary window of a secondary application	Presentation of another application called from the parent window	Help window in an application

Design Principle 12: Use Controls Correctly Controls are the visual elements that let the user interact with the application. GUI designers are faced with an unending array of controls from which to choose. Each new control brings with it expected behaviours and characteristics. Choosing the appropriate control for each user task results in higher productivity, lower error rates, and higher overall user satisfaction. Use the table in Figure 4 as a guideline for control usage in your screens.

Figure 4 - **Guidelines for Using Controls**

Control	Number of Choices in the Domain Shown	Type of Control
Menu bar	Maximum of 10 items	Static action
Pull-down menu	Maximum of 12 items	Static action
Cascading menu	Maximum of 5 items, 1 cascade deep	Static action
Pop-up menu	Maximum of 10 items	Static action
Push button	1 for each button, maximum of 6 per dialogue box	Static action
Check box	1 for each box, maximum of 10 to 12 per group	Static set/select value
Radio button	1 for each button, maximum of 6 per group box	Static set/select value
List box	Maximum of 50 in the list, display 8 to 10 rows	Dynamic set/select value
Drop-down list box	Display 1 selection in the control at a time, up to 20 in a drop-down box	Dynamic set/select single value
Combination list box	Display 1 selection in the control at a time in standard format, up to 20 in a drop-down box	Dynamic set/select single value; add a value to the list
Spin button	Maximum of 10 values	Static set/select value
Slider	Dependent on the data displayed	Static set/select value in range

Finally, try to keep the basic behaviour and placement of these controls consistent throughout your application. As soon as you change the behaviour of these basic controls, your user will feel lost. Make changes thoughtfully and apply the changes consistently.

Applying Design Principles

Understanding the principles behind good GUI design and applying them to your applications can be a challenge. Let's examine an application to see how these principles can result in an improved interface.

Part 1: Exploring a GUI in Need of Redesign The interface in Figure 5 is used by an ambulance-dispatching company to maintain customer data, provide billing information, and dispatch ambulances. The application was a port from a character-based system and contains several design errors that affect the user's performance with this mission-critical application. Keep in mind that GUI ease of use and clarity is especially important in a critical application such as this where the rapid handling of a request can make the difference between life and death. Here is what is wrong with this screen:

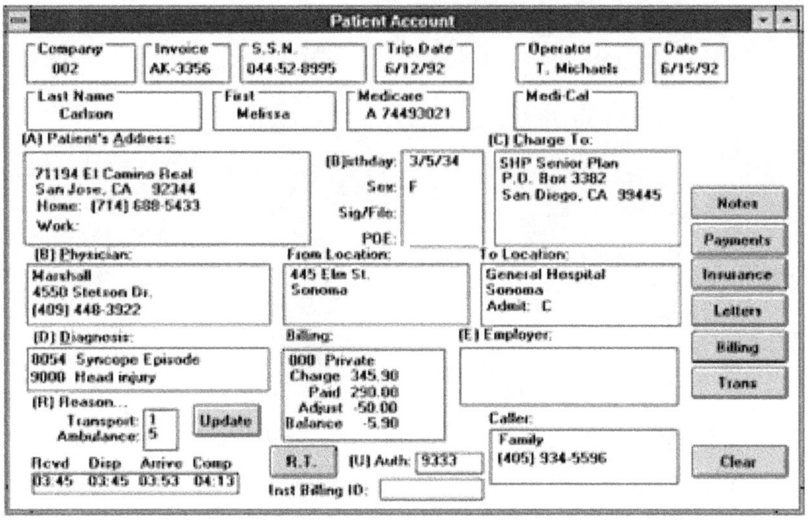

Figure 5

- **Too many functions at the top level.** The users requested that the new application provide all of the information at their fingertips. This results in the screen being used for both customer maintenance and ambulance dispatching. If you enter extensive customer information and then press the Update button, the record is updated. However, if you enter minimal customer information, such as social security number, diagnosis, from-location, and to-location, and then press the Trans button, an ambulance will be dispatched. Updating and dispatching functions need to be in separate dialogue boxes.
- **Too many buttons.** The buttons along the right should be on the application's parent window, possibly in a toolbar, but not on this child window.
- **Poor navigational assistance.** GUI controls should be positioned according to frequency of use. The most important field should be in the upper left; the least important field should be in the lower right. It's hard to imagine how the company and invoice number could be the most important fields when dispatching an ambulance.
- **Inappropriate use of controls.** The designer chose to use text labels rather than group boxes to identify which groups of data would be placed in the boxes. This many group boxes with text labels in these positions makes the screen appear convoluted and makes it difficult to distinguish the data from the labels. Also, the editable fields should be identified with a box around them, so that it is intuitively obvious which fields can be changed.
- **Lack of symmetry.** Just lining up fields, group boxes, and buttons will make this GUI much easier to use. Our brains like order, not chaos.

Part 2: Looking at an Improved Interface Figures 6 and 7 show a much-improved interface for this same application:

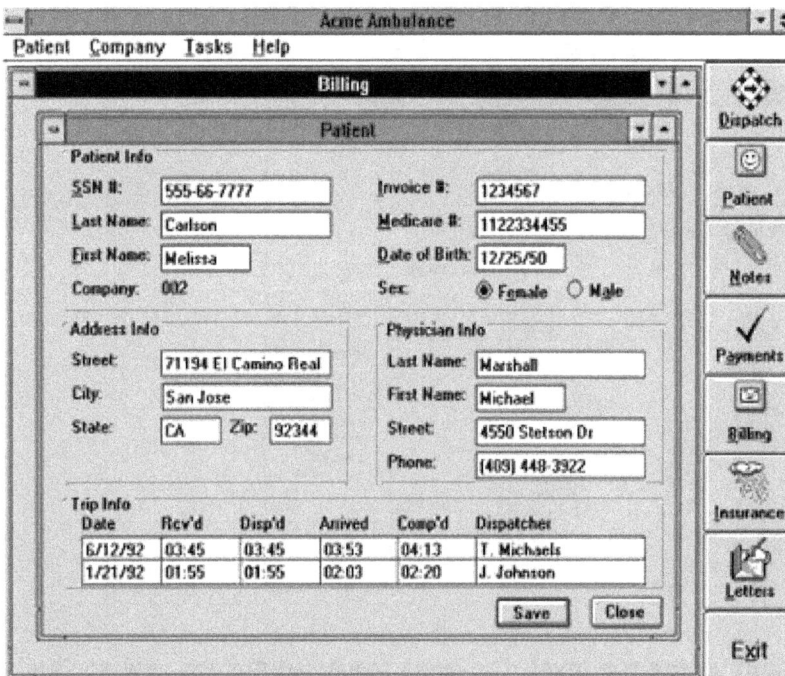

Figure 6

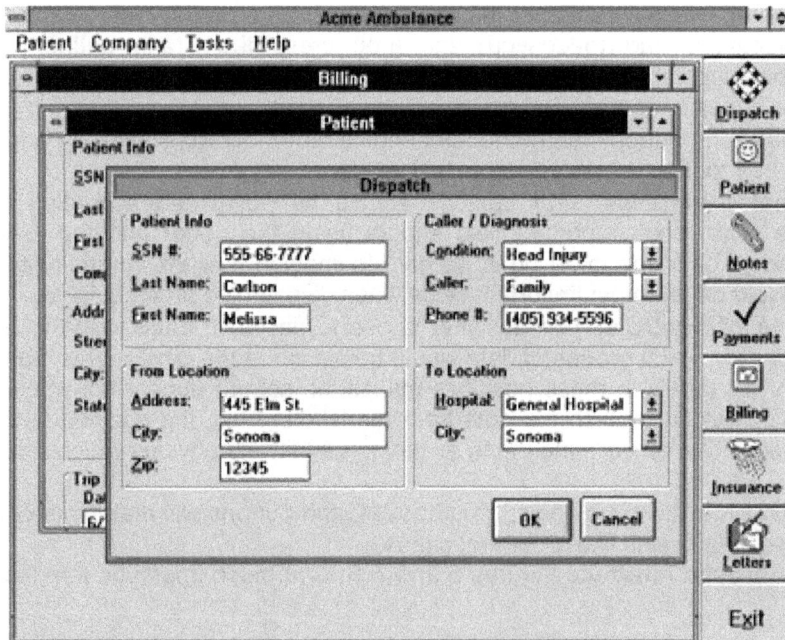

Figure 7

- **Order out of chaos.** This application should contain several child windows for the different tasks that a user might perform. These tasks can be accessed easily through the Tasks menu or by pushing a button on the vertical toolbar. The Dispatch button invokes a modal dialogue box instead of a modeless child window. That way, you can require the user to acknowledge the completion of the dispatching task. If it were a modeless window, the user might overlay it without ever dispatching the ambulance.
- **Reordering input fields.** The confusing order of fields has been more logically structured based on importance and frequency of use.

- **Improved controls.** The revised interface features a consistent use of data-entry fields. Any field in which a user can enter data is surrounded by a border. Group boxes are used to group related fields together or to illustrate a domain.

These changes, suggested by the principles that we have previously discussed, make for a clean and more intuitive interface.

Implementing Effective Standards

Once you implement some good design practices into your GUI applications, how do you ensure others in your organisation will do the same? The most cost-effective way to ensure consistency among your GUI applications is to implement GUI standards that are easy to use, clear, and concise. We've all experienced the "standards" manual that is energetically distributed to co-workers only to be placed immediately on the developer's shelf next to other unread manuals. To ensure that your standards do not meet this same fate, provide them in an online hypertext format. Divide your standards into rules -- which must be followed or the developer will have some explaining to do -- and recommendations. Developers like to know what is mandatory and where they have discretion.

Conclusion

Designing good GUIs is a critical skill for application developers in the 1990s, regardless of the GUI platform for which they are designing. Good GUI designs don't happen naturally. They require that the developer learn and apply some basic principles, including making the design something the user will enjoy working with every day. They also require that the developer get as much experience as possible in working on and being exposed to good GUI designs.

Remember that if you apply the principles and get some experience in good GUI design, your users will have an easier time getting their jobs accomplished using the GUIs you produce for them.

[http://www.classicsys.com/css06/cfm/article.cfm?articleid=20]

INDEX

4

4+1 view of software architecture · 37

A

Abstract modelling · 30
Abstraction · 19
Activity diagram · 53
Aggregation · 23
Agile methods · 120, 121
Algorithmic design notation for sequence, iteration and selection · 8
Ambiguities · 72
Architecture models · 37
Associations · 23
Availability · 127

B

Behaviour models · 32
Benchmark tests · 173
Benefits of a requirements specification · 67
Black box and White box testing features · 168
Black Box or Functional Testing · 172
Boehm's basic Model for cost estimation: · 197

C

Choosing a prototyping approach · 121
Class diagram · 48
COCOMO cost estimation model · 199
COCOMO II Effort Equation · 212
COCOMO II Schedule Equation · 212
COCOMO II Software Cost Estimation Model · 211
COCOMO Model types · 202
Collaboration diagram · 56
Communication diagram · 58
Component diagram · 50
Composite structure diagram · 50
Conflicts · 72
Context models · 27
Cost estimation methods · 199
Cost Estimation Models · 201
Costing-Organic Mode · 204
Costing-Semidetached Mode · 204
Costing-Embedded Mode · 205
Costing-Development Mode · 203
Criticality Analysis of risk · 152

D

Data-flow model · 32
Debugging · 163
Defect Testing · 167
Dependability of software · 125
Deployment diagram · 51
Design stages in RTS · 102
Detail Design-Driven Prototypes · 114
Development view · 37, 85
DFD Notation symbols · 33
Dimensions of Dependability · 126
Documenting the architecture · 43
Domain Testing: · 172
Dynamic analysis techniques for testing · 161
Dynamic analysis tools · 162

E

Effects of Dependability · 128
Emulators · 163
Encapsulation · 22
Equivalence partitioning and boundary value analysis · 174
Evolutionary Prototypes · 114
Experimental Prototypes · 114
Explorative Prototypes · 114
Exploratory programming · 3, 25
Extreme programming (XP) · 118, 123

F

Failure classification · 131
Failure mode and effects analysis · 150
Failure Protection · 129
Fault-tree analysis · 133
Fault-tree diagram · 139
FCFS-First Come First Serve scheduling policy · 98
Feasibility analysis Case Study · 63
Field tests · 173
Five state Diagram · 95
FMEA concept in software lifecycle management · 153
Formal Transformation · 4, 25, 215
Functional requirements · 69

G

Gantt Chart · 65
Group Working · 86
GUI design considerations · 106

H

Hard real time systems · 90
Hazard and Operability Studies (HAZOP) ·
    154
Hazard and Risk Analysis · 133
Hazard and Risk Analysis in safety-critical
    systems · 149
HAZOP flow diagram · 155
Highest Response Next (HRN) scheduling
    policy · 99

I

Identifying a Class · 19
Incremental development prototyping · 117
Interaction diagrams · 55
Interaction overview diagram · 57
Interactions between classes · 21
Interface testing · 164
Interface types · 107
Intermediate COCOMO Model: · 209
Interrupt driven control · 91

L

Laboratory tests · 173
Levels of testing · 165
Logical view · 37, 85
Loop Testing: · 171

M

Maintainability · 128
Message passing · 22
Methodologies · 23
Metrics application · 187
Metrics characteristics · 189
metrics in software engineering · 189
Metrics methodology · 184
Multi-level feedback queues (MFQ)
    scheduling policy · 101

N

Natural language specifications · 71
non pre-emptive principle · 98
Non-functional requirements · 69
Non-functioning prototypes · 114

O

Object diagram · 52
Object-oriented design considerations · 18

Object-oriented programming · 16
Omissions · 72
Oracles · 163

P

Package diagram · 52
Path Testing · 170
PDL Uses · 79
Performance · 129
Physical view · 37, 85
Planning of projects · 62
Polling based control · 91
Polymorphism · 22
Pre-emptive scheme · 96
Priority-based interrupt · 97
Procedural programming · 7
Process considerations · 84
Process view · 37, 85
Program Design Language (PDL) · 75
Programming paradigm · 8, 6, 7, 24, 84,
    108
Project management · 61
Project planning · 87
Properties of classes · 20
Prototype process · 113
Prototyping · 3, 25, 111, 112

Q

Quality assurance · 192
Quality Control · 193
Quality Planning · 193
Quick and Dirty Prototypes · 113

R

Real Time Operating Systems (RTOS) · 92
Real-time systems · 89
Recovery tests · 173
Regression tests · 163
Reliability · 127
Reliability Metrics · 131
Repository model · 30
Requirement specification · 71
Requirements definition · 70
Requirements engineering · 67
Research in natural language methodology
    · 75
Risk Assessment · 141
Risk Priority Numbers · 152
Round Robin scheduling policy · 100
RTOS Kernel function · 93

S

Safety · 128
Safety and reliability · 130
Safety argument · 138
Safety lifecycle · 140
Safety-critical systems · 149
Scheduling · 94
Scheduling policies · 96
Security · 128
Sensors and Actuators in RTS · 90
Sequence diagram · 55
Simulators · 163
SJF–Shortest Job First scheduling policy · 99
Soft real time systems · 90
Software costing · 196
Software design · 83
Software development methodology · 7
Software modelling · 26
Software prototyping · 111
Software quality · 183
software quality attitudes · 192
Software quality factors · 88
Software reuse · 4
SRT-Shortest Remaining Time scheduling policy · 99
Stages in project management · 62
State machine diagram · 54
State machine models · 34
State transition table · 36
Static analysis techniques for testing · 159
Stress tests · 173
Structure diagrams · 48
Structure of a feasibility report · 64
Survivability · 128
Systems Engineering · 83

T

Test data generators · 162
Testing Effectiveness Assessment · 176
Testing Strategies · 163
Testing to validate the system · 159
Testing Tools · 162
Three state diagram · 94
Throw away Prototyping · 115
Timing diagrams · 58
Total Quality Management (TQM) · 183
Types of models · 26
Types of prototype · 113

U

UML description · 46
UML Diagrams · 47
UML model types · 47
Unified Modelling Language · 46
Use-case diagram · 54
User and System requirements · 68
User Interface design · 105

V

Validation and verification · 159
Volume tests · 172

W

Waterfall approach · 2
White Box or Structural Testing · 169

www.ingramcontent.com/pod-product-compliance
Lightning Source LLC
Chambersburg PA
CBHW081407200326
41518CB00013B/2267